SOURCE MATERIAL ON THE
HISTORY AND ETHNOLOGY
OF THE CADDO INDIANS

SOURCE MATERIAL ON THE HISTORY AND ETHNOLOGY OF THE CADDO INDIANS

By

JOHN R. SWANTON

Foreword by

HELEN HORNBECK TANNER

UNIVERSITY OF OKLAHOMA PRESS
NORMAN AND LONDON

Library of Congress Cataloging-in-Publication Data

Swanton, John Reed, 1873–1958.
    Source material on the history and ethnology of the Caddo Indians / by John R.
Swanton ; foreword by Helen Hornbeck Tanner.
      p.   cm.
    Originally published: Washington, D.C. : U.S. G.P.O., 1942, in series: Smithsonian
Institution. Bureau of American Ethnology. Bulletin 132.
    Includes bibliographical references and index.
    ISBN 0-8061-2856-9 (alk. paper)
    1. Caddo Indians—History. 2. Caddo Indians—Social life and
customs.   I. Title.
E99.C12S83 1996
970.004′979—dc20   96-18016
                                       CIP

Published by the University of Oklahoma Press, Norman, Publishing Division of the
University. First published in 1942 as Bureau of American Ethnology Bulletin 132 by
the Smithsonian Institution, Washington, D.C. Foreword by Helen Hornbeck Tanner
copyright © 1996 by the University of Oklahoma Press. All rights reserved. Manufactured in the U.S.A. First printing of the University of Oklahoma Press edition, 1996.

1 2 3 4 5 6 7 8 9 10

CONTENTS

ILLUSTRATIONS

FOREWORD

Since it first appeared in 1942, John R. Swanton's *Source Material on the History and Ethnology of the Caddo Indians* has remained the basic compendium of information on the Caddo Indians, who are the present-day descendants of a group of southeastern chiefdoms that existed in the Red River region of Arkansas, Louisiana, Texas, and Oklahoma. The modern Caddo, with close to three thousand five hundred enrolled tribal members, have a small reservation near Binger, Oklahoma, about forty miles southwest of Oklahoma City.

Although their present headquarters lies on the edge of the western plains, the Caddo earlier were among the great Mississippian chiefdoms, including Cahokia, that flourished between 1000 and 1400 A.D. Culturally linked to the Southeast, and particularly to the neighboring Natchez and Taensa, they were the only major chiefdoms located west of the Mississippi River. In the seventeenth century, the Caddo people were separate communities in four regional alliances. The name Caddo is a contraction of Cadohadacho, signifying "the real chiefs," a term that identifies the regional alliance along the bend of the Red River. (Swanton chose to spell Cadohadacho as Kadohadacho, which is not in common usage today). Another small cluster of communities in central Arkansas, known as the Cahinnio, gradually joined the leading Caddo. Farther south on the Red River was Natchitoches, the leading town of a third cluster. Finally, to the west in present-day Texas, an alliance of eight or nine towns known as the Hasinai occupied the valleys of the Neches, Angelina, and upper Sabine Rivers.

Although diminished to an estimated 4,000 population by the year 1800, the Caddo retained control of their own territory up to 1834. Their world then collapsed, however, and they lived a hazardous existence during a diaspora lasting twenty-five years. The loss of their great leader, Tinhiouen, the cession of their lands in Louisiana in 1835, and their unwilling involvement in Texas Indian warfare left them in an insecure location on a reserve in west Texas in 1854. Aggressively opposed by local settlers, in 1859 this segment of the dispersed Caddo was guided to relative safety in Oklahoma by a dedicated Indian agent. The

IX

Caddo had fought their traditional enemies, the Osage, and also
the Kiowa, Apache, and Choctaw, when they encroached on Caddo
hunting lands, but their real talent was in diplomacy rather than
warfare. Because of their status and influence, the Caddo were
identified up to the beginning of the nineteenth century as the
most important tribe between the Mississippi River and the
Rio Grande.

Although interest in the Caddo has increased steadily since
the 1970s, only recently has the tribe emerged from the obscurity
noted by Swanton in his 1942 publication. In the first sentence,
Swanton points out that he is calling attention to "a group of
tribes of the very first importance, but one which has been almost
lost to sight by our ethnological students and its significance
seriously underrated."

The long neglect of the Caddo tribes is probably more the
responsibility of historians and ethnohistorians than of ethnologists.
Only a limited picture of the highly organized Caddo society could
be gleaned by investigators conducting fieldwork in Oklahoma
during the early twentieth century, when government policy still
suppressed use of Indian languages, and dances were performed
in secrecy. The surviving fragments of data collected by Swanton
scarcely indicated the governmental hierarchy and elaborate religious rituals described by seventeenth-century Spanish and French
missionaries and travelers. For early twentieth-century ethnologists
the more prominent and numerous tribes, such as the Comanche
and Pawnee, provided more interesting research opportunities.
American historians paid scant attention to the small number of
Caddo, who played no conspicuous role in the dramatic Indian
military campaigns on the southern plains.

The full story of the Caddo tribes still remains to be untangled
from the diverse sources identified by Swanton more than a half-
century ago. An adequate overview is hampered by the compart-
mentalization of research. For example, archaeologists have collected data about the earliest developments in Caddo history,
rooted in the first human occupation of the districts adjoining
the Red River and the western side of the Mississippi. Because
archaeological research tends to be divided by present-day state
boundaries, however, an aspiring Caddo historian must piece
together the results of locally focused enterprises in each of the
four states bordering the great bend of the Red River. The
changing Euro-American political jurisdictions over the contested
international borders encompassing the territory of the Caddo
have proved to be a challenge for historians seeking reports of the
Caddo in archives of Spain, France, Texas, and the United States.

The Swanton volume is an introductory sampling of parts of these major resources. Since his landmark enterprise, there have been significant additions to the Caddo literature. In 1954, William J. Griffith published "The Hasinai Indians of East Texas as Seen by Europeans, 1687-1722," *Philological and Documentary Studies* 2, no. 3 (New Orleans: Middle American Research Institute, Tulane University). This publication synthesized material from a number of documents selected by Swanton. The confusing period when the Caddo were involved with twenty refugee tribes in Texas is illuminated by correspondence in Dorman H. Winfrey, *Texas Indian Papers,* 5 vols. (Austin: University of Texas Press, 1959-61, 1966).

One stimulus to Caddo research was the need to gather evidence for Indian Claims Commission litigation over terms of the Treaty of 1835, which ceded Caddo land in Louisiana to the U.S. government. The series of hearings up to 1972 produced five volumes of expert-witness reports published as part of the *American Indian Ethnohistory Series,* compiled and edited by David Agee Horr (New York: Garland Publishing, 1974).

Since the 1970s, a new generation of archaeologists has contributed new insights into Caddo society, and ethnohistorians have become aware of the Caddos' role in regional history. Noteworthy among the steady accumulation of research reports has been the new review of the earliest Spanish incursion into the Caddo country, Gloria A. Young and Michael P. Hoffman, eds., *The Expedition of Hernando de Soto West of the Mississippi, 1541-1543: Proceedings of the De Soto Symposia, 1988 and 1990* (Fayetteville: University of Arkansas Press, 1993).

Meetings of the Caddo Conference are the forum for predominantly archaeological research, focusing on regional variations in pottery types, some of exceptionally fine quality. A group of Caddo archaeologists first convened in Shreveport, Louisiana, in 1942, the year the Smithsonian Institution published Swanton's *Source Material.* The first organized symposium did not occur until 1946, and the Caddo Conference has met annually only for the past two decades.

When I attended the conference in 1971, I believe I was the first historian to participate. At that time, the Caddo people appeared to have conserved more of their cultural past than Swanton would have believed, based on his observations in 1912. The Caddos' link to their ancestors was not particularly visible in their lifestyle, but it did remain deep within their community consciousness. Leading singers, for example, had memorized a fourteen-hour-long sequence of songs and dances reenacting their history. Fortunately, most of this music has been recorded. In recent years there has been a resurgence of interest in learning the language and teaching the songs and dances. This movement has been promoted by the Caddo Culture Club, a group that meets regularly on the reservation and brings drums, singers, and dancers to the annual Caddo Conferences.

The Caddo people themselves have been active in fostering the renewed interest in their heritage and recording it for posterity. For many years prior to her death in 1982, Vynola Beaver Newkumet of Norman, Oklahoma, collected records of tribal traditions, music, and dances. The result of her work, in collaboration with Howard L. Meredith, appeared as *Hasinai: A Traditional History of the Caddo Confederacy* (College Station: Texas A & M University Press, 1988). Each chapter in this unusual volume focuses on a particular dance, with an accompanying essay commenting on a special aspect of Caddo life and values. Most recently, Cecile Elkins Carter completed a long quest to understand the past experience of her people. Combining archaeological fieldwork, scholarly research, and interviews with elders conducted principally in the 1970s, she blends historical narrative and contemporary vignettes in *Caddo Indians: Where We Come From* (Norman: University of Oklahoma Press, 1995), a valuable contribution to Caddo scholarship.

None of the new Caddo literature, however, replaces Swanton's volume. Scholars, students, and the Caddo people themselves will all be gratified to have this new edition available, an indication of the long-delayed appreciation of the Caddos' role in America's diverse history.

Helen Hornbeck Tanner
Senior Research Fellow
The Newberry Library, Chicago
March 1996

MAPS

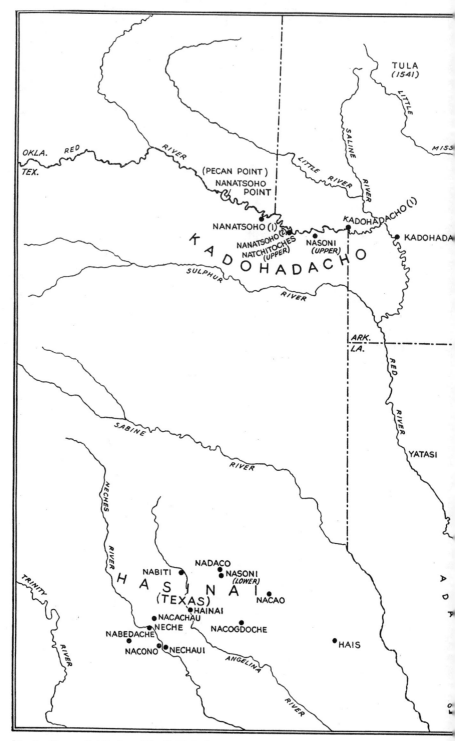

Map 1.—Former distribution of the Caddo Indians.

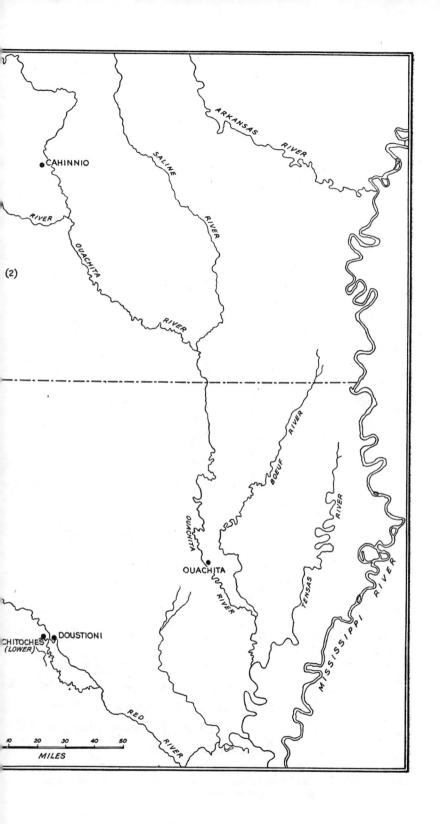

ARKANSAS RIVER

SALINE RIVER

CAHINNIO

RIVER

OUACHITA RIVER

(2)

BOEUF RIVER

OUACHITA RIVER

OUACHITA

TENSAS RIVER

MISSISSIPPI RIVER

DOUSTIONI

CHITOCHES
(LOWER)

RED RIVER

10 20 30 40 50
MILES

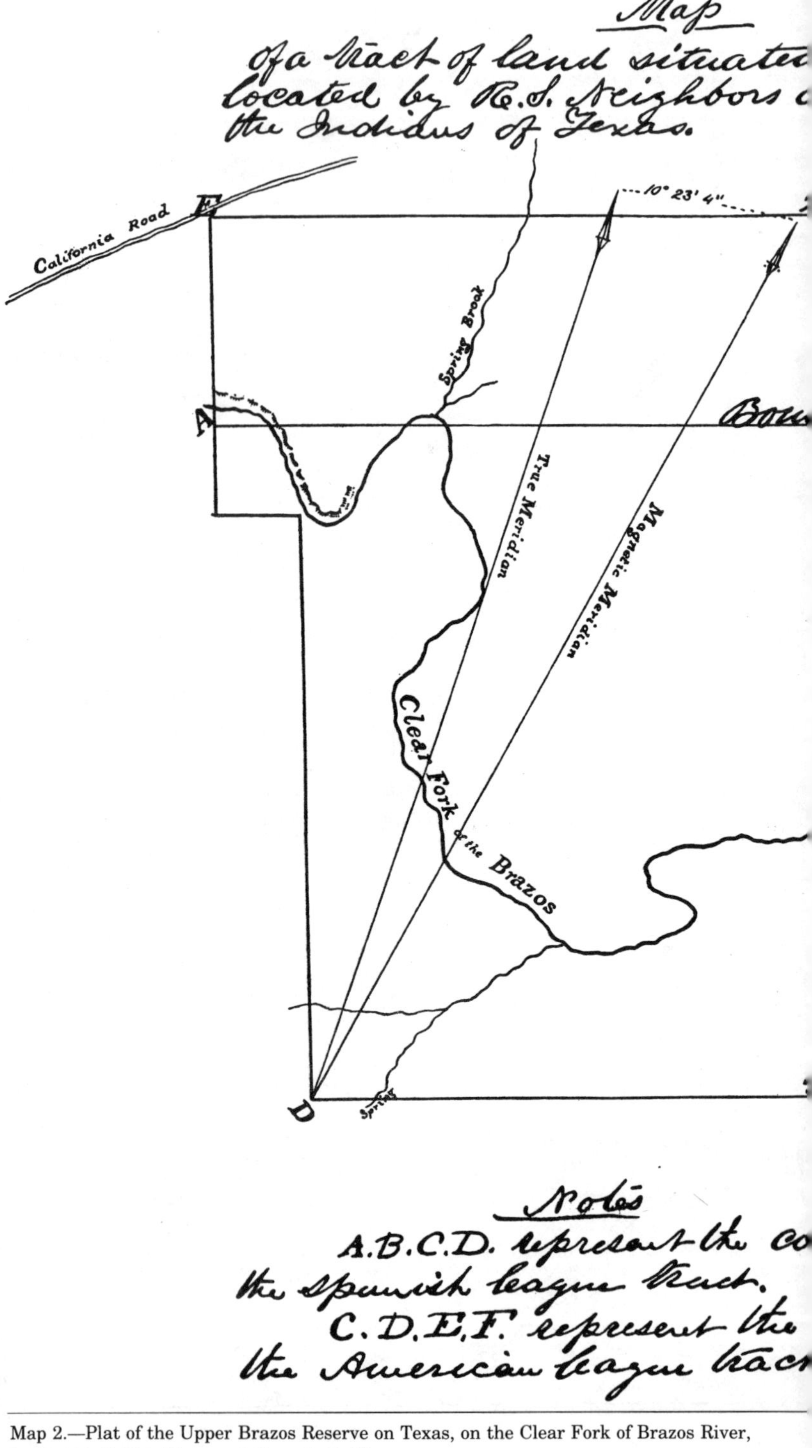

Map

Of a tract of land situated
located by R. S. Neighbors a
the Indians of Texas.

California Road

...10° 23' 4"...

Spring Brook

Bou...

True Meridian

Magnetic Meridian

Clear Fork of the Brazos

Spring

Notes

A.B.C.D. represent the co
the Spanish league tract.
C.D.E.F. represent the
the American league tract

Map 2.—Plat of the Upper Brazos Reserve on Texas, on the Clear Fork of Brazos River, by Maj. R. S. Neighbors and Capt. R. B. Marcy.

upon the Clear Fork of the Brazos river
.. Capt. R. B. Marcy for the site of

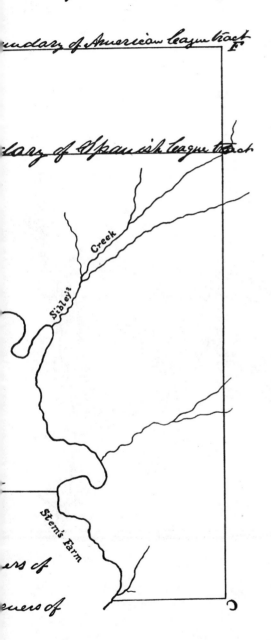

..undary of American league tract

..dary of Spanish league tract

Creek

Sibley's

Stem's Farm

..rs of

..ders of

Map 3.—Region surveyed by Rector in preparation for the removal of the Indians from Texas.

Rough chart accompanying
Sup't Rector's Report of exploration
of the Leased District.

Original in the National Archives: Records of the Department of the Interior,
Office of Indian Affairs, Map No. 50.

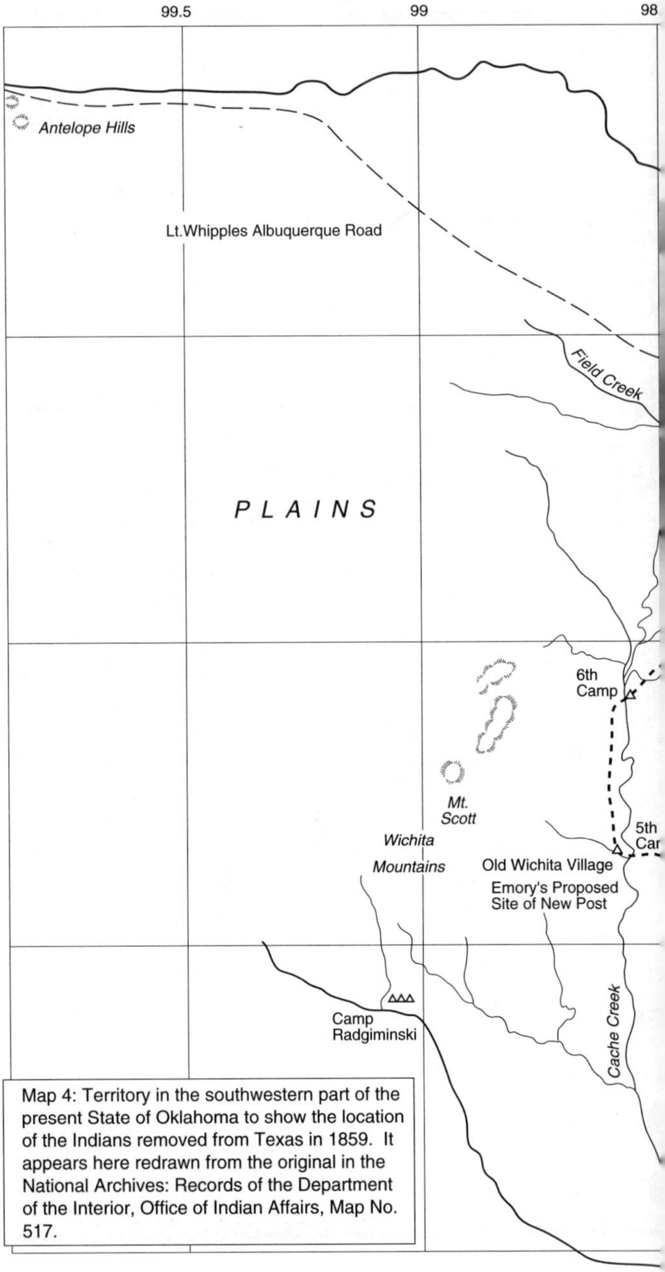

99.5 99 98

Antelope Hills

Lt.Whipples Albuquerque Road

Field Creek

P L A I N S

6th
Camp

Mt.
Scott

Wichita

5th
Car

Mountains

Old Wichita Village

Emory's Proposed
Site of New Post

Camp
Radgiminski

Cache Creek

Map 4: Territory in the southwestern part of the
present State of Oklahoma to show the location
of the Indians removed from Texas in 1859. It
appears here redrawn from the original in the
National Archives: Records of the Department
of the Interior, Office of Indian Affairs, Map No.
517.

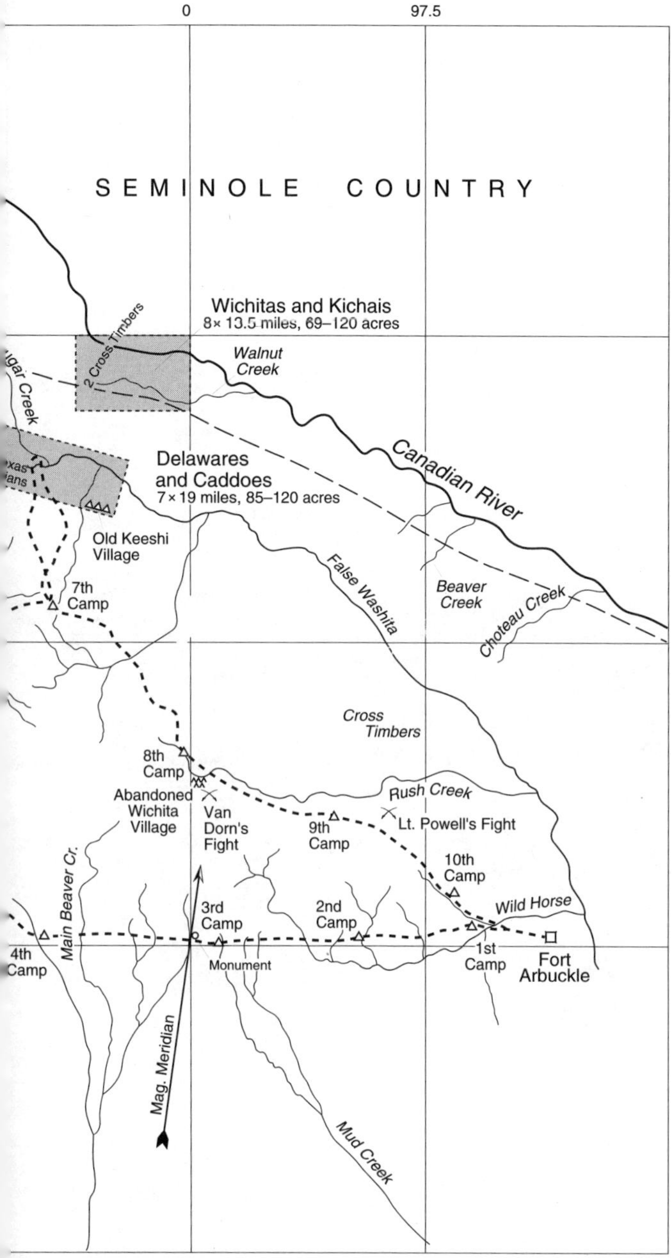
0
97.5
SEMINOLE COUNTRY
Wichitas and Kichais
8× 13.5 miles, 69–120 acres
2 Cross Timbers
Walnut Creek
Canadian River
Delawares and Caddoes
7× 19 miles, 85–120 acres
Old Keeshi Village
7th Camp
False Washita
Beaver Creek
Choteau Creek
Cross Timbers
8th Camp
Abandoned Wichita Village
Van Dorn's Fight
Rush Creek
9th Camp
Lt. Powell's Fight
10th Camp
Wild Horse
Main Beaver Cr.
3rd Camp
2nd Camp
4th Camp
Monument
1st Camp
Fort Arbuckle
Mag. Meridian
Mud Creek
Red River

SOURCE MATERIAL ON THE HISTORY AND ETHNOLOGY OF THE CADDO INDIANS

By John R. Swanton

INTRODUCTION

In a wide area beyond the Mississippi River within the boundaries of the great States of Arkansas, Louisiana, Texas, and Oklahoma, there lived, at the earliest period of which we have historical record—that is, the first half of the sixteenth century—a group of tribes of the very first importance, but one which has been almost lost to sight by our ethnological students and its significance seriously underrated. This is owing in a measure to the fact that the period when these tribes played a prominent part in history was before they and their lands came under the control of the United States and the records of that period, preserved in foreign languages and largely buried in long unfrequented archives, were little known even to American students, and in part because by the time professional ethnologists were prepared to take the field the Caddo tribes had been uprooted from their historic seats, broken up, their separate rites and dialects extinguished or confounded, and the merest shreds of their ancient culture preserved. The attention of students was naturally drawn away to tribes still retaining their early usages and ceremonials in some vigor.

When I undertook to assemble materials from the original sources bearing on the tribes of the lower Mississippi, the Caddo were not included, partly because they did not reach the Mississippi and partly because consideration of them was believed to involve a study of the stock to which they belonged, and work was at that time being conducted in it by Dr. George A. Dorsey of the Field Museum of Natural History.

Thanks to the work of Dr. Dorsey, Dr. Wissler and his collaborators, Mr. Murie, Miss Fletcher, and more recently Dr. Gilmore, Dr. Lesser, Dr. Weltfish, and others, we now have a large body of material on the northern representatives of the Caddoan stock, but the little that has been done on Caddo proper shows clearly that, except in the matter of language, not much bearing upon the real aboriginal lives of these people may be expected through direct studies. It is hoped that Dr. Lesser and Dr. Weltfish will be enabled to complete the investigations on the Caddoan languages they have so well begun. In the present work I have undertaken to bring together the principal materials relating to these Indians from Spanish and French sources. For the translation and publication of them we are particularly indebted to the Texas State Historical Society and the students of the University of Texas, to Prof. Herbert E. Bolton, now librarian of the Bancroft Library in San Francisco, Dr. Carlos E. Castañeda, Latin-American Librarian at the University of Texas, the Quivira Society, Mr. Frederick M. Chabot, Miss Mattie Austin Hatcher, and others who have brought these invaluable documents regarding well-nigh forgotten people to the attention of historians and ethnologists.

The Caddo Indians are noteworthy in many ways. They have given their name to one of the large lakes of northwestern Louisiana and a parish in that State, and contributed many place names to the region which they formerly inhabited. Their name has also been extended to one of the principal linguistic families of North America. To the western Caddo we owe the name of the largest State of our Union. Although not the first Texas tribe to appear in history, they made the greatest impression upon the explorers who visited the territory now occupied by it, so that finally, as just noted, the name which had become fixed to them was transferred to the Spanish, and later Mexican, province, and to the Republic and State which in turn succeeded. Fate decreed that the lands of the Caddo tribes should lie in the debated region between French and Spanish claims, and later between the possessions of the United States and those of Spain, and the Republic of Mexico, whose authority succeeded to that of Spain. Hence, they constituted a factor in the history of the Southwest of peculiar significance.

Moreover, what we know of aboriginal Caddo culture, particularly the excellence of Caddo pottery, and its developed social and ceremonial organizations, and the influence exerted by them upon the surrounding peoples, make the Caddo a center of interest in their own right. There can be little doubt that they played a part in the history of the area before white contact even more important than their role after the advent of Europeans.

In the subjoined material there are but few original notes, the greater part, as the title implies, being a compilation from the productions of earlier writers, including mainly the letters and reports of the missionaries Francisco Casañas de Jesus Maria, Francisco Hidalgo, Isidro Felix de Espinosa, and Gaspar José de Solís, the Historia and Memorias of Juan Agustín Morfi, and the relation of La Salle's companion, Henri Joutel.

The translations from Joutel are my own. Those from Casañas, Hidalgo, and Espinosa are mainly the ones made by Miss Hatcher; those from Solís are mainly those of Miss Kress, while those from Morfi's Memorias are essentially reproductions of the translations printed by Chabot, but I have found it necessary to introduce certain alterations and in one or two cases these are extensive. For the historical sections I have drawn upon numerous authors, early and late. I am particularly indebted to Dr. Castañeda for his assistance on many occasions and particularly in securing a photocopy of the Letter and Report of Fray Francisco Casañas. I am indebted to my friend, the late David I. Bushnell, Jr., for his interest and suggestions and for the use of the sketch by Eastman which constitutes plate 15.

After most of the above was in type, Dr. Parsons' memoir made its appearance, its modest title, Notes on the Caddo, undoubtedly concealing the fact that it contains about all the ethnological material that may be expected from the remnants of the many tribes now covered by the name "Caddo." Of course, one can never say that one has secured absolutely *all* such information, but it may be confidently assumed that this is as perfect a sample of these fragmentary materials as will ever be recovered. That which remains will be acculturation processes rather than the restoration of what we are pleased to call, but never is, primitive.

Comparison of this with the insight into the customs and usages of the tribe furnished by the missionaries is interesting as showing in what direction and to what extent cultural losses have taken place, although there are preserved also data from the earlier time which were entirely missed by them. As might have been anticipated, the ancient tribal cult connected with the temples has disappeared along with those collective functions such as are assumed by our Departments of State and War. The Ghost Dance and Peyote cults have acted powerfully to affect the former and immersion in white institutions the latter. What have survived are the minor social relations between individuals and families, much of the kinship terminology, customs connected with naming and marriage, with the relations brought about by marriage, some of the burial customs, and customs connected with medical practices and witchcraft. Notes regarding certain of these will appear below under the separate heads.

DESIGNATIONS

The name Caddo is applied collectively to a people now regarded as a single tribe, but which, when they were first known to Europeans, consisted of something like 25 tribes forming 3 or more confederated groups besides some units that held themselves entirely separate. The largest confederation was in eastern Texas in the present counties of Nacogdoches, Rusk, Cherokee, and Houston. They called themselves Hasinai, a word which appears in the historical narratives as Asinai, Assoni, Asenay, Cenis, etc., but since these tribes were on terms of closest intimacy and were constantly calling one another "friends," or "allies," the Spaniards early heard the native term meaning "friends" used and came to apply it to them. This word appears in the forms *texas, texias, tejas, tejias, teysas, techan,* etc., and hence these Indians were called Texas Indians and the word was subsequently applied to the province of Texas and taken over by the American colonists as that of the Republic and later State of Texas. The *x* in this word was not, however, pronounced by the Spaniards as it is in English. Sometimes it was made equivalent to Spanish *j,* which resembles German *ch,* but I have usually found that in the early Spanish narratives it is employed for the English *sh,* for which the Spanish language provides no specific sign. This fact is often indicated by synonyms which use *s* or *ch,* just as we find in the present instance. I, therefore, believe that the original pronunciation of Texas was Tayshas, although, as Bolton suggests, it may have been Taychas. It was not a specific term for the Hasinai but became such by accident.

Casañas says:

I notice that this name Tejas includes all the friendly tribes. The name is common to all of them, even though their language may be different. And, since this name is a general term, it must be used for no other reason than to indicate the long-standing friendship which they entertain towards each other. And, therefore, among all these tribes "Tejias" means friends. [Casañas, 1927, p. 286.]

And Solís:

We crossed the San Pedro River and afterwards came to a village that was very large and thickly settled with the Tejas Indians. This name comes from the word *techi,* which in our language means *friend,* and so *Tejas Indians* is the same as saying *friendly Indians.* [Solís, 1931, p. 60.]

Bolton considers the terms "Texas" and "Hasinai" at some length:

The testimony of the sources warrants the conclusion that before the coming of the Spaniards the word Texas, variously spelled by the early writers, had wide currency among the tribes of eastern Texas and perhaps over a large area; that its usual meaning was "friends," or, more technically, "allies"; and that it was used by the tribes about the early missions, at least, to whom especially it later became attached as a group name, to designate a large number of tribes who were customarily allied against the Apaches. In this sense, the Texas included tribes who spoke different languages and who were as widely separated as the Red River and the Rio Grande. It seems that the Neches-Angelina tribes designated did not apply the term restrictively to themselves as a name, but that they did use it in a very untechnical way as a form of greeting, like "hello, friend," with which they even saluted Spaniards after their advent . . .

The name Texas has been variously applied by writers, but it was most commonly used by the Spaniards, from whom the French and the English borrowed it, to designate those tribes of the upper Neches and the Angelina valleys, and this in spite of their knowing full well that among the natives the word had a wider application that has been indicated. There are many variations from this usage in Spanish writings, it is true, but this, nevertheless, is the ordinary one. As a tribal name the term was sometimes still further narrowed to apply to a single tribe. When this occurred, it was most commonly used to designate the Hainai, the head tribe of the group in question, but sometimes it was applied to the Nabedache tribe. As a geographical term, the name Texas was first extended from these Neches-Angelina tribes to their immediate country. Thus for the first quarter of a century of Spanish occupation, the phrase "the Province of Texas" referred only to the country east of the Trinity River; but with the founding of the San Antonio settlements the term was extended westward, more in harmony with its native meaning, to the Medina River, and then gradually to all of the territory included within the present State of Texas.

While the name Texas, as used by the tribes in the eastern portion of the State, was thus evidently a broad and indefinite term applied to many and unrelated tribes occupying a wide area, it is clear that the native group name for most of the tribes about the missions in the Neches and Angelina valleys was Hasinai, or Asinai. Today the term Hasinai is used by the Caddoans on the reservations to include not only the survivors of these Neches-Angelina tribes, but also the survivors of the tribes of the Sabine and Red River County. It seems from the sources, however, that in the early days the term was more properly limited to the former group. In strictest usage, indeed, the earliest writers did not include all of these. A study of contemporary evidence shows that at the first contact of Europeans with these tribes and for a long time thereafter writers quite generally made a distinction between the Hasinai (Asinai, Cenis, etc.) and the Kadohadacho (Caddodacho) group; these confederacies, for such they were in the Indian sense of the term, were separated by a wide stretch of uninhabited territory extending between the upper Angelina and the Red River in the neighborhood of Texarkana; their separateness of organization was positively affirmed, and the details of the inner constitution of both groups were more or less fully described; while in their relations with the Europeans they were for nearly a century dealt with as separate units. Nevertheless, because of the present native use of the term and some early testimony that can not be disregarded, I would not at present assert unreservedly that the term formerly was applied by the natives only to the Neches-Angelina group. If, as seems highly probable, this was the case, in order to preserve the native usage we should call these tribes the Hasinai; if not, then the Southern Hasinai.

The name Hasinai, like Texas, was sometimes narrowed in its application to one tribe, usually the Hainai. But occasionally the notion appears that there was an Hasinai tribe distinct from the Hainai. This, however, does not seem to have been the case. As now used by the surviving Hasinai and Caddos, Hasinai means "our own folk," or, in another sense, "Indians." [Bolton, 1908, pp. 250–252.]

Just as the Hainai were sometimes regarded as the Hasinai tribe par excellence, so in the confederacy on Red River were the Kadohadacho eminent above all the rest. The name is derived from kadi,

or rather kaadi, ka'-ede, meaning "chief," and Kadohadacho signifies
"real chiefs." Strictly, it was applied to one of a group of four bands
(five, if one counts in the Cahinnio) but was first extended in the contracted form Caddo to all of the bands of this group and later to all of
the related tribes, including the Hasinai. It is likely that the fact that
it prevailed was owed as much to the simple character of the word as
to the dominant position of the tribe.

Since Caddo appeared as the name of a group of languages in Gallatin's classification (Gallatin, 1836) a few pages before his similar use
of "Pawnee," it was selected by Powell in the form "Caddoan" to designate a linguistic stock which included, besides the Caddo in the broad-
est sense of the term, the Kichai, the Wichita, with the Tawakoni,
Waco, and their allies, the Pawnee, and the Arikara. The Adai were
at first supposed to constitute a distinct family called Adaizan, but
very shortly the connection of their language with Caddo was demonstrated by Dr. A. S. Gatschet. (Powell, 1891, pp. 45–46, 58–62). In
the present study I shall use Caddoan as the name of the stock, Caddo
to cover all the southern tribes the remnants of which are now classed
under that term, and Kadohadacho for the group of four tribes on
Red River which included the Kadohadacho proper, the Nasoni,
Upper Natchitoches, and Nanatsoho. When I wish to designate the
original Kadohadacho I will call it the Kadohadacho tribe or town.

Following are names applied to the Caddo by various tribes:

Arapaho: Tani'bänĕn, Tani'bänĕnina, Tani'bätha (Mooney).
Cheyenne: Otä's-itä'niuw' (Mooney), U-tai-sǐ-ta (Ten Kate), Utásĕta
(Gatschet).
Choctaw: Ka-lŏx-lá-tce (Ten Kate).
Comanche: At'-ta-wits (Ten Kate), Witúne (Gatschet).
Creek: Kul-hŭl-atsĭ (Grayson).
Kiowa: Ma'se'p (Mooney), Mósi (Ten Kate).
Omaha: Pa'thi"waçabe (Fletcher and La Flesche).
Pawnee: Édawika, Érawika (Gatschet).
Osage: Hiⁿ-sha (La Flesche).
Quapaw: Soudayé (La Harpe), Su'-d¢ĕ (Dorsey).
Tonkawa: Kalu-xnádshu, Karo-xnádshu, Kásseya, Kasseye'-i (Gatschet).
Wichita: Dä'sh-i, Dĕ'sa, Ni'ris-häri's-kǐ'riki (Mooney), Táshash,
Táwitskash (Gatschet).[1]

The Choctaw and Creek names and the two first Tonkawa terms
are corruptions of Kadohadacho. The Arapaho, Cheyenne, and
Kiowa terms signify "Pierced Noses," and the Caddo were so-called
because of their custom of wearing nasal ornaments. The gesture
indicating them in the sign language refers to the same custom. The
Omaha name means "Black Pawnee."

---

[1] Hodge, 1907, 1910, *Articles* Caddoan, Caddo, Kadohadacho, etc.; Mooney, 1896, pp.
953, 1043, 1081, 1102–1103.

The following terms are used by the Caddo to designate other tribes:

Apache, Kiowa Apache: Ka'ntsi (Mooney), Gántsi (Gatschet), Cancey (early writers).
Apache (Lipan): Sow-a-to (Neighbors).
Arapaho: Detse-ka'yăă (Mooney), "Dog Eaters."
Cheyenne: Ba'hakosĭn (Mooney), "Striped Arrows."
Comanche: Saúhto (Mooney), Sau'-tux (Ten Kate), Sow-a-to (Neighbors).
Kiowa Apache (see Apache).
Pawnee: Awáhi (name applied by Caddo and Wichita—Gatschet).
Quapaw: Ima (Gatschet).

THE CADDO TRIBES

(Map 1)

Early in the seventeenth century, when Caddo came to the attention of French and Spanish explorers and traders for the first time except for the De Soto expedition, most of them were gathered into three or four loose confederations. The Hasinai, often called Texas by the Spaniards, were the largest of these, occupying the greater part of the land now included in the Texas counties of Nacogdoches, Rusk, Cherokee, and Houston. The Kadohadacho, or Caddo proper, were at the bend of Red River in southwestern Arkansas and northeastern Texas. A third group lay farther south about the present city of Natchitoches, La., which perpetuates the name of its leading tribe. Between these last two lay a tribe known as Yatasi which at an earlier day appears to have belonged to still another group, but shortly after first contact with the whites it separated into two bands one of which united with the Kadohadacho and the other with the Natchitoches.

Besides these groups there were certain tribes which had an independent status though they were related to the others. The Cahinnio lived in a town on the upper Ouachita in 1687 and in the sixteenth century had probably been settled along Caddo River and about Caddo Gap, where they became known to the followers of De Soto as Tula Indians. They were, it is believed, closely connected with the Kadohadacho, with whom they undoubtedly ultimately united.

The Adai lived in the neighborhood of the present Robeline, La., and camped at times along Red River above Natchitoches. They spoke a divergent dialect of Caddo and seem to have had a ruder culture than the other tribes excepting only the Eyeish. They had the unique distinction of harboring within their territory the first capital of Texas, and this, curiously enough, fell outside of Texas' later boundaries.

The Eyeish lived almost directly west of the Adai, about the present San Augustine, Tex. They are called barbarous by early writers and were looked down upon by the surrounding Indians.

The tribes above enumerated, excepting the two last, did not live in groups which maintained the same constituent elements unchanged from generation to generation. Several, as noted in the case of the Yatasi, split into two or more divisions which, from time to time, established new associations. These will be noted as we take up the several groups.

In the De Soto documents the following tribes or "provinces" are mentioned which were undoubtedly Caddo: Tula, Amaye or Maye, Naguatex, Hacanac, Nissohone, Lacane, Nondacao, Hais (or Aays), Soacatino (or Xuacatino or Xacatin), Guasco, Naquiscoça, Naçacahoz. Daycao is given as the name of a river and the word is undoubtedly from the Caddo language. From the De Soto map we may add Animay and perhaps Cenoa. The word Tula is probably not from Caddo but it is believed that the province so named was occupied by the tribe later called Cahinnio. Amaye or Maye seems to contain the Caddo word signifying a male human being. It may have been recorded by the Spaniards from the misunderstanding of an informant. Naguatex or, as we should pronounce it, Nawataysh, signifies "place of salt" and the people so designated may be set down as a branch of that tribe later known as Namidish. Hacanac, which appears but once, may be identical with Lacane, and the latter certainly is a form of Nacanish. The Nissohone or Nisohone were the later Nasoni, the Nondacao the later Anadarko, and Hais the later Eyeish. Guasco appears in a list of Hasinai tribes given by Casañas, but I am unable to identify the Soacatino, Naquiscoça, and Naçacahoz although they bear undoubted Caddo names. Joutel mentions a tribe allied to the Hasinai called Daquio whose name is possibly related to that of the river Daycao. In Animay we seem to have Hainai, perhaps with maye, "male person," added. Cenoa might be an attempt at Hasinai. (Bourne, 1904, vol. 1, pp. 135–141, 169–183; vol. 2, pp. 32–34, 148; Robertson, 1933, pp. 194–201, 238–257, map p. 418; Garcilaso, 1723; Final Report of the U. S. De Soto Expedition Commission, 1939, pp. 230, 261–263, map 1.)

Joutel in 1687 gives a long list of tribes said to be allied to the Hasinai and another long list of tribes hostile to them. In the first of these I am able to identify the following as Caddo:

Joutel list	Identity
Cenis	Hasinai
Nassoni	Nasoni
Natsohos	Nanatsoho
Cadodaquis	Kadohadacho
Natchittos	Natchitoches
Nondaco	Anadarko
Nadaco	Anadarko (?)
Cahaynohoua	Cahinnio
Nacodissy	Nacogdoche
Haychis	Eyeish

The following are possible identifications:

Joutel list	Identity
Douesdonqua	Doustioni
Dotchetonne	People of Bayou Dauchite
Sacahayé	Soacatino
Daquio	Dacayo River people
Nouista	Neches

The following tribes listed as allies were non-Caddo people:

Joutel list	Identity
Tanico	Tunica
Cappa	Quapaw
Tanquinno	Tunica(?)
Cassia	Kichai
Nadamin	Sadamon (Apache or Tonkawa)
Annaho	Osage(?)
Choumay	Chouman or Shuman (Jumano)

The following seem to be Caddo tribes but are listed as enemies:

Joutel list	Identity
Nadaho	Adai
Nacassa	Yatasi(?)
Nahacassi	Yatasi(?)
Chaye	Choye (a tribe placed by Tonty with the Yatasi)

The other names either belong to non-Caddo people or cannot be identified (Margry, 1875–1886, vol. 3, pp. 409–410).

Jesus Maria de Casañas, after enumerating the nine tribes which made up the Hasinai nation, gives another list which partly repeats the first but contains some names which it is difficult to identify with any in his first list and he adds some new ones, including the tribes of the Caddo group and two non-Caddo tribes, the Kichai and the Bidai. The two lists are compared below.

First List	Second List	Indentity
1. Nabadacho or Ineci	Nabaydacho	Nabedache
2. Necha	Nesta	Neches
3. Nechavi		
4. Nacono	Nacan	Nacanish
5. Nacachau	Nacoz(?)	Nacachau
6. Nazadachotzi	Neticatzi(?)	Nacogdoche
7. Cachae	Caxo	Hainai
8. Nabiti	Naviti	Namidish
9. Nasayaha	Nasayaya	Nasoni(?)
	Nazones	Nasoni
	Guasco	Guasco
	Cataye (cf. Caxo)	
	Dastones	Doustioni
	Nadan	Anadarko
	Tadivas	
	Nabeyeyxa	
	Caynigua	Cahinnio
	Cauddachos	Kadohadacho
	Quizi	Kichai (not Caddo)
	Natsoos	Nanatsoho
	Nasitox	Natchitoches
	Bidey	Bidai (not Caddo)

He lists another group of tribes about 80 leagues to the south and west which contains no Caddo names unless the Guaza are intended for Guasco. Towards the southwest he lists still another but again it contains no Caddo. In enumerating the tribes at enmity with the Hasinai, however, he gives the Nabiti, Nondacau, and possibly the Eyeish ("Hauydix"), besides the Osage, Tunica, Quapaw, Kichai ("Quitxix"), Tonkawa, Kiawa, Lipan, and probably the Wichita ("Canabatinu") (Casañas, 1926, pp. 215–216; 1927, pp. 286–287).

In his declaration before the Spanish authorities, St. Denis, who should have known these Indians well, stated that there were 11 Caddo tribes, the chief of which were the Asinai and their allies, the Navedachos, Nacaos, Namidis, Nacogdoches, Ainays, Nadacocos, Nacitos, and Nachoos. The last two belonged to the Kadohadacho, the Nadacocos were evidently the Anadarko, and the others are all readily recognizable except that we do not know what tribes were included under the "Asinai and their allies," though they were perhaps the Neches and Nasoni.

While the greater number of Casañas' tribes are identifiable in subsequent lists, there are some which seem to disappear completely after his time. Among these are the Nechavi, but Nachawi (signifying "Osage orange") was the native name of Neches River and this was probably a band of Neches Indians or a syononym for the Neches Tribe itself since both are placed on Neches River not many miles apart. The Nacachau may be the Naquiscoça of the De Soto chronicles but it seems to have disappeared from history at an early date. Bolton thinks that the Nasayaya were a part of the Nasoni. The Guasco are important because of the fact that De Soto's followers met them in 1542. The Cataye are not heard of again. They may have been identical with the Caxo and Cachae. The Tadivas and Nabeyeyxa also cannot be identified after this time unless it is possible that the latter is a synonym for Nabedache.

We seem to get hints that the complication exhibited by Caddo tribes was late and that, had we more data regarding them, we should find that there were actually a relatively small number of tribes and that the complication arose because these had separated into two or more sections the constituents of which not infrequently changed their associations. One case of the sort is supplied by the Yatasi, which divided at a very late date, part settling with the Natchitoches and part with the Kadohadacho. There was also a lower and an upper Natchitoches town connected respectively with the same larger groupings. While the Nasoni formed one town of the Kadohadacho, which sometimes bears their name, there was a second close to the Hasinai but, significantly enough, not rated as a true Hasinai division. Indeed, Bolton (1908, p. 270) suggests a third which appears under the name Nasayaha or Nasayaya. At least these last lived close to the true Nasoni. The Nacono may also have been divided. We hear of a tribe called Nacao not reckoned among the true Hasinai but located on a creek called today Naconicho. A tribe called Lacane was encountered by Moscoso some distance farther east and it is altogether probable that it was a part of the same people. In other words, it looks as though the Nacono, Nacao, Naconicho, and Lacane were fragments of one tribe, and to these may be added Mooney's "Nakanawan." I was told, indeed, by Caddo Jake that Nakanawan, or "Nakahanawan," as he pronounced it, was another name for the Hainai but the Nacanish very likely united with them. It is possible that we should add the Nacachau to this list, a tribe which disappears very early in Hasinai history. Bolton (1908, pp. 260–261) has demonstrated that the Hainai were also called Cachae by Casañas—in his later list referred to as Caxo, or, possibly Cataye. My own informants stated that the Hainai had several different names. A tribe early associated with the Hasinai, yet not constituting, according to Casañas, one of the original group, was the Nadaco or Anadarko. It is evidently the one he calls Nadan in the list just quoted and goes back to the time of Moscoso, when we have the name in the form Nondacao. It retained its designation until a very late period and gave it finally to Anadarko, Okla.

More puzzling than any of these cross-connections is that which is suggested between Casañas' Nabadacho and Nabiti, listed as two of the original Hasinai group. The first of these, usually called Nabedache but spelled more correctly by Casañas in another place Nabaydacho, was located on San Pedro Creek and it was in the Nabedache town that the first Spanish mission was established. The Nabedache are sometimes called San Pedros. The Nabiti he also calls Naviti, and they are evidently the Nabiri of St. Denis. But Bolton notes that this tribe seems to occupy a spot where Joutel found a tribe called Noadiche, and this latter appears to bear the same name as the Naouydiche of La Harpe, a band of whom was found in 1719 well north of Red River in what is now Oklahoma (Bolton, 1908, p. 270; Margry, 1875–1886, vol. 6, p. 286; Beaurain, 1831, p. 204). In a French list in a letter by the Duc de Linares (Margry, 1875–1886, vol. 6, p. 217), we find the form Namidis, and knowing that one of the dialectic differences between eastern and western Caddo was a change from m to w, and that b and v are often used for w in Spanish, we seem to find a family relationship between the names Nabiti, Naviti, Nabiri, Namidis, Noadiche (for Nowadish) and Naouydiche. To these must also be added the Naguatex of the De Soto narratives which would be transliterated in English as Nawatāysh. This does not prove, of course, that these Nabiti-Namidis people were related to the Nabedache. The names are distinguished in later times, the former meaning "place of salt" while the latter is said to be the term for a berry like a blackberry borne on thorny trees. The philologist Gatschet, however, asserts that the ancient name of the Nabedache was Nawadishe (Hodge, 1910, vol. 2, *art.* Nabedache), and if his source of information was reliable, the two would appear to be brought together. Such an identification would reconcile two confusing statements by Morfi (1935, pt. 1, p. 82; 1932, p. 5), one to the effect that the Texas proper inhabited the banks of the San Pedro though that was the country of the Nabedache when the San Pedro mission was founded, and the other that the Nabedache lived about the head waters of the Neches. It is true that Casañas does not locate his Nabiti *on* the Neches but he places them to the north of the other Hasinai towns—except the Nadaco and Nasoni which lay farther east—and the Nabiti were probably nearer than any others to the headwaters of the Neches River. Undoubtedly we have two tribes called Nabedache and Namidi or Namidish distinguished at a very early period, and it must always remain doubtful whether they stemmed from one original group or whether the resemblance in their names is purely accidental.

To sum up, then, we seem to have the following original Hasinai tribes: Hainai, Neches (or Neche), Nacogdoche, Nacono or Nacao or Naconish, Namidish (Nabiti) or Nawidish, Nasoni, Anadarko, and perhaps Nabedache, two of which, the Nasoni and Anadarko, were not reckoned as original Hasinai tribes while two others, the Nacono and Namidish, were represented by divisions outside of the Hasinai.

The Kadohadacho confederation presents to us fewer difficulties. When first visited in 1687 it was found to consists of four tribes, Kadohadacho, Nanatsoho, Nasoni, and Natchitoches—the last two represented also in the Hasinai and Natchitoches confederations respectively—which lived close together and to which a fifth tribe, the Cahinnio, was sometimes added though this was established near the upper Ouachita. In early historic times part of the Yatasi were added to these after that tribe had been disrupted by the Chickasaw (Beaurain, 1831, pp. 185–186). The location of the Nasoni town in this group was pretty certainly that of the "Principal Caddo village" on the King map (pl. 2), and the site of the Kadohadacho village the "Old Caddo village," northeast of it beyond Red River.

The Natchitoches group consisted primarily of the tribe which gave it the name and the Doustioni. By 1690 a part of the Ouchita of the lower Ouachita River had joined these, and it may be assumed that the remainder did so at a later period but we have no information on that point. Tonti speaks of a tribe called "Capiché" as constituting part of this group but none bearing a similar name appears in any later document and it may be assumed that the tribe intended was the Doustioni or that it is a bad misspelling of Nakasa (or Nakasé) (Cox, 1905, vol. 1, p. 45; Beaurain, 1931, pp. 32–33). The identity of these Nakasa causes some difficulty since they are mentioned only by Bienville (*in* Margry, 1875–1886, vol. 4, p. 439) in the account of his expedition from the Taensa villages to Red River in 1700 and in the account of this same expedition by Beaurain (1931, p. 33). The only Indians encountered on this part of the river by later travelers before reaching the Yatasi were Adai, and Bienville himself, in his discussion of the Indian tribes of Louisiana written about 1718, although making mention of his earlier expedition, drops the Nakasa from his narrative. He speaks merely of the Natchitoches, Doustioni, and Yatasi (those already brought down to unite with the two former) and the Adai living by themselves 7 leagues west (Bienville ms.). Since the Nakasa were found close to the Yatasi, they may have been a part of that tribe, a form of the name with the Caddo prefix *na-* and the *k* a misreading or miscopying of *t*. Such an identification is strengthened somewhat by Tonti, who encountered a tribe in about the same region which he calls "Natchés" (Cox, 1905, vol. 1, p. 45). This may be interpreted as Yatasi plus the prefix *na-* and with the loss of a vowel between *t* and *ch*. The *ch* in French is, of course, pronounced like English *sh* and would therefore approximate *s*. The loss of the vowel is rendered probable by the mention by Iberville of a tribe on Red River called "Nataché." Such analyses may seem far-fetched to the ordinary reader, but not to one familiar with the manner in which Indian terms became distorted in copying. The name of the Avoyels tribe, for instance, appears in one or two documents as "Houjets" and in that case the identification is undoubted.

The Yatasi, as has been said above, lived at an early period midway between the Natchitoches and Kadohadacho and subsequently separated into two parts, one of which united with each of these others. At one time they themselves may have constituted a group of the tribes since Tonti speaks of the three villages of "Yatachés, Nadas, and Choye" which were "together" (Cox, 1905, vol. 1, p. 45). The Nadas may possibly have been part of the Adai, the name here carrying the *na-* prefix. The Choye were seemingly the "Chaye," listed by Joutel among enemies of the Hasinai (Margry, 1875–86, vol. 3, p. 409), but this helps us little in the determination of their relationship except that we may assume from the association they were a Caddo band.

Lesser and Weltfish (1932, pp. 13–14), very recent students of the living Caddo, found the following tribes remembered: Hainai, Nabedache, Anadarko, Natchitoches, Yatasi, Nacogdoche, Haish, and Kadohadacho. They list one more, evidently referring to a band living on the Kiamichi River and named for it, though this may have been substituted for a more ancient appellation. Mooney's list (1896, pp. 1092, 1093), made about 40 years earlier, contains no name resembling Kiamichi but adds those of the Adai, the Nakanawan (probably intended for the Nakanish), the I'măha, a band of Quapaw, and the Yowa'ni, a band of Choctaw. These last are named from the southernmost Choctaw town from which it is to be assumed many of them came. The I'măha undoubtedly represented a hold-over from the time when the Quapaw Tribe lived beside the Kadohadacho and consisted of individuals which remained behind after the rest of their nation had gone to Oklahoma. (See pp. 86 to 89.)

Lesser and Weltfish quote native informants to the effect that at one time all bands of the Caddo spoke divergent dialects except the Hainai and Nabedache whose speech was identical. In fact, they claimed that the Nabedache were a branch of the Hainai rather than of the Caddo in general. The Hainai were the largest band and the Kadohadacho the second largest. They continue:

The divergence of Hainai dialectically from Caddo proper is supported by a little evidence still obtainable in the form of a few remembered differences in words. These are of two types: Slight phonetic differences of a dialectic character; and complete difference of word. In some cases the latter type of difference suggests adoption of foreign words, particularly of Spanish words; such occur prominently for words which must be relatively recent in use, such as the word for horse. In Caddo proper, the vocabulary shows instances of multiple synonymy, and more than one word for the same object, which may prove to have resulted from two factors: Adoption of foreign words, as Spanish, and preservation of usages of a number of the Caddo bands in the contemporary Caddo proper. Hainai kinship terms and usages also differ from those of Caddo proper. [Lesser and Weltfish, 1932, pp. 13–14.]

By Caddo proper they mean the Caddo of the Kadohadacho "which seems to have gradually eliminated whatever former dialectic differentiation existed, in favor of a common speech." The ancient separation between the Kadohadacho and Hasinai seems to have been perpetuated to the present day in the northern and southern bands of Caddo reported by Dr. Parsons (1941, pp. 8–9).

This information agrees in almost every particular with what I learned when I visited the Caddo in 1912. Caddo Jake, one of the oldest of the Caddo at that time and one of the few Indians who knew the eastern or Natchitoches dialect, said that Nabedache was the same as Hainai, and that the Anadarko (Nadako) and Kadohadacho were "somewhat related." He affirmed that in some places you cannot understand Hainai, assuming that you are a speaker of Kadohadacho. The Nacogdoche was the same as the Anadarko. He added that he had heard the Adai, or "Hadai" as he called them, and the Haish converse and that their languages were "about the same."

Another Caddo, White Bread, confirmed the close relationship between Hainai and Nabedache, and held that the Kadohadacho, Nacogdoche, and Anadarko were related but considered the last mentioned a little different from the first two. In assigning the Adai to the same group he was evidently in error.

Caddo Jake stated that the Natchitoches and Yatasi languages were the same and gave the following examples of their dialect:[2]

NATCHITOCHES AND YATASI	KADOHADACHO	ENGLISH
ha'dĭkya	do'haya	now
kya'ashĭk	wa'ásha	I can't
ĭ'ntcĭ hayŏ'k'o	waasha't okȧna'sĭwa	I am not going to talk
ĭ'mĭ	íwĭ'	eagle
hĭ'dĭk'u	nȧsaik !û'na	in the evening
nȧ'nuwa	nȧ'bȧ	in the night
hĭntĭ'sak'	sa'onts sao'	house
	(sao also=a tent)	
kōho'n	kō'ho	alligator
watȧ'n	bā'tȧ	fish
tc !aŏ'k	t !ao'ẋ	beaver
kĭ'dĭn	yŏ'sā	muskrat
nȧ'mtsĭ	na'otsĭ	bear
mȧdo''	wȧdo''	wildcat
do'	do'o	rabbit
tā'nȧ'	tȧ'nȧhȧ	buffalo
dŏ'ot	dȧt	mouse
sĭ'n'ȧnk'aĭ	cĭ'waẋ	squirrel
hȧ'dĭk !ya hȧnĭk tsȧk kom-payŏ'kȧn	hȧme'tcai tca-yŏ'konȧn	now I am very tired of talking
kȧwa'yoĭ' (Sp. *caballo*)	dĭ'tȧma	horse
dĭ'	dĭ'ĭtsĭ	dog
kȧwa'yoĭ'do'tsĭ	do'tĭtẋ	colt
kȧmta'gĭdȧn	hȧha'otsaso (or) ha'owĭdȧ	wind
ĭ'tok'	nĭ'k !o	fire
kȧto'k !	koko	water
mā'dȧt	wā'dȧt	dirt
kû'nakĭskayā'mtȧ'ksȧ	kwĭska'oka	east
akȧnĭ'gĭdaha'gȧdĭsa	hā'nĭdā'dĭs	creek
de'mȧs	de'wȧs	pine

The words for quail, duck, tame goose, a kind of wild goose, pigeon, parrot, chicken hawk, screech owl, two other species of owl, crane,

---

[2] The letters in the above words and those following carry values similar to those associated with them in English: *a*, *ā̇*, the sound of *a* in "barn"; *ȧ* like *a* in "ability"; *e* like *ai* in "fail"; *ĭ* like *ee* in "seek"; *ĭ* like *i* in "it"; *o*, *ō*, the sound of *o* in "roll"; *û* like *u* in "pull"; *ꞷ̇*, a spirant; ', a breathing; ', a pause; !, gives an explosive sound to the consonant preceding; *c* is like *sh* in "shall"; *tc* like *tch* in "catch."

heron, wolf, fox, south, west, north, doctor, cedar, ash, elm, walnut, oak, tobacco, apple, sweetpotato, snake, deer, panther, raccoon, opossum, antelope, elk, and rat were said to be the same in all dialects.

RIVER NAMES IN CADDO
(Said to be in the Anadarko and Hainai dialects)

Brazos	Baha′tsĭ, Little River."
Canadian	Ko′ko akä′yo.
Cibolo Creek	Kä′ndácka, "Swift, strong water."
Colorado	Nawä′kȧs.
Guadalupe	Kä′n′tĭno, "Red, swift water."
Mississippi	Ba′hȧt sa′sĭn, "Mother River," *or* Ba′hȧt hȧĭ′mĭ, "Big River."
Neches	Natca′wi, "Osage orange."
Pecos	Kä′ndácka (according to a second informant) "Swift, strong water."
Red	Ba′hȧt, "River."
Sabine	Ka′yaẋci (this ran between the Kadohadacho and Anadarko).
San Antonio	Kaí′saẋko.
Washita	Kene′di ko′ko.

Sodo Lake preserves its Caddo name, from Tso′to, "water thrown up into the drift along the shore by a wind." The above identifications were mainly from Caddo Jake. Others identified the Kä′n′tĭno with the Colorado, the Kä′ndácka with the Pecos (as given in parenthesis), and the Kaí′saẋko or Kaí′saẋko-sa′hako with the Guadalupe, but Caddo Jake was positive that these three rivers were near or northeast of San Antonio, and that they all ran into the Nawä′kȧs before reaching the sea. This might mean that they all ran into connecting bays.

POPULATION

Statements regarding the population of the various Caddo groups in early times are very general and very unsatisfactory. We will take them in chronological order, considering first the Hasinai, then the Kadohadacho and Natchitoches groups, and finally the Adai and Eyeish.

Father Anastasius Douay, in his account of La Salle's expedition into the Hasinai country in 1686, says of the confederation, which he terms a "village," it "is one of the largest and most populous that I have seen in America. It is at least twenty leagues long, not that it is evenly inhabited, but in hamlets of ten or twelve cabins, forming cantons, each with a different name" (Cox, 1905, vol. 1, p. 232). He adds that there were two families to a house, but Joutel, during his passage through the same country a year later, notes that the grass houses of the Hasinai held "usually eight or ten families, some [dwellings] being sixty feet in diameter." The houses of the Nasoni were not as tall as those of the Hasinai proper but it is not clear that they accommodated fewer people (Margry, 1875–1886, vol. 3, pp. 345, 393).

In 1691 the Spanish Franciscan missionary Casañas says that these people were "numerous." Farther on he informs us that "some three or four hundred persons—more or less—had died in that province during the month of March" of the same year in consequence of an epidemic. Still farther on he is more detailed—and somewhat more moderate:

According to the information I have received about three thousand persons among all the friendly tribes of the *Tejias* must have died during the epidemic which the Lord sent during the month of March, 1691. The disease was worse in some provinces than in others. As to our own province, I have already stated that the deaths probably reached the number of three hundred—in other provinces the number was sometimes greater, sometimes less. [Casañas, 1927, pp. 294, 303.]

As he has already classed as "Tejias" all the Caddo tribes of every connection as well as the Kichai and Bidai, the larger figure must be interpreted as applying to them. In 1699 a Canadian who had lived several years among the Hasinai reported that they "form but one village and the same nation" and he estimated "that they do not exceed six hundred or seven hundred men." [Margry, 1875–1886, vol. 4, p. 316.] Here the Hasinai alone seem to be meant, and they are called the most populous tribe of the region as they were by the missionaries Casañas and Hidalgo. According to Ramón, the four missions resulting from his expedition of 1716 "would comprise from four thousand to five thousand persons of all ages and both sexes" (Bolton, 1908, p. 274). In the same year the missionary Espinosa recorded in his diary that he believed "the Indians grouped around the three Queréteran missions, not including the mission among the Nacogdoche and the Nacao, would number three thousand"; and after a residence there of some years he estimated the number of persons within the range of each mission at "about one thousand" (Bolton, 1908, p. 274). Ramón's estimate is probably the basis of Morfi's statement (1935, p. 187) that "over 5000 Indians" were gathered into the missions established by the former. A slight addition should be made to the sedentary Hasinai population by adding that "Naouydiche" band met by La Harpe on a northern branch of Red River. The chief had 40 warriors under him which would indicate 100 to 150 souls. (Margry, 1875–1886, vol. 6, p. 286). In a note to the original manuscript of his History, Morfi adds that the Nacogdoche Indians were "divided into twenty-two rancherías, in which there were one hundred and twenty warriors." The mission "was established in the center of these rancherías, which spread for a distance of ten leagues from south to north" (Morfi, 1935, vol. 1, p. 230). Populations of 400 to 450 and 100 to 150 are indicated. Bolton furnishes the following figures from the records of the Aguayo expedition of the year 1721:

When Aguayo in that year re-established the missions that had been abandoned some two years before, he made a general distribution of presents and clothing among the Indians at the different villages. At the mission of San Francisco de los Neches he gave the Neche chief the Spanish *baston*, token of authority, and "clothed entirely one hundred and eighty-eight men, women, and children." . . . West of the Neches Aguayo had been visited by a hundred Nacono from down the river. At the mission of Concepción he requested the Hainai chief, Cheocas by name, to collect all his people. This took some time, as they were widely scattered, but several days later they were assembled, and Aguayo gave clothing and other presents to four hundred, including, possibly, eighty Kadohadachos, who happened to be there on a visit [in fact to confer with St. Denis]. Similarly, at the Nacogdoche mission he provided clothing "for the chief and all the rest," a total of three hundred and ninety; and at the Nasoni mission for three hundred. This gives us a total of less than fourteen hundred Indians who came to the missions during Aguayo's *entrada* to take advantage of the ever welcome presents. This number apparently included the majority of the five most important tribes, and probably included some from the neighboring smaller tribes attached to the missions. [Bolton 1908, p. 275.]

In 1777–1779 De Mézières discovered that the Nasoni and Anadarko together had 25 men, the Nabedache 30, and the "Texas" (presumably the Hainai) 80 (Bolton, 1914, vol. 2, pp. 145, 263). Morfi (about 1783) notes that the Texas (Hainai) had 80 warriors, and the Nabedache were reduced to less than 40, but that the Nacogdoche numbered 300 warriors. He mentions also a tribe called "Ahijitos" almost as numerous as the last named but these were probably the Kichai (Morfi, 1935, p. 82). In 1805 Sibley (*in* Amer. State Pap., Indian Affairs, 1832, p. 722) reported about 40 men of the Anadarko, and 80 each of the Nabedache and Hainai. The Cincinnati Gazette (1818–20) states, on the authority of an Indian agent recently returned from Natchitoches, that the Anadarko numbered 120–130 including 30 warriors, the Nacogdoche 150 including 40 warriors, the San Pedro (Nabedache?) 130 with 30 warriors, the "Naradachoes" (Namidish?) 100 with 20 warriors, and the Texas (Neches or Hainai) 150 with 30 warriors (Sibley, 1922, p. 96). It is probable that the Texas were really the Hainai although the "Eynies" are said to be "dispersed and mingled with other tribes of the vicinity." The Mexican Padilla (1820) has a somewhat exaggerated idea of the sizes of the tribes. He gives the Nacogdoche a total of 200, the Nadacos (Anadarko) 200, the San Pedro (presumably Nabedache) 500, the Texas (Hainai?) 400, and a tribe he calls "Yuganís" 150.[3] In 1828

---

[3] Padilla, 1919, pp. 49, 52; the "Yuganís" may have been the Yowani band of Choctaw.

Sanchez says there were 29 families of Anadarko (Sanchez, 1926, p. 279), and in 1934 Almonte (1925, p. 222) enumerates 100 "Tejas" and 300 Nacogdoche. In 1837 the Caddo, Anadarko, Nacogdoche, Nabedache and Eyeish together were said to number 225 (Muckleroy, 1922, p. 232). In 1847 Governor Burnet estimates about 50 families each of the Hainai, San Pedro, Nabedache, and Nacogdoche (Schoolcraft, 1851, vol. 1, pp. 39–40). From another source we get 450 Anadarko in 1847 and in 1849, 450 Hainai (Schoolcraft, 1857, vol. 6, pp. 686–687). The first careful census was made by Jesse Stem in 1851 and showed 202 Anadarko and 113 Hainai, but a few others were then living apart in the Choctaw Nation, Indian Territory. There were over 100 warriors (Indian Affairs, 1851, p. 261). In 1855 Neighbors reported 205 Anadarko but seems to have omitted the Hainai though in a letter to him Hill notes that there were then about 200 Waco, Tawakoni, Kadohadacho, and Anadarko north of Red River (Indian Affairs, 1855, pp. 178, 184). In 1856 the number of Indians on the Brazos reservation had increased to 948 but the tribal affiliations are not in evidence (Indian Affairs, 1856, p. 173). In 1857 Neighbors reported 210 Anadarkos but some Caddo were still north of Red River (Indian Affairs, 1857, p. 265). When the Indians were removed to the north in 1859 they numbered 1,050 but the tribal affiliations were not recorded (Indian Affairs, 1859, p. 328). After the outbreak of the Civil War most of the Caddo fled to Kansas, and in 1864 150 Hainai were there (Indian Affairs, 1864, p. 319). In 1872, some years after their return to the reservation, 85 Hainai were counted in addition to the Caddo proper (Indian Affairs, 1872, p. 254). In 1873 the number had sunk to 50 but they were not separately enumerated again until 1876, when there were 30 (Indian Affairs, 1873, p. 224; 1876, p. 64). In 1877 the Caddo, Hainai, and some Delaware had a population of 643, which had been increased over the preceding year by the addition of 63 former absentees, principally Hainai (Indian Affairs, 1877, p. 112). In 1878 the Hainai are mentioned but not enumerated separately and they are omitted from all subsequent censuses of the Caddo population. Undoubtedly some of the Hasinai were returned under the heading of Caddo; not all were covered by the name Hainai.

If the Cahinnio are to be regarded as part of the Kadohadacho, Joutel's statement that they occupied 100 cabins in 1687 is the first information vouchsafed us regarding the population of any part of this group, except that the De Soto chroniclers represent their supposed ancestors, the Tula Indians, as numerous (Robertson, 1933, p. 194; Bourne, 1904, vol. 1, p. 137). In 1718 Bienville (ms., see pp. 55–56 below) says that the Kadohadacho, under whom he seems to include

the Kichai, had about 200 men but that they had formerly counted
500–600. About the same time La Harpe estimated that there were
then in the four Kadohadacho tribes, and including some Yatasi
who had recently joined them, not more than 400 souls but that 10
years before they had counted 2,500 (Margry, 1875–1886, vol. 6, p.
264). In 1773 De Mézières found 60 warriors among the Little
Caddo, 10 more on the Prairie des Ennemis, and 90 among the Great
Caddo (Bolton, 1914, vol. 2, p. 83). He states that the great epidemic
of 1777 had carried off more than 300 Kadohadacho, and about 1800
Sibley tells us that smallpox had destroyed about half of them. In
1805 the latter estimated 100 warriors belonging to the old nation,
and as many more old men and strangers, and adds that there were
40 or 50 more women than men (Sibley, in Amer. State Pap., Indian
Affairs, 1832, p. 721). An estimate dated about 1818–20 gives a
Caddo population of 500 to 600 including 120 warriors (Sibley, 1922,
p. 95). Padilla (1919, p. 49) raises the population figure to 2,000,
perhaps including more tribes under that head, though he enumerates separately the Nacogdoche, Ais, San Pedro Indians, Texas, and
Anadarko. Schoolcraft (1853, vol. 3, pp. 585, 596) gives a population figure of 450 in 1825 and Peter B. Porter, 4 years later,
the same. In 1834 Almonte estimates 500 over all and in 1836
there is another estimate of 250 warriors (Almonte, 1925, p. 222;
Muckleroy, 1922, p. 241). However, a careful census by Stem, taken
in 1851, showed 161 Caddo on the Brazos Reservation (Indian Affairs,
1851, p. 261). As the Chickasaw Agent Upshaw had stated that there
were then 167 Caddo among his people, the total at that time would
seem to have been about 300 (Foreman, 1930 a, p. 181). In 1855
Neighbors reported 188 Caddo on the Brazos Reserve, and Hill reported that 200 Waco, Tawakoni, Caddo, and Hasinai were still north
of Red River (Indian Affairs, 1855, pp. 178, 184). In 1856 the Indians under Neighbors had increased to 948 but the tribes are not
separately enumerated (Indian Affairs, 1856, p. 173). In 1857, 235
Caddo are returned, and still all had not been brought together, nor
are we told what proportion of the 1,050 which Neighbors led out
of Texas in 1859 were Caddo (Indian Affairs, 1857, p. 265). In 1864,
after the greater part of the Caddo and Hasinai had fled to Kansas,
there were 370 in that state (Indian Affairs, 1864, p. 319). In 1872,
392 were back on their old reservation, and in 1873, 401 are returned
(Indian Affairs, 1872, p. 254; 1873, p. 224). In 1874 and 1875 they
are not enumerated separately from the Hasinai (Hainai) and a
band of Delaware, but in 1876 467 are separately listed (Indian
Affairs, 1874, p. 100; 1875, p. 289; 1876, p. 64). In 1877 the Caddos,

including Hainai and Delaware, numbered 643 and the same figure is given in 1878 (Indian Affairs, 1877, p. 112; 1878, p. 112).

In Beaurain's account (1831, pp. 32–33) of Bienville's expedition to the Natchitoches Indians and their allies in 1700, he states that the Natchitoches themselves had 200 men, the Doustioni 50 and the Yatasi, who had not yet settled with the Natchitoches and Kadohadacho, 200 men more. In Bienville's own memoir of 1718 (ms., see p. 56), however, he says that the three tribes had 400 men when he visited them but that at date of writing they had been reduced to 80. La Harpe, who visited these people 1 year after Bienville penned his memoir, states that they totaled 200 souls, but Beaurain in his account of La Harpe's expedition reduces this to 150 (Margry, 1875–1886, vol. 6, p. 254; Beaurain, 1831, p. 179). It is not clear whether the earlier estimates include the Ouachita or not, though as Bienville himself found part of them living on Ouachita River in a village of about 5 cabins and counting 70 men, it would seem as though they must have been left out of his later estimates of the Natchitoches (Margry, 1875–1886, vol. 4, p. 434). Part of the tribe had already joined the Natchitoches (Cox, 1905, vol. 1, pp. 44–45) and the rest probably followed them before 1718. It is, at any rate, a fair inference that the remnant are included in the later estimates of Bienville and La Harpe.

In 1773 De Mézières reports that there were only three warriors in the Yatasi town (Bolton, 1914, vol. 2, p. 78), but in 1805 Sibley found 8 men there belonging to the original Yatasi tribe and 25 women besides children. Other men had come in, however, so that there were about 40 men altogether. The same year he reports that there were but 12 men and 19 women left of the Natchitoches (Sibley, in Amer. State Pap., Indian Affairs, 1832, pp. 722, 724). Schoolcraft (1853, vol. 3, p. 585) quotes a census taken in 1825 which reported 36 Yatasi and 25 Natchitoches. Some of these undoubtedly married with and became lost in the white and Negro population about them, but a part united with the larger bodies of Kadohadacho and Hasinai and followed their fortunes to Texas and Oklahoma. Caddo Jake, one of the principal informants of Mr. Mooney and myself, was a Natchitoches Indian.

There now remain for consideration the two small aberrant tribes, the Adai and Eyeish.

According to Beaurain (1813, p. 33), Bienville in 1700 visited an Adai village containing 50 warriors. In 1716 three French traders came upon an Adai village in which there were about 30 inhabitants (Beaurain, 1831, p. 135). Two years later, however, Bienville (ms., see p. 56) estimates 100 men alone. In 1721, according to Morfi, Aguayo found more than 400 Adai Indians (Morfi, 1935, pt. 1, p. 219). In 1805 Sibley (*in* Amer. State Pap., Indian Affairs, 1832, p. 722) reported that there were 20 men but a larger proportion of women. In 1825 an informant of Schoolcraft (1853, vol. 3, p. 585) gives the total Adai population as 27, and they are now entirely merged with the other Caddo.

In 1716 the three Frenchmen mentioned above found that the Eyeish village consisted of 10 cabins (Beaurain, 1831, p. 135). The same year Morfi says there were "seventy families settled in eight rancherías, occupying a distance of two leagues" (Morfi, 1935, pt. 1, p. 230). In 1779 De Mézières reported 20 families there (Bolton, 1914, vol. 2, p. 257). In 1801 most of this tribe is said to have been destroyed, but Sibley (*in* Amer. State Pap., 1832, pp. 96, 722c) reported 25 souls in 1805 and an estimate made in 1818-20 doubles the number, while Padilla (1919, p. 49) gives a population of "about 300" and in 1828 we are told that there were 160 families (Muckleroy, 1922, p. 233). These last figures are evidently very much in error. Although the tribal name is remembered, the tribe itself is now wholly merged with the peoples which go under the name of "Caddo."

The more important of these estimates may conveniently be tabulated as follows, the figures in parentheses being obtained by multiplying the number of warriors by four:

HASINAI

Year and authority	Warriors	Total population
1699 (Anonymous Canadian)	600–700	(2, 400–2, 890)
1716 (Ramón)		4, 000–5, 000
1721 (Aguayo)		1, 378+
1779 (De Mézières)	135	(540)
1783 (Morfi)	380 (?)	(1, 520)
1805 (Sibley)	200	(800)
1818–20 (Cincinnati Gazette)	150	650–660
1820 (Padilla)		1, 450
1834 (Almonte)		400
1847 (Burnet)	200 (families)	(800)
1851 (Stem)	100+	315+
1864 (Indian Office)		150
1872 (Indian Office)		85
1873 (Indian Office)		50
1876 (Indian Office)		30

KADOHADACHO

Year and authority	Warriors	Total population
1700 (Bienville)	500–600	(2, 000–2, 400)
1709 (La Harpe)		2, 500
1718 (Bienville)	200	(800)
1719 (La Harpe)		400
1773 (De Mézières)	160	(640)
1805 (Sibley)	200	(800+)
1818–20 (Cincinnati Gazette)	120	500–600
1820 (Padilla)		2, 000
1825 (from Schoolcraft)		450
1829 (Porter)		450
1834 (Almonte)		500
1836 (H. M. Morfit)	250	(1, 000)
1851 (Stem)		300
1857 (Neighbors)		235+
1864 (Indian Office)		370
1872 (Indian Office)		392
1873 (Indian Office)		401
1876 (Indian Office)		467

NATCHITOCHES GROUP

Year and authority	Warriors	Total population
1700 (Bienville in Beaurain)	450	(1, 800)
1700 (Bienville's Memoir)	400	(1, 600)
1718 (Bienville's Memoir)	80	(320)
1719 (La Harpe Narrative)		200
1719 (La Harpe in Beaurain)		150
1773 (De Mézières)	3 (Yatasi)	(12)
1805 (Sibley)	52	(208)
1825 (From Schoolcraft)		61

ADAI

Year and authority	Warriors	Total population
1700 (Bienville in Beaurain)	50	(200)
1716 (French traders)	30	(120)
1718 (Bienville)	100	(400)
1721 (Aguayo)		400+
1805 (Sibley)	20	(80)
1825 (From Schoolcraft)		27

EYEISH

Year and authority	Warriors	Total population
1716 (French traders)	10 (cabins)	320
1716 (Morfi)	70 (families)	100–150
1779 (De Mézières)	20 (families)	80
1805 (Sibley)		25
1818–20 (Cincinnati Gazette)		50
1820 Padilla		300
1828 (Muckleroy)		640

The population figures for 1880 and subsequent years, after all of the tribes of this linguistic group had been brought under the one name "Caddo" are as follows:

1880: 139 men, 156 women, 123 boys, 120 girls.
1881: 151 men, 151 women, 127 boys, 123 girls.
1882: 151 men, 151 women, 128 boys, 123 girls.
1883: 535, total population.
1884: 271 males, 285 females (including 60 children of school age).
1885: 278 males, 292 females (including 88 children of school age).
1886: 521, total population (125 of school age incl. some Delaware).
1887: 256 males, 269 females (including 121 children).
1888: 491, total population.
1889: 517, total population.
1890: 538, total population.
1891: 545, total population.
1892: 526, total population.
1893: 507, total population.
1894: 507, total population.
1895: 498, total population.
1896: 476, total population.
1897–1903: Not reported separately from the Wichita, Tawakoni, Waco, and a band of Delaware.
1904: 535, total population.
1905: 274 males, 222 females.
1906: 277 males, 274 females.
1907: 555, total population.
1908–1929: Not reported separately from the Wichita, Tawakoni, Waco, and a band of Delaware.
1910: 452, total population (census).
1930: 353 males, 355 females (total population, 1930 census, 625).
1931: 362 males, 367 females.
1932: 383 males, 377 females.
1933: 386 males, 387 females.
1934: 391 males, 408 females.
1935: 456 males, 472 females.
1936: 466 males, 481 females.
1937: 479 males, 488 females.[4]

If we omit from the Hasinai enumerations that of De Mézières which is evidently partial, that of Padilla, which is probably exaggerated like all of his figures, and that of Burnet, which is superficial, and if we remember that the Aguayo reckoning does not profess to be complete, the remaining early figures tell a fairly consistent story of decline. The same is true of the Kadohadacho figures if we omit those of Padilla, H. M. Morfit, and perhaps Sibley. Relative consistency is introduced into the last three groups if we allow for

[4] U. S. Indian Office Reports for 1880, p. 71; 1881, p. 77; 1882, p. 64; 1883, p. 70; 1884, p. 79; 1885, p. 83; 1886, p. 128; 1887, p. 81; 1888, p. 96; 1889, p. 188; 1890, p. 187; 1891, p. 352; 1892, p. 386; 1893, p. 702; 1894, p. 576; 1895, p. 372; 1896, p. 528; 1994, p. 606; 1905, p. 300; 1906, p. 308; 1907, p. 48; 1930, p. 44; 1931, p. 51; 1932, p. 44; 1933, p. 129; 1934, p. 139; 1935, p. 165; 1936, p. 216; 1937, p. 257.

the increase by immigration into the Yatasi tribe between 1773 and 1805, remember that the first two estimates of Adai population do not profess completeness, and ignore the last two estimates of Eyeish population which are patently too high.

A possible check on Hasinai population is furnished by Father Anastasius' comment that their cantons contained 10 or 12 houses apiece. He also says, as already noted, that each house accommodated 2 families, but Joutel raises the number to 8 or 10. If we assume a dozen cantons, a very conservative estimate, and 4 individuals to the family, we should attain a population of 10 or 12 by 2 by 4 by 12, accepting Anastasius' allocation of families to the house, or 10 or 12 by 8 or 10 by 4 by 12, using Joutel's estimate, anywhere from 960 to 5,760. This is not very satisfactory and it would seem that Aguayo's figures supply a more rational basis for determination since he claims to have clothed 1,378 adults, though this probably includes 80 Kadohadacho visitors. Although it is quite probable that there were some repeaters in this interesting process, if we subtract the 80 Kadohadacho, assume that the children were about as numerous as the adults, and that as many more may not have been reached, we shall arrive at a figure of nearly 4,000, which is as satisfactory as anything that could be suggested. About half that number should account for the 4 Kadohadacho tribes and the Cahinnio, and 1,000 for the Natchitoches group, while 400 apiece would be an ample estimate for the Adai and Eyeish. This makes a grand total of somewhat less than 8,000, more than 500 below Mooney's estimate. I regard even that as an outside figure, and believe that the sudden diminution of the Kadohadacho, Natchitoches, and their allies, asserted by Bienville and La Harpe during the first 20 years of white contact, not to have reached the proportions they indicate in spite of the epidemic of 1691. Reduction in the numbers of these Indians was certainly real and it continued apparently with no considerable interruption until about 1870, after which date a recovery began which has raised the Caddo from about 450 to nearly 1,000. If we regard 8,000 as an outside figure, it appears that they are not as far behind their numbers when the French and Spaniards first met them as the great losses they have suffered might lead one to expect. Blood from other races has undoubtedly entered into the present Caddo population, but the amount of Indian blood itself must have increased in the doubling of population which has taken place in the last 60 or 70 years.

ORIGIN LEGENDS

Like most tribes of the Southeast and Southwest, native Caddo myths pointed to an original home under the earth. According to Caddo Jake, an Indian of the Natchitoches tribe whom I interviewed in 1912, his people came out of the ground where two rivers met and in the point of land between them. It was said to have been in the neighborhood of Sodo Lake, La. One of the two rivers was of course the Red. The other was perhaps a river mentioned by him called the River Kī'si, reputed to have originated from a vine called naatco'ot, "raccoon intestines," which grows to a great length and has a smooth black surface. The Caddo were then very numerous and immediately began spreading out into villages in all directions. But the Choctaw lived near by, between them and the sea, and they killed many Caddo by waylaying them at night and clubbing them to death. Later many died of the smallpox, and the Caddo moved westward around the end of the lake and began hunting in the country beyond. They also began to divide and the several bands came to be called after the names of the foods they lived upon. The Hainai—apparently a part of them only—went to a place where there were many black berries growing on thorny trees which are called be'idatco. Hence they came to be known as Nabedache. Some Yatasi went out hunting and discovered pawpaws, which they began to eat, and these were afterwards known as "Pawpaw People" (Natchitoches, from Nâshitōsh). José Antonio Pichardo, however, was told that Natchitoches was from an Indian word "nacicit," signifying "A place where the soil is the color of red ochre," and that it was applied originally to a small creek running through red soil. (Hatchett's translation of Pichardo's work quoted by Castañeda in Morfi (1935, vol. 1, p. 76).) A part of the Kadohadacho found in the ground some bumblebee honey, which they started to feast upon. From that they were called Da'ko, and hence Nadâko, (Anadarko). Still later the Anadarko and Hainai crossed the Sabine and lived beyond it.

Mooney supplies us with the following origin myth:

They came up from under the ground through the mouth of a cave in a hill which they call Cha' kani'nă, "The place of crying," on a lake close to the south bank of Red river, just at its junction with the Mississippi. In those days [the story continues] men and animals were all brothers and all lived together under the ground. But at last they discovered the entrance to the cave leading up to the surface of the earth, and so they decided to ascend and come out. First an old man climbed up, carrying in one hand fire and a pipe and in the other a drum. After him came his wife, with corn and pumpkin seeds. Then followed the rest of the people and the animals. All intended to come out, but as soon as the wolf had climbed up he closed the hole, and shut up the rest of the people and animals under the ground, where they still remain. Those who had come out sat down and cried a long time for their friends below, hence the name of the place. Because the Caddo came out of the ground they call it ină', "mother," and go back to it when they die. Because they have had the pipe and the drum and the corn and pumpkins since they have been a people, they hold fast to these things and have never thrown them away. From this place they spread out toward the west, following up the course of Red river, along which they made their principal settlements. For a long time they lived on Caddo lake, on the boundary between Louisiana and Texas, their principal village on the lake being called Sha'ʻchildī'ni, "Timber hill." [Mooney, 1896, pp. 1093–1094.]

A version of this story given by Freeman, however, represents the events as having taken place after a universal deluge. He says:

From the similarity of one of their traditions to the Mosaical account of the deluge it deserves notice. They say that long since, a civil war broke out amongst them, which so displeased Enicco, the Supreme Being, that he caused a great flood, which destroyed all but one family; consisting of four persons, the father, mother, and children. This family was saved by flying to a knoll at the upper end of the prairie, which was the only spot uncovered by the water. In this knoll was a cave, where the male and female of all the kinds of animals were preserved. After the flood had continued one moon, they set a bird, called by them O-Wah, at liberty, which returned in a short time with a straw. The family then set out on a raft in search of the place, from whence this straw was brought, and, pursuing a west course for two leagues, they came to land; where they saw a fish Toesha, and being much alarmed at its enormous size, they all shed tears; from this circumstance, they named the place Chacanenah, or ground upon which tears have been shed. This fish remained for many years after, and was large enough for 30 men to encamp under. All the Mexican and Louisiana Indians are supposed to be the offspring of this family. It is said that some other of the nations have a similar tradition; and that many of the tribes used to meet, on a certain day in every year, at the knoll upon which this family was supposed to have been preserved; and there offer sacrifices to the Supreme Being, for not destroying the whole race. [Freeman-Custis Expedition, 1806, pp. 28–29.]

The site of this cave is here said to have been at an old village on the east side of Red River in the latitude of Hervey, but Sibley places it at an older town site still higher up the river, on the south side about on the meridian of Ogden, Ark.

They have a traditionary tale [he says] which not only the Caddoes, but half a dozen other smaller nations believe in, who claim the honor of being descendants of the same family; they say, when all the world was drowning by a flood, that inundated the whole country, the Great Spirit placed on an eminence, near this lake, one family of Caddoques, who alone were saved; from that family all the Indians originated. [Sibley, in Amer. State Pap., Indian Affairs, 1832, p. 721.]

Part of this story appears again in Morfi's Memorias, quoted from a letter written November 17, 1763, by Cavallero Macarti, commandant of the post of Natchitoches, to Don Angel de Marto y Navaryete, governor of the province. Speaking of the Kadohadacho proper he says:

Their history refers to their origin in this manner. On a hill some two leagues distant from the pueblo where they lived, there appeared a woman, called by them Zacado, and venerated by them as the first of their divinities, who in the same place raised her first children, instructing them to hunt, fish, to construct houses, and to dress themselves, and when they were skillful in these things she suddenly disappeared from sight. The hill is still held in great veneration by those Indians, who consider themselves as the progenitors of the other nations. [Morfi, 1932, p. 6.]

No myth describing the origin of man or his emergence above the surface of the earth has been collected from the Hasinai. All refer to the Kadohadacho and their associated tribes, unless we except some items of the origin legend contained among the Traditions of the Caddo, collected by G. A. Dorsey. The first of these relates how the people lived in a village called Old-Home-in-the-Darkness under ground, how they chose the Moon as their leader and traveled westward until they came to the surface of the earth. We also have the common story that part of the people were turned back before reaching the surface. The rest continued on westward. Their first village was called Tall-Timber-on-top-of-the-Hill, for the place was in black-jack timber near the top of a high hill. Going on farther west, they came to some mountains which they climbed, finding a lake on the top. Before this, Moon left them and was succeeded by Medicine-Screech-Owl, apparently the first child born after they had attained the surface of the earth. Gathering his people together along the banks of the lake, the new leader said:

These waters which are before you are the tears of your great chief, Moon, for before he was taken up into the heavens he came up to this mountain and shed tears for the wrongs he had done to his people. So we shall call this mountain Moon's-Tears-on-the-Mountain. [Dorsey, 1905, pp. 7–13.]

This is interesting because it again brings in a place named from the shedding of tears, evidently an old element in the several myths.

Another fragment of the origin myth is preserved in a letter written to Henry R. Schoolcraft, by William B. Parker, and dated March 14, 1855. According to this, the Caddo, Hainai, and Anadarko "issued from the hot springs of Arkansas" (Schoolcraft, 1854, vol. 5, p. 682).

The several narratives agree in one important item, in locating the point of origin, or emergence, of the Caddo in the eastern part of their territories, or indeed east of their territories, and in representing their movement as from east to west.

This is contrary to an opinion regarding the origin of the Caddoan tribes which has been widely held and would bring them from the Southwest. It is partly due to a Pawnee legend, but I was told by the late James Murie that this legend belonged to only one of the Pawnee tribes and that two of the others claimed to have come from the east. It is also thought to have received confirmation from mention of Jumano Indians, supposedly Caddoans, on the Rio Grande. This tribe, or one of similar designation,—a name which should really be spelled Shumano—was on the steppe east of the Pueblo Indians in later times and was probably incorporated with the Wichita (Hodge, 1907, *art.* Jumano). Sauer (1934, p. 68) thinks he has evidence that it was really a Nahuatlan group, and it was perhaps a part of the Suma disrupted by Apache invaders. Wichita traditions seem to agree with those of the Caddo and the majority of the Pawnee in pointing to a movement from the east and north rather than the south and west (Gatschet, 1891, pp. 249–252). This conclusion would be further supported if the linguistic relationship affirmed to exist between Caddoan and Iroquoian languages is borne out by future investigations. In the meantime we must wait upon the linguists and archeologists.

HISTORY

Our first historical references to the Caddo Indians are in the narratives of the De Soto expedition. The Atayos visited by Cabeza de Vaca in 1528 were the Toho or Tohaha, both Tonkawan tribes, and not the Adai as has sometimes been thought (Cabeza de Vaca, 1905, p. 105). Cabeza encountered no Caddo.

On or about the first day of October 1541, when De Soto's army was in a province called Cayas or Tanico in southern Arkansas, he set out with 13 horsemen and 50 foot to view another province known as Tula, which Biedma describes as fertile, and "to see whether it was a land through which he might pass with all his men," or "in which he could winter the people" (Bourne, 1904, vol. 2, p. 32; Robertson, 1933, p. 194). "And," says Ranjel, "he returned from there in a hurry, and the Indians killed one horse and wounded four or five." The Cayas chief had described this province as "the best populated land thereabout," and "situated to the south." He added "that he could give him a guide, but that he did not have an interpreter, for the speech of Tula was different from his; and because he and his forebears had always been at war with the lords of that province, they had no converse, nor did they understand each other." Elvas, from whom the last two quotations are taken, amplifies Ranjel's terse comment on the ensuing struggle by saying:

As soon as he arrived and was perceived by the Indians, the band was summoned. When fifteen or twenty Indians had gathered together, they came to attack the Christians. On seeing that they handled them roughly, and that when they took to flight the horses overtook them, they climbed on top of the houses, where they tried to defend themselves with their arrows; and when driven from some would climb on top of others; and, while they were pursuing some, others would attack them from another direction. In this way, the running lasted so long that the horses became tired and could no longer run . . . Fifteen Indians were killed there and captives were made of forty women and young persons; for they did not leave any Indian alive who was shooting arrows if they could overtake him.

On October 5 the entire Spanish army set out for Tula and they reached it on the 7th, but, found it abandoned. De Soto had carried along the chief of Cayas, in accordance with his usual custom, but Elvas says that among the Cayas Indians "he did not find a single one who understood the speech of Tulla."

On Saturday morning, the day after their arrival,

the Indians came to give them a brush, or a battle, and they had large, long poles, like lances, the ends hardened by fire, and they were the best fighting people that the Christians met with, and they fought like desperate men, with the greatest valour in the world. That day they wounded Hernandarias, the grandson of the marshal of Seville, and, thank God, the Christians defended themselves so valiantly that they did not receive much damage, although the Indians tried to round up the whole force. [Bourne, 1904, vol. 2, p. 148; cf. Robertson, 1933, pp. 194–196.]

So Ranjel; Elvas describes this encounter at greater length:

As soon as [the Indians] knew [De Soto] was in Tulla, at the hour of dawn of the first night, they came in two bands from two different directions with their bows and arrows and long poles resembling pikes. As soon as they were perceived both those of horse and those of foot sallied out against them and there many Indians were killed, and some Christians and horses wounded. Some Indians were captured, six of whom the governor sent to the cacique with their right hands and their noses cut off. He ordered them to tell him that if he did not come to make his excuses and obey him, he would go to get him; and do to as many of his men as he found what he had done to those whom he sent to him. He gave him the space of three days in which to come. This he gave them to understand the best he could by signs as he had no interpreter. After three days came an Indian whom the cacique sent laden with cowhides. He came weeping bitterly, and coming to the governor cast himself at his feet. He raised him up, and he made him a talk, but no one could understand him. The governor told him by signs that he should return and tell the cacique to send him an interpreter whom the people of Cayas could understand. Next day, three Indians came laden with cowhides and three days after that twenty Indians came. Among them was one who understood those of Cayas. After a long discourse of excuses from the cacique and praises of the governor, he concluded by saying that he and the others were come thither on behalf of the cacique to see what his lordship ordered; and that he was ready to serve him. The governor and all the men were very glad, for they could in no wise travel without an interpreter. The governor ordered him under guard and told him to tell the Indians who had come with him to return to the cacique and tell him that he pardoned him for the past and that he thanked him greatly for his gifts and for the interpreter whom he had sent him and that he would be glad to see him and for him to come next day to see him. The cacique came after three days and eighty Indians with him. Both he and his men entered the camp weeping in token of obedience and repentance for the past mistake, after the manner of that land. He brought many cowhides as a gift, which were useful because it was a cold land, and were serviceable for coverlets as they were very soft and the wool like that of sheep. Nearby to the north were many cattle. The Christians did not see them nor enter their land, for the land was poorly settled where they were, and had little maize. The cacique of Tulla made his address to the governor in which he excused himself and offered him his land and vassals and person. No orator could more eloquently express the message or address both of that cacique and of the other caciques and of all those who came to the governor in their behalf. [Robertson, 1933, pp. 196-199.]

Biedma tells much the same story. According to him, De Soto had 20 horsemen in his reconnaissance, and he mentions no infantry, but his account is probably defective in that particular.

In attempting to seize some Indians, [he says] they began to yell and show us battle. They wounded of ours that day seven or eight men, and nine or ten horses; and such was their courage, that they came upon us in packs, by eights and tens, like worried dogs. We killed some thirty or forty of them.

In the attack made upon the main army after it reached their country, he says they were divided into "three very large squadrons" which came upon them from as many different directions. Later five or six Indians were sent who understood the Spaniards' interpreters. "They asked who we were, and of what we were in search" (Bourne, 1904, vol. 2, pp. 32–33).

Garcilaso, as is his wont, enlarges considerably on these encounters and adds various details which we can neither confirm nor deny. However, he agrees with Biedma that the attacking Indians were divided into three bands, and he agrees with our other authorities as to the valor of this tribe, their linguistic separateness, and their use of long lances. He also states that they deformed their heads, referring apparently to frontal head deformation, and he notes that they tattooed their faces, and particularly their lips (Garcilaso, 1723, pp. 189–194).

After leaving these people De Soto marched to the southeast and came among others who seem to have been of an entirely different connection. The Caddo relationship of these Tula people is not, of course, proved by the mere fact that their language was different from that of their neighbors, but is clearly shown by the fact that during the attempt of De Soto's followers to reach Mexico by land, they came among tribes that were undoubtedly Caddo and noted the resemblance in customs between them and the Tula people. Their western connection is also indicated by the use of lances and the fact that they were much addicted to buffalo hunting. The name Caddo, moreover, persists in Caddo River and Caddo Gap, which correspond to the location of these people as indicated in the relations.

In any event, the later contact, to which reference has just been made, undoubtedly did occur with true Caddo tribes. On June 5, 1542, about 2 weeks after De Soto's death, his successor in the governorship, Luis de Moscoso, led the surviving Spaniards westward and, after passing through two provinces where salt was made, he arrived among Caddo tribes near Red River about the middle of July. The first of these was called Amaye and lay perhaps 20 miles east of the river. It is esteemed to have been Caddo from its association with known Caddo tribes and the resemblance between its name and the Caddo word designating a male human being. The next tribe or "province" lay on Red River and bore a Caddo name, Naguatex or Nawatesh, meaning "Place of Salt." This is represented as the most fertile and populous of all the provinces through which the army passed during this expedition, and though they plundered its granaries in July on their way west, when they returned in October these were refilled. Mentioned with the Amaye and Naguatex was a third tribe called Hacanac, identical, it may be, with the Lacane. Here our Spaniards seem to have turned toward the southwest. They passed through two very poor provinces bearing Caddo names, Nissohone and Lacane, after which they reached a more populous one known as Nondacao. These three were evidently the Nasoni, Nacanish, and Nadako or Anadarko of later times. Beyond they came to the Hais Indians, the Eyeish or Haish of the more recent historical period, who were represented as warlike and much addicted to buffalo hunting. Next they reached Soacatino, a province in wooded country. It bears a Caddo name but is not certainly identifiable in later Caddo history. Still farther on toward the south or west they reached a considerable province called Guasco, one which is barely noted in Casañas' list. There they obtained considerable corn. Two other places bearing Caddo names, Naquiscoça and Naçacahoz, were visited and finally they came upon a river which bore the name Daycao, apparently derived also from the Caddo langauge. This was quite certainly the Trinity since beyond it their scouts captured some Indians living in wretched hovels whose speech none of the other Indians could understand. They were evidently Tonkawa or Bidai. On their return to the Mississippi River they followed the same route (Bourne, 1904, vol. 2, pp. 36–38; Robertson, 1933, pp. 239–258).

Just before Moscoso and his men penetrated the Caddo country from the east, Coronado approached it from New Mexico, and it has been believed by some that he came in direct contact with these people. The belief is based upon his report that he encountered Indians called "Teyas" living in the northwestern part of what is now Texas, and the apparent impossibility of identifying them with any other tribe. Coronado describes his first encounter with these Indians as follows. After reaching extensive plains, probably the Staked Plains,

with no more landmarks than as if we had been swallowed up in the sea . . . and while we were lost in these plains, some horsemen who went off to hunt cows fell in with some Indians who also were out hunting, who are enemies of those that I had seen in the last settlement [the Querechos], and of another sort of people who are called Teyas; they have their bodies and faces all painted, are a large people like the others, of a very good build; they eat the raw flesh just like the Querechos, and live and travel around with the cows in the same way as these. [Winship, 1896, p. 581; Hammond and Rey, 1940, p. 186.]

It was the information obtained from these men, in many respects contradictory to what he had before been told, that induced Coronado to leave the greater part of his army and push on with 30 horsemen to the province of Quivira. Castañeda notes that one of these Teya Indians was

seen to shoot a bull right through both shoulders with an arrow. These people [he continues] are very intelligent; the women are well made and modest. They cover their whole body. They wear shoes and buskins made of tanned skin. The women wear cloaks over their small under petticoats, with sleeves gathered up at the shoulders, all of skin, and some wore something like little sanbenitos with a fringe, which reached half-way down the thigh over the petticoat. [Winship, 1896, p. 507; Hammond and Rey, 1940, p. 239.]

The Relacion del Suceso states that

two kinds of people travel around these plains with the cows; one is called Querechos and the other Teyas; they are very well built, and painted, and are enemies of each other. They have no other settlement or location than comes from traveling around with the cows. They kill all of these they wish, and tan the hides, with which they clothe themselves and make their tents, and they eat the flesh, sometimes even raw, and they also even drink the blood when thirsty. The tents they make are like field tents, and they set them up over some poles they have made for this purpose, which come together and are tied at the top, and when they go from one place to another they carry them on some dogs they have, of which they have many, and they load them with the tents and poles and other things, for the country is so level, as I said, that they can make use of these, because they carry the poles dragging along on the ground. The sun is what they worship most. The skin for the tents is cured on both sides, without the hair, and they have the skins of deer and cows left over. They exchange some cloaks with the natives of the river for corn. [Winship, 1896, p. 578; Hammond and Rey, 1940, pp. 292–293.]

Castañeda describes the Plains people as follows:

These people are called Querechos and Teyas. They described some large settlements, and judging from what was seen of these people and from the accounts they gave of other places, there are a good many more of these people than there are of those at the settlements [on the Rio Grande]. They have better figures, are better warriors, and are more feared. They travel like the Arabs, with their tents and troops of dogs loaded with poles and having Moorish pack saddles with girths. When the load gets disarranged, the dogs howl, calling some one to fix them right. These people eat raw flesh and drink blood. They do not eat human flesh. They are a kind people and not cruel. They are faithful friends. They are able to make themselves very well understood by means of signs. They dry the flesh in the sun, cutting it thin like a leaf, and when dry they grind it like meal to keep it and make a sort of pea soup [mush] of it to eat. A handful thrown into a pot swells up so as to increase very much. They season it with fat, which they always try to secure when they kill a cow. They empty a large gut and fill it with blood, and carry this around the neck to drink when they are thirsty. When they open the belly of a cow, they squeeze out the chewed grass and drink the juice that remains behind, because they say that this contains the essence of the stomach. They cut the hide open at the back and pull it off at the joints, using a flint as large as a finger, tied in a little stick, with as much ease as if working with a good iron tool. They give it an edge with their own teeth. The quickness with which they do this is something worth seeing and noting. [Winship, 1896, pp. 527–528; Hammond and Rey, 1940, pp. 261–262.]

Castañeda gives the name of the large settlement of the Teyas, the first which they reached, as "Cona." Guides were taken from them for Quivira, and though the first ran away in a few days. Coronado sent back for others and they were supplied promptly.

Another important reference to these people is also furnished by Castañeda:

There is a village, small and strong, between Cicuye [Pecos] and the province of Quirix [the Keres Indians], which the Spaniards named Ximena [Galisteo], and another village almost deserted, only one part of which is inhabited. This was a large village, and judging from its condition and newness it appeared to have been destroyed. They called this the village of the granaries or silos, because large underground cellars were found here stored with corn. There was another large village farther on, entirely destroyed and pulled down, in the yards of which there were many stone balls, as big as 12-quart bowls, which seemed to have been thrown by engines or catapults, which had destroyed the village. All that I was able to find out about them was that, sixteen years before, some people called Teyas, had come to this country in great numbers and had destroyed these villages. They had besieged Cicuye but had not been able to capture it, because it was strong, and when they left the region, they had made peace with the whole country. It seems as if they must have been a powerful people, and that they must have had engines to knock down the villages. The only thing they could tell about the direction these people came from was by pointing toward the north. They usually call these people Teyas or brave men, just as the Mexicans say chichimecas or braves, for the Teyas whom the army saw were brave. These knew the people in the settlements, and were friendly with them, and they [the Teyas of the plains] went there to spend the winter under the wings of the settlements. The inhabitants do not dare to let them come inside, because they cannot trust them. Although they are received as friends, and trade with them, they do not stay in the villages over night, but outside under the wings. The villages are guarded by sentinels with trumpets, who call to one another just as in the fortresses of Spain.

There are seven other villages along this route, toward the snowy mountains, one of which has been half destroyed by the people already referred to. These were under the rule of Cicuye. [Winship, 1896, pp. 523–524; Hammond and Rey, 1940, pp. 257–258.]

Later he notes that the people of Quivira "are almost of the same sort and appearance as the Teyas" (Winship, 1896, p. 528; Hammond and Rey, 1940, p. 263).

If these descriptions of the Teyas Indians are trustworthy, it is impossible to regard them as Caddo. They were evidently a Plains tribe with all the typical Plains characteristics. They were living in skin tents, and there is no evidence that these were mere temporary lodges occupied during the hunting season. Only 1 year later, Moscoso passed completely through the Caddo country and seems to have found them occupying semisedentary villages with no intimation that their houses were of skins. If that had been the case the Spaniards would certainly have noted it as a singular differentiation from the houses of the Mississippi tribes. And inasmuch as the Indians of Quivira, who are generally regarded as Wichita, were already inhabiting grass houses, we should have to assume that the Caddo were roving about in a wild state and inhabiting tipis, while their relatives to the north were in good-sized grass dwellings. This is contrary to all of the information that has come to us regarding the Caddo and is not in accord with common sense. Assuming that the Querecho were Apache, as is generally believed, and that the Kiowa, Kiowa Apache, and Comanche, as well as the Arapaho and Cheyenne, had not in Coronado's time got so far south, we find some difficulty in identifying the Teyas with any known people. J. P. Harrington (*in* Swanton Ann. Vol., 1940, p. 512) reports, however, "that Teya is the Pecos-Jemez word for eastern Apache," and this perhaps solves the difficulty, Querecho being apparently a corresponding term for the western Apache. At the same time the differences between Apache bands would not seem sufficient to call for two distinct, all-inclusive terms, and one wonders whether "Teya" has always been applied in the same manner. The only possible alternative, however, would be some tribe connected with the Wichita or Kichai, or perhaps those ubiquitous Jumano. These Teyas, indeed, occupied a territory close to that in which the Jumano later dwelt, but it is assumed by Sauer, who has made a careful study of the tribes of the Rio Grande region, that the Jumano lived along that river in the early part of the sixteenth century and adapted themselves to a Plains life only gradually. And besides Castañeda understood from his Pecos informants that the Teya had come from the north. For the present the identification indicated by Mr. Harrington must be regarded as the most probable.

In any case, it is possible that the word "Teyas" may have a similar origin to that of Texas, whether it was originally a Caddo term or not, for it may have enjoyed currency among many otherwise unrelated peoples. Note particularly that Castañeda states the Teyas settled close to the Pueblo Indians during the winter, evidently in large measure for the purpose of buying corn, as is actually said in the Relacion del Suceso, just as the Assiniboin came to the Mandan towns on the upper Missouri.

After 1542 the Caddo drop out of sight for more than a hundred years and do not reappear above the horizon of history until 1650, when knowledge of them was resurrected as one of the results of an expedition from New Mexico to the country of the Jumano, under Hernando Martin and Diego del Castillo. This particular tribe of

Jumano was upon the headwaters of the Colorado, Bolton thinks the Concho. While staying in that region, part of these Spaniards went 50 leagues beyond through the country of the Cuitaos, Escanjaques, and Aijados, to the borders of a people called Tejas. Quoting the chronicler, Bolton continues: "They did not enter their territory as they learned that it was very large and contained many people," and adds that a "lieutenant" of the Tejas "king" went to see Castillo. "This, so far as I know," continues Bolton, "is the first information acquired by the Spaniards unquestionably concerning the people from whom Texas got its name" (Bolton, 1912, pp. 9–10). With the exception, of course, of Moscoso's brief sojourn among them.

From this time on trading relations seem to have continued between the Spaniards and the Jumano, and it is safe to conclude that the latter soon assumed that profitable position as middlemen in passing on European goods to the Hasinai which we find them occupying in 1676, when the Bishop of Guadalajara visited Coahuila. One of the reasons the bishop gave for favoring the establishment of four Franciscan missions in that region, as had just been recommended by Fernando del Bosque, was the opportunity they would afford of reaching the more important Hasinai. He says, quoting from Bolton:

Coahuila has as a neighbor on the north, inclining somewhat to the east, a populous nation of people, and so extensive that those who give detailed reports of them do not know where it ends. These [who give the reports] are many, through having communicated with the people of that nation, which they call Texas, and who, they maintain, live under an organized government (*en policía*), congregated in their pueblos, and governed by a casique who is named by the Great Lord, as they call the one who rules them all, and who, they say, resides in the interior. They have houses made of wood, cultivate the soil, plant maize and other crops, wear clothes, and punish misdemeanors, especially theft. The Coahuiles do not give more detailed reports of the Texas because, they say, they are allowed to go only to the first pueblos of the border, since the Great Lord of the Texas does not permit foreign nations to enter the interior of his country. There are many of these Coahuiles who give these reports, and who say that they got them through having aided the Texas in their wars against the Pauit, another very warlike nation. The Coahuiles once pacified, the Spaniards can reach the land of the Texas without touching the country of enemies. [Bolton, 1912, p. 16.]

Another reason why the Coahuilteco Indians visited the Tejas periodically was to carry objects of Spanish origin thither in trade, including Spanish horses, and, as the latter at least were not always come by in honorable ways, they were naturally not anxious to call attention to it. Every spring, for an unknown period before this, as Dr. Carlos Castañeda informs us, Juan Sabeata, a Jumano Indian, was in the habit of leading his followers to the east to hunt buffalo and to trade with the friendly Indians of the Hasinai Confederacy on the Neches and Trinity Rivers of East Texas. Here it appears that each year the Indians held a fair in which the plunder obtained from the Spanish outposts along the whole northern frontier of New Spain was bartered and traded. In the fall, before cold weather set in, Juan Sabeata led his people back to the region of La Hunta de los Rios [a Presidio opposite the mouth of the Conchos] where they spent the winter. [Castañeda, 1936, vol. 1, p. 326.]

This trading route is also mentioned by French writers. Le Page du Pratz (1758, vol. 2, pp. 241–242) alludes to the other end of it in his account of the Avoyel Indians on lower Red River.

It is they who have brought to the French of Louisiana horses, oxen, and cows; I do not know in what fair they purchase them, nor in what money they pay for them; the truth is that these beasts cost only 20 pounds (*livres*) apiece. The Spaniards of New Mexico have such a great quantity that they do not know what to do with them, and it pleases them to be relieved of some. At present the French have more than they need and especially of horses.

If by "oxen and cows" Du Pratz means domesticated cattle he must be speaking of a very late period, but it is possible that the informants upon whom he relied had in mind buffalo skins. There can be no doubt that trade in horses was actively carried on. It is probable, too, that although stimulated by the approach of Spanish settlements, trade followed much the same routes in pre-Columbian times. Elvas, the chronicler of the De Soto expedition, notes that when the Spaniards were in the country of the Guasco, a Hasinai tribe, they saw "turquoises and cotton blankets, which the Indians gave them to understand by signs were brought from the west" (Robertson, 1933, p. 256). This was in 1542, and it is evident that the European settlers in Mexico could have had nothing to do with them. There were two articles of trade for which the Caddo were noted, salt and bow wood, the latter from the Osage orange or bois d'arc. Of course, there were plenty of salines west of the Caddo country, so that we should not expect to find them exporting salt in that direction, but it was otherwise with bow wood, and Robbins, Harrington, and Freire-Marreco say:

The wood of this shrub was considered better for making bows than any which grew in the Tewa country. It was brought from the east by the Tewa, or obtained from the Comanche or other eastern tribes. [Robbins, Harrington, and Freire-Marreco, 1916, p. 68.]

On October 15, 1683, seven Indians of the Jumano and other tribes appeared before Governor Cruzate, of New Mexico, to repeat requests for missions which had been made in previous years. Juan Sabeata was the leader of this delegation and he told the governor of thirty-odd tribes to the eastward including "the Great Kingdom of the Texas," which was situated at a distance of 15 or 20 days' march from La Junta, i. e., the point where the Conchos joins the Rio Grande. Cruzate sent this information on to the viceroy, but without awaiting further instructions, on January 1, 1684, dispatched an expedition in that direction under Juan Domínguez de Mendoza. The explorers spent most of their time among the Jumano Indians upon the head-waters of the Colorado, but Father Nicolas Lopez, who went with them, says in his letter to the king, "we had ambassadors from the Texas, a powerful kingdom, . . . and we came to tread the borders of the first settlements of this nation." He speaks also of a nation called "Aijados," 70 leagues from Quivira and within 25 leagues of the Texas (Bolton, 1912, pp. 20–22).

Two years later, and then owing to the accident which carried La Salle west of the Mississippi River, Frenchmen succeeded where the Spaniards had failed in effecting an entrance into the Hasinai country. During his descent of the Mississippi River in 1673, Marquette learned of the existence of the Pawnee and Wichita and he makes one possible reference to a Caddo tribe. Upon, or south of, the Arkansas River is entered upon his map the name "Aiaichi," which on the Thevenot map appears as "Ahiahichi" (Shea, 1852, p. 268). This has been identified, plausibly enough, with the Eyeish. But since it is placed beside the Tunica who were near the Mississippi and no prominent Caddo tribe is entered, it is possible that Marquette had heard of a town discovered by De Soto on Ouachita River in 1542 and named "Ayays" (Robertson, 1933, p. 208). If the latter supposition is correct, the tribe was probably not Caddo.

Early in 1685, La Salle, having missed the mouth of the Mississippi, established himself on Garcitas River, which enters the Gulf of Mexico through Lavaca Bay, and began to explore the surrounding country in order to locate the great river he had overshot. The first of his expeditions to reach the Hasinai set out the following year, on April 28, according to Joutel, or April 22, if we rely on Father Anastasius Douay, a Franciscan priest, who formed one of the party of 10 accompanying the French commander (Cox, 1905, vol. 1, p. 223; Margry, 1875–1886, vol. 3, p. 225). In May or June they reached a village of the Hasinai ("Cœnis") [evidently the Nabedache town], and their adventures in that country are thus described by Father Anastasius:

Still marching east, we entered countries still finer than those we had passed, and found tribes that had nothing barbarous but the name; among others, we met a very honest Indian returning from the chase with his wife and family. He presented the Sieur de la Salle with one of his horses and some meat, invited him and all of his party to his cabin, and, to induce us, left his wife, family, and game as a pledge, while he hastened to the village to announce our coming. Our hunter and a servant of the Sieur de la Salle accompanied him, so that two days after they returned to us with two horses loaded with provisions, and several chiefs, followed by warriors very neatly attired in dressed skins adorned with feathers. They came on bearing the calumet ceremoniously, and met us three leagues from the village; the Sieur de la Salle was received as if in triumph and lodged in the great chief's cabin. There was a great concourse of people, the young men being drawn out and under arms, relieving one another night and day, and, besides, loading us with presents and all kinds of provisions. Nevertheless, the Sieur de la Salle, fearing lest some of his party might go after the women, encamped three leagues from the village. Here we remained three or four days and bought horses and all that we needed.

This village, that of the Cœnis [Sp. Asinais], is one of the largest and most populous that I have seen in America. It is at least twenty leagues long, not that this is evenly inhabited, but in hamlets of ten or twelve cabins, forming cantons, each with a different name. Their cabins are fine, forty or fifty feet high, of the shape of bee-hives. Trees are planted in the ground and united above by the branches, which are covered with grass. The beds are ranged around the cabin, three or four feet from the ground; the fire is in the middle, each cabin holding two families.

We found among the Cœnis many things which undoubtedly came from the Spaniards, such as dollars, and other pieces of money, silver spoons, lace of every kind, clothes and horses. We saw, among other things, a bull from Rome, exempting the Spaniards in Mexico from fasting during summer. Horses are common; they gave them to us for an axe; one Cœnis offered me one for our cowl, to which he took a fancy.

They have intercourse with the Spaniards through the Choümans [see p. 28], their allies, who are always at war with New Spain. The Sieur de la Salle made them draw on bark a map of their country, of that of their neighbors, and of the river Colbert, or Mississippi, with which they are acquainted. They reckoned themselves six days' journey from the Spaniards, of whom they gave us so natural a description that we no longer had any doubts on the point although the Spaniards had not yet undertaken to come to their villages, their warriors merely joining the Choümans to go to war on New Mexico. The Sieur de la Salle, who perfectly understood the art of gaining the Indians of all nations, filled these with admiration at every moment. Among other things, he told them that the chief of the French was the greatest chief in the world, as high as the sun, and as far above the Spaniard as the sun is above the earth. On his recounting the victories of our monarch, they burst into exclamations, putting their hands on their mouths as a mark of astonishment. I found them very docile and tractable, and they seized well enough what we told them of the truth of God.

There were then some Choüman ambassadors among them, who came to visit us. I was agreeably surprised to see them make the sign of the cross, kneel, clasp their hands, and raise them from time to time to heaven. They also kissed my habit, and gave me to understand that men dressed like us instructed tribes in their vicinity, who were only two days' march from the Spaniards, where our religious had large churches, in which all assembled to pray. They expressed very naturally the ceremonies of the mass; one of them sketched me a painting that he had seen of a great lady, who was weeping because her son was upon a cross. He told us . . . that if we would go with them, or give them guns, they could easily conquer them, because they were a cowardly race, who had no courage, and made people walk before them with a fan to refresh them in hot weather.

After remaining here four or five days to recruit, we pursued our route through the Nassonis, crossing a large river which intersects the great Cœnis village. These two nations are allies, and have nearly the same character and customs.

Four or five leagues from there, we had the mortification to see that four of our men had deserted under cover of night and retired to the Nassonis; and, to complete our sorrow, the Sieur de la Salle and his nephew, the Sieur de Moranget, were attacked with a violent fever, which brought them to extremity. Their illness was long, and obliged us to make a long stay at this place, for when the fever, after frequent relapses, left them at last, they required a long time to recover entirely.

The length of this sickness disconcerted all our measures, and was eventually the cause of the last misfortunes which befell us. It kept us back more than two months, during which we had to live as we could; our powder began to run out; we had not advanced more than a hundred and fifty leagues in a straight line, and some of our people had deserted. In so distressing a crisis the Sieur de la Salle resolved to retrace his steps to Fort [St.] Louis; all agreed and we straightway resumed our route, during which nothing happened worth note but that, as we repassed the Maligne, one of our men was carried off with his raft by a crocodile of prodigious length and bulk.

After a good month's march, in which our horses did us good service, we reached the camp on the 17th of October [or August], in the same year, 1686, where we were welcomed with all imaginable cordiality, but, after all, with feelings tinged alike with joy and sadness as each related the tragical adventures which had befallen both since we had parted. [Cox, 1905, vol. 1, pp. 231–236.]

La Salle brought back with him five horses laden with corn, beans, pumpkin seeds, and watermelons (Margry, 1875–1886, vol. 3, p. 249). During this visit we are told that he recorded some words of the Hasinai language (Margry, 1875–1886, vol. 3, p. 304).

A more determined attempt to reach the Mississippi was made by La Salle the following year. He set out on January 12, 1687 (so Joutel; Douay says the 7th), with 16 companions (Cox, 1905, vol. 1, p. 238; Margry, 1875–1886, vol. 3, p. 259). Toward the end of February they met a Hasinai Indian and others were presently encountered, but before they came into the country itself, near the present site of Navasota it is believed, the commander and his nephew, De Moranget, were murdered by some members of the party. The survivors continued to the main Hasinai town and passed beyond it to that of the Nasoni, where the murderers fell out and part were destroyed by the rest. All then returned to the Hasinai village, where some of the Frenchmen accompanied their Indian friends on a war expedition against the Kanoatino. Later six of the remaining whites, including the Sieurs Cavelier, uncle and nephew, the Sieur Joutel, and Father Anastasius Douay, set out for the Mississippi. An extended narrative of this expedition by the pilot Joutel is left us, which will be drawn upon frequently. They visited two Hasinai towns 5 leagues apart, and passed to that of the Naodiche (Namidish) 9 leagues off. The Nasoni town was 3 leagues farther on. Continuing toward the northeast they came to the towns of the Kadohadacho at the bend of Red River, the one at which they arrived first being a second Nasoni village located on the south side. One of the party, named

De Marle [or De Marne], was drowned in the river here, and his body was buried on an eminence near the village. They reached and crossed Red River after passing a league and a half farther, and a journey of 2 leagues more brought them to the town of the Kadoha-dacho, which Father Anastasius calls the town of the "Ouidiches," meaning evidently the Namidish. In the same town they met two Cahinnio Indians who had come after Osage orange bows, and these accompanied them back to their own people living a league and a half from the Ouachita and apparently in the neighborhood of the present Arkadelphia. July 11 they set out from the Cahinnio town and on July 24 reached Arkansas River some miles above its mouth (Margry, 1875–1886, vol. 3, pp. 260–438).

In the meantime the ubiquitous Juan Sabeata had brought to the Spaniards in Coahuila news of this French enterprise and the destruction of the colony by neighboring Indians, and Alonso de Leon set out from Monclova on March 23, 1689, to visit the spot and clear any remaining Frenchmen out of the country. On his way he came to a rancheria of Emet, Toaa, and Cavas Indians, probably related to the Tonkawa. Its inhabitants at first fled to the woods but presently the chief and some of his companions came out and began calling "Thechas, techas," which was explained as meaning "Friends, friends." This was undoubtedly the Hasinai term discussed elsewhere. Either it had been adopted by tribes of different linguistic connections or this band had learned it from some Hasinai ("Tejas") who had recently been in their country and had passed through shortly before with two Frenchmen. Indeed, the chief of this band of Hasinai and eight followers presently came to the Spanish camp, and De Leon seems to say that the Indian town belonged to them. As the Hasinai occupied a dominant position among most of the surrounding peoples, it is probable that they assumed a tone of superiority in their attitude towards the Indians of this place, but it was far outside of their own country and the village cannot properly be regarded as one of theirs (Bolton, 1916, pp. 353–367, 388–404).

Both Massanet and De Leon were very much impressed by the Texas chief. The latter says:

Although unable to speak Castilian he was an Indian in whom was recognized capacity. He had a shrine with several images. The governor gave him and the other Indians who had come with him generously of what was left of the cotton garments, knives, blankets, beads, and other goods. He was very much pleased and promised to come with some Indians of his nation to the province of Cohaguila. [Bolton, 1916, p. 403.]

Massanet presented this chief with "two horses, and the blanket in which I slept, for I had nothing else which I could give him." Using one of the former French companions of La Salle as an interpreter, he promised to visit the Hasinai country next year at planting time accompanied by other priests, at which the Indian seemed pleased (Bolton, 1916, pp. 363–364).

The day after this interview, May 3, 1689, the chief left to rejoin his tribe and De Leon departed 10 days later for Monclova. In his report to the Viceroy of Mexico, the Spaniard gave a glowing account of the Texas province from the information he had obtained, though he had not visited it. He reported nine permanent settlements there and "went so far as to declare that, in his opinion, the Texas were as civilized as the Aztecs had been when the Spaniards first came to Mexico" (Castañeda, 1936, vol. 1, pp. 341–342).

When Henri de Tonti learned at Fort St. Louis on the Illinois River of the death of La Salle and the misfortunes of his former companions, he determined to proceed to "Naondiché" (the Namidish) in the Hasinai country in order to bring back the French who remained there and those upon the seacoast. He left the fort October 3, 1689, and reached the Quapaw villages January 1690. At the Uzutiuhi village on Arkansas River he was given two Kadohadacho women to take along as he was bound for their country. Returning to the Mississippi, he descended to the Taensa towns on Lake St. Joseph, which he reached early in February, and set out from that point for the Caddo country accompanied by three Frenchmen, a Shawnee Indian, and two slaves, besides the two women who had been given him at Uzutiuhi and some Taensas Indians. His own account continues as follows:

We set off on the 12th [of February] with twelve Taencas, and after a voyage of twelve leagues to the northwest we left our boat and made twenty leagues portage, and on the 17th of February, 1690, came to Natchitoches. They made us stay at the place, which is in the midst of the three villages called Nachitoches, Ouasita and Capiché. The chiefs of the three nations assembled, and before they began to speak the 30 Taencas who were with me got up and, leaving their arms, went to the temple, to show how sincerely they wished to make a solid peace. After having taken their God to witness, they asked for friendship. I made them some presents in the name of the Taencas. They remained some days in the village to traffic with salt, which these nations got from a salt lake in the neghborhood. After their departure they gave me guides to Yatachés, and, after ascending the river, always towards the northwest, about thirty leagues, we found fifteen cabins of Natchés [Bienville's Nakasa], who received us pretty well. We arrived on the 16th of March at Yatachés, about forty leagues from thence.[5] The three villages of Yatachés, Nadas and Choye are together. As they knew of our arrival, they came three leagues to meet us with refreshments, and on joining us we went together to their villages. The chief made many feasts for us. I gave presents to them, and asked for guides to the Cadadoquis. They were very unwilling to give us any, as they had murdered three ambassadors about four days before who came to their nation to make peace. However, by dint of entreaties, and also assurances that no harm would

---

[5] It is probable that "40 leagues from thence" means from the Natchitoches town and not from that of the Natchés.

happen to their people, they granted me five men, and we got to Cadadoquis on the 28th. At this place where we were encamped we discovered the trail of men and horses. The next day some horsemen came to reconnoitre us, and, after speaking to the wife of the chief, whom I brought back with me, carried back the news. The next day a woman, who governed this nation, came to visit me with the principal persons of the village. She wept over me, demanding revenge for the death of her husband, and of the husband of the woman whom I was bringing back, both of whom had been killed by the Osages. To take advantage of everything, I promised that their death should be avenged. We went together to their temple, and after the priests had invoked their God for a quarter of an hour they conducted me to the cabin of their chief. Before entering they washed my face with water, which is a ceremony among them. During the time I was there I learned from them that eighty leagues off were seven Frenchmen whom M. Cavelier had left. I hoped to finish my troubles by rejoining them, but the Frenchmen who accompanied me, tired of the voyage, would go no further. They were unmanageable persons over whom I could exercise no authority in this distant country. I was obliged to give way. All that I could do was to engage one of them, with a savage, to accompany me to the village of Naovediché [or "Nacondiché"], where I hoped to find the seven Frenchmen. I told those who abandoned me that, to prevent the savages knowing this, it was best to say that I had sent them away to carry back the news of my arrival, so that the savages should not suspect our disunion.

The Cadadoquis are united with two other villages called Natchitoches and Nasoui [Nasoni] situated on the *Red River*. All the nations of this tribe speak the same language. Their cabins are covered with straw, and they are not united in villages, but their huts are distant one from the other. Their fields are beautiful. They fish and hunt. There is plenty of game, but few cattle (*boeufs*). They wage cruel war with each other, hence their villages are but thinly populated. I never found that they did any work, except making very fine bows, [with] which they make a traffic with distant nations. The Cadadoquis possess about thirty horses, which they call "cavali" [Sp. *caballo*, a horse]. The men and women are tattooed in the face and all over the body. They call this river the Red River, because, in fact, it deposits a sand which makes the water as red as blood. I am not acquainted with their manners, having only seen them in passing.

I left this place on the 6th of April, directing our route southwards, with a Frenchman, a Chaganon (Shawnee), a little slave of mine, and five of their savages, whom they gave me as guides to Naouadiché. When I went away I left in the hands of the wife of the chief a small box, in which I had put some ammunition. On our road we found some Naouadiché savages hunting, who assured me that the Frenchmen were staying with them. This gave me great pleasure, hoping to succeed in my object of finding them. On the 19th the Frenchman with me lost himself. I sent the savages who were with me to look for him. He came back on the 21st, and told me that, having lost our trail, he was near drowning himself in crossing a little river on a piece of timber. His bag slipped off, and thus all our powder was lost, which very much annoyed me, as we were reduced to sixty rounds of ammunition. On the 23d we slept half a league from the village, and the chiefs came to visit us at night. I asked them about the Frenchmen. They told me that they had accompanied their chiefs to fight against the Spaniards, seven days' journey off, that the Spaniards had surrounded them with their cavalry, and that their chief having spoken in their favor, the Spaniards had given them horses and arms. Some of the others told me that the Quanouatins had killed three of them, and that the four others were gone in search of iron arrow-heads. I did not doubt that they had murdered them. I told them that they had killed the Frenchmen. Directly all the women began to cry, and thus I saw that what I had said was true. I would not, therefore, accept the calumet. I told the chief I wanted four horses for my return, and, having given him seven hatchets and a string of large glass beads, I received the next day four Spanish horses, two of which were marked on the haunch with an R and a crown (*couronne fermée*) and another with an N. Horses are very common among them. There is not a cabin which has not four or five. As this nation is sometimes at peace and sometimes at war with the neighboring Spaniards, they take advantage of a war to carry off the horses. We harnessed ours as well as we could and departed on the 29th, greatly vexed that we could not continue our route as far as M. de la Salle's camp [on the seacoast]. We were unable to obtain guides from this nation to take us there, though not more than eighty leagues off, besides being without ammunition, owing to the accident which I related before.

It was at the distance of three days' journey from hence that M. de la Salle was murdered . . .

We reached Cadadoquis on the 10th of May. We stayed there to rest our horses, and went away on the 17th with a guide, who was to take us to the village of Coroas. [Cox, 1905, vol. 1, pp. 44–50, 55.]

Meanwhile De Leon's rose-colored report on the kingdom of the Texas and his and Father Massanet's sanguine expectations regarding a rapid conversion of its inhabitants to Christianity, coupled with fear of French intrusion, rumors of which were continually filtering across the Rio Grande, determined the Mexican government to undertake an expedition into the Hasinai country for the purpose of beginning missionary labors there and clearing out Gallic intruders. Alonso de Leon was again commissioned to lead, and with him went four Queréteran friars headed by Father Damian Massanet, and cattle and horses for the new missions were driven along. The expedition left Monclova March 26–28, 1690, and, following closely the route of the first, continued beyond to the Hasinai country. On the way they remained about the site of La Salle's fort for several days in hopes of discovering some Frenchmen or Texas Indians, and on May 4 one Texas Indian was found whose family was encamped nearby. The gift of a horse and some other presents induced one of these Indians to take a message to the Texas chief, whose town is said to have been rather more than 30 leagues away. He left his wife and a brother-in-law to guide the army. On the 18th, as the expedition neared Trinity River, this Indian met them accompanied by 14 more of his tribe including the chief, who appeared very happy to see them again. On May 22, 18 leagues farther on toward the northeast, they came upon the first Texas rancheria in a valley surrounded by planted fields, and a quarter of a league beyond was another village. To the valley they gave the name of San Francisco Xavier. The second village they called San Francisco de los Texas. That afternoon De Leon accompanied the chief to his house, "where his mother, his wife, a daughter of his, and many people who were expecting him" came out to receive them, bringing out a bench upon which to seat their visitor and providing him with a luncheon of corn tamales and *atole*, "all very cleanly" (Bolton, 1916, pp. 368–387, 405–423). De Leon narrates the events of the succeeding days as follows:

Tuesday, the 23d, I set out with the reverend missionary fathers over the half-league intervening between the camp and the house of the [Indian] governor, in a procession with the officers and soldiers, who were followed by a large number of Indians with the said Indian governor. Having reached his house, the missionaries sang the Te Deum Laudamus. After remaining a while at his house seated upon benches which the said governor ordered brought, they served us, in jars and crocks, a luncheon of boiled beans, *atole*, and *pinole*, which the said fathers and soldiers ate. . . .

Wednesday, the 24th, a chapel was prepared in which to celebrate the feast of Corpus Christi, having this day bestowed upon the Indians clothing and the other commodities. This day I notified the governor to summon all his people to come to the feast of Corpus Christi.

Thursday, the 25th, the feast of the Most Holy Sacrament was celebrated with all solemnity and a procession, all the officers and soldiers, the Indian governor, and many of his people accompanying the procession and witnessing the high mass. Mass having been completed, the ceremony was enacted of raising the flag in the name of his Majesty (whom God protect), and I, the said General Alonso de Leon, as the superior officer of all the companies which, by order of his Excellency, the Señor Conde de Galve, viceroy of this New Spain, had come on this journey in the name of his Majesty, accepted the obedience which they rendered to his Majesty, and in his royal name promised to befriend and aid them. I delivered to the governor a staff with a cross, giving him the title of governor of all his people, in order that he might rule and govern them, giving him to understand by means of an interpreter that which he should observe and do, and the respect and obedience which he and all his people ought to have for the priests, and that he should make all his families attend Christian teaching, in order that they might be instructed in the affairs of our holy Catholic faith so that later they might be baptized and become Christians. He accepted the staff with much pleasure, promising to do all that was desired of him, and the company fired three salutes. Likewise, the Reverend Father Commissary of these conversions in this mission, Fray Damian Masanet, was given possession, in order that he might instruct them in the mysteries of our holy Catholic faith. The governor and his people having begged us to leave them religious to teach them the Christian doctrine, as a pledge of friendship we asked the said governor to give us three of the principal Indians of this province, among them being a brother, a nephew, and a cousin of the governor, who with much pleasure promised to go with us to see the most Excellent Señor Conde de Galve, viceroy and captain-general of New Spain. This day the sun was observed and we found ourselves in 34° 7'.

Friday, the 26th, I set out with the missionary fathers, some soldiers and officers, and the said Indian governor, towards the northeast, to find the most suitable place to put the mission, and after having seen three small valleys [about three leagues away], we came to where they told us two Frenchmen had died, where they had wished to make a settlement, and where we saw the graves. We placed a cross in a tree for them and went to a river which we found could be crossed only by means of a tree which the Indians have athwart it, and a rope of which they take hold. We named the river San Miguel Arcangel, and from there we returned to camp, having travelled six leagues.

Saturday, the 27th; *Sunday*, the 28th; *Monday*, the 29th; *Tuesday*, the 30th; and *Wednesday*, the 31st, they labored to build the church and the dwelling of the apostolic fathers, in the midst of the principal settlement of the Texas.

Thursday, June 1st, I gave possession of the said mission, the reverend father commissary, Fray Damian Masanet, having sung mass in the said church, the said Indian governor and his people attending mass and the blessing of the church. This afternoon I sent the company to begin the return march to the province of Coahuila, over the same road by which we came. They halted this night at the camp of San Carlos, having marched five leagues.

Friday, the 2d, with the reverend father commissary, Fray Damian Masanet, and six soldiers, I set out from the pueblo of San Francisco de los Texas to follow the company, there being with us a brother of the governor, a nephew, and a cousin of his, and another Indian of the said pueblo. Having joined the company we advanced to the Real de San Bernardino, a little over half a league. [Bolton, 1916, pp. 415–418.]

Massanet gives a more extended account of the happenings in the Hasinai country during this expedition and many interesting details regarding the customs of the people which will be noted elsewhere.

Governor Leon wished to leave a garrison of 40 or 50 men, but the Texas chief objected to the presence of so many unmarried soldiers, not without reason, and, after consultation with the padres and the chief, the number was reduced to 3. The 3 friars who had accompanied Massanet remained to take charge of the mission. Before they recrossed the Rio Grande, where they were detained a week by high water, 2 of the Indians gave up and returned to their own country, 1 of the others was killed accidentally in Querétero, and only 1 finally reached the City of Mexico (Bolton, 1916, pp. 383–387, 416–423).

On their return both De Leon and Massanet recommended the establishment of 7 new missions. It was proposed to place 4 of these among the Kadohadacho and 2 more among the Texas while the seventh was to be on the Guadalupe and so outside of Caddo territory. They were to be cared for by 14 missionaries and 7 lay brothers. These recommendations were adopted by the Fiscal and approved by the Junta de Hacienda. On January 23, 1691, Domingo Teran de los Rios, Governor of Coahuila, was commisisoned to carry out the recommendations adopted by the Junta. On May 16 the expedition set out. On June 19 they came to the Guadalupe River and found Juan Sabeata encamped there with a large body of Jumano Indians and their allies, estimated to number 2,000 souls.

From him and his companions it was learned, through two letters they brought from the missionaries who had remained at San Francisco de los Tejas, that a serious epidemic had visited the new mission, that many of the Indians had perished, and that the devout and zealous Father Fray Miguel de Fontcuberta had died of a malignant fever on February 5, after an illness of eight days. The Indians also reported rumors of renewed French activities among the Cadodachos.

On August 4, Teran reached San Francisco de los Texas whither he had been preceded by the missionaries, impatient at his slow movements.

That same afternoon the main body of the expedition pitched camp a short distance from San Francisco de los Tejas, where the governor of the Indians and many of his people came to welcome him. Two days later, he made his formal entry into the *rancheria* where he officially reinvested the Indian chief as governor and distributed many presents to him and his people. The soldiers held a parade that morning, and with bugles blowing and drums beating they marched to the church of the Mission of San Francisco de los Tejas, where, preceded by the missionaries, they fired six volleys before entering to hear High Mass. [Castañeda, 1936, vol. 1, pp. 361–367.]

In June of the preceding year (1690) Fray Francisco Casañas de Jusus Maria had founded a new mission on the banks of the Neches River to which he gave the name Santísimo Nombre de María. It was about 5 miles east of San Francisco de los Texas and here he prepared that account of the Hasinai Indians which is one of our chief sources of information regarding the Caddo peoples. But the subjects of that sketch grew increasingly cold toward his teachings and after the arrival of Teran their hostility became more and more manifest. After remaining among the Texas 20 days, Teran decided to go to the coast in hopes of obtaining supplies expected from Vera Cruz. When he reached the site of the French fort with the larger part of his men, he found there Captain Salinas Varona with supplies and also with instructions that he carry out the exploration of the Caddo country before returning to Mexico. Therefore, with great difficulty he made his way back to the Hasinai and arrived on October 26, but found the attitude of the Indians worse even than before.

The attacks upon the cattle and horses had become more frequent and open. The chief, who had welcomed the first Spaniards with so much kindness and friendliness, had by now tired of his associates. He had gone on the warpath to chastise a hostile tribe. Before leaving, he had warned his friends, the missionaries, that he did not want to find them among his people upon his return. Such a state of affairs had cooled the ardor of the energetic and zealous *Padres*, some of whom were already beginning to show signs of discouragement. [Castañeda, 1936, vol. 1, pp. 368–369.]

However, in pursuance of his instructions, Teran surveyed the surrounding country and on November 6 set out for the Kadohadacho accompanied by Massanet and a number of other missionaries, Capt. Gregorio de Salinas, and a party of soldiers, and after considerable hardship, for the weather had turned cold with snow and sleet, reached the Kadohadacho on November 28 with 30 of his party. In the towns of that tribe they spent a week exploring the surrounding country and taking soundings of Red River. The map shown in plate 1 is one of the results of their work. The Indians treated them in a friendly manner, but Teran was unable to carry out his instructions regarding the foundation of the four missions because of the lack of supplies. However, "the *Padres* were well impressed with the country and with the character and attitude of the Indians and declared their intention of returning at some later date to establish missions among these natives." They set out on their return December 5 and reached the Mission of Santísimo Nombre de María on the 30th after renewed hardships and the loss of nearly all their horses.

Four days later Teran went on to the Mission of San Francisco de los Texas, from which he deemed it necessary to commandeer a sufficient number of horses and cattle for his return to Mexico. On January 9 he set out for the Bay of St. Bernard taking with him all of the missionaries except Father Massanet and two companions and all but nine soldiers. On March 5 they reached their objective, and Teran remained there 2 weeks to write up his report before returning to Mexico.

After this, interest in the east Texas missions subsided and it was not until November 25, 1692, that the Viceroy of Mexico ordered the Governor of Coahuila, Capt. Diego Ramón,

> to make a report of the latest news from the Tejas and to suggest the best means of communicating with them. Diego Ramón replied on January 11, 1693. The most recent news from Texas had been brought by two Indians who had come to Coahuila the previous October. According to them, the missionaries were in good health but in dire need of supplies. Their provisions had been exhausted and most of their cattle had died, the crops had been a failure, and they were daily expecting relief to be sent from Mexico. [Castañeda, 1936, vol. 1, p. 372.]

Heusinger speaks of their difficulties in the following terms:

> To start with, the small guard that had been left to protect the Padres was not large enough to be of any real service. Then the Indians were beginning to show signs of duplicity: they were accepting gifts which were frequently given to them and professing a friendship for the missionaries, yet whenever they had the opportunity they would steal from the missions anything that could be stolen. To add to the missionaries' troubles a severe drought caused two successive crop failures, and a disease spread among the stock causing many cattle to die. A good number of the natives also fell victims to the disease and the Indians, attributing their misfortune to the baptismal water which the missionaries used, became actually hostile. To cap the entire situation the soldiers were offensive in their relations with the natives. The missionaries attempted to meet this last problem by their efforts to lead the soldiers to live in a more Christian manner, for their bad example was not only an obstacle to, but was actually undoing, the work which the missionaries had accomplished. The soldiers did not respond, discord increased and this, added to the other difficulties, made life very disagreeable and discouraging at the missions. [Heusinger, 1936, pp. 51–52.]

Diego Ramón suggested that a party of 20 men from Monclova could take the missionaries the desired supplies, since the road was well known. This plan was adopted, and on May 3 the men set out under Captain Gregorio Salinas "taking ninety-seven pack loads of provisions and gifts for the Indians, and one hundred and eighty horses for the use of the twenty soldiers who made the trip." They arrived at the mission of San Francisco de los Texas on June 8 just in time to prevent the abandonment of the country which the missionaries had decided to effect in July. Salinas found that the mission of Santísimo Nombre de Maria had been destroyed by a flood shortly after Teran left and that the missionaries and soldiers had all retired to San Francisco de los Texas.

The native *Cona* or medicine men

had convinced the Indians that the waters of baptism were fatal to them, because most of those who were baptized in *articulo mortis* died . . . Father Massanet deplored deeply that the Indians refused to believe that there was but one God. He explained that the Indians declared there were two: one who gave the Spaniards clothing, knives, hatchets, and all the other things they had, another who gave the Indians corn, beans, nuts, acorns, and rain for their crops. They had lost all respect for the priests and had on various occasions threatened to kill them. [Castañeda, 1936, vol. 1, p. 373.]

Massanet recommended to the Viceroy that, unless a new policy were adopted, the missions should be abandoned and an expedition sent to withdraw him and his associates from the country.

Salinas set out on his return on June 14, 1693, accompanied by two of the friars, and reached Coahuila on July 17. Massanet's letter and official report were dispatched at once to the Viceroy and referred successively to the Fiscal and a Junta General, with the result that it was decided to discontinue the missions and send the missionaries back to their college "until a more fitting occasion arose for the continuance of these labors."

In October Salinas received orders to proceed to East Texas and bring back all of the Spaniards remaining there, but the council which he summoned decided that the season was too far advanced and postponed the expedition until spring. However, events in East Texas moved much too rapidly for him. Castañeda thus describes the concluding events of this mission period:

On October 6 . . . the Tejas chief personally warned the corporal of the mission guard that his people were angry and did not want the Spaniards to stay in their country any more. The few horses and cattle that remained were frequently attacked by the Indians. Father Massanet called the chief and asked him if the story of the corporal was true. The chief replied with a sneer that it was only too true; that the Spaniards ought to leave if they did not want to die. Father Massanet replied with warmth that he and his men were well armed and could defend themselves, but he told him that since the Indians did not want the Spaniards any more they would leave. Secretly the valuable ornaments were packed, the heavier articles, such as cannon, bells, and other things of similar nature were buried, and, when everything was in readiness, on October 25, 1693, fire was applied to the Mission San Francisco de los Tejas, founded with so many sacrifices and so much expense. In the fitful glare of the conflagration, the fugitives stole away. For several days, they were followed at a distance by their former friends, who although they threatened the runaways, did not attack them. Four of the soldiers, Joseph Urrutia, Nicolás Rodelo, Francisco González and Marcos Juan, deserted the little group to join the Indians. At the Colorado, one of the faithful Indians of the mission overtook the fugitives and informed the *Padres* that the soldiers who had deserted had gone back to the mission and helped the Indians dig up the buried articles. For forty days they wandered over the trackless wilderness, completely lost. Finally they drifted to the coast and there found their bearings. After suffering incredible hardships and dangers, the worn-out little band finally arrived in Monclova on February 17, 1694. [Castañeda, 1936, vol. 1. pp. 375–376.]

On March 11, 1694, the Viceroy of Mexico ordered that the province of Tejas, to which Teran had given the name El Nuevo Reyno de la Nueva Montaña de Santander y Santillana, be definitely and formally abandoned (Heusinger, 1936, p. 53).

French activity had been largely responsible for the stimulation of Spanish interest in Texas in the first instance and it was destined to repeat the performance. The scene, therefore, shifts temporarily to the French and to their colony of Louisiana which came into existence in 1699. In 1700 Le Moyne d'Iberville, founder of that colony, returned to it a second time, began the construction of a fort near the mouth of the Mississippi, and undertook an expedition up that river to a point considerably above the mouth of Red River. The names of several tribes living on the latter were reported to him and among them we seem able to make out the Yatasi ("Yataché"), Nanatsoho ("Natsvtos"), and Kadohadacho ("Cadodaquis"), the others being perhaps the Natchitoches ("Nactythos"), Nakasa ("Nataché"), Adai ("Natao"), Ouachita ("Yesito"), and Cahinnio ("Cachaymons") (Margry, 1875–1886, vol. 4, p. 178).

The same year, a little later, Iberville's brother Bienville was sent to the Caddo country from the Taensa towns on Lake St. Joseph. He was accompanied by a young Canadian, Louis Juchereau de St. Denis. They set out March 22 and on the 28th came to the Ouachita village on the river which bears the name of that tribe. It was reduced to five cabins, part of the tribe having gone to live with the Natchitoches, and this removal must have taken place at least 10 years earlier because Tonti had found them there in 1690. Bienville reached Red River at the town of the small Souchitiony tribe, the Doustioni of other writers, 1 league from which was the village of the Natchitoches. From the latter town he ascended the river to a village of 15 cabins occupied by a tribe he calls Nakasa (perhaps part of the Yatasi) and to another village of this same tribe higher up but of 8 cabins. Still farther on were the cabins of the Yatasi scattered along Red River for 2 leagues. From their settlements to those of the Kadohadacho it was said to take only 2 days in the summer, but the Indians affirmed that at that season (April) it required 10 nights by boat along the river. Bienville returned, however, without ascending farther and reached Iberville's vessels May 18 (Margry, 1875–1886, vol. 4, pp. 432–444). The same month— immediately after Bienville's return, it would seem—St. Denis was commissioned to travel westward with 25 men in order to keep watch of the Spaniards. Accordingly he ascended to the country of the Natchitoches, where he obtained a native chief called the White Chief as a guide and then continued on to the country of the Kado-hadacho. These Indians informed him that they had not seen a Spaniard for more than 2 years (Clark, 1902, pp. 5–6; Margry, 1875–1886, vol. 5, p. 421).

Soon after his return St. Denis was placed in command of the Mississippi fort. At least he was there in 1702 when, having lost their crops, the Natchitoches Indians descended to the French fort. St. Denis sent them to live beside the Acolapissa on the north shore of Lake Pontchartrain whither the latter had but lately moved from Pearl River. Pénicaut places this among the events of 1705 but Beaurain's testimony is to be preferred.[6] The same year their war-riors and those of the Acolapissa participated in an expedition led by St. Denis against the Chitimacha, (Margry, 1875–1886, vol. 4, p. 405, vol. 5, p. 460; Beaurain, 1831, p. 73). Pénicaut states that St. Denis abandoned the public service in 1705 and retired to Biloxi (Clark, 1902, vol. 6, p. 6; Margry, 1875–1886, vol. 5, p. 460), and he implies that he remained in retirement until called upon in 1713 by Governor Cadillac to head an expedition into the Texas country. St. Denis' own testimony, however, establishes a much greater range of activity within this period. He went to the Choctaw Indians, from Mobile, perhaps after a stop at Biloxi as Pénicaut would suggest, and then to the Natchez on the Mississippi. From them he crossed to the old country of the Natchitoches Indians and after a short stay there, vis-ited the Hasinai and kept on to the Presidio of San Juan Bautista on the Rio Grande. Testimony is adduced by Castañeda to indicate that St. Denis made several visits to the Hasinai before 1714 and had spent a number of months among them during which he acquired some knowledge of their language (Castañeda, 1936, vol. 2, p. 19).

In 1707 four Natchitoches Indians took part in an attack upon the Chitimacha to avenge the death of the missionary St. Cosme (Beau-rain, 1831, p. 102).

In 1709, acting on information that the Texas Indians had moved west to the Colorado River, Captain Pedro de Aguirre, commander of the Presidio of Rio Grande del Norte, was ordered to escort two Franciscan friars, Antonio de San Buenaventura Olivares and Isidro

---

[6] Margry, 1875–1886, vol. 5, p. 459; Beaurain, 1831, p. 73, date implied by contemporary events, particularly St. Denis' expedition against the Chitimacha.

Espinosa, to them, but on arriving there they learned from some
Yojuane Indians

that the Asinai Indians, commonly called Tejas, were in their own country
where they had always lived; that they had not moved to the place we inquired
about; that only a few were in the habit of going in search of buffalo meat to
the Colorado River and its neighborhood. Asked again, if they knew this
to be the truth, they maintained what they had said and declared further that
Bernadino, a Tejas Indian, who knew Spanish and was very crafty, having
lived many years among the Spaniards, was the chief of all the Tejas, and
this they knew well. All this caused us sorrow on the one hand, because we
wanted to see the Tejas, and joy on the other hand, because it relieved us of
the uncertainty under which we had labored concerning the whereabouts of
the Tejas. The Indians said also that it was a three-day journey from the
place where we were to the village of the Tejas. Not having planned to stay
any longer, and the Captain of the military expedition not having instructions
to go any farther, and having been told by all who knew him that the chief
of the Tejas was very adverse to all matters of faith, never having been made
to live like a Christian, and that he had escaped from the mission of Rio
Grande with some Indian women who had been left there, we decided not to
proceed any farther. [Castañeda, 1936, vol. 2, p. 23.]

The next entrada of the Spaniards among the Hasinai came
about in this way. In 1709 Francisco Hidalgo, one of the Queré-
teran friars who had been with Massanet at San Francisco de los
Texas and had afterward labored in the missions along the Rio
Grande, set out for the Texas country alone, and, single-handed,
ministered to the spiritual wants of that province for several years.
Receiving no answer to his various petitions to the Viceroy for help,
Hidalgo finally (on January 17, 1711) sent a letter to Lamothe
Cadillac, Governor of Louisiana, asking cooperation in founding a
mission among the Hasinai, and Cadillac at once saw an opportunity
to push the trade of France by this means. Cadillac, therefore, selected St. Denis, then commander of the Biloxi fort, to carry the
project through and the latter set out from Mobile in September
1713 (Heusinger, 1936, pp. 57–58). He sent Pénicaut to gather the
Natchitoches together and bring them to him at the fort on the
Mississippi—or so Pénicaut says—but from some motive which we
are unable to divine, as soon as the Acolapissa heard that the Natchitoches Indians were to remove, they fell upon them, killed 17, and
captured 50 women and girls. The remainder scattered and rejoined
Pénicaut during the following night, and he led them to St. Denis.
That explosive officer was deeply angered at what had taken place
and promised at some future day to take vengeance upon the Acolapissa and recover the captives. However, we learn that 30 reached
St. Denis later and it is probable that the rest were released without
an open rupture (Margry, 1875–1886, vol. 5, pp. 496–499). These
events evidently occasioned the postponement of the St. Denis date of
departure, for he did not set out from Dauphin Island until August

23, 1714, when he took with him 24 Canadians and "30 braves from the Natchitoches," and picked up on the way the chief of the Tunica Indians and 15 of his hunters (Margry, 1875–1886, vol. 6, p. 193; Castañeda, 1936, vol. 2, p. 28). Arrived at the old village of the Natchitoches, he built 2 houses in which to store the merchandise he had brought and left a guard of 10 men to protect the new post. He then proceeded to the villages of the Hasinai, reaching them on November 15, and began among them a profitable trade, bartering guns, beads, knives, and cloth for cattle and buffalo hides. Later he returned to the Natchez post to render an account of his expedition to M. de La Mothe, reascended Red River to the Natchitoches with five Canadians and crossed again to the Hasinai. Fray Hidalgo had by then returned to the Spanish settlements on the Rio Grande, but the Indians were so much attached to him that they offered to accompany the French officer to the Spanish country if he would use his influence to bring about Hidalgo's restoration to them.

Acceding to this request, St. Denis set out for Coahuila with the Hasinai chief Bernadino and 25 other Indians. At the River San Marcos he met and defeated 200 coast Indians, after which all of the Hasinai returned to their homes except the chief and 3 companions. Six weeks after leaving the Hasinai towns they came to the Presidio of San Juan Bautista, and its commander, Capt. Don Diego Ramón, sent his French guest on to Mexico City, which he reached early in June. At a meeting of Spanish officials on August 22, 1715, it was determined to reoccupy eastern Texas and reestablish missions—the number later fixed at four—among the Indians there. On September 30 Don Diego Ramón was appointed captain and leader of the expedition. The viceroy also engaged St. Denis to accompany it as second in command, and, accordingly, he left Mexico on October 26, but made several stops on the way, one of them apparently at the mission of San Juan Bautista to espouse Doña Maria Ramón, the granddaughter of Don Diego Ramón, though it is claimed by some that the marriage took place in Natchitoches. This expedition consisted of 75 people, including 6 Queréteran missionaries, and 2 Zacatecans besides 2 lay brothers. Father Margil, President of the Zacatecans, was taken seriously ill, however, and it was decided to push on without him, so that the final start was made from the Presidio of San Juan Bautista on April 27, 1716, and it was not until June 24 that they came into the neighborhood of their objective. On approaching the first town St. Denis went forward with a son of Captain Ramón and soon returned (on June 26) with a delegation of chiefs. The usual pipe-smoking ceremony having been performed, the latter led the way to their village where other Indians came bringing presents of corn, watermelons, and tamales. On

June 28 they reached the site of the abandoned Mission of San Francisco de los Texas, but Captain Ramón, the missionaries, and some
of the Indian chiefs thought it best to pick out another site for the
new establishment, and they chose one 4 leagues farther inland and
on the other side of Neches River. Here on July 3, 1716, they established the Mission of San Francisco de los Neches (or de los Texas)
and placed Father Hidalgo in charge. This mission was intended to
serve the Neches, Nabedache, Nacogdoches, and Nacono tribes. A
short distance away Ramón established the Presidio of Nuestra
Señora de los Dolores de los Texas.

The Mission of Nuestra Señora de la Purisima Concepción was
founded 4 days later among the Hainai, 8 or 9 leagues northeast of
the first, and placed in charge of Father Vergara. The third,
Nuestra Señora de Guadalupe, was established July 9 for the Nacogdoche and Nacao in the village of the former, and placed in the
care of Father Margil for the Zacatecans; and next day, one called
San José de los Nazones was created for the Nasoni and Nadaco
(Anadarko) in the Nasoni village, and given to the care of the
Queréteran Father Sánchez. Heusinger continues:

At all these places log houses and small wooden churches were hastily erected
with the assistance of the Indians. Of the four missions, that of Concepción
became the most famous. Because of its strategic location it became the
headquarters of the province of Texas of the College of Santa Cruz de Querétero. The president of the Queréteran missions, Padre Ysidro Felix de Espinosa,
personally took charge of this establishment and from it he directed the
activities of the other two. . . . .

The Spaniards soon learned that the French had established a post at
Natchitoches, close to their territory. Since this would serve the French as
a convenient point for communication with the Indians it was determined
to investigate conditions. Ramón and Margil with a small following made an
expedition to the French post. As only two Frenchmen were found, Ramón and
Margil thought it best to found a mission as close as possible to the point where
the French would most probably enter into Spanish territory. Thus, returning
westward eight leagues—near the present Robeline, Louisiana—they came to
the village of the Adaes and founded a mission among them on January 29,
1717 [but Castañeda says it was late in 1716], calling it San Miguel de Linares.

Padre Margil, urged on by missionary zeal, pushed forward to found a mission
among the Yatasi, but was prevented by floods from reaching his goal. On
his return he founded a second mission. This was among the Ays Indians, at
the site of modern San Augustine, Texas. Like its predecessor it was a Zacatecan mission, and it was named Nuestra Señora de los Dolores. Margil placed
Padre Augustín Patrón de Guzman and a lay brother in charge [Heusinger,
1936, pp. 58–66; Morfi, 1935, vol. 1, p. 229; Castañeda, 1936, vol. 2, pp. 33–69],
but also made it his own headquarters [Castañeda, 1936, vol. 2, p. 57].

Meanwhile St. Denis had passed on to Mobile where he arrived
August 25. There he organized a trading company and early in October 1716 set out—with or without his partners—for Mexico with a
large quantity of merchandise. He reached Natchitoches on November

25 and soon departed alone for the Hasinai country, where he was joined by his partners late in December. Among the Eyeish at this time were 2 Franciscan missionaries, 3 soldiers, and a Spanish woman. At Nacogdoches were 4 Franciscans, a brother, 2 soldiers, and another Spanish woman. Among the Hasinai (Hainai), where the Frenchmen met, they found two Franciscans, a soldier, and a Spanish woman. The same month St. Denis started with a large part of his company's merchandise for the Rio Grande. The first day he came to the Spanish presidio where were a captain, an ensign, and 25 soldiers. The second day, March 22, he made 10 leagues and passed the last Hasinai mission, evidently that of the Nabedache, where were 2 religious and a few soldiers, who supplied them with some relief horses. Between the 23d and 24th they covered 18 leagues and reached Trinity River for the night. St. Denis arrived at the Presidio of San Juan Bautista in April, after suffering some losses at the hands of the Indians. There, however, his merchandise was seized and when he went on to the City of Mexico to secure its release, he himself was imprisoned. His partners thereupon entrusted their trading goods to the missionaries, who obtained a good price for them in Nuevo Leon, and then returned to Mobile, which they reached on October 25, 1717. After varying fortunes in Mexico, St. Denis, with the aid of his wife's relatives, made his escape September 5, 1718, returned to the Presidio of San Juan Bautista, and reached Natchitoches February 24, 1719. Some years later his wife was sent by her relatives to rejoin him. On March 24 he was at Dauphin Island. (Morfi, 1935, vol. 1, pp. 187–190; Margry, 1875–1886, vol. 5, pp. 494–505, 527–535, vol. 6, pp. 200–202; Beaurain, 1831, p. 203.)

Meanwhile, in January 1717, Bienville had forestalled any designs of the Spaniards upon the post at Natchitoches by sending thither a sergeant and six soldiers. The sergeant was probably that M. de Tissenet who assisted the Spanish missionaries in 1718 (Bienville ms.).

The condition of the Caddo tribes on Red River as revealed to Bienville through his explorations is given in a short Manuscript Memoir by that commander written about this time, from which we quote the following:

Twenty leagues from the Tchetimachas one finds the mouth of Red River, an affluent of the Missicipy. One must ascend six leagues before coming to a little branch of this river on the left hand of which are settled the Houbiels [Avoyels] the Natchitoches, the Louchetehona [Doustioni], and Yatacés, the Adayés, the Cadodakios, the Nassonites, the Natchitouches, Natsohos, Quitchiaiches [Kichai]. The four last mentioned nations are gathered in one village 80 leagues above the Natchitoches, that is to say 150 leagues up Red River. They make war on the Cannecy [Apache] allies of the Spaniards. They travel on horses and are still able to put 200 men into the field. They are respected by their enemies although they have few firearms. They formerly numbered 500 to 600 men.

The Natchitoches, Louchetehonis, and Yatacés also form one village. When I passed in the year 1700 they numbered at least 400. Now they are unable to furnish more than 80 men. They are by nature cowardly and lazy, little given to agriculture, but very good hunters. These are the first savages I have found with a kind of religion, which has in it much idolatry. They have a temple filled with many (idols) which have the shapes of toads and many other animals.

Seven leagues directly west of and behind the village of the Natchitoches are the Adayés numbering 100 men as cowardly and lazy as their neighbors. The Spaniards have a little establishment among them, the foundations of which were laid in 1715, a feeble obstacle to us if the interest of the nation compels us to advance farther. [Bienville ms.]

The Quitchiaiches (Kichai) may have got misplaced in Bienville's narrative, for the four tribes which formed one village were the four whose names precede it. The Kichai seem to have been in the habit of attaching themselves now to one tribe and now to another, sometimes with a Caddo group but more often with the Wichita and their confederates. The Houbiels or Avoyel were not a Caddo tribe.

In each community where the Spaniards had established a mission a captain-general was chosen by the Indians subject to the approval of Captain Ramón. The French remained an element of danger because of the many presents they were in the habit of making at Natchitoches and the Viceroy was petitioned to offset these by equal generosity (Heusinger, 1936, pp. 67–68). Between October 14 and November 28, 1718, Martin de Alarcon visited the East Texas missions, distributed gifts and left supplies for the soldiers and missionaries, and visited the French post at Natchitoches, but his expedition resulted in no changes of consequence (Heusinger, 1936, pp. 71–76; Castañeda, 1936, vol. 2, pp. 102–109).

The next important French expedition into the Caddo country set out from New Orleans, December 17, 1718, under Bernard de la Harpe, who had been commissioned to establish a post in the country of the Kadohadacho and to carry on explorations among the tribes of that imperfectly known section. January 15, 1719, he entered Red River and presently arrived at the Natchitoches post, which he found under the command of a lieutenant named Blondel. Father Manuel of the Adai mission was there at that time and informed him of the expedition of Alarcon who, he said, intended to return later and set up a post among the Kadohadacho. Besides the original inhabitants of the region, the Natchitoches and Doustioni, a part of the Yatasi had come there, having been brought down from their old country by Bienville in 1717. Desiring to forestall the expected second expedition of Alarcon, La Harpe left Natchitoches on March 6, 1719. Next day he passed a little Yatay (Adai) village 1 league overland from Natchitoches. March 9 he encamped in the country of the Adai, and passed another Adai village on the 10th, noting that these people lived on the river only when the water was low. April 1 he encamped at the mouth of a river which he called Rivière de l'Ours, the modern Sulphur River, along which he determined to make his way to the village of the Nassonites, the distance being 5 leagues by the smaller river plus 10 of land travel, while by Red River it would have been 52 leagues. At the Nasoni village he was met by its chief and the chiefs of the Kadohadacho, Nanatsoho, and the upper Natchitoches town. He learned that the Naouydiches and other wandering nations had made peace with them, that the village of the Nadacos was 60 leagues south, and the Amediche (Namidish) village 70 leagues south by southeast, the two being not far from 10 leagues apart. On April 7 he ascended Red River 10 leagues to a site once occupied by the Nanatsoho.

The Indians of the assembled tribes prepared for him on his arrival at the Nasoni town a feast of smoke-dried fish, and, after it was consumed, the venerable chief of the Kadohadacho delivered a speech of welcome "which moved his people to tears." With these tribes lived a second section of the Yatasi who had been so severely handled by the Chickasaw that they had left their own town in 1717, another part of them, as we have seen, removing to the Natchitoches post. The Indians had been in the habit of living in scattered settlements and for that reason had been decimated by their enemies to such an extent that they had been reduced, it was claimed, from 2,500 to 500. La Harpe expressed a desire to restore the Yatasi to their old country.

On April 21 the boats which had pursued the longer course by Red River arrived, and on the 25th he began the establishment at a place previously selected by him, on the south bank of the stream, a gunshot distance from the dwelling of the Nasoni chief. He was obliged to buy from the Nasoni chief his cabin and his land, an eighth of a league inland. La Harpe's dwelling was enclosed in a stockade, and the Indians aided him in its construction. On May 20 he sent some of his men to obtain salt at a small stream 3 days' journey away, and they returned with 200 pounds. On June 6 some Nadaco chiefs came to visit him. He also learned that the chief of the Naouydiches and 40 warriors were on a branch of the "rivière des Ouachitas"—which seems to have been the Boggy and not the Washita River of Oklahoma, as might be assumed. After completing his post, La Harpe sent St. François, the corporal of the garrison, who spoke many Indian tongues, to the Hasinai with letters to Martin de Alarcon from Bienville and himself. June 6 the messenger returned accompanied by several Nadaco chiefs and with a letter from Alarcon. June 24 a "Dulchioni" man from Natchitoches came to inform the Nasoni that the French and Spaniards were at war and to solicit them to declare for the former.

They answered that they did not care to be mixed up in the affair but would defend their guests if they were attacked. July 29 [7] an officer named Du Rivage who had been sent up Red River on an exploring expedition returned and reported that he had encountered several bands of Indians among which he mentions one called Nouydiches (or Nahouidiches), which appears to have been an errant band of Caddo of the Namidish subdivision.

August 1, 1719, the corporal who had been sent to the Hasinai returned with some chiefs of that nation who came to assure him of their neutrality. They brought news that (on June 19) M. Blondel with seven men had attacked the Adai mission.[8] The priest happened to be absent on a visit to his superior, Father Margil, but the lay brother who had charge in his absence escaped and carried the news to the latter. The French captured a ragged soldier and carried off the sacred vessels and all the other belongings of the mission as well. The escaped lay brother had been informed that a hundred more men were soon expected to take possession of all of the other missions, and upon hearing this through Margil, Ramón, the soldiers, and the missionaries withdrew to the west side of Trinity River and finally to Villa de Bejar, which they reached in October 1718 (Castañeda, 1936, vol. 2, p. 118). Margil and Espinosa remained at Concepción for a time but later joined the others.

Relieved of any fears on account of the Spaniards, La Harpe now undertook an expedition to the northwest, taking with him two officers, three soldiers, one of whom spoke "the Indian tongue," two laborers, and two negroes, besides two "Quidehais and Nahouidiches" who had come up with him, and a Nasoni Indian. He set out on August 11 with 12 horses laden partly with provisions and merchandise. On the 28th they met a "Naouidiche" scout who informed them that they must be on their guard against 60 Canecy (Apache) raiders and that 6 leagues farther on the head chief of his own nation was encamped on the banks of the Rivière des Ouatchitas (the Boggy) with 40 warriors and that they were on their way to the Touacaro (Tawakoni). Two days later they came upon this band on the banks of the river in question "occupied in smoke-drying 'lions', animals of the size of a horse but not so long, the skin red, the legs thin, and the foot cloven. Its flesh is white and delicate." [9] The "Naouidiches" accompanied them to a branch of Arkansas River, probably the Canadian, and all continued on until September 3, when they encountered the chief of the Touacaros (Tawakoni) and chiefs of six other

---

[7] The Margry narrative seems to imply June 29, but Beaurain has July 29 and is probably correct.
[8] Morfi is evidently in error in attributing this attack to St. Denis.
[9] This "lion" was evidently a buffalo.

tribes who had come to meet him. They communicated with the French officer through a "Naouidiche" Indian who spoke the Nassonite language, and he went on to their town, which was on high banks along the river in latitude 37°45' [about 34°45']. These people belonged for the most part to the Wichita Confederation. September 13 La Harpe set out on the return journey and reached his post on October 13. On the 27th he started for New Orleans and was overtaken by sickness by the time he reached the Natchitoches portage on November 21, where he remained until December 4, being visited in the meantime by many Adai Indians. This tribe was reputed to have the most famous jugglers or sorcerers and they used every effort to cure him, finding him in the last extremity. Two days afterward they took him to the lake on a litter and placed him in a dugout in which he was carried 10 leagues toward Natchitoches and the rest of the way by land, although he suffered unbelievably from pain. He reached that place December 10, and, after recovering somewhat, left for New Orleans January 3, 1720, and arrived there on the 26th (Margry, 1875–1886, vol. 6, pp. 243–306; Beaurain, 1831, pp. 179–219).

On July 1, 1720, St. Denis was appointed commandant of the post of Natchitoches (St. Jean Baptiste aux Nachitos) and he had conferred upon him the cross of St. Louis, but at what time is uncertain (Margry, 1875–1886, vol. 6, pp. 220–221; Morfi, 1935, note, p. 231). The same spring word was brought to him that a French officer named Simars de Belle-Isle was held in captivity by the Arkokisa and Bidai Indians of the lower Trinity. Belle-Isle was the surviving member of a party which had gone ashore in Trinity Bay from the vessel le Maréchal–d'Estrées and fallen into the hands of the Indians. St. Denis thereupon solicited the Hasinai to rescue him and they did so promptly, the coast Indians all standing in awe of their neighbors to the north. Belle-Isle finally arrived in New Orleans April 4, 1721 (Margry, 1875–1886, vol. 6, pp. 230–347).

Meantime French activities had alarmed the Spaniards to such an extent that they determined upon another expedition into East Texas. This was led by the Marquis de San Miguel de Aguayo, Governor of Coahuila. While the party was on the Rio Grande, where they were delayed 3 months, rumors reached them that St. Denis and other Frenchmen were holding councils with the Sana Indians, and these were presently confirmed by a scout who reported that the conference was being held "above the Texas road between the two branches of the Brazos." On May 13, 1721, Aguayo set out from the Presidio of San Antonio under the guidance of Juan Rodriguez, chief of the Rancheria Grande Indians, and accompanied by the Padres Margil, Gabriel Vergara, and José Guerra, and Friars José Albadejo and José Pita. On July 9 they reached the Trinity, the crossing of which required 16 days, and here they were met by the Hainai chief, eight other native chiefs, and four Indian women, including the famous Angelina from whom the Texas River so-called received its name.

On July 27 Father Espinosa went forward with the new captain general of the Texas to arrange for the reception of Aguayo by the Indians at the site where the first mission had been founded. The next day he arrived and was met by "a great number of Indians, of all ages and of both sexes," who "came from the surrounding country to greet the Spaniards, all bringing some gifts, such as flowers, wild fruit, watermelons, *pinole*, or beans, in proof of their love. Aguayo received them kindly and dressed every one of them, and they all went away very happy and grateful."

Morfi continues as follows:

There came also one of the chiefs of the Neches with sixty men and women of his tribe. They entered the encampment and fired several salutes with their guns, whereupon they were welcomed with pleasure. After the ceremony of the peace pipe, the chief made an address in which he expressed their joy at witnessing the return of the Spaniards and the fear their stay would be temporary. He offered, in his name and that of his followers, to cooperate with Aguayo to enable him and his men to establish a settlement. Thanks were extended to him, as were due, but the distribution of clothes was postponed until the site of the mission of San Francisco was reached, which was near to their pueblo. They were given food supplies to last them until that time. . . .

At dusk that same day, a Frenchman arrived in camp, sent by Saint Denis, commander of the French on that frontier, who declared that his superior officer was at the site on which Concepción mission and the capital of the province [of the Texas] had been. He solicited a passport for Saint Denis, who, if granted permission, was ready to call on the Marquis of Aguayo to acquaint him with the instructions he had received from the governor of Mobile. Aguayo replied that he [St. Denis] was free to come whenever he pleased, and gave his [Aguayo's] word of honor to assure his personal safety. The messenger left the next morning.

The expedition continued its march and, after crossing the plain on which the presidio was established in 1716, set up its camp, July 29, on the bank of the Neches. The following day about one hundred Indians came, of both sexes and all ages, all of the Nacono tribe, who lived five leagues away from where our camp was situated and belonged to the mission of San Francisco de los Neches. They were led by a chief who was also their high priest and of whom it was said he had put his eyes out in his old age in order to obtain his dignity, there being the custom among them that the high priest be blind. He made a long speech and accompanied his words with the most pathetic gestures to express his joy and that of his people for the return of the Spaniards. Aguayo replied through the interpreter, and his words so pleased the chief that he addressed his followers and pointed out the blessings that would accrue to them from living together [with the Spaniards] and winning their friendship. [He urged them] to look upon us as brothers who were the friends of their friends and the enemies of their enemies, and he entreated them to prove their love by going immediately in search of game to present to their new neighbors.

The next day they brought tamales, fresh ears of corn, pinole, beans, and watermelons, which, though in a moderate amount, made a bountiful present considering their poverty. Aguayo was deeply impressed by their action and dressed all of them, distributing many pocket- and butcher-knives, scissors, combs, and sundry trinkets, all of which are highly prized by them. To the chief he gave a silver-mounted cane and a complete suit of Spanish clothes, and to his wife twice the number of presents given the others. This pleased and over-joyed all the Indians, who were delighted to see their chief in his new attire. [Morfi, 1935, pp. 204–206; Heusinger, 1936, pp. 96–110; see also Castañeda, 1936, vol. 2, chap. 4.]

Saint Denis arrived the same day, July 31, and on the following morning a conference was held between the two commanders at which the Frenchman stated that he was disposed to observe the truce then existing between the two nations and inquired whether Aguayo was disposed to do likewise. The Spaniard replied in the affirmative on condition that the Frenchmen should withdraw entirely from the province of Texas including Los Adaes, all of which he intended to reoccupy. Saint Denis acceded to these terms, though making some remarks in disparagement of the Adai post, which he would probably have prefered that they should abandon on account of its proximity to Natchitoches.

On the second of August, while still west of the Neches, Aguayo sent ahead two detachments, one with Father Joseph Guerra to the site of the second mission of San Francisco, the other under Fathers Gabriel Vergara and Benito Sánchez to the mission of Concepción, to rebuild the churches and houses. [Buckley, 1911, p. 45.]

On the 3rd the expedition crossed the river [Neches], and on the 5th witnessed the formal re-establishment of the Mission of San Francisco de los Neches, "commonly called de los Téxas." Due solemnity and appropriate exercises marked the refounding, the order of ceremony being what in general was observed at the founding and refounding of all missions. Solemn high mass was celebrated, salutes fired, bells rung, bugles blown, and drums beaten; next Aguayo formally invested with a cane the one whom he had chosen captain of the tribe; then followed the distribution of clothing and gifts,—which in this case, we are told, was more lavish than had ever before been witnessed by the Indians. [Buckley, 1911, pp. 45–46.]

Father Espinosa then made a speech to the Indians, since he knew their language, a speech containing a judicious mixture of religion and politics.

Finally came the formal acts of possession, by which Aguayo, in the name of the king, gave the Indians the lands and waters nearby, and left in charge of the mission Father Joseph Guerra of the College of Querétaro. [Buckley, 1911, pp. 45–46.]

The Spaniards, as was their wont, urged these Indians to gather into large towns, and Aguayo named the town which it was expected they would form here San Francisco de Valero. The Indians promised to come together after gathering their crops, which had been planted in different places.

On the very day on which this ceremony took place Aguayo and his party set forward, crossed the Angelina on the 6th, and reached the Mission of La Purisima Concepción, the only one that had not been entirely destroyed, half a league east of the river. They encamped on the site of the old presidio 1 league beyond, so that the horses would not eat the Indians' corn.

The church was completed on the 7th, and Aguayo arranged that on the next day, the battalion, the companies of Alonzo Cardenas and Juan Cortinas, and the eight companies that had made up the expedition from Monclova, making ten in all, should be present at the refounding. Father Margil celebrated mass, Father Espinosa preached "an eloquent and touching" sermon, while the Indians, "among them some eighty Cadodachos," were awed by the simultaneous discharge of the artillery and at the presence of so many Spaniards. Aguayo assured the natives that their occupation would this time be permanent. And to gain the good will of Cheocas, the Aynay chief, seeing that he had a large following, he requested the Indian to assemble his people, that gifts might be distributed among them. When the day came the eighty Cadodachos [who had come to attend the convocation called by Saint Denis] were present among the four hundred to be regaled. The Spanish commander took special pains to please these, sending clothes and trinkets to their people at home,—hoping thereby to gain their good will in advance of his arrival. The day's work was closed by the formal act of placing the College of Querétaro in possession through its representatives, Espinosa and Vergara, and by the formal investiture of Cheocas as governor. [Buckley, 1911, p. 47.]

On the 9th Aguayo sent a lieutenant with an escort and Father Benito Sánchez, to rebuild the church and priest's house at the Mission of San Joseph de los Nazonis, eight leagues northeastward from Concepción. On the 13th [or 12th], leaving the main part of the force to rest at Concepción, Aguayo passed to the Nazonis, and solemnly re-established the mission, leaving as missionary Benito Sánchez of the College of Querétaro. [Buckley, 1911, p. 48.]

On the 14th Aguayo returned to Concepción and installed Juan Cortinas and his company of 25 soldiers in the old presidio 1 league away.

It occupied an advantageous position on a hill, overlooking the country, with the arroyo of Nuestra Señora de la Assumpción (evidently the first eastern branch of the Angelina) running at its base. The fortifications were not outlined until Aguayo's return from Los Adaes. The fort was to be square, with two bastions on diagonal corners, each to cover two wings, which were to be sixty *varas* in length. The diary gives the impression that the company installed had formerly occupied the *presidio*. The company may have been the same, but Cortinas was evidently the captain at this time. [Buckley, 1911, p. 48.]

Margil and two other friars were sent to this mission on August 10 (Morfi, 1935, p. 212, and note, p. 238). To resume:

On the same day, the 15th, the expedition took up the march for the next mission, at Nacogdoches [Our Lady of Guadalupe of Albuquerque of the Nacogdoches]. On the 18th the new church was dedicated. Father Margil, on behalf of the College of Zacatecas, received possession, and Father Joseph Rodríguez remained as missionary. Aguayo repeated the presentation of the silver-headed cane to the chosen captain, enjoined upon the Indians the formation of *pueblos*, distributed gifts lavishly, and clothed one hundred and ninety Indians. [Buckley, 1911, pp. 48–49.]

On the 21st of August, after traveling three days through lands of walnuts, pines, oaks, and glades, having had to bridge several streams, the expedition camped one-fourth of a league beyond where the mission of Dolores had stood. The mission was rebuilt here, beside a stream, and near a spring of water, where the high and clear grounds and the surrounding plains offered inducements for planting. [Buckley, 1911, pp. 50–51.]

It was dedicated on the 23d.

On the 24th, Aguayo left Dolores for San Miguel. The route lay for six days of his travel east-northeast, through brushy lands of walnuts, pines, and oaks, over glens and plains, and across many streams. The most important of these were the modern Palo Guacho, the Patroon, and the Sabine. [Buckley, 1911, p. 50.]

On the 26th, it was necessary to reenforce the vanguard to enable it to cut a road through woods so thick that they blocked the way (Morfi, 1935, vol. 1, p. 218). On the 29th, Aguayo reached the site of the mission and camped half a league beyond it because there was no running water in the creek. No Indians were found at Los Adaes and parties were sent out to hunt for them, which discovered that their nearest rancherias were some 10 to 12 leagues off.

On September 1, the cazique of the Adaes nation with many of his following visited the Spanish camp. All expressed themselves as joyful at the return of the Spaniards, and explained that at the time of the French invasion they had been driven out of their land because they had shown regret at the departure of the Spaniards. The French had, moreover, they said, taken some of the Adaes women and children as slaves, and had shown such hostility that the Indians were compelled to leave that locality and retire to a less fertile one higher up, hence their absence when the Spanish arrived. [They complained particularly of ill-treatment by the Natichitoches Indians.] Learning now of Aguayo's intention to erect a *presidio* and a mission, they decided to return to their old home. [At that time they were said to number more than 400.]

The same day, September 1, Aguayo received a letter from Rerenor, the French commandant at Natchitoches. After the usual courtesies, it stated that Saint Denis on his return from Texas in August, had immediately proceeded to Mobile, to inform the governor of the coming of the Spaniards. Therefore, Rerenor, not having orders to let the Spaniards settle, asked the commander to abstain from definite action till Saint Denis could return. In answer Aguayo wrote that, as "the matters of war could not be well settled by pen," he was sending his lieutenant Almazán and Captain Gabriel Costales to have a personal conference with the commandant at Natchitoches. The former were instructed to observe the situation and condition of the French post. Almazán explained to Rerenor that the Spaniards had come determined to occupy Los Adaes, as they had already done at Los Téxas, to rebuild the mission of San Miguel, and to erect a *presidio* on that frontier where it might seem most fit. Rerenor replied that he had no definite orders either to agree to or to prohibit such an act, and that he would therefore be content with a mutual observation of the truce between Spain and France. [Buckley, 1911, pp. 51–52.]

Immediately on the return of the envoys the marquis, without losing time, looked for a suitable place for the erection of a presidio. The ground in the neighborhood was carefully explored, and after many considerations, there was no place found more suited [for the purpose] than the one where the camp had been established, on the road to Natchitoches itself, seven leagues distant from that place, and one league from the lake through which the Cadodachos river flows before entering Red river. The rest of the country was found to be too thickly covered by heavy woods. Furthermore, in the location chosen there were good plains or valleys on which to establish the mission near the fort, with abundant land for both the Indians and the Spanish soldiers to have their separate fields, and an abundant supply of water suitable for irrigation. Here then, the marquis established the presidio, the foundations of which gave considerable trouble, it being necessary to dig them with bars in the solid rock. Taking into account the character of the ground, the number of the garrison that was to be left, and the scant artillery at his disposal for its defense, Aguayo constructed a hexagonal fort with three bastions. Each of these was provided with two small cannon mounted in such a manner as to protect two curtains of fifty-five varas each. He left a garrison of one hundred men in order that thirty could always watch the horses of the fort and seventy be left free at all times for its defense. Of these, thirty-one had families. It was the intention that these, and such others as might come later, should gradually form a settlement, without causing new expense to the royal treasury. The water supply was protected by the artillery, being only a gunshot's distance, but, to prevent contingencies, orders were issued for the excavation of wells within the fort, which was enclosed by a stockade, the bastions being protected by earthwork, until they could be replaced by stone defenses. To the fatigue of this work was added that of cutting down many thick trees that covered the ground in order to clear the approaches,—this to keep the enemy from approaching under cover and surprising the fort . . . The Indians informed him of a saline located fifteen leagues from the fort. A lieutenant was sent with twenty men to reconnoiter it, who brought back twenty-five mules laden with salt ore, of such high grade that it yielded fifty per cent; that is, one arroba of salt ore yields half an arroba of excellent salt. [Morfi, 1935, vol. 1, pp. 217-219.]

The mission was finally reestablished on September 29, the feast of St. Michael the Archangel (Morfi, 1935, vol. 1, p. 219), but the buildings were not erected until later. San Miguel de los Adaes was on a hill one-fourth of a league from the presidio and with a creek between.

Father Margil, president of the Zacatecan missions, remained there in charge. The relative position of mission and *presidio* is shown by Le Page du Pratz; the intervening arroyo was probably the arroyo Hondo. [Buckley, 1911, p. 52.]

Buckley continues:

As near as can be ascertained from distance and direction from the other missions and from other evidence, the establishment was near the present town of Robeline, La. A mission was founded for a colony of Mexicans in the early part of last century, about two miles west of Robeline, and went by the name of Adayes in the records and directories down to the seventies. This continuity of name, and, as far as can be ascertained, the approximate location, give reason to believe that the Mexican colony was settled at the site of the Spanish mission of 1721.[10]

Meantime, on September 8, a ship laden with provisions had reached La Bahia from Mexico and on October 20 part of the cargo

[10] Buckley, 1911, pp. 52-53; the expedition is exhaustively covered by Castañeda (1936, vol. 2, chap. 4).

was brought on to Los Adaes on mules left at San Antonio for that purpose. On November 1, 400 sheep and 300 cattle reached Los Adaes from Nuevo Leon. Aguayo set out on his return on November 17. On the 29th he reached the Presidio of Nuestra Señora de los Dolores and outlined its fortifications. December 9, near Trinity River, he met a second train of provisions from La Bahia and sent part of it back to Los Adaes. The expedition reached San Antonio on January 22–23, 1722 (Buckley, 1911, p. 54).

News of the reoccupation of Los Adaes seems to have reached Mobile on September 16. Beaurain (1831, p. 350) appears to have the date 2 years too late and he calls Aguayo "the Marquis de la Guallo." On December 10 Bienville "entered a vigorous protest against it," but Aguayo had by that time accomplished his work, as we have seen, and was on the way back to Mexico. Los Adaes became the capital of the province of Texas and so continued for half a century. Father Margil remained there until June 1722, when he returned to Mexico, where he died on August 6, 1726 (Heusinger, 1936, pp. 104–105).

The east Texas missions thus appeared to have been resurrected with the most brilliant prospects. These, however, were soon clouded over. During the Governorship of Don Melchor de Mediavilla y Azcona, 1726–30, a *visitador* in the person of Gen. Pedro de Rivera was sent to the province and, according to his report (dated March 23, 1728),

there was not a single Indian at San Miguel de los Adaes; at Nuestra Señora de los Ais there was one small *ranchería*, but not a single convert; at Nuestra Señora de Guadalupe de Nacogdoches, although there were many Indians, industrious and well-disposed, they were all still heathens; at three missions, Nuestra Señora de la Concepción, San Francisco de los Neches, and San José de los Nazones, there were no Indians at all, with little hope of ever getting any. [Heusinger, 1936, pp. 111, 112.]

He recommended that the Presidio of Nuestra Señora de los Dolores be suppressed and the garrison of Nuestra Señora del Pilar de los Adaes be reduced to 60 men, which was presently done.

The missionaries of the Querétaran missions, now having been deprived of protection, and themselves despairing of making any headway with the Indians, asked permission of the viceroy to transfer their establishments to a more favorable location. [Heusinger, 1936, p. 114.]

The request was granted and on March 5, 1731, three new missions were (formally) founded in the neighborhood of the present City of San Antonio. Nuestra Señora de la Purisima Concepción de los Hainai (or de los Hasinai) became Nuestra Señora de la Purisima Concepción de Acuña, San Francisco de los Neches became San Francisco de la Espada, and San José de los Nazones became San Juan Capistrano, the radical change in the name of the last having been made in order to distinguish this mission from one already existing there called San José de Aguayo. The Queréteran missions thus pass out of the history of the Hasinai people (Heusinger, 1936, pp. 114–117.)

The Adai post was now left more and more isolated on the side of Texas and it is not surprising that relations between its inhabitants and those of the neighboring Natchitoches post should improve although they were under different flags. To quote Bolton:

In spite of these various forms of border friction, the relations of the two lonely outposts, Los Adaes and Natchitoches, were, on the whole, friendly, as might well be expected. When, for example, Bustillo, the new governor, arrived in Texas in 1731, the French officials went to Adaes to pay their compliments. When in the same year the Natchez Indians attacked Natchitoches, Saint Denis appealed to Bustillo for help. In response the Spanish governor sent eleven soldiers and a contingent of Indian allies. For twenty-two days they took part in the defense of besieged Natchitoches, one Spanish soldier being killed. Out of gratitude for this aid, Saint Denis sent Bustillo a present of some captive Indian women, which, however, the Spanish governor declined with thanks. In after years the aid thus given by the Texas Indians against the Natchez seldom failed to be recalled in the oratory of the border councils. [Bolton, 1915, p. 40.]

Charlevoix describes this affair with the Natchez as follows:

The Flour chief, after the miscarriage of his plot at the Tonicas, proceeded to join those of his nation who had escaped Perrier on the Black river, led them to Natchitoches, where De St. Denys was with but a few soldiers, and besieged him in his fort. St. Denys at once sent an express to the Commandant-General to ask relief, and on the 21st of October Mr. De Loubois set out from New Orleans at the head of 60 men to reenforce him. He had advanced six leagues up Red River, and was only seven or eight days' march from the Natchitoches, when the Sieur Fontaine, sent by De St. Denys to Perrier, informed him that the Natchez had been defeated; that the Natchitoches had at the outset wished to attack them, but being only 40 against 200, they had been compelled to retire, and even abandon their village after losing 4 of their men; that the Natchez had seized the village, and intrenched themselves there; that then De St. Denys, having received a reinforcement of Assinais and Attacapas, who were joined by some Spaniards, had attacked the enemy's intrenchments and killed 82, including all their chiefs; that all the survivors had taken flight, and that the Natchitoches were in close pursuit. [Charlevoix, 1872, vol. 6, pp. 117–118.]

The three Zacatecan missions remained among the eastern Caddo, but they can hardly be said to have flourished.

The removal of the French post at Natchitoches to the west side of the Red River in 1735, in consequence of the overflow of that stream, occasioned a heated exchange of communications between Governor Sandoval, then absent at Béxar, and his lieutenant José Gonzales at Los Adaes on one side, and St. Denis on the other, the Spaniards claiming that the Red River had always been the boundary between the two nations. The protests were of no avail, however; it was shown to the satisfaction of the higher Spanish authorities that the recognized boundary between the two nations had been the Arroyo Hondo and La Gran Montaña, and Sandoval was rewarded for his zeal in the Spanish cause by imprisonment in 1736 at the Presidio of Los Adaes by his successor Carlos Benites Franquis de Lugo, a Canary Islander (Bolton, 1915, pp. 33–34). The new governor was soon in trouble himself, however. Morfi says:

Franquis was accused of taking the Indians from the missions to make them work outside of their pueblos. Being maltreated, the Indians fled to the woods, diminishing thereby the number of the converted and keeping the unconverted informed of this violence through the deserters. An appeal was made to the viceroy for a remedy, and his excellency ordered the governor, in his communication of March 6, 1736, to abstain, under pain of being fined, from taking Indians out of the missions, since these could be used only at the discretion and with the consent of the religious. [Morfi, 1935, vol. 2, pp. 285–286.]

Franquis refusing to change his conduct, an investigation was ordered, but he was ultimately acquitted. Nevertheless, he was superseded in the government by Don Prudencio de Orobio y Basterra. Meanwhile, the influence of the French traders was becoming more and more pronounced every year. We quote again from Bolton:

More important than any question of the precise boundary was that of the activities of French traders among the tribes of Texas. While the expedition of the Marqués de Aguayo to eastern Texas in 1721 had determined the ownership of Texas—or of what is now southern Texas—in favor of Spain, it did not by any means give the Spaniards undisputed sway over the natives. The missionaries, unsupported by an adequate military force, failed almost completely to convert the Indians of eastern Texas, and they rightfully regarded this failure as due in no small degree to the baneful influence of the neighboring French. The men of the latter nation were skillful Indian traders, and readily affiliated with the savages. On the other hand, the narrow commercial policy of Spain permitted trade with the Indians only under the strictest regulations, and entirely prohibited supplying them with firearms. As a consequence the Indians of eastern and northern Texas continued to look to the French for their weapons, ammunition, and most of their articles of commerce, for which they gave in exchange their peltry and, to some extent, their agricultural products. As time went on the complaints, in Spanish circles, of French trade and French influence among the Indians of Texas, increased.

The French traders operated even among the Hasinai, in whose very midst the Spaniards were established, though not without liability to apprehension and punishment, for such trade was strictly forbidden by law. Northern Texas the Spaniards scarcely entered before the middle of the century, and there the French traders were practically unimpeded. Among the Cadodacho the French had founded the Nassonite post in 1719. This establishment, which was maintained till after the Louisiana cession in 1762, was an effective barrier to the Spaniards. A regular trail led from Natchitoches by way of the Sabine to the Cadodacho. Depots were established at the villages of the Petit Cado and Yatasí, further down the Red River. These trading stations, together with the influence of Saint Denis, the imperious and blustering French commander, were the basis of an almost undisputed French domination over the Caddoan tribes of the northeastern Texas border. More than once the Spanish authorities contemplated driving the French from the Cadodacho village, and erecting there a Spanish post, but the thought was never carried into action. Indeed, any attempt to curtail the French trade among the natives was made at the risk of bringing down upon the Spaniards the wrath of the Indian tribes. [Bolton, 1915, pp. 34–36.]

In June 1744, when the distinguished French commandant, St. Denis, passed away, Governor Boneo and Father President Vallejo from Los Adaes were present to assist in the funeral honors (Bolton, 1915, p. 41). St. Denis was succeeded by his son, Louis de St. Denis, who enjoyed an equally commanding influence with the Caddo. In 1750

the Indians had openly rebelled and threatened to expel the Spaniards merely because Governor Barrios had interfered with the trading operations of [young] Saint Denis. In the following year Barrios sent Manuel Antonio De Soto Vermúdez among the tribes to report on the operations of the French, but in attempting to go from the Nasoni to the Nadote village, where Saint Denis had a trading post, he was driven back by the Nadote chief. Immediately after De Soto left, an assembly of five hundred warriors gathered at the Nadote village and threatened to massacre all the Spaniards on the frontier, but they were calmed by Saint Denis. [Bolton, 1915, p. 70.]

Early in 1754 Governor Barrios was instructed "to order Saint Denis to withdraw his commission to the Nadote chief; to require the commander of Natchitoches [César de Blanc] to recall the French interpreters from the Indian villages on Spanish soil; and to 'prevent the commerce of the French with the Indians of Texas' " (Bolton, 1915, p. 72). Relations between the Adai and Natchitoches posts continued friendly, however, for the most part, until the cession of Louisiana to Spain in 1762 put an end to national rivalry in that quarter.

With this cession, moreover, radical changes were made possible in the government of East Texas. In August 1767, the Marques de Rubí came to that section on a visit of inspection under commission from the King, and as a result of his examination he recommended that the Presidio del Pilar de los Adaes be abandoned

since danger was no longer to be apprehended in that quarter, neither from the Indians, who had always been peaceful, nor from the French, now that Louisiana belonged to the crown of Spain . . . Los Ays and Nacogdoches missions could also be abandoned since they involved a useless expenditure, and the territory extending from Espíritu Santo to Los Adaes could be left untouched. [Heusinger, 1936, pp. 166–167.]

The next year Padre Gaspar José de Solís of the College of Zacatecas visited the missions of his order. He found that the mission

of Señor San Miguel de Cuellar de los Adaes, to give it its full title as he does, was beautifully rather than hygienically situated. It was on the side of a hill that dominated a plain covered with a dense forest of pines, oaks, and other trees, but its only supply of water was a small arroyo through which trickled a thin and unsanitary stream. The church was built of logs and had a shingle roof; though strongly constructed it had grown shabby with age. The ecclesiastical ornaments and sacred vessels were also considerably the worse for wear. The forty log houses which served as habitations for the Indians likewise bore signs of decrepitude.

The spiritual condition of the mission was scarcely better than the material. The proximity of the French fort and settlement of Natchitoches brought sad results in its train; well supplied with liquors and wines, the Indians easily fell prey to bad habits, and were disinclined to bear the restraints of life in the mission. Still, at the hour of death, they would send for the missionary and ask for baptism. The records on May 7, 1768, showed a total of 103 baptisms for the mission, 256 baptisms, 64 marriages and 116 burials for the presidio, and 20 baptisms, 13 marriages and 15 burials for Natchitoches. This last set of entries can be explained by the fact that Padre Margil, shortly after founding the mission, hearing that there was no priest at the French post, took it upon himself to visit it periodically, and kept record of his ministrations in his own register.

The second mission of this group, Nuestra Señora de los Dolores de Benavente de los Ays, was likewise placed in a romantic setting, entirely surrounded as it was by a dense forest. Its buildings were in a better state of preservation than those of the other, but its spiritual condition was far inferior. Only eleven baptisms, seven burials, and three marriages are recorded in its registers. This fact is easy to explain: the Ais Indians were the most corrupt in the Province of Texas. They made fun of the missionary and told him they would rather deal with the devil than with him. Hence it is rather surprising that any success at all greeted his efforts. And we are forced in a way to admire his perseverance, even in the face of the proposal made by Padre Camberos that this mission be transferred to the vicinity of Espíritu Santo in favor of the Cujanes.

The third mission in this sector was called Nuestra Señora de Guadalupe de Albuquerque de los Nacogdoches. Founded for less savage Indians, and advantageously situated so as to be accessible to four important tribes, it had nevertheless no greater spiritual conquests to boast of. Twelve baptisms, eight burials, and five marriages are all that grace its books. Materially it was in excellent condition. Its ornaments and jewels showed less wear than those of the other two missions, and the dwellings of the missionaries were better constructed. The granary, soldiers' quarters and other buildings were also made of good material and roomy enough for all needs. Like its two neighbors, it was well enough provided with livestock, but in this respect the missions of the eastern frontier could not compare with those of the San Antonio district. [Heusinger, 1936, pp. 164–166.]

Rubí's recommendations were adopted in substance in September 1772, after long delay, and along with them the decision to remove the Texan capital from Los Adaes to San Antonio de Béjar. In May 1773, the Governor, the Baron de Ripperdá, set out for Adaes to remove the soldiers, missionaries, and settlers, and on his arrival issued an order that within 5 days all must be ready to set out. The short time allowed caused such universal protest that an extension was granted while he himself set out for San Antonio. A number of the settlers took to the forests or to Natchitoches, and others dropped off at Nacogdoches and other points along the route, but the majority, after a journey of 2 months, entered San Antonio on September 26, 1773. The three Zacatecan missions were abandoned at the same time (Heusinger, 1936, p. 171; Bolton, 1915, pp. 108, 114).

After Louisiana had been brought under Spanish rule and discontent had been suppressed, Athanase de Mézières, a son-in-law of the elder St. Denis, was appointed lieutenant governor of the Natchitoches district in the year 1770, and almost immediately he undertook a series of expeditions to the Indian tribes on Red River in order to win them to the Spanish alliance. In the year last mentioned he held a great council at the Kadohadacho village of San Luis, at which the chief of that tribe, Tinhiouen, acted as mediator (Bolton, 1914, vol. 1, p. 208). In 1772 he followed with an expedition among the Hasinai, Tonkawa, and Wichita Indians as far as the upper Brazos. He gives an interesting list of the presents which were annually made to the Great and Little Caddo, the Natchitoches, and the Yatasi. In an agreement made with the Kadohadacho and Yatasi Indians on April 21, 1770, he says that those two tribes "have ceded him [the King] all proprietorship in the land which they inhabit, . . . [and promise] not to furnish any arms or munitions of war to the Naytanes [Comanche], Taouayaches [Wichita], Tuacanas [Tawakoni], Quitseys [Kichai], etc." (Bolton, 1914, vol. 1, p. 157). The principal town of the Caddo, Tinhiouen's town, known to the Spaniards as San Luiz de Cadodachos, was situated 100 leagues from the post at Natchitoches and 80 from that of the Arkansas, and on the banks of Red River. "It is surrounded by pleasant groves and plains, is endowed with lands of extreme fertility, and abounds in salines and pastures" (Bolton, 1914, vol. 1, p. 208). The chief of the Yatasi at this time was named Cocay; the head-chief of the Natchitoches, Sauto; and that of the Texas Indians, Vigotes (Bolton, 1914, vol. 1, pp. 211, 255, 264). This year De Mézières visited the village of the Petit Caddo, who gave him a horse to pass to the Yatasi.

Here, most excellent Sir, shortly before arriving at the village, I met the Indian chief in a field tent which they make of hides or skins of the deer which they kill. It was so small that there was scarcely room in it for a bench of reeds with a buffalo [hide], which was his bed. There was another little tent where he had the fire, which this people are never without. I arrived at night when it was raining, and was all wet, for it had rained the whole day. This Indian arising on the instant, took me down from the horse and ordered the Indian woman, his wife, to get up from the bed where she had already retired with her little doughter, who was very ill, and very tenderly and charitably made me retire into it. [Bolton, 1914, vol. 2, pp. 76–77.]

It is not evident whether the humanity of the white man equaled the hospitality of the red one.

In 1773–74 one J. Gaignard ascended Red River. On the third day he reached the town of the Natassee (Yatasi), 25 leagues from Natchitoches and found they had only three warriors. There was, however, a trader. October 9, 1773, he came to the village of the Little Kadohadacho, 25 leagues farther on, and found 60 warriors. "They are friendly with the French." On the 14th he arrived at the "Prairie des Ennemis" and reports that there were about 10 Caddo living in that vicinity.

> On the twenty-third, [he says] I arrived at the village of the Great Cados, who are thirty leagues distant from the Petit Cados. There are ninety warriors. They are brave and employ themselves only at war and in the chase, the women having to tend the crops. They are friendly with the French. They are situated on the banks of the Red River straight west [north?] from Natchitoches. During the eighty-four days which I spent with the Great Cados I observed nothing except that they told me that there was a silver mine twelve leagues from the Cados toward the northeast, and another on the Cayaminchy [Kiamichi] River, fifty leagues from the Cados toward the north-west. [Bolton, 1914, vol. 2, pp. 83–84.]

Evidence of the bitter warfare waged by the Osage against all of their neighbors is already apparent. In a letter dated May 2, 1777, De Mézières informs the Governor-general that they had killed five Kadohadacho men and two women. For an expedition planned against the Osages, he says that the Kadohadacho would be able to furnish 50 men; the Anadarko and Nasoni, 25 men; and the Nabedache, 30 men. In this same year there was an epidemic which worked havoc among many tribes including the Nasoni and the Kadohadacho, carrying off more than 300 of the latter. The Adai were said to be almost extinct as a result and since they were "given extremely to the vice of drunkenness, cannot be useful or of any advantage." The Texas Indians

> divided into various bands, known under the names Azinays, Nevadizoes, Nadacogs, and Nacogdoches . . . are very industrious in agriculture, are lovers of and beloved by the Spaniards, and are ready to serve them with that efficiency that they proved in 1730 (which may still be remembered in Louisiana), when the hostile Natches invaded the territory of the Natchitoches and perished by their arms. [Bolton, 1914, vol. 2, pp. 131, 145, 173, 231–232.]

Further on we read:

> As the Cadaudakioux is very much enfeebled by the continual war of the Osages, and since the last epidemic has still more diminished its numbers, it has created a faction amongst them who desire to abandon the great village. This would leave the interior of the country exposed to incursions of foreigners and its Indian enemies, a design so fatal that it will not succeed if Monsieur the governor uses his prodigious influence to frustrate it. [Bolton, 1914, vol. 2, p. 250.]

In April 1779 the settlers of Bucareli—an attempted settlement on the lower Trinity—were removed to Nacogdoches (Bolton, 1915, p. 119).

In a letter written May 27, 1779, De Mézières confirms the low esteem in which, as we have seen, the Eyeish were held:

Near this river [the Sabine] is the little village of Ais, for whose benefit the mission of Nuestra Señora de los Dolores, of that name, was founded. It was so unfruitful that all the ministers gained were labor, sorrow, and expense; for these lazy, insolent and greedy people so satiated themselves with material food that they would not accept that [spiritual food] which was longed for by their [ministers'] apostolic zeal. They number twenty families; their vices are without number; and the hatred which they have won from the natives and Europeans, general. Their country is one of the richest in this province. [Bolton, 1914, vol. 2, p. 257.]

He adds the following regarding the other Caddo:

The Mission of Nuestra Señora de Guadalupe was founded with no more profit than the foregoing with respect to the conversion of the Nacogdoches Indians, who soon deserted it, and to the Texas and Navedachos, who constantly lived at it without giving up their heathen ways. At the foot of the hill, on which its buildings remain, flows a beautiful creek of large volume. If it were adapted to the irrigation of the land, there could be no more desirable place to live in; but since the lands are very elevated and consequently sterile when the rains do not fertilize them, they have value only for stock ranches, and none—or only accidental—for cultivation. This has been the experience of the inhabitants from Bucarely in their removal from the Trinity River to this place; for, seeing their labor to be vain through a total loss of their plantings, they wander scattered among the heathen, offering them clothing for food, and exchanging hunger for nakedness. [Letter of August 23, 1779; Bolton, 1914, vol. 2, p. 260.]

Three days later he writes:

[The Angelina River] crosses the territory of the Texas, and is not navigable. On one of the banks of the second, which flows near the village of the Navedachos, one sees a little mound, which their ancestors erected in order to build on its summit a temple, which commanded the nearby village, and in which they worshipped their gods. It is rather a monument to the multitude than to the industry of its individuals. The distance from the source of the Angelinas to its ford is two ordinary days' journey, and from there to its junction with the Neches the same. The latter, which is larger, flows into the sea, affording easy entrance. . . .

The number of the Texas is eighty men, that of the Navedachos being less than one-half as great. Both maintain intercourse and friendship [with the Spaniards], which time has proved. In the last epidemic their chiefs, who were held in much esteem, perished. Their principal men having presented themselves to me, in order that I might elect another, I denied their petition, telling them that this nomination was a prerogative of the governor of the province, since they are included in his jurisdiction, and since he is an officer of higher rank and authority than I. [Bolton, 1914, vol. 2, p. 263.]

On August 30, he writes that he found only women in the village of the Nabedache as in that of the Texas, the men having departed to hunt buffalo or visit friendly tribes (Bolton, 1914, vol. 2, p. 264).

De Mézières was finally appointed Governor of Texas on October 12, 1779, but died November 2 following (Morfi, 1935, vol. 2, pp. 439, 440).

In 1783 there passed away the one man upon whom more than any other historians have depended for their narratives of the early Spanish period in the Province of Texas. This is Fray Juan Augustin de Morfi, an Austrian Spaniard, who came to America in 1755 or 1756 and was for a time professor of theology at the College of Santa Cruz de Tlaltelolco in Mexico. He became a Franciscan friar in 1761, and as chaplain of Don Theodore de Croix, the Commandant General of the Internal Provinces, he accompanied that official in his journeys of inspection. The information acquired in this way he incorporated into two great works, the Memorias para la Historia de Texas, which carried the history down to the year of his death in 1783, and the Historia de la Provincia de Texas, 1673–1779. The Memorias have been constantly drawn upon by writers on early Texas history, but the Historia lay unused in manuscript until translated and printed as volume 6 of the Publications of the Quivira Society (Albuquerque, 1935) (Morfi, 1935).

From the earliest days of Spanish and French colonization in the Southwest, the position of the Caddo peoples on and near the disputed boundary line made them of particular interest to the rival governments and, as we have seen, the first capital of the Province of Texas was in Caddo country, so far east, indeed, as to be actually outside of the limits of the present State. Between 1762 and 1803, however, Texas and Louisiana were under one government, the Spanish, the significance of the boundary line disappeared, and with it the special interest in the Caddo. But in 1803, after passing for a brief period again into the hands of France, Louisiana was sold to the United States and the boundary between it and the Spanish territories had renewed significance. This naturally involved an interest in the aboriginal inhabitants of the newly acquired territories and those adjacent on the part of the great Republic, and it was satisfied largely through the labors of Dr. John Sibley, a New England doctor, born at Sutton, Mass., in 1757. After a somewhat varied career, Sibley drifted to Louisiana shortly before the purchase. Here he became known to Governor Claiborne and through him to President Jefferson. By a letter of March 20, 1804, he put himself at the President's disposal, and was appointed "surgeon's mate for the troops stationed at Natchitoches, and later as Indian agent for Orleans Territory and the region south of the Arkansas." He is known particularly for his Historical Sketches of the Indian Tribes of Louisiana and Texas, and an account of Red River based on his own travels and information obtained from his assistant, François Grappe. These have been supplemented for the student in recent years by the publication of a manuscript Report from Natchitoches in 1807, edited by Miss Annie H. Abel (Sibley, 1922, pp. 5–9; *in* Amer. State Pap., Indian Affairs, 1832, pp. 721–722). Following are his accounts of the condition of the Caddo (Kadohadacho), Yatasi, Anadarko, Adai, Eyeish, Hainai, Nabedache, and Natchitoches:

Caddoques.—Live about thirty-five miles west of the main branch of Red river, on a bayou or creek, called, by them, Sodo, which is navigable for pirogues only, within about six miles of their village, and that only in the rainy season. They are distant from Natchitoches about 120 miles, the nearest route by land, and in nearly a northwest direction. They have lived where they now do, only five years. The first year they moved there, the small pox got amongst them, and destroyed nearly one half of them; it was in the winter season, and they practised plunging into the creek, on the first appearance of the irruption, and died in a few hours. Two years ago they had the measles, of which several more of them died. They formerly lived on the south bank of the river, by the course of the river 375 miles higher up, at a beautiful prairie, which has a clear lake of good water in the middle of it, surrounded by a pleasant and fertile country, which had been the residence of their ancestors from time immemorial. They have a traditionary tale, which not only the Caddoes, but half a dozen other smaller nations believe in, who claim the honor of being descendants of the same family; they say, when all the world was drowning by a flood, that inundated the whole country, the Great Spirit placed on an eminence, near this lake, one family of Caddoques, who alone were saved; from that family all the Indians originated.

The French, for many years before Louisiana was transferred to Spain, had, at this place, a fort and some soldiers; several French families were likewise settled in the vicinity, where they had erected a good flour mill, with burr stones brought from France. These French families continued there till about twenty-five years ago, when they moved down and settled at Compti, on the Red river, about twenty miles above Natchitoches, where they now live; and the Indians left it about fourteen years ago, on account of a dreadful sickness that visited them. They settled on the river nearly opposite where they now live, on a low place, but were drove from there on acount of its overflowing, occasioned by a jam of timber choking the river at a point below them.

The whole number of what they call warriors of the ancient Caddo nation, is now reduced to about one hundred, who are looked upon somewhat like Knights of Malta, or some distinguished military order. They are brave, despise danger or death, and boast that they have never shed white men's blood. Besides these, there are of old men, and strangers who live amongst them, nearly the same number; but there are forty or fifty more women than men. This nation has great influence over the Yattassees, Nandakoes, Nabadaches, Inies or Tachies, Nacogdoches, Keychies, Adaize, and Natchitoches, who all speak the Caddo language, look up to them as their fathers, visit and intermarry among them, and join them in all their wars.

The Caddoques complain of the Choctaws encroaching upon their country; call them lazy, thievish, &c. There has been a misunderstanding between them for several years, and small hunting parties kill one another when they meet.

The Caddoes raise corn, beans, pumpkins, &c. but the land on which they now live is prairie, of a white clay soil, very flat; their crops are subject to injury, either by too wet or too dry a season. They have horses, but few of any other domestic animal, except dogs; most of them have guns, and some of them have rifles. They, and all other Indians that we have any knowledge of, are at war with the Osages. The country, generally, round the Caddoes, is hilly, not very rich; growth, a mixture of oak, hickory, and pine, interspersed with prairies, which are very rich, generally, and fit for cultivation. There are creeks and springs of good water frequent.

Yattassees.—Live on Bayou river, (or Stony creek) which falls into Red river, western division, about fifty miles above Natchitoches. Their village is in a large prairie, about half way between the Caddoques and Natchitoches, surrounded by a settlement of French families. The Spanish Government, at present, exercise jurisdiction over this settlement, where they keep a guard of a non-commissioned officer and eight soldiers. A few months ago, the Caddo chief, with a few of his young men, were coming to this place to trade, and came that way, which is the usual road; the Spanish officer of the guard threatened to stop them from trading with the Americans, and told the chief, if he returned that way with goods, he should take them from him. The chief and his party were very angry, and threatened to kill the whole guard; and told them, that that road had been always theirs, and that, if the Spaniards attempted to prevent their using it, as their ancestors had always done, he would soon make it a bloody road. He came here, purchased the goods he wanted, and might have returned another way, and avoided the Spanish guard, and was advised to do so, but he said he would pass by them, and let them attempt to stop him if they dare. The guard said nothing to him as he returned. This settlement, till some few years ago, used to belong to the district of Natchitoches, and the rights to their lands given by the Government of Louisiana before it was ceded to Spain. Its now being under the Government of Texas, was only by an agreement between the commandant of Natchitoches and the commandant of Nacogdoches. The French formerly held a station and factory there, and another on the *Sabine* river, nearly a hundred miles northwest from the Bayou Pierre settlement. The Yattassees now say the French used to be their people, and now the Americans; but of the ancient Yattassees there are but eight men remaining, and twenty-five women, besides children; but a number of men of other nations have intermarried with them, and live together. I paid a visit to their village the last summer; there were about forty men of them altogether. Their original language differs from any other; but now, all speak Caddo. They live on rich land, raise plenty of corn, beans, pumpkins, tobacco, &c, have horses, cattle, hogs, and poultry.

Nandakoes.—Live on the Sabine river, sixty or seventy miles to the westward of the Yattassees, near where the French formerly had a station and factory. Their language is Caddo; about forty men of them only remaining. A few years ago they suffered very much by the small pox. They consider themselves the same as Caddoes, with whom they intermarry, and are occasionally visiting one another in the greatest harmony; have the same manners, customs, and attachments.

Adaize.—Live about forty miles from Natchitoches, below the Yattassees, on a lake called Lac Macdon, which communicates with that division of Red River that passes by Bayou Pierre; they live at, or near, where their ancestors have lived from time immemorial. They being the nearest nation to the old Spanish fort, or mission of Adaize, that place was named after them, being about twenty miles from them, to the south. There are now but twenty men of them remaining, but more women. Their language differs from all other, and is so difficult to speak, or understand, that no other nation can speak ten words of it; but they all speak Caddo, and most of them French, to whom they were always attached, and joined them against the Natchez Indians. After the massacre of Natchez, in 1798 [1729], while the Spaniards occupied the post of Adaize, their priests took much pains to proselyte these Indians to the Roman Catholic religion, but, I am informed, were totally unsuccessful.

Aliche, (commonly pronounced Eyeish).—Live near Nacogdoches, but are almost extinct as a nation, not being more than twenty-five souls of them remaining; four years ago the small pox destroyed the most of them. They were some years ago a considerable nation, and lived on a bayou which bears their name, which the road from Natchitoches to Nacogdoches crosses about twelve miles west of Sabine river, on which a few French and American families are settled. Their native language is spoken by no other nation; but they speak and understand Caddo, with whom they are in amity, often visiting one another . . .

Inies, or Tachies, (called indifferently by both names.)—From the latter name, the name of the province of Tachus or Texas is derived. The Inies live about twenty-five miles west of Natchitoches, on a small river, a branch of the Sabine, called the Natchez; they are like all their neighbors, diminishing; but have now eighty men. Their ancestors, for a long time, lived where they now do. Their language the same as that of the Caddoes, with whom they are in great amity. These Indians have a good character, live on excellent land, and raise corn to sell.

Nabedaches.—Live on the west side of the same river, about fifteen miles above them; have about the same number of men; speak the same language; live on the best of land; raise corn in plenty; have the same manners, customs, and attachments. [Sibley, in Amer. State Pap., Indian Affairs, 1832, pp. 721–722.]

Natchitoches.—Formerly lived where the town of Natchitoches is now situated, which took its name from them. An elderly French gentleman lately informed me, he remembered when they were six hundred men strong. I believe it is now ninety-eight years since the French first established themselves at Natchitoches; ever since, these Indians have been their steady and faithful friends. After the massacre of the French inhabitants of Natchez, by the Natchez Indians, in 1728 [1729] those Indians fled from the French, after being reinforced, and came up Red river, and camped about six miles below the town of Natchitoches, near the river, by the side of a small lake of clear water, and erected a mound of considerable size, where it now remains. Monsieur St. Dennie, a French Canadian, was then commandant at Natchitoches; the Indians called him the *Big-foot;* were fond of him, for he was a brave man. St. Dennie, with a few French soldiers and what militia he could muster, joined by the Natchitoches Indians, attacked the Natchez in their camp, early in the morning; they defended themselves desperately for six hours, but were at length totally defeated by St. Dennie, and what of them that were not killed in battle, were drove into the lake, where the last of them perished, and the Natchez, as a nation, became extinct [which is, of course, erroneous]. The lake is now called by no other name than the Natchez lake.

There are now remaining of the Natchitoches, but twelve men and nineteen women, who live in a village, about twenty-five miles, by land, above the town which bears their name, near a lake called by the French, *Lac de Muire.* Their original language is the same as the Yattassee, but speak Caddo, and most of them French.

The French inhabitants have great respect for this nation, and a number of very decent families have a mixture of their blood in them. They claim but a small tract of land, on which they live, and, I am informed, have the same rights to it from Government, that other inhabitants, in the neighborhood, have. They are gradually wasting away; the small pox has been their great destroyer; they still preserve their Indian dress and habits; raise corn, and those vegetables common in their neighborhood. [Sibley, in Amer. State. Pap., Indian Affairs, 1832, p. 724.]

In 1806 a United States Government expedition set out to explore Red River (see pl. 2). It consisted of Thomas Freeman, surveyor,

"Dr. Peter Custis, whose attention was directed to botany, and natural history, Captain Sparks and Lieutenant Humphreys, two noncommissioned officers; seventeen private soldiers, and a black servant. They left Fort Adams, on the Mississippi," April 19, reached Natchitoches in May and left it June 2. The next day they reached the second raft where "they were overtaken by Talapoon, a guide and interpreter, hired at Natchitoches" to accompany them to the Panis nation. "He had a mule and a package of goods, for the purchase of horses" among the latter in order to continue the exploration after the river ceased to be navigable. In order to escape the third raft, they entered a bayou on the east side called "Datche (which in their language, signifies a gap eaten by a bear in a log, from the circumstance of the first Indian who passed this way, seeing a bear gnawing at a log at this place)." They then entered Lake Bistineau, "called by the Indians Big Broth, from the vast quantity of froth which collects in, and floats along it, during the time of high water." They came to a prairie on the left, beyond which, at a distance of 30 miles from the river, was the main Caddo village. Presently they were overtaken by a canoe containing their interpreter, who had detoured by way of the Caddo town, and an Indian sent by the Caddo chief, the latter to inform them that about 300 Spanish dragoons were encamped near his village with intent to stop the explorers. At sunset, June 26, they reached a village of Koasati Indians who had come from Alabama. There they were met on July 1 by the Caddo chief with 40 of his young men and warriors, who arrived about noon, and a salute was fired as the chief entered their camp (Freeman-Custis Expedition, 1806, pp. 3, 11–23).

The Chief and the United States party being seated under the shade, with the young men and warriors of the Caddo Nation in a semicircle behind them, the chief after a short pause observed, that they must have suffered a great deal of hardship in passing the great swamp, with their boats, and expressed his wonder at their success.

He was informed that they had suffered much, but were not to be deferred by obstacles of that nature, from paying a visit to him, and the other chiefs and nations on this river. Mr. Freeman then explained to them the wishes of the President of the U. States and the American people, respecting the Indians of that country; as also the rout [sic.] they proposed, and distance they expected to go.

The chief said he was glad to see them in his land, as he should be to see them in his village; but was too poor to receive them in the manner he wished. The red people were always poor; he was sensible the Supreme Being had made a difference between the people of the U. States and his people; that he had endowed the former with more sense, and had given them means of which the Indians were entirely destitute: he should therefore look to them for protection and support; to be his fathers, brothers and friends. He said they had had a Spanish and a French father, who had treated his people well and against whom he had no complaints to make. He had now an American father, and in the two years he had known the Americans, he liked them also, for they too had treated his people well. His fathers and their fathers always told their children to live in peace with the white people, and never to spill white blood in their land. The nation never did, and he hoped [they] never would stain their ground with it. For some days he had been rendered very uneasy, because a large party of Spanish soldiers were encamped at the back of his village. The commander waited on him in the village, took him by the hand, and asked if he loved the Americans: to which he had replied that he did not know what to say; he did not understand him; but he did love the Americans and the Spaniards too, for he was treated well by both, and wished to be friends with them both. If the Spaniards wanted to fight with the Americans, they must go to Natchitoches to fight, for they should not spill blood on his land. The Spanish officer then retired and had not returned, so that he knew not what they intended to do.

He then said he wished the U. States party to proceed and see all his country and all his neighbors, in doing which however they would have far to go, and many difficulties to encounter; his friends, the *Panis*, would be glad to see them, and would treat them well. He professed to be highly gratified by the party explaining to him so fully the objects of their voyage; it was treating him with a respect and candor, which the Spaniards did not evince by their conduct. He said it was possible the party might be harassed by the Osages, who had always been the inveterate enemies of his nation. Should the party kill any of them he should dance for a month; and if they killed any of the Americans, he would turn out with his warriors, although few, make it his cause, and get revenge.

He then apologised for bringing so many of his men with him; but they wished to see their new brothers, the Americans. Most of them were young and had not been so far as the Post.

After this communication, provision was given to the visitors; and some liquor was furnished, that the soldiers of the party and the young Indians might drink together.

The soldiers were then drawn up in a single file in open order. The Caddos marched along shaking hands with them from right to left; after which they formed a line in front of the soldiers, about three paces distant, with their faces towards the soldiers. On their principal warrior coming opposite to the United States serjeant, he stepped forward, and addressing his men, observed—"that he was glad to see his new brothers had the faces of *men*, and looked like men and warriors;" then addressing the serjeant by the interpreter, he said—"here we are all men and warriors, shaking hands together, let us hold fast, and be friends forever."

The Caddo chief dined and spent the 2nd of July at the American camp. He informed the party that he should return to his village on the next day early, with his people; he had already kept them several days from hunting; not knowing with what intentions the Spaniards came so near; and hearing of the United States party, he thought it best to keep all his people together, that they might prevent hostilities in his land.

He had now seen the United States party, knew their business, and had been well treated by them. He believed what they told them, and would hold them fast by the hand as fathers and friends.

He said that the day before he left his village, three Spanish soldiers came to it from their camp, and informed him, that their commander had sent an express to Nacogdoches, and as soon as it returned, with dispatches and orders from the government, they should go to the Americans on Red river, stop them, and drive them back or take them prisoners. The chief supposed the express from Nacogdoches would arrive at his village, as early as his party could effect their return; and might be waiting for him. He would endeavor to find what their object was, would return with the Spanish officer to the American camp, if he wished to visit it, when he should hear the talks of both parties. Should he find the Spaniards determined to be cross, and to spill blood, he would supplicate them not to do so on his land: not through fear, because he did not fear man! Although his men were small, and might appear like nothing, they were unacquainted with fear! If entreaty had not the desired effect, he would order the Spanish officer immediately to return to his camp, and move from the land, and not to trouble the party nearer than fifty leagues above the old Caddo village (800 estimated leagues higher than this place). When he arrived at his village, if the express had not returned, and he could not learn that their intention was to interrupt the party, he would send three of his best warriors to the camp, with whatever information he could obtain.

It was found advisable to engage three Caddo Indians, to proceed up the river with the party; to act as guides, spies, or on express, as circumstances might require. One Indian will not go with a party of strangers; two are company for each other; and by engaging the third, he could be dispatched on express, to the Caddo nation, or to Natchitoches in case of necessity.

The Caddos reside 50 miles from the Coashuta village, on a small creek, which empties into a lake that communicates with the river a little above the raft. It is now eleven years since they fixed on that place for their residence. They formerly lived on the river, in a large prairie; said to be 150 leagues higher up: from which the Osages drove them. They are a very small people, without any appearance of that savage ferocity, which characterises some other tribes of Indians. They have some firearms among them, but their principal weapon is the bow and arrow, which they use with astonishing dexterity and force. It is said they can with ease shoot the arrow through a buffaloe.

The Caddos engaged as guides, arrived at the camp on the evening of the 10th, with information that the Spaniards had retired to the Sabine. It was believed to be only a sham, and that they intended to meet the party at a little distance above; for this expedition up the river seems to have thrown this whole country into a ferment.

This suspicion was afterwards justified, so that the expedition was turned back by the Spaniards a short distance above the great bend. Before reaching that point, however, the Americans passed several former town sites of the Caddo. The first of these was reached on the ninth day after leaving the Koasati village.

On the evening of the 19th they passed a beautiful prairie, on the north-east side of the river, 125 miles from the Coashutta Village. This prairie was the scite of an old Caddo village, deserted by that nation in consequence of a surprize, and the massacre of the greatest part of the inhabitants, by the Osage Indians. The Caddos with the exploring party, expressed a wish to visit this place when they were approaching it; and shewed a remarkable hill in its rear, on which their old chiefs used frequently to meet in council. They proposed to visit it with a bottle of liquor, that they might take a drink and talk to the Great Spirit!

This remarkable mount or hill stands on a level plain about two miles from the river, having the prairie on which the Caddo Village stood in front, or between it and the river. It is about two miles in length, 250 or 300 feet in elevation, very narrow at the top, in many places not exceeding two or three paces, and so steep, that it is with difficulty it can be ascended. The angle formed with the plain on which it stands, is from 45 to 50 degrees: in some places almost perpendicular.

This bill is an irregular mass of iron colored porous rock, in which there is a great number of small round pebbles. It has the appearance of having been in fusion at some former period. There is very little clay or soil on the surface, but a red colored gravel; it produces small scrubby Oaks and Pines only. In front of this mount lies a beautiful and rich meadow, extending from its base to the river, and downwards for about two miles. It is interspersed with small clumps of trees, and has a small lake or pond in its centre. Around and near to this pond, are to be seen the vestiges of the Caddo habitations; it was the largest of their villages, and their cultivated fields extended for five or six miles from it in every direction.

From the summit of this hill, the high ground, which bounds the valley on both sides, is distinctly seen; the distance to the opposite side appeared to be about ten miles. In the rear of the hill the land was nearly level, and the ascent from the base very gentle. The soil good, covered with White and Black Oak and Hickory.

Later they came upon another site.

On the 25th, at about 20 miles above the Little River, on the right hand side, ascending, is a prairie, considerably above the water, of a rich soil, and now overgrown with high grass, bushes and briars. This prairie extends back from the river about half a mile, and is bounded by open woods of Oak and Hickory.

Here was formerly a considerable Caddo Village; many of the Cedar posts of their huts yet remain, and several Plumb trees, the fruit of which is red and not good. A bunch of hemp, of several stems, nearly an inch in diameter, and ten feet high, was found on the left bank of the river opposite this village. From Red river across to Little River, is about eight miles, over a level and rich plain, and open woods.

A quantity of clay, of a high blue color, and so hard as to resist the current of the water, appeared in the bank of the river at this prairie, projecting some yards beyond the general line of the bank. At the head of this prairie, a bar of stones and coarse gravel, crosses the bed of the river, on which was found not more than 14 inches of water. [Freeman-Custic Expedition, 1806, pp. 23–35.]

On the 26th they discovered three runners sent by the Caddo chief to warn the party that "the day before they left their village, the Spanish troops upwards of 1,000 in number entered it, and cut down the staff on which the American flag was flying, and carried off the flag with them." They also threatened to kill the Americans or carry them off in irons. "They had taken away with them two young Caddos as guides to a handsome bluff on the river, a few miles above the old Caddo Village, and 230 miles (by water) higher than the Coashutta Village." The Spaniards were said to number 1,050 or 1,060 (Freeman-Custis Expedition, 1806, pp. 35–36).

Towards evening [of the same day] they were opposite to a lake on the south of the river, round which the Caddos had cornfields, when they occupied their principal village, which was situate in the prairie just above it. This lake is about two miles in length, and parallel to the river. Astronomical observations taken this evening, determined their latitude to be 33 deg. 34 min. 42 sec. north.

The next morning they selected a spot on the north side of the river, where they deposited part of their provisions, ammunition, and astronomical instruments; near which, and in a more secret place, they left a trunk of stationery, with the field notes of their survey to this part of the river. Round the place of deposit they made a small enclosure of saplings. The bank where this was done, was about 40 feet higher than the water in the river, and formed a barrier or mound between the river and a lake of considerable extent. A thick growth of Oak, Ash, Hickory and Walnut timber, made a complete cover, and rendered it capable of defence, to a small and active party, should they, as was expected, have had to retreat to it.

On the side of the river opposite to this deposit, the Indians said *the French once had a small military post;* and there also, was one of the principal villages of the Caddos. The prairie in which they were is very extensive, and now grown up with bushes. The growth of briars and bushes was so rank as to prevent them from ascertaining exactly, where the French post was, unless some Cedar posts which were found standing denoted the place. [Freeman-Custis Expedition, 1806, p. 37.]

A short distance above this point they were met by the Spaniards, whose numbers so far exceeded their own that they agreed to bring their explorations to an end there and return. Setting out on July 30, they reached Natchitoches August 23 (Freeman-Custis Expedition, 1806, p. 42).

Sibley's "Report" of 1807 gives some interesting items regarding events in the Caddo country at that period.

He notes, for instance, that on January 5, 1807, "I gave an Aiche [Eyeish] woman a Shawl for attending and giving me a Vocabulary of the Aiche Language" (Sibley, 1922, p. 12). If it is still in existence, this vocabulary would fill a serious gap in our knowledge of the Caddo dialects. The same day he learned through two Caddo that

a party of their Nation have been on a friendly visit and to trade with the Panis and were on their return home Rob'd of Seventy two Horses by a party of Ozages, and left on foot about 200 Miles from home with Considerable quantity of Baggage, Consisting Principally of Buffalo Robes.

To add to their misfortunes, after their chief had information of this and set out to relieve them with all the horses he could muster, his house caught fire and was burned "with a quantity of corn and Other Valuable property" (Sibley, 1922, p. 11). On February 21, another party came and complained that game was scarce "there being no acorns," and the loss of so many horses to the Osage prevented them from going into the prairie after buffalo. Sibley adds:

I gave *Cut Finger*, who is a particular friend & Companion of the great Caddo Chief a Hat and had made for him a Blue half Regimental frock Coat which I presented him with, [because] he was particularly friendly & attentive to Major Freemans exploring Party. [On February 26, Sibley purchases] two Brass Kittles to keep to lend to Indians who Come in On business from a distance and bring no Cooking Utensils with them. [Sibley, 1922, pp. 13–14.]

On March 20, he

received information that a Party of Alibamis & Appalaches were in the Prarie above the Caddo Village hunting Buffelo & fell in with the Same party of Ozages who Rob'd the Caddos of their Horses, Attack'd them in the Night in their Camp killed five of them & defeated the whole Party & Retook Most of the Horses, there were more than twenty Ozages & only eight of the other Partie who Sustained no loss, the Scalps of the five they killed had arriv'd at the Conchetta Village where all the Neighbouring Tribes were Collecting to hold the War Dance; my informant was one of the Alibamis who belonged to the Party. [Sibley, 1922, pp. 15–16.]

That day there also arrived a small party of Cherokee in two pirogues, descending Red River. They had deer skins to use in barter at the trading house and were said to be "the first Cherokees that ever were here." They had also taken occasion to make friends with the Caddo with whom they had had a misunderstanding.

Seven or eight years Ago there was by Accident a Cherokee Killed in the Caddo Country, the brother to the Man who was killed was one of the party that was here, he told me they had talk'd it over with the Caddo Chief, who entirely Satisfied him, he did not blame the Caddos in the Least, & spoke highly of the Caddo Chief. [Sibley, 1922, p. 16.]

On April 14

the Grand Caddo Chief and a party of 15 men of that Nation in Perogues loaded with Skins arriv'd. I gave them Provisions & a carrot [i. e., roll of] Tobacco. I gave the Caddo Chief a Scarlet Regimental Coat trim'd with Black Velvet and white Plated Buttons. The Cloth I bought of the factor the Making & Trimings Cost Eight Dollars. At the same time gave the Son of Carody the Old Caddo Chief a Blue Half Regimental Coat trim'd with Scarlet and a White Linnen Shirt. And Sent by the Caddo Chief a Regimental Coat to a friend of his Called the Grand Ozages. (Called so from his having in a Battle with a party of Ozages been wounded with a Ball in his forehead) and who particularly attach'd himselfe to Maj' Freeman in his exploring expedition & accompanied him from the Caddo Village as far up the River as he went, and back again to Natchitoches, and was Particularly Servisable in hunting, as a Guide & keeping the Other Indians together, and is in Major Freemans Opinion one of the Best Indians he ever saw. [Sibley, 1922, pp. 20–21.]

On May 5

three Caddos Arriv'd Special Messengers from the Caddo Chief to inform me that a party of Chactas consisting of Eight persons from the great Nation Under a Leader Called *Stamelachee* had lately been at a Camp of Nandacos at a Saline on the River Sabine above where the Nandacos live, the Men being out hunting & left their Women to Make Salt & had Murdered two of the Women & wounded Some Others, without any provocation and brought the Scalps of the women through the Conchetta Village on their way to the great Chacta Nation. [Sibley, 1922, pp. 22–23.]

On representations made by Sibley to the Choctaw chiefs, several of them met at Natchitoches and agreed to make reparations to the Caddo and do all in their power to have the murderers punished (Sibley, 1922, p. 27).

SWANTON]CADDO HISTORY AND ETHNOLOGY

Sibley continued to reside in Natchitoches until his death in 1837. In the American State Papers (Public Lands, 1834, vol. 3, No. 6) we seem to have recorded the sale of their lands by the Natchitoches Indians. One Hypolite Bordelin claims

a tract of land of about four arpents and eight poles in front, on each side of Red river, with all the depth thereunto belonging, and claimed under a purchase from an Indian chief of the Natchitoches village, by deed, bearing date the 23d of June, 1808, for the price and sum of eighty dollars.

With this claim was filed the following document:

Louis C. DeBlanc, *Commandant of the post of Natchitoches, &c.* In consequence of the death of Tomoc, chief of the Natchitoches nation of Indians, and finding that the said Indians are now inhabiting land not belonging to them, in the settled parts of this post, I grant to them, subject to the will of the Governor, Don Estevan Miro, twenty arpents of land on each side of Red river, at a place called Lac de Meures, about ten leagues above the post of Natchitoches.

This was, of course, the land to which Bordelin laid claim. Miro was governor between 1785 and 1792. In connection with this claim one François Grapp testified on July 19, 1812, that he

was called about seven years ago, by the Indian tribe Natchitoches, to be interpreter for them in making a sale of a portion of the land granted to them by the Spanish Government, on Lake de Mure, above Compte, to erect their village, and that, to his knowledge, the said portion of land was then adjudged to Hypolite Bordelin for ninety dollars, by consent of all the Indians; which sum of ninety dollars was paid down by said Bordelin.

In the judgment of the court, however,

the Indians had only a provisional grant of the land claimed from the commandant. No evidence has been adduced of the ratification of the title by any Governor of Louisiana. Even if their title was valid, the land was purchased from them at a time when the laws of the United States, then in force in Louisiana, forbade such purchases. The claimant can have no pretensions to a right from occupancy; his occupancy could not have commenced previous to the purchase, and the occupancy of the Indians could vest no right in a person to whom they could not legally sell. The claim, therefore, in the opinion of the Board, ought not to be confirmed. [Amer. State Pap., Public Lands, 1834, vol. 3, p. 79.]

Another claim involving title to property derived through the Natchitoches tribe, and apparently part of the ground occupied by their village, is the following:

No. 30. Pierre Gagnier, two hundred and thirteen and thirteen-hundredths acres, claimed under a purchase from John Sohano, an Indian, with settlement, &c. The notice of the claim is accompanied by a plat of survey, dated in 1806, embracing forty-two and twenty-hundredths acres on the left [right?] and one hundred and sixty-eight and ninety-three-hundredths acres on the left bank of Red river; and a deed of conveyance from said Sohano to Pierre Gagnier, dated 26th of September, 1804, for two arpents and a half, and twelve feet front, with the ordinary depth, on the right bank of Red River, at a place called Lac aux Mures, and four arpents front by the ordinary depth, on the left bank of said river. Pierre Elie, before the Board, 15th of June, 1812, hath deposed "that the land claimed has been inhabited more than twenty years by John Sohano, a civilized or Christian Indian, and other Indians of the Natchitoches village, and those claiming under the said John Sohano. No evidence has been offered to establish that John Sohano was of that class of Indians denominated Christians, under the Spanish Government, by which he might have been entitled to the privilege of holding and conveying land in his own right." [Amer. State Pap., Public Lands, 1834, vol. 3, p. 83.]

The above-mentioned François Grapp (properly Grappe) himself filed a claim for a tract of land on Lake Bastiano (Bistineau),

under a purchase from Cahada, an Indian. The notice of this claim is accompanied by a plat not signed by any surveyor; a certificate by John Paul Badin, stating that the said Badin was employed by the claimant to make an improvement on the land claimed; and that he resided on the land three years before 1790; that he heard, from the Indians, that the claimant purchased the land three years previous to that time, (1790) from an Indian called Cajadet. The certificate bears date the 14th of September, 1806. Another certificate of Louis C. de Blanc, dated 5th of October, 1806, in Attakapas, stating that, in the year 1788, when he was commandant of Natchitoches, the Indian of the Cado tribe, called Cajadet, came before him, and declared to have sold to François Grapp a tract of land, which was known by his nation to have been his property by inheritance, from his ancestors; and which had been inhabited and cultivated by him and them at a place called Lake Bastiano, on the east side of Red river, on the road from Compté to the little Cado village; that he had received pay for the purchase and relinquished his right and claim to the said land.

One Andre Rambin claimed a tract of land under a purchase from an Indian Cayacaillé, and his wife, in the year 1790. The name of the tribe is not given (Amer. State Pap., Public Lands, 1834, vol. 3, pp. 82–83, 89).

Another group of cases concerns the later history of the Adai tribe. The most important is the following:

[No.] 87. Joseph Valentine, of the parish of Natchitoches, filed his notice claiming, by virtue of a Spanish grant in his favor, a tract of land lying within the late neutral territory, situated on the Bayou Pierre branch of Red river, in the settlement of Bayou Pierre, having, on the south side of said river, Bayou Macdown for its northern boundary, its eastern boundary being Red river, being one mile and a half square, and on the other side of said river beginning at a certain bayou, and running down the river ten acres, with the ordinary depth, if it can be had. The following is a translation of the grant on which the claim is founded: "Don Antonio Gil y Barvo, captain of militia, lieutenant governor, and judge delegate of smuggling and forfeitures, and chief justice of the town of Na. Sa. del Pibar [Pilar] of Nacogdoches and its jurisdiction. Whereas Jph. V. [torn] has appeared by petition, bearing date August 5, in the present year, one thousand seven hundred and ninety-one, praying with due submission that the tract of land called Adaes, because the tribe of the Adaes occupy it, may be granted him, I do grant it to him for the object in his petition mentioned— the raising of horses, herds of cattle, flocks of sheep, and the cultivation of grains of husbandry—with the condition of remaining subject, as ought to be, and are all those domiciliated in this province, and under my jurisdiction, to the royal laws, mandates, and dispositions, and orders of his superiors. In virtue whereof, I have given this grant and signed it with witnesses of my assistance, for want of a notary, there being none, August 13, 1791. Signed Antonio Gil y Barvo; paraphd Christival de Cordoba, Jacinto de Ignono." In support of the claim the following testimony was taken before the board:

"Pierre Laffitt, being sworn, says that he knows the land claimed by Joseph Valentine in his above notice; that the same is situated and lying as described; that the grantee, Joseph Valentine, twenty-one years ago established and lived on the land claimed with his family; that he kept his horses, cattle, &c., and planted corn and other grains thereon at that time, and that he has continued to live on, cultivate, and occupy said land, to raise horses, cattle, &c., and to plant and raise corn and other grains thereon, from the time of its first establishment until the present time." [Amer. State Pap., Public Lands, 1859, vol. 4, pp. 105–106.]

Title to this was confirmed to the claimant.
In No. 110.

Emanuel Prudhomme, of the parish of Natchitoches, filed his notice claiming a tract of land lying within the late neutral territory, situated at the Adaise, and around the village of Adaise, containing one league square, claimed by virtue of a concession signed by the lieutenant governor and commandant of Nacodoches, which concession the claimant alleges he cannot procure, because the same was carried off with the archives of that post in the year 1812; claimed also by virtue of habitation, occupation, and cultivation for upwards of thirty years.

Three other "Adaise" claims are mentioned, and all were confirmed, but it is uncertain whether the "village of Adaise" was Indian or white (Amer. State Pap., Public Lands, 1859, vol. 4, p. 110). As we have seen, in 1805, according to Sibley, the tribe was living at Lake Macdon and about 20 miles north of the old Spanish mission (Sibley, Amer. State Pap., Indian Affairs, 1832, p. 722). Some of these references may be to the later Mexican settlement of "Adaize" (p. 75).

In 1797, while Andrew Ellicott was at Natchez, a body of Choctaw Indians crossed the Mississippi to make war upon the Caddo. "They were very successful and returned in June with a number of poles filled with scalps" (Foreman, 1930, p. 32). This war was ended, for a time at least, by the peace concluded by Sibley in 1807 (Sibley, 1922).

Their great enemies, however, were the Osage. In 1804 William Dunbar reported that the Caddo were unable to defend themselves against these Indians (Foreman, 1930, p. 25). One Osage chief was named Caddo Killer, his native name being He-sha-ke-he-ree (Foreman, 1930, p. 198). In 1819 Gov. James Miller of Arkansas found a party of Caddo and Choctaw Indians ready to join the Cherokee in an expedition against the Osage. He ordered them to disperse (Foreman, 1930, p. 89).

In 1815 a number of white traders made a settlement at Nanatscho, or Pecan Point, on the south bank of Red River, south of the present Kullituklo in McCurtain Co., Okla. The Caddo chief immediately complained of this intrusion to the Caddo agent, Jamison, at Natchitoches, because this was the only crossing place for buffalo for miles and the only one from which the Caddo derived any advantage. In April 1816, Jamison, supported by a military detachment, removed a dozen families from this settlement to the north side of Red River, arrested several unlicensed traders there, and seized their merchandise (Foreman, 1930, p. 160).

We have a report on the condition of the Indian tribes of Texas in 1820 by Juan Antonio Padilla, which devotes considerable space to the Caddo. Speaking of the Caddo proper, he says:

> Considering the fact that they are heathens, the moral customs of these natives are good, since they are not ambitious like the Comanches nor deceitful like the Lipanes. They live by farming and hunting. From the former industry they obtain large quantities of corn, beans, potatoes, and other vegetables which are sufficient for their families; and from the latter they obtain a large supply of furs from the bear, the deer, the beaver, the otter, and other animals. These they carry to Natchitoches and exchange for carbines, munitions, merchandise, tobacco, and firewater, of which they are very fond. Their houses are of straw, some are of wood, but all are well built. They enjoy social intercourse, dislike theft, and treat Spaniards well, entertaining them in their houses and aiding them in every possible manner. They are faithful in keeping their contracts; for the merchants of Natchitoches advance them munitions, trifles, and liquors at a good rate of exchange for furs. For all these they pay punctually, in spite of the fact that there are among them foreigners who come from Natchitoches and other points of the United States for the purpose of trading their wares to the said Indians for their products. Still, there are some swindlers and scoundrels who do not pay the debts they contract. . . . They, of all the Indians, perhaps, are the most civilized. . . . At their dances, they drink great quantities of firewater—some of them drinking until they tumble over. In these gatherings, there are never lacking some disorders resulting in personal injuries because of their drunkenness. They raise hogs, chickens, and dogs, and have horses and mules to make their journeys and hunting trips. . . . Because of the commerce they have with foreigners, many of them have learned the French language, and a few the Spanish, poorly pronounced. . . . At the present time they are in the Neutral Ground. [Padilla, 1919, pp. 46–49.]

Many other items given by him show little intelligent examination of the people under discussion. His estimate of the Hasinai tribes is upon the whole more favorable.

On November 15, 1824, there was signed at Harrington's in the Territory of Arkansas, a treaty between the United States and the Quapaw Indians, the fourth article of which reads thus:

> The Quapaw tribe of Indians will hereafter be concentrated and confined to the district of country inhabited by the Caddo Indians, and form a part of said tribe. The said nation of Indians are to commence removing to the district allotted them before the twentieth day of January, eighteen hundred and twenty-six. [Amer. State Pap., Indian Affairs, 1834, p. 530.]

July 1, 1825, Governor Izard of Arkansas wrote as follows to the Secretary of War:

> On the 20th of last month the principal chief of the Quapaw tribe, attended by a small suite, visited me at this place, and in a formal conference requested

that I would communicate the wish of his people to their great father, that they may remain a few years longer on the land ceded to the United States by the treaty of November, 1824. I expressed to Hecketon (the hereditary chief) my conviction that such permission could not be granted; but that I would nevertheless comply with his request, and would inform him of the President's decision. The deputies were satisfied with their reception; and I have no doubt that the removal of the tribe to the Caddo country will be effected without difficulty, even before the term stipulated. They asked permission to send a few of their chiefs to investigate the lands which they are to settle on, previously to the migration of the whole nation: to this I consented. They will be attended by an acting Indian sub-agent, Mr. Barraqué, an intelligent Frenchman, who has lived much among them, and who was particularly designated as the person they wished to accompany them. [Amer. State Pap., Indian Affairs, 1834, p. 705.]

September 3 he wrote again as follows:

I informed you on the [1st] of July, that a small party of Quapaw (more properly Gappa) chiefs were to visit the country of the Caddoes, to examine the lands on which they are to settle themselves next winter. They returned ten days ago, and I was gratified to hear from themselves that they were pleased with their destined residence, and with their reception by the Caddo tribe. In this transaction, the characteristic improvidence of the Indians is strongly exhibited; they had concluded their treaty with us, and had remained since last November in their own country, without informing the tribe to whom they have stipulated to aggregate themselves of their intentions. The Caddoes and Gappas have a tradition of having been allied in some wars, many years ago; but they have had no intercourse with each other for a long time, and their languages are totally different. The accidental circumstance of a Gappa hunter having resided some months with the former tribe furnished them with an interpreter; they would otherwise have been obliged to employ two of ours to translate their speeches into French and English, and thence again into their respective tongues.

From a humane regard for the weak and infirm part of their population, the emigrants are desirous of commencing their removal early in the autumn. I am in daily expectation of learning the time of their departure, which was to be fixed upon at one of their councils. The last visit of the chiefs to me was made previously to seeing their own people on their return from the South. As soon as I shall have due notice, the advertisement for their supplies shall be published, in conformity with the instructions in your despatch of the 8th of July, received by the last week's mail. [Amer. State Pap., Indian Affairs, 1834, p. 706.]

On September 24 the Governor wrote the Secretary as follows:

I have the honor to inform you that the Quapaw Indians will be ready to commence their removal to the Caddo country on the 12th of December. Their population is ascertained to be four hundred and fifty-five individuals; of whom one hundred and fifty-eight are men, one hundred and twenty-three women, and one hundred and seventy-four children under fourteen years of age. The proposals for their supplies will be published in the next Arkansas Gazette. [Amer. State Pap., Indian Affairs, 1834, p. 706.]

September 30 George Gray, Indian agent on Red River, wrote to the Secretary of War:

Some short time since the Quapaw chiefs visited the Caddoes, and selected a situation to settle on, in about half a mile of my agency, by consent of the

Caddo chief. I furnished the Quapaw chiefs with a small quantity of rations, as they were entirely out of provisions. It must acknowledge I was much at a loss whether to furnish the Quapaws with rations or not, as I had never received any instructions respecting them; but, on examining the treaty, I found they were to form a part of the Caddo tribe, and, of course, I should become their agent; which induced me to give them rations. [Amer. State Pap., Indian Affairs, 1834, p. 706.]

At the advice of the Caddo agent, a gratuity was given the Caddo chief for his willingness to take other Indians on his lands.

According to a Mexican document, by 1828 there were 150 families of Quapaw on Sulfur Creek (Hodge, 1910, *art*. Quapaw). By a letter of January 16, 1826, we learn that a mill was to be built for the Caddo. One from the Indian Agent, April 30, 1826, states that most of the beeves which had been given to them had run away and they were in a destitute condition. Corn was selling at $1.25 a bushel (Amer. State Pap., Indian Affairs, 1834, pp. 707, 708).

In 1828 José Maria Sanchez visited Texas and has left us an interesting account of his experiences. The Ais, Tejas, and Nadaco chiefs were complaining of the entrance of northern tribes into their territory and stated that they would declare war upon them if they had more warriors (Sanchez, 1926, p. 279). A little more than a league from the Angelina River, he says,

we found some houses, or huts, a camp of *Nacogdochitos* Indians, a peaceful tribe. They were in the greatest inaction, while the women worked the fields with the greatest fatigue in this burning climate to maintain their tyrants. This work is a burden especially heavy on the old women because the charms of the young girls cause them to be treated more tenderly, in a way, by the lazy males, while old age groans oppressed under this arbitrary burden. While crossing a fairly large creek called *El Loco*, we saw other huts of Tejas Indians where we witnessed the same tyrannical scenes as in the village of the *Nacogdochitos*.

Different tribes of Indians such as the Tejas, Nadacos, Yguanes [Yowani Choctaw?], Savanos, Cherokees, Kickapoos, Delawares, Cutchates [Koasati], Alabamas, Quichas [Kichai], and Cados, continually enter Nacogdoches, but they are all peaceful and carry on their trade in the city with skins, corn, pumpkins, and beans. These tribes are located in the neighborhood of Nacogdoches, their *Pueblos* being intermingled with the settlements of the Americans who are scattered throughout Texas. [Sanchez, 1926, pp. 282, 283.]

His description of the dress of these people is very good (Sanchez, 1926, pp. 284–285).

In 1830 Col. Peter Ellis Bean of the Mexican army, superintendent of Indian affairs in the Province of Texas, visited Pecan Point for the purpose of establishing a garrison, but his plans were opposed by Governor Pope of Arkansas and by the Caddo Indians, who threatened to attack him.

Bean, in turn, declared he would send the Cherokee Indians to destroy the Caddo, and their agent, Jehiel Brooks, at Natchitoches, called on Col. James

B. Many stationed at Fort Jessup for troops to protect his wards. [Foreman, 1933, p. 108.]

The Red River floods, which had frequently inflicted great losses on the Caddo, occasioned suffering as well to the Quapaw, and on May 13, 1833, they signed another treaty relinquishing and conveying to the United States "all their right and title to the lands given them by the Caddo Indians on the Bayou Treache of Red river," obtaining in exchange 150 sections of land in the northeastern part of what is now the State of Oklahoma (Royce, 1899, pp. 748–749). This seems to have terminated the intimate relations between these two tribes, but a few Quapaw may have remained with the Caddo, because the I'măha, a name of one of the Quapaw towns, was given to Mooney as that of a band among the Caddo. The same authority also noted a band of Yowa'ni Choctaw, the Yowa'ni having occupied the southernmost of all Choctaw towns before they left their old country in Mississippi (Mooney, 1896, pp. 1092–1093).

July 22, 1834, 33 Caddo, in charge of Capt. James Dean, reached Camp Washita to accompany the troops led by Leavenworth and Dodge into the Kiowa and Comanche country (Foreman, 1933, p. 131).

By the following treaty, signed on July 1, 1835, at the Caddo Agency in the State of Louisiana, the Caddo relinquished all of their territory within the limits of the United States and agreed to remove at their own expense within 1 year beyond its boundaries:

Articles of a treaty, made at the Agency house in the Caddo nation, and State of Louisiana, on the first day of July, in the year of our Lord one thousand eight hundred and thirty-five, between Jehiel Brooks, commissioner on the part of the United States, and the chiefs, head men, and warriors of the Caddo nation of Indians

ART. 1. The chiefs, head men, and warriors of the said nation, agree to cede and relinquish to the United States all their land, contained in the following boundaries, to wit: Bounded on the west by the north and south line which separates the said United States from the Republic of Mexico, between the Sabine and Red rivers, wheresoever the same shall be defined and acknowledged to be by the two governments. On the north and east by the Red river, from the point where the said north and south boundary line shall intersect the Red river, whether it be in the territory of Arkansas or the State of Louisiana, following the meanders of the said river down to its junction with the Pascagoula bayou. On the south by the said Pascagoula bayou to its junction with the bayou Pierre by said bayou, to its junction with bayou Wallace by said bayou and lake Wallace to the mouth of the Cypress bayou; thence, up said bayou to the point of its intersection with the first mentioned north and south line, following the meanders of the said watercourses; but if the said Cypress bayou be not clearly definable, so far then from a point, which shall be definable by a line due west till it intersects the said first mentioned north and south boundary line, be the content of land within said boundaries more or less.

ART 2. The said chiefs, head men, and warriors of the said nation, do voluntarily relinquish their possession to the territory of land aforesaid, and

299671—42——7

promise to remove at their own expense out of the boundaries of the United States, and the territories belonging and appertaining thereto, within the period of one year from and after the signing of this treaty, and never more return to live, settle, or establish themselves as a nation, tribe, or community of people within the same.

ART. 3. In consideration of the aforesaid cession, relinquishment, and removal, it is agreed, that the said United States shall pay to the said nation of Caddo Indians, the sums in goods, horses, and money hereinafter mentioned, to wit:

Thirty thousand dollars to be paid in goods and horses, as agreed upon, to be delivered on the signing of this treaty.

Ten thousand dollars in money to be paid within one year from the first day of September next.

Ten thousand dollars per annum, in money, for the four years next following, so as to make the whole sum paid and payable eighty thousand dollars.

ART. 4. It is further agreed, that the said Caddo nation of Indians, shall have authority to appoint an agent or attorney in fact, resident within the United States, for the purpose of receiving for them, from the said United States, all of the annuities stated in this treaty, as the same shall become due, to be paid to their said agent or attorney in fact, at such place or places within the said United States, as shall be agreed on between him and the proper officer of the Government of the United States.

ART. 5. This treaty, after the same shall have been ratified and confirmed by the President and Senate of the United States, shall be binding on the contracting parties.

In testimony whereof, the said Jehiel Brooks, commissioner as aforesaid, and the chiefs, head men, and warriors of the said nation of Indians, have hereunto set their hands, and affixed their seals at the place and on the day and year above written.

J. Brooks,			
Tarshar, his x mark,	L. S.	Tiohtow, his x mark,	L. S.
Tsauninot, his x mark,	L. S.	Tehowahinno, his x mark,	L. S.
Satiownhown, his x mark,	L. S.	Tooeksoach, his x mark,	L. S.
Tennehinum, his x mark,	L. S.	Tehowainia, his x mark,	L. S.
Oat, his x mark,	L. S.	Sauninow, his x mark,	L. S.
Tinnowin, his x mark,	L. S.	Saunivoat, his x mark,	L. S.
Chowabah, his x mark,	L. S.	Highahidock, his x mark,	L. S.
Kianhoon, his x mark,	L. S.	Mattan, his x mark,	L. S.
Tiatesum, his x mark,	L. S.	Towabinneh, his x mark,	L. S.
Tehowawinow, his x mark,	L. S.	Aach, his x mark,	L. S.
Tewinnum, his x mark,	L. S.	Sookiantow, his x mark,	L. S.
Kardy, his x mark,	L. S.	Sohone, his x mark,	L. S.
		Ossinse, his x mark,	L. S.

In presence of

T. J. Harrison, *Capt. 3d. Reg. Inf.* D. M. Heard, M. D., *Act. Assist. Surgeon, U. S. A.*
  commanding detachment,
J. Bonnell, *1st Lieut. 3d Reg. U. S.* Isaac Williamson,
  Inf. Henry Queen,
J. P. Frile, *Bvt. 2d Lieut. 3d Reg.* John W. Edwards, *Interpreter.*
  U. S. Infantry,

Agreeably to the stipulations in the third article of the treaty, there have been purchased at the request of the Caddo Indians, and delivered to them, goods and horses to the amount of thirty thousand dollars.

As evidence of the purchase and delivery as aforesaid, under the direction of the commissioner, and that the whole of the same have been received by the said Indians, the said commissioner, Jehiel Brooks, and the undersigned, chiefs and head men of the whole Caddo nation of Indians, have hereunto set their hands, and affixed their seals, the third day of July, in the year of our Lord one thousand eight hundred and thirty-five.

J. Brooks,	L. S.	Oat, his x mark,	L. S.
Tarshar, his x mark,	L. S.	Ossinse, his x mark,	L. S.
Tsauninot, his x mark,	L. S.	Tiohtow, his x mark,	L. S.
Satiownhown, his x mark,	L. S.	Chowawanow, his x mark,	L. S.

In presence of

Larkin Edwards,	John W. Edwards, *Interpreter*,
Henry Queen,	James Finnerty.

SUPPLEMENTARY ARTICLES

Articles supplementary to the treaty made at the Agency house in the Caddo nation, and State of Louisiana, on the first day of July, one thousand eight hundred and thirty-five, between Jehiel Brooks, commissioner on the part of the United States, and the chiefs, head men, and warriors of the Caddo nation of Indians, concluded at the same place, and on the same day, between the said commissioner, on the part of the United States, and the chiefs, head men, and warriors of the said nation of Indians, to wit:

Whereas, the said nation of Indians did, in the year one thousand eight hundred and one, give to one François Grappe, and to his three sons then born and still living, named Jacques, Dominique, and Belthazar, for reasons stated at the time, and repeated in a memorial which the said nation addressed to the President of the United States in the month of January last, one league of land to each, in accordance with the Spanish custom of granting land to individuals. That the chiefs and head men, with the knowledge and approbation of the whole Caddo people, did go with the said François Grappe, accompanied by a number of white men, who were invited by the said chiefs and head men to be present as witnesses, before the Spanish authorities at Natchitoches; and then, and there, did declare their wishes touching the said donation of land to the said Grappe, and his three sons, and did request the same to be written out in form, and ratified and confirmed by the proper authorities agreeably to law.

And whereas, Larkin Edwards has resided for many years to the present time in the Caddo nation; was a long time their true and faithful interpreter, and though poor he has never sent the red man away from his door hungry. He is now old and unable to support himself by manual labor, and since his employment as their interpreter has ceased, possesses no adequate means by which to live: Now, therefore,

ART. 1. It is agreed that the legal representatives of the said François Grappe, deceased, and his three sons, Jacques, Dominique, and Belthazar Grappe, shall have their right to the said four leagues of land reserved to them and their heirs and assigns forever. The said land to be taken out of the lands ceded to the United States by the said Caddo nation of Indians as expressed in the treaty to which this article is supplementary. And the said four leagues of land shall be laid off in one body in the southeast corner of their lands ceded as aforesaid, and bounded by the Red river four leagues, and by the Pascagoula bayou one league, running back for quantity from each, so as to contain four square leagues of land, in conformity with the boundaries established and expressed in the original deed of gift, made by the said Caddo nation of Indians to the said François Grappe, and his three sons Jacques, Dominique, and Balthazar Grappe.

ART. 2. And it is further agreed that there shall be reserved to Larkin Edwards, his heirs and assigns forever, one section of land, to be selected out of the land ceded to the United States by the said nation of Indians, as expressed in the treaty to which this article is supplementary, in any part thereof not otherwise appropriated by the provisions contained in these supplementary articles.

ART. 3. These supplementary articles, or either of them, after the same shall have been ratified and confirmed by the President and Senate of the United States, shall be binding on the contracting parties, otherwise to be void and of no effect upon the validity of the original treaty to which they are supplementary.

In testimony whereof, the said Jehiel Brooks, commissioner as aforesaid, and the chiefs, head men, and warriors of the said nation of Indians, have hereunto set their hands and affixed their seals at the place, and on the day and year above written.

J. Brooks,	L. S.	Tiohtow, his x mark,		L. S.
Tarshar, his x mark,	L. S.	Tehawahinno, his x mark,		L. S.
Tsauninot, his x mark,	L. S.	Toackooch, his x mark,		L. S.
Satiownhown, his x mark,	L. S.	Tchowainin, his x mark,		L. S.
Tinnehinan, his x mark,	L. S.	Sanninow, his x mark,		L. S
Oat, his x mark,	L. S.	Sauninot, his x mark,		L. S
Tinnowin, his x mark,	L. S.	Hiahidock, his x mark,		L. S
Chowabah, his x mark,	L. S.	Mattan, his x mark,		L. S.
Kianhoon, his x mark,	L. S.	Towahinnek, his x mark,		L. S.
Tiatesun, his x mark,	L. S.	Aach, his x mark,		L. S.
Tehowawinow, his x mark,	L. S.	Soakiantow, his x mark,		L. S.
Tewinnun, his x mark,	L. S.	Sohone, his x mark,		L. S.
Kardy, his x mark,		Ossinse, his x mark,		L. S.

In presence of

T. J. Harrison, *Capt. 3d Reg't. com'g. detach't.*
J. Bonnell, *1st Lieut. 3d Reg't. U. S. Inf.*
G. P. Field, *Bv't. 2d Lieut. 3d Reg. U. S. Inf.*

D. M. Heard, M. D. *Act. Ast Surg'n. U. S. A.*
Isaac C. Williamson,
Henry Queen,
John Edwards, *Interpreter.*

(This treaty was ratified on Feb. 2, 1836.)
[Treaties between the United States of America and the several Indian Tribes, 1837, pp. 621–625.]

The money payment, it was asserted, was not really to extinguish a valid Indian claim but to induce the Indians to remove peaceably. It was contended that the Caddo actually had no right to the lands they then occupied near the white settlements but had come to live there in recent times after having been driven out of their old country by enemies. Information regarding this claim is contained

in the following document in the American State Papers, Public
Lands, 1861, vol. 8, p. 914:

24th Congress, 2d session

On Claims to Land in Louisiana

Communicated to the House of Representatives, December 30, 1836

Mr. Huntsman, from the Committee on Private Land Claims, to whom were
referred the documents pertaining to various land claims, for lands lying
between the Rio Hondo and Sabine rivers, reported:

That the register and receiver of the southwestern land district was directed
by the act of Congress of the 3d of March, 1823, and a supplemental act
thereto passed on the 25th of May, 1824, as commissioners to examine into the
claims, take testimony, &c., recommend for confirmation or rejection, to Congress,
such claims as should be submitted [to] them in a given time, as will more
fully appear by a reference to said acts. The register and receiver, in pursuance of said authority, proceeded in the performance of the duty assigned
them, took testimony, and adjudicated many claims, confirming some and
rejecting others. Among those which were recommended for confirmation,
were a certain number which were suspended by Congress in the passage of an
act of the 24th of May, 1828, (which confirmed the balance,) as the act
recites that they should be suspended until it is ascertained whether they
are situated in the country claimed by the Caddo Indians.

There has been no information obtained upon this point; but it is believed
there has been sufficient information obtained to supersede the necessity of
that inquiry. It is believed by the committee, from the best information
within their reach, that the Caddo Indians had no right of any sort there,
except a permissive right, and that the citizens who claimed by habitation,
cultivation, or otherwise, were not trespassers or intruders upon the Indian
lands. A thorough inquiry has been made of the Secretary of War, for such
information as was in possession of his department in relation to the country
whence the Caddoes came; what time they settled in the country in question;
and what right they hold and claim in these lands.

The Secretary has communicated all the information at his command, which,
taken with his correspondence with one of your committee, is too voluminous
to incorporate in this report. And although there is no direct evidence which
is absolutely conclusive, yet there is much circumstantial testimony which is
extremely persuasive to establish these facts:

That, anciently, these Indians inhabited a country much farther southwest
[northwest?] than the one which is now the subject of inquiry; that about
thirty years ago they were driven by their enemies (the Osages) from the
country they then inhabited upon the white settlements, where they were
permitted to remain until the late treaty with them, in the making of which
it appears that the Secretary of War did not consider that they had any title
to the country, but were induced to give them the sum, perhaps $80,000, to re-
linquish their possessions and go off *peaceably*, as will more fully appear by the
correspondence upon that subject.

The committee are therefore of opinion that those cases which were suspended
by the first section of the act of 1828, are as meritorious as those which were
confirmed, and have reported a bill for the confirmation of those claims which
were suspended. [Amer. State Pap. Public Lands, 1861, p. 914.]

These words of wisdom may embody good law but leave us in the dark regarding certain very vital matters. The statement is valid only as to the Kadohadacho or Caddo proper and their immediate allies. If it was meant to include all the Caddo tribes of northwestern Louisiana, it is egregiously false since the Natchitoches, Yatasi, and Adai had occupied their lands from earliest French contact. It is also very doubtful whether there were any valid white claims to the lands upon which the Caddo settled about Lake Caddo at the time when they settled. If no tribe was conceived to have had a right to any lands into which it had been driven in the historic period, a very large number of them would have no claims to much of the land to which their claims were admitted and for which they were actually paid. And finally, if late occupancy of land by Indians invalidated their claims, how did the claims of post-Columbian whites happen to be better? That might have been the case, of course, if the Indians had come among the white settlements, but the western shores of Lake Caddo were far from white settlements, and any claims to ownership of them stand suspect. In a letter dated "Washington, Feb. 21, 1835," Col. J. Brooks, evidently the Commissioner whose name appears in the treaties, states that in May 1805, the Caddo claimed to be the original inhabitants of the land they occupied, and in a memorial of January 28, 1835, 23 chiefs and head men affirmed that their villages had been established where they then stood "ever since the first Caddo was created." [11]   History certainly contains record of no other tribes than Caddo in the entire region in spite of later shiftings.

The unceremonious dumping of these Indians into Texas had consequences as to which the Federal Government was probably indifferent. Part of them associated themselves with the Cherokee chief Bowl, and Cherokee Indians informed C. H. Sims in 1836 that "a large body of Caddo, Kichai, Eyeish, Tawakoni, Waco, and Comanche were expected to attack the settlements and in all probability the Cherokee would join them" (Muckleroy, 1922, p. 6). In view of the specific wording of the treaty of 1835, the reaction of the Texans to the movement of Caddo Indians into their republic is hard to understand. Instead of repressive measures against the Indians, it would have seemed to call for a protest to the United States Congress or else negotiations for the peaceful accommodation of the new comers. But on March 1, 1837, instead of protesting against the ejection of these Indians and their removal to Texas, Houston wrote to his Secretary of State instructing him to urge upon the United States the necessity of restraining the Caddos with two companies of mounted men. In his message to the Texan Congress on May 5, 1837 he

[11] United States Archives.

said that the [Caddo] tribe had recently ceded certain of their lands to the United States, and that in consequence the Caddos had shown a disposition to unite with the wild Indians of Texas. He had received information that the United States agent had issued rifles and ammunition to the warriors. [Muckleroy, 1922, p. 24.]

The next year Rusk found a Captain Tarrant on the Louisiana border at the head of a company of soldiers "about to attack the Caddo Indians from the United States. It was believed that these Indians were about to cross into Texas to commit depredations. Rusk forced the Caddo to surrender, and turned their arms over to their agent at Shreveport," although it would seem that, more than a year having elapsed since the ratification of the Caddo treaty, their agent would have ceased to function except to make the annual payments agreed upon. And our authority goes on to say that Rusk "promised the Indians that the government of Texas would support them" (Muckleroy, 1922, pp. 15–16).

This sinister interpretation of the issuance of rifles intended doubtless for hunting reminds us of those race riots in which, the homes of the negroes being searched, the remarkable discovery is made that they have firearms—like everybody else in the region. However, Houston continues: "The principal aggressions on our frontier have either been instigated or perpetrated by the Caddos" (Muckleroy, 1922, pp. 24–25). Houston was a friend of the Indians and it would seem that he might have looked far enough behind these depredations to discover that a people cannot well be uprooted from their homes without creating more or less disturbance in their endeavors to obtain new ones. The greater part of them naturally allied themselves with the Hasinai and other related tribes. In 1837 the affiliated tribes included the Kadohadacho, Anadarko, Nacogdoche, Nabedache, and Eyeish (Muckleroy, 1922, p. 232). Henry M. Morfit, sent by President Jackson in 1836 to investigate the military, civil, and political condition of Texas, states that the Caddo had recently destroyed the village of Bastrop (Muckleroy, 1922, p. 241). But as Bastrop is 200 miles from the Caddo country and in territory raided rather by the Lipan and Comanche than the Caddo, one is permitted to doubt that the criminals were properly identified.

In 1842 Gen. Ethan Allen Hitchcock was informed by Colonel Upshaw, the Chickasaw Indian agent, that

the Caddos were reduced, he thought, to about 250; that 167 were in the Choctaw Nation and that the last annuity due them was paid this year and now they are without a country and without an annuity and are living here by sufferance of the Choctaws. [Foreman, 1930 a, p. 181.]

On July 29 of that year four Muskogee chiefs wrote to Red Bear, chief of the Caddo, advising against having anything to do with

Mexican emissaries (Foreman, 1933, p. 168). Meanwhile the Caddo
Indians had been sending messages to Robert M. Jones, an intelligent
and influential Choctaw, suggesting that he act as intermediary between the Republic of Texas and her Indian enemies, and that same
month

a number of Indians from that tribe, bearing a letter from the Caddo chief,
Red Bear, came to Boggy Depot to see Jones. Soon after, a delegation of
Texans headed by Colonel Stroud, authorized by President Houston to negotiate
treaties with the hostile Indians, reached Boggy Depot and showed Jones their
credentials and their "talk" from President Houston. On the thirtieth three
of the Caddo young men departed for their home with the peace "talk" and
a long letter to Red Bear written by Jones urging the Indians to make peace
with the whites. The letter contained some sage advice on the folly of main-
taining war against the whites in which history showed that the Indians
were invariably losers. He told Red Bear to ascertain whether his neighboring
Indians were for peace and if so to send word to him when and where they
would meet the Texans in a peace conference "and make a white road that
you and all others who choose, may travel in peace and safety; by this you
will bury the war hatchet which is stained with blood and let the red path
which has brought distress to the doors of your people as well as those of
the white man, grow up with grass and weeds and be traveled no more . . . .
I send you a medal and some tobacco and white beads as an emblem of the
long friendship existing between your people and the Choctaws and Chickasaws,
and Col. Stroud has sent you, the Ironeyes [Hainai] and Madargoes
[Anadarkos], tobacco in token of his favorable reception of your request for
peace." [Foreman, 1933, pp. 167–168.]

In 1843 the Caddo were visited by the artist J. M. Stanley and his
catalog shows that he made sketches of seven prominent members
of the tribe, all of which suffered in the Smithsonian fire the same
irreparable loss as the rest of his work. We particularly regret the
loss of his painting of José Maria, which appears to have been the
only likeness ever made of that great chief. From the catalog I
quote the following descriptions of the seven paintings:

Caddoes [meaning Kadohadacho]: . . . 74. Bin-tah, the Wounded Man
(painted 1843). Principal Chief of the Caddoes. He derived his name from
the fact of his having been wounded in the breast by an Osage; he wears a
piece of silver suspended from his nose, as an ornament.

75. Ah-de-bah, or the Tall Man (painted 1843). Second or Assistant Chief of
the Caddoes. Painted in the act of striking the drum.

76. Se-hia-ah-di-you, the Singing Bird (painted June, 1843). Wife of
Ah-de-bah, seated in her tent. A view on Tiwoccany Creek, Texas.

77. Ha-doon-cote-sah (painted 1843). A Caddo Warrior.

Anandarkoes [Anadarko]: 78. José Maria (painted 1843). Principal chief
of the Anandarkoes. This chief is known to the Mexicans by the name of
José Maria, and to the Caddoes as Iesh. He has fought many battles with
the Texans, and was severely wounded in the breast in a skirmish with them.

Natchitoches: 80. Cho-wee, or the Bow (painted 1843). Principal Chief of
the Natchitoches. This man had a brother killed by the Texans, some four or
five years since, while on a hunting expedition, whose death he afterwards
avenged by taking the scalps of six Texans. [Stanley, 1852, pp. 48–49, 51.]

On September 29, 1843, a treaty of peace was signed at Bird's Fort on the Trinity River between the Republic of Texas and a number of Indian tribes, including the Caddo, Anadarko, and Hainai. It was approved by the Texas Senate on January 31, 1844, and signed by President Houston February 3 following (Muckleroy, 1923, pp. 188–191). Another treaty was concluded on October 7, 1844, of which the three above-mentioned tribes were also signers. This was ratified by the Texas Senate January 24, 1845, and signed by President Jones on February 5, 1845 (Muckleroy, 1923, pp. 193–196). The same tribes were represented at a peace council in September 1845 (Muckleroy, 1923, pp. 197–198).

Eight Caddo attended a convocation of Indians of different tribes on Deep Fork River, summoned by the Creeks for the purpose of adjusting intertribal differences. It was called for May 1, 1845, but the delegations were slow in coming in and the Caddo did not reach the council ground until the 14th (Foreman, 1933, pp. 225–226). One of the Caddo chiefs, Cho-wa-wha-na, was a principal speaker, and the Cherokee agent, Pierce M. Butler, comments:

He was a striking man of great personal beauty and commanding appearance; small in stature, yet beautiful and attractive features; dressed in what would be called Indian magnificence—feathers, turbans, and silver bands. His speech was looked for with interest and was very well received. Approving the council—deploring the past and probable future fate of the Red Man; had been gloomy—future prospects worse; hostility among themselves would bring the destruction of their race and ruin of their children.

The council broke up on the 16th, the leave-taking being in accordance with the several tribal customs. The Creeks, Choctaws, etc., shook hands. The Osages, Quapaw, and others took hold of the right arm above the elbow with the right hand and gave it a hearty grip and shake, while the Caddo gave "a real lover's embrace, warm, affectionate, and delightfully intimate" (Foreman, 1933, pp. 228–229).

William Armstrong, acting superintendent of Indian affairs for the West, reporting the same year, says of the Caddo:

The Caddoes unlike the other bands mentioned have no regular homes of their own. A few of them have settled among the Choctaws by permission of that tribe. These endeavor to support themselves by labor, the rest, like the Kickapoos, depend on the chase, and lead a wandering life. [Foreman, 1933, p. 234.]

By a law of January 14, 1843, the Republic of Texas had engaged itself to establish a line of trading posts which were to form a boundary between the Indians and whites. However, only one of these was established that year, by the Torrey brothers on the Brazos River near the present City of Waco, and it was 100 miles below the point where, according to the law, it should have been placed. It served to preserve friendship with the Indians. Later Mathias Travis established another trading house on the south fork of Trinity River. It was completed in September 1845.

Torreys' Trading House was the residence of the Indian agents. On January 10, 1845, three chiefs came to agents Sloan and Williams at this place and informed them that tales were being circulated to the effect that when their corn was ripe, the whites intended to fall upon the Indians and exterminate them. Williams promptly went around to reassure them.

After the accession of the Republic of Texas to the United States in 1846, Robert S. Neighbors was appointed Special Commissioner to the Texas Indians and on May 30 of that year he reached the village of the Kadohadacho, Hainai, and Anadarko, "situated on the Brazos River, 45 miles from Torreys' trading house." He says:

> I found everything perfectly quiet in their village, and the Indians well satisfied and friendly. They are cultivating large fields of corn, and appear to be in a prosperous condition. The village consists of about 150 houses, built of wood and covered with grass. I held a talk with the chiefs, and found everything in a healthy condition. [Indian Affairs, 1847, p. 894.]

No hint is supplied as to the time when they had moved over from their former country. It may have been in 1843 when the Torreys' trading house was erected.

Neighbors learned at this time that frequent depredations, meaning in particular horse stealing, had been committed on these people by the Wichita, Waco, Tawakoni, and Kichai to the north, and he determined to make peace between the two parties.

> On application to the chief of the Onadakoes, he sent Pow-iash, second chief, with six of his warriors with me; Jose Maria, the principal chief, having been thrown from his horse and badly injured, was unable to accompany me in person.

The mission was accomplished successfully. Visiting the village of the three tribes again on August 23, he found the chiefs peaceable and friendly, but he says:

> the drought has been excessive during the whole summer; and although the crops were very promising in the early part of the season, there was a perfect failure in the corn crop. They complain of great scarcity of provisions, and their chief, Jose Maria, said that it was with much difficulty their people were able to subsist; the tribes were necessarily much scattered in pursuit of game, and other means of subsistance. I found also that large quantities of whiskey had been introduced among them since my former visit, which has in some degree disorganized them. These Indians are very fond of spirits, and it is with much difficulty that I can get sufficient information from them to arrest the trade. The chiefs have now pledged themselves to give me information in future, that will enable me to stop its importation into their country. [Indian Affairs, 1847, pp. 894-895, 899.]

On arriving at the village of the Wichita and their allies "about 175 miles this place," he found some Caddo and Hainai there, possibly as visitors. He notes that, finding an additional interpreter necessary, he had, on August 20, employed Col. L. H. Williams, as interpreter for the Caddo, Hainai, and related tribes.

He reports rumors being industriously spread among the Indians that the whites intended to massacre all of them after they had been brought together (Indian Affairs, 1847, pp. 899, 903, 904).

In 1848 a Caddo boy was killed by a company of soldiers and the Indians demanded satisfaction, threatening to take vengeance on the company responsible if it was not given. Haso-dib-bar is mentioned as the Caddo chief at that time but he cannot have been the head chief unless this is the Indian name of José Maria (Indian Affairs, 1848, pp. 591, 593). Otherwise he must have been chief of the Kadohadacho only. The following account of these tribes is contained in the report for 1849 (p. 33):

The Caddoes, Annadarcoes, and Ionies, although having each their separate chief or head man, and living in separate villages, are associated together under the government of one principal chief. The Caddoes and Ionies live upon the Brazos and its northern tributaries in the upper Cross Timbers, about 140 miles above the settlements on Red River, 120 miles from those on the Trinity, and about 160 miles from those of the Brazos. The Annadarcoes have their village on the Brazos, about 40 miles above the settlements, but spend most of their time some 100 miles within the settlements between the Brazos and Trinity rivers, where they have been permitted to go at their pleasure in violation of the laws of the State, greatly against the will and much to the annoyance of the citizens, and greatly jeopardizing the peace and safety of the frontier, which was several times, during the last year, on account of this very tribe, and the fact that they were permitted to go into the settlements, near being involved in a general war with all the border tribes and bands; and if not stopped, must inevitably, and within the next six months, bring about that much to be deplored and fatal result.

The three last named bands migrated from Louisiana; small parties of them have been in Texas for a number of years, and have been gradually increasing in strength by migrating parties of their own people, who have followed them, until they now number about 1,200 souls. They live in wigwams and tents, and raise some corn, pumpkins, &c.

The agent is in error regarding the origin of two of these tribes. The Caddo proper did, indeed, come from Louisiana, but the other two had been established in eastern Texas from earliest white contact.

There was further trouble between Caddo and Wichita the same year. The latter having stolen some horses from the former,

the Caddo with Jim Ned, a Delaware, and a few Biloxi Indians made a descent upon the Wichita village and drove off some of the horses of the Wichita. The latter fired on them and precipitated a general fight in which two Caddo and a number of Wichita Indians were killed. The Wichita who escaped the massacre, came into the Creek country, and implored them to save their tribe from extermination.

saying that 30 of their people—men, women, and children—had been killed in the attack.

The Caddoes and their leader told the Wichitaws that Col. Upshaw the Chickasaw Sub-agent had given them liberty to kill the Wichitaws, as they were a very bad people. [Indian Affairs, 1849, p. 191; Foreman, 1934, pp. 119–120.]

In 1850 the Chickasaw sent a memorial to the President against the continuance in their country of bands of wild Indians, among them being enumerated the Caddo (Indian Affairs, 1849, p. 122). February 23, 1851, Col. Dixon S. Miles reported about 300 Caddo located in the Chickasaw District, "near the oil spring and not over 15 miles from where Capt. Marcy is ordered to locate a post on Wild Horse Creek [Fort Arbuckle]." "They are," he adds, "disposed to cultivate the soil and live peaceably and friendly" (Foreman, 1934, p. 128).

In 1851, Jesse Stem, Special Agent for the Indians in Texas, sent a lengthy report, parts of which follow:

On the 15th [of June], I saw and held talks with Jose Maria and Towash, and the principal men of their bands, (the Caddoes, Audaicos, and Ionois,) near their villages on the Brasos, about twenty miles below the Waco village.

These tribes [including also the Waco, Kichai, and Tawakoni] have maintained friendly relations with the whites, and are regarded as peaceable and well disposed. In these talks with me, they professed the most cordial feelings toward our Government and people; expressed great anxiety that their relations with the Government should be established on a more certain and permanent basis; that a permanent boundary should be fixed, so that they might have a country where they could be secure from encroachments of the white settlements, and where they could build up their villages and cultivate their corn fields without the constant fear of being driven further back, and compelled to abandon their homes, the fruits of their labor, and the graves of their kindred.

Jose Maria said: "That now there was a line below which the Indians were not allowed to go; but the white people came above it, marked trees, surveyed lands in their hunting grounds, and near their villages, and soon they would claim the lands; if the Indians went below they were threatened with death; that this was not just: . . . that a party of white men had recently been in his country, surveying land and marking trees; that he followed them, told them that they must mark no more trees, and must leave the country; that he would not molest them, but they should not survey his lands." There can be no more prolific source of strife, jealousy, and bloodshed on the frontier, than the want of a fixed boundary, above which the white men are not allowed to go.

These tribes are more fixed in their location, and more advanced in the arts and comforts of civilization, (slight as they are,) than any other of the Indians in Texas. They are making very creditable efforts at raising Indian corn, beans, pumpkins, and melons; their lodges are made of a frame or net-work of sticks, thatched with coarse grass, and are large, warm, and comfortable. Their corn fields looked well, and were comparatively well cultivated.

They have no farming instruments but hoes, most of which they said they had bought. They wanted some light ploughs and plough harness, and more hoes.

I took pains to encourage them in the cultivation of corn, &c., and went around with them and looked at their corn fields, promised them some ploughs and harness, and more hoes this fall, and next spring would endeavor to provide them with some seed potatoes, (which they have not yet cultivated,) and other seeds.

There has been, and still is, a great want of certain information as to the numbers and condition of the various tribes in Texas. While among these Indians I endeavored to ascertain their exact numbers, and with this view induced the chiefs to go among their people and count them. Having no system of numbers they enumerated only with their fingers, or by means of bundles of sticks. They brought me a bundle of sticks for each tribe.

The following is the enumeration furnished me as above, which I consider very accurate:

Towaccarros_____ 141				
Wacoes_____ 114	Total 293	Warriors	90	
Keechies_____ 38				
Caddoes_____ 161				
Andaicos _____ 202	" 476	"	161	
Ionies_____ 113				
Delawares_____	" 63	"	31	
Shawnees_____	" 70	"	35	
	902		317	

[He adds an enumeration of the Tonkawa.]

It will be seen, upon examining the files of the department, that the tribes above enumerated, including the Wichitas, were in 1849 reported officially as having 800 warriors, and numbering 4000 persons. The Wichitas were represented to me as a small tribe, numbering 100. They, together with about 80 warriors from the Caddoes, Wacoes, and Keechies, (including about two-thirds of the latter tribe.) together with a small proportion of women and children, have, within the last two years, left Texas, and are now inhabiting the Wichita mountains beyond Red river. But deducting these, the above enumeration shows that former estimates have been very much too large, and I entertain no doubt that, upon actual enumeration, it will be found that there has been a proportionate over-estimate of the other Indians in Texas. [Indian Affairs, 1851, pp. 260–261.]

In a letter dated November 1, of the same year, Stem says:

The tribes on the Brasos, especially the Caddoes, Aud-dai-coes, and Ionies, are the most peaceable and well disposed of the Indians of Texas, and for several years, by their uniform good conduct, and readiness in delivering up stolen property brought among them, have maintained a good reputation among the citizens of this State. They desire, and should receive, encouragement and proper consideration from the Government.

Since my former report a military post has been established on the Clear fork of the Brasos, some 150 miles further up than Fort Graham. This post is beyond the several Indian villages on the Brasos, and unites [extends] the location and settlement of the adventurous citizens of this State on the hunting grounds, and perhaps upon the corn fields, and in villages of these Indians, or otherwise demand their removal [unless they remove] beyond this line of posts; in either case it involves serious hardship upon the Indians. They have built up villages, cleared off corn fields, and established homes, which they are forced to yield up without compensation; already have several of these tribes been compelled to yield up homes thus established. [Indian Affairs, 1851, p. 263.]

Stem's report for 1852, dated at Fort Graham, Tex., October 8, contains the following paragraphs:

The Caddoes, Ana-da-kos, and Ionis have remained on the Brazos, and have peaceably and quietly tilled their corn-fields and followed the chase, occasionally calling on me for slight aid to make out the measure of their subsistence. The efforts of these people are much embarrassed by the constant reflection that the tenure by which they hold their homes and improvements is so slight and precarious. With the constant anticipation that the fields which they have subjugated, the warm lodges they have erected, the clear cold springs they have discovered, are to be given up to the adventurous white man, whose surveys have already enclosed and surrounded their villages and "marked their trees," they have no courage for vigorous and hopeful effort.

José Maria, after the close of his "winter hunt," would not go back to his old village on the Brazos. His lands had been surveyed, (a subject about which he has been extremely sensitive), and perhaps he feared interruption. The consequence has been that, upon new land, the corn-crop of his people (limited at best) has been unusually small; and their frail and imperfect lodges failing to afford the accustomed protection, they have experienced an unusual amount of sickness and mortality. I have adverted in my former reports to the obvious policy of the general government, in connection with the State of Texas, assigning some territory to those tribes in Texas who have manifested a desire to establish homes for themselves, and to cultivate the arts of civilization.

I cannot resist the inclination to again call attention to this subject, as a step fundamental to any enlightened policy in the administration of Indian affairs in Texas.

These remarks do not, at present, apply to the Comanches and other wild tribes, whose habitations are as shifting as the winds of their own prairies; but the three tribes to whom I have just alluded, together with several others, deserve this consideration, and are prepared to be benefited by it. The Caddoes are now indebted to the liberality of Major H. H. Sibley, in his capacity of a private citizen, that they have an hour's security in their homes and in the cultivation of their crops. He has generously given them written permission to occupy, for the term of five years, their present home, (which is his property). He has made the same offer to José Maria, and, for want of any present expectations from the government, he will probably avail himself of the offer.

Surely a great government, such as ours, and a great State like Texas, with her vast public domain, will not permit the burden to rest upon a private citizen of furnishing these people with a home.

An effort was made in the Texas legislature last winter to confer a grant of lands upon these tribes. It received the earnest support, I believe, of a number of enlightened and liberal gentlemen; but from some cause the measure failed, legislation ending in vesting the Governor with the power to appoint commissioners to confer upon this subject with the commissioners to be appointed by the general government. [Indian Affairs, 1852, pp. 145–146.]

It must be added with regret that Stem, evidently a good friend of the Indians, was murdered by some miscreants of their race the year after this was written. On February 16, 1852, "the [Texas] Legislature approved a resolution authorizing the Governor to conduct negotiations with the national authorities concerning territory for the use of Texas Indians" (Koch, 1925, p. 98).

On February 6, 1854, the legislature passed an act providing for reservations, and authorizing the National Government to select and survey twelve leagues of land for these reservations. This land was not to be located over twenty miles south or east of the most northern line of military posts of the United States from Red River to the Pecos. As soon as the land was surveyed and marked, the Federal Government was to settle thereon Indians belonging to Texas, and to have control of them, and establish such agencies and military posts as were necessary. The act provided for the reversion of the land to the state, when it was no longer used for the Indians.

The departments of War and of the Interior appointed Captain R. B. Marcy and Major R. S. Neighbors to survey the land. Captain Marcy wrote Governor

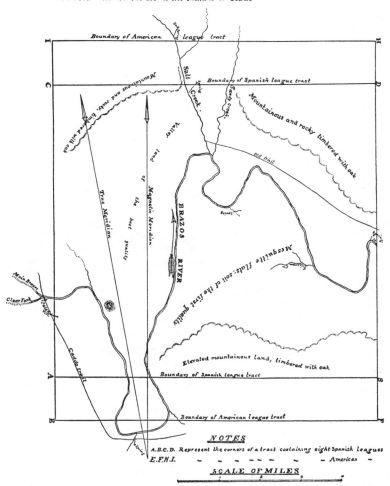

Map 5.—Plat of the Lower Brazos Reserve in Texas, by Maj. R. S. Neighbors and Capt. R. B. Marcy.

Original in the National Archives: Records of the Department of the Interior, Office of Indian Affairs, Map No. 723.

Pease, January 10, 1855, that he had surveyed and marked the boundaries of the land, and inclosed copies of the plots and field notes [maps 2 and 5]. He marked the tracts in both Spanish and English measurements since the act did not specify which was to be used. Marcy said he and the secretary of war thought the American measurements should be used, since the reservations were small at best. He recommended that the American league be adopted. Major Neighbors also wrote Governor Pease, February 20, 1855, saying that they had used great care in selecting the land, consulting the Indians as to their preferences. He stated that he had submitted his field notes and plots to the departments of the General Government, and was now sending them to the Governor in order that he might have them entered on the maps of the General Land Office. He requested that the Governor report to him any error in them for the Indians had already begun to settle on the land. [Koch, 1925, pp. 98–99.]

The Brazos Agency on which the Caddo and their allies were placed together with the Waco, Tawakoni, Kichai, Tonkawa, and some Delaware, consisted of eight leagues, or 37,152 acres. "It was located on the main fork of Brazos River, about twelve or fifteen miles south of Fort Belknap" (Koch, 1925, p. 99).

In a communication to Schoolcraft written at about this period, Marcy says that the Hainai, Anadarko, and Caddo

live in permanent villages, where they plant corn, peas, beans, and melons. They, however, live for a great portion of the year upon the fruits of the chase, are well armed with fire-arms, but also make use of the bow and arrow . . . [They] have heretofore been engaged in hostilities with the Texans, but are now quiet and friendly, and are already availing themselves of the opportunity extended to them by the Government, of settling upon the lands donated by the State of Texas for their use. They are commanded by a very sensible old chief, called "*José Maria*," who feels a deep interest in the welfare of his people; and is doing every thing in his power to better their condition. [Schoolcraft, vol. 5, p. 712.]

The progress made in settling the Indians upon this reservation is thus described by Neighbors, the Supervising Agent of the Texas Indians, in a letter to the Acting Commissioner of Indian Affairs, dated "Brazos Agency, Texas, September 10, 1855":

Under your instructions of February 2, (as soon as I could possibly make the necessary arrangements,) I commenced the new policy of colonizing the Texas Indians on the lands set apart for them, but it was the 1st of March before it was possible to commence, which was so late in the season that it was impossible to expect any considerable success in farming this year.

As soon as the reservations were opened for settlement all the Indians immediately in the neighborhood assembled and selected their lands for farming purposes; and, although late, I instructed the special agent in charge to have some land prepared, and to assist such of the Indians as were willing to work in planting corn; the result was that there were about 400 acres of land planted, but owing to the extremely dry season experienced in this section, the yield has not been commensurate with the exertions made by the Indians to make their own bread. The Caddoes, Anadahkoes, Wacoes and Tahwaccorroes are the tribes who have been most forward in farming, and there is no doubt but they will, after the next crop, be able to make their own bread. Accompanying, I beg leave to submit Special Agent Hill's report of 31st August, which will inform you more in detail in regard to his operations.

There are now settled on this reservation, as you will perceive by reference to the census rolls herewith enclosed, 794 Indians of the following tribes, to wit: 205 Anadahkos, 188 Caddoes, 136 Tahwaclorroes [Tawakoni], 94 Wacoes, and 171 Tonkahwas. They embrace a majority of the above tribes, and it is confidently expected that before the end of the present fiscal year, the whole of them will be settled down permanently. As regards the Indians already settled down on this reservation, I must say that, for good behavior, morality, and industry they have far exceeded my most sanguine expectations; there has not been, within my knowledge, a single case of drunkenness, and not a gallon of spirits sold on the reservation; this is simply the result of the wishes of the Indians themselves, as there has been no police, and there has been but one depredation committed, as far as known, upon any of the white settlers in the neighborhood; when application was made to the chief, the offender was immediately given up and reparation made. I must say that a more peaceful and quiet settlement does not exist in any portion of Texas than is now found on this reservation, and all that visit it are astonished at the progress made by the Indians in the arts of civilized life. So far as the tribes above named are concerned, the policy now pursued can no longer be called an experiment. [Indian Affairs, 1855, pp. 177–178.]

In his report to Neighbors, Hill says:

In obedience to your instructions of March, 1855, covering a copy of those from the Indian Bureau to you of February 2, 1855, I have located and settled on this reservation seven hundred and ninety-two Indians; there are yet north of Red river near two hundred Wacoes, Tawaccoroes, Caddoes, and Anadahcoes, entitled to settlement here. [Indian Affairs, 1855, pp. 184.]

We now quote from articles by Clara Lena Koch on "The Federal Indian Policy in Texas, 1845–1860":

Near the center of the reservation, in a grove of mesquite trees, the Federal Government erected a group of buildings for the transaction of business. There were two houses for the employees, a house for the agent, a kitchen, a store room, and a blacksmith's shop. . . . The government of the reservation was fairly simple. Neighbors wrote Charles Mix shortly after the opening of the agency that he had established temporary rules for the control of the Indians. They acknowledged the treaty of 1846 to be still binding so the agents based their action on it, adding articles of government as a supplement to the treaty. Neighbors wrote Major General Twiggs, July 17, 1857, that never since the opening of the reservations had he found it necessary to call on the military department to enforce orders. The agents with the assistance of the Indians organized and conducted a police force. The Federal Government had stationed two companies of dragoons and two companies of infantry at Fort Belknap, altogether about 850 men. This was in September of 1854. The accounts show that there was always some force here because this fort was on the frontier. The troops there, after the establishment of the reservations, were designed for the protection of the agency Indians. as well as of the frontier settlers. . . .

The Government neglected the matter of education for the Agency until just about a year before it abandoned the reservation system in Texas. Reverend John W. Phillips of the Methodist Episcopal Church wanted to establish a mission school for the Indians, and Neighbors wrote Mix September 10, 1855, that he hoped Mix would consider the plan favorably. The tribes were anxious for a school, and he thought the Indians ought to be educated; the children ought to learn English. Five days later, September 15, Neighbors wrote to Mr. Phillips saying that it would be of little use to establish a mission for two or three years yet, until the Indians had made some advances in civilization. Whether Phillips ever established a mission or a mission school, the writer [i. e., Miss Koch] has been unable to discover. Ross in a letter to

Neighbors, September 30, 1856, urged him to call the attention of the Indian Department to the fact that schools had been promised the Indians, and they were expecting the Federal Government to fulfill the promise. The children ought to be trained for citizenship, said Ross. By September, 1857, Neighbors had made contracts for school buildings at the Agency, according to instructions which he had received in March. The buildings were then nearly completed, and he expected school to open in November. School did not open, however, until June 1, 1858. Z. E. Coombes, the teacher, wrote Ross on September 7, 1858, giving an account of progress. There were sixty pupils enrolled, forty-seven boys and thirteen girls. He advised the employment of an assistant teacher. There had been continued excitement, he said, among the Indians on the reservation, due to the depredations committed on and near the Agency by wild Comanches and their allies, and this had interfered greatly with the school progress. On January 29, 1859, Coombes wrote Neighbors that he had been unable to open school until the tenth of the month because of the excitement due to the killing of Agency Indians, and threats of extermination made by those guilty of murders, an account of which follows shortly. The pupils, the number of whom had decreased to fifty, were in fear of being murdered and brought their bows and arrows to school.

The first agent for the Brazos reservation was G. W. Hill. He wrote Neighbors, August 31, 1855, that he was then about to retire from duty as agent, and go to his farm near the frontier, where he had lived for twenty years. He had spent the past twenty-six months almost constantly among the Indians. Captain Shapley P. Ross succeeded Hill at Brazos Agency. He entered on duty September 1, 1855, and continued as agent until the reservation system was abandoned. . . . Ross was very successful in his work for the Indians. Neighbors attributed the progress of the Agency to his efficiency. [Koch, 1925, pp. 101–104.]

Jim Shaw was the principal interpreter and George Williams, a Delaware, was made assistant interpreter in 1858, his services being needed at school and in cases of sickness (Koch, 1925, p. 104).

In 1856 the number of Indians on this reservation had increased to 948. Ross reported:

The Indians at the several villages have neat cottages, with good gardens and fields adjacent, and the many conveniences to be seen on every hand give me abundant evidence of the progress made by the Indians since their settlement. The Caddoes and Anahdahkos show a great desire for the adoption of the customs as well as the habits of the white men. They have also held themselves ready and willing to assist in rescuing any property stolen from the citizens on this frontier by the roving bands of hostile Indians. I also noticed that the Indians are conquering to a great extent their old disposition for roving; there seems to be now more attraction for them at home among their families. This marked advancement in their civilization is evident to all who visit this reservation.

There had been but one case of drunkenness. The farms had, however, suffered from drought.

The Caddoes have in cultivation about 150 acres of land; the Anadahkos about 140; the Wacoes and Tahwaccanos 150; and the Tonkahuas 100; all of which . . . are in good condition for next crop. [Indian Affairs, 1856, pp. 179, 180.]

In 1857 Neighbors reported that the Caddo had 130 acres in corn and 20 in wheat; the Anadarko 115 in corn and 20 in wheat (Indian

Affairs, 1857, p. 262). The members of these tribes not on the reserve were beyond Red River, in the Chickasaw and Choctaw country and with the Wichita.

They frequently visit the reserve, and on several occasions the census roll of the agent showed over one thousand Indians. All of the above tribes have been perfectly peaceable since the reserve was opened, and no depredations have been traced to them. They have made considerable progress in agriculture and stock raising, built themselves good cabins, and have under fence and cultivation about seven hundred acres of land, and it is confidently expected that they will raise an abundance of bread and vegetables to sustain them the next year. It has never been necessary since the opening of the reserve to ask the aid of the military to enforce the orders of the agent, the whole police of the reserve being conducted by the agent, with the assistance of the Indians, who are well organized for that purpose. [Indian Affairs, 1857, p. 265.]

Samuel Church, Farmer for the Caddo and Anadarko, reported that "the Caddoes have ploughed twenty acres of new land the past month, and also built, during the past year, seven good log houses, and the Anadahkoes ten houses" (Indian Affairs, 1857, p. 271). There were then 1,014 settlers on the reservation, and they had

a fair stock of horses, cattle, and hogs, and are paying particular attention to stock raising; and I am satisfied [writes Ross,] that in a few years their condition will bear comparison with our frontier citizens. I have thought it proper to give permission to a portion of the Caddoes and Anadakoes, who have proved themselves perfectly reliable, to make small hunting and scouting parties, after securing their crops this fall; this was more a matter of recreation than profit, and I deemed it bad policy to confine the Indians on the reserve, with nothing to employ them. It was supposed that the information obtained from them, concerning the movements of hostile Indians, would greatly aid us in checking their depredations on our frontier. [Indian Affairs, 1857, p. 269.]

During this period warriors from these reservations accompanied both Federal and State troops in their expeditions against the northern Indians. In April 1858, a hundred went with Capt. John S. Ford in his attack on the camp of the Comanche chief Iron Jacket. One hundred and thirty-five Indians from the same place were with Major Van Dorn of the U. S. Cavalry in his fight with the Comanche on the False Washita (Koch, 1925, pp. 33, 34). The Indian agent, J. R. Baylor, wrote Neighbors that Indian troops under the command of white officers were the best protection to the whites. The same year 100 Indians of the Brazos tribes went out on a scout with Capt. William Martin of the ranger service. They accompanied several expeditions and Koch says that "these Indians, who were faithful to the whites and assisted them, were the agricultural tribes who had been settled on reservations, and who had to some extent adopted the manners, customs, and habits of the white people" (Koch, 1925, pp. 34, 35).

Nevertheless, friction developed between the reservation Indians and the settlers, caused in part by whites who hated all Indians equally, or who wished to get them out of the way and occupy their lands, and in part, as was claimed by Neighbors, by the hostility of J. R. Baylor who nursed an animosity against the Federal Government and the reservation system, because he had been discharged from his position as agent. It was asserted on the other hand that many depredations which the agents were wont to charge on the more northern Indians had actually been committed by those on the reservations and that they had even killed some white men. This bad feeling culminated on the morning of December 27, 1858, in an attack by a body of whites upon 17 Indians, including men, women, and children, who were "encamped, grazing their horses on a bend of the Brazos, above the mouth of the Reichie [Keechi]." One Caddo man, one Caddo woman, three Anadarko men, and two Anadarko women were killed. The rest were wounded but got back to the reservation. One of the dead was a nephew of José Maria, the Anadarko chief. These facts are taken from a letter dated December 28, 1858, written by J. J. Sturm, the Farmer for the Brazos reserve. In a second letter, sent two days later, Sturm says that those who had been killed were "seven of the best and most inoffensive Indians on the reserve" (Indian Affairs, 1859, pp. 220–222).

The whites who participated in this attack had the support of the greater part of their neighbors and it was found impossible to bring them to justice. The peace commissioners appointed by Governor Runnels to examine the matter were unable to put an end to the disturbances. The attitude of the white settlers bears all the earmarks of one of those emotional outbreaks on the part of men who have suffered real losses but are not in a frame of mind to consider questions judicially. And if, as Neighbors affirmed, they were being egged on by men who believed they had grievances and hoped to advance their personal fortunes in the situation created, the momentum of the movement would have been increased thereby. Since offenses committed against other tribes are often held up as models for imitation before the minds of growing Indian boys, the theft and slaughter of domestic animals may well have been perpetrated occasionally by reservation Indians. Such atrocities, and murders of men and women as well, by the more distant Indians were of constant occurrence, and the desire for vengeance could easily be deflected to satisfy the grudges of self-interested leaders from real culprits to others more readily available. If there were no excuse, one could soon be manufactured. If there were some excuse it could readily be augmented. Whatever the actual truth may have been, the following facts make the case for the settlers appear rather weak.

Firstly, the general peaceable character and excellent reputation of the Caddo and their allies and their past services to the whites to which Baylor himself testified. Secondly, the failure of the white men to adduce any specific cases of depredations that could be pinned definitely upon the reservation Indians, the evidence being wholly circumstantial, and involving no murders. Thirdly, granted that the settlers felt assured that such acts had been committed by the reservation Indians and that summary action was necessary, an attack on a body of campers, the slaughter of both men and women, and the wounding of children,—whether or not these Indians were among "the best and most inoffensive Indians on the reserve"—was not a very heroic performance, and was not calculated to dramatize the wrongs of the settlers to the best advantage (Indian Affairs, 1859, p. 221).

But the situation had now become so tense that not only the white settlers but also the State Government and the Indian agents were agreed that it would be necessary to remove the Indians from Texas to the territories north of Red River (Indian Affairs, 1859, p. 237). Already the United States Government had been considering leasing land from the Choctaw and Chickasaw for this purpose, and in the summer of 1858 Douglas Cooper, agent for the latter tribe, reported, as the result of a personal investigation, that the area around Medicine Bluff west of Fort Arbuckle and including the old Wichita village was suitable for the purpose. In 1859 Major Emory, the commander at the fort, went over the same ground to determine upon a location for the new post and chose the site of the old Wichita village (Nye, 1937, p. 83). The final decision rested, however, with Elias Rector, Superintendent of Indian Affairs for the Southern Superintendency, and he set out June 18, 1859, from Fort Smith to begin an examination of the country in the neighborhood of the Wichita Mountains for a prospective reserve. He finally fixed upon a region lying along the False Washita, being completely disappointed in the character of that which had commended itself to Cooper and Emory.

Finding myself thus compelled to the conclusion that another locality must be looked for, since this is wholly unfit for the purposes intended, and that the War Department, when fully advised, will certainly not select, as a position for a military post, the site of the old Wichita village, or any point in its vicinity, I had to turn either to the main or little Fausse Ouachita, and accordingly proceeded to the former.

From the sandstone hills before mentioned, about forty miles northeast of the Blue mountain, and in the country to the northward, a number of small streams, draining the prairie, with barren ridges between, thickly covered with stunted oaks, uniting together, flow northward to the Fausse Ouachita, which is about twelve miles in that direction from those hills. A mile or two further to the westward, is another similar system of drainage, terminating in another small stream. The most easterly of these systems, at its lower end, opens out into an open valley of moderate width, covered with rich grass and in places with large trees. Here was the old Kichai village; and a little way below, the valley debouches into that of the Fausse Ouachita, extending above and below some eight or ten miles, bounded on the south by a range of low barren hills, the lower half about one and a half miles in width, and around the upper half, the hills retreating still further back and forming almost a semicircle, enclosing between them and the river a broad level plain from two to two and a half miles in width, a large part of it of great fertility, and covered with the thickest and finest grass. The most westerly valley, towards its mouth, is wide and fertile, and covered with a thick growth of timber. My guides informed me that above this river valley are three others on the south side of the river, after which there are no more.

Crossing this alluvial plain, passing through a body of timber some hundred yards in width, I reached and forded the river, here of a deep red color, about three feet in depth and thirty yards in width, and emerged from a similar belt of timber, on the north side, into another wide and level alluvial plain, round which, on the north and east, ran Sugar Tree creek from the northwest, flowing into the river below. This plain, between the creek and river, some two and a half miles in width in its widest part, is bounded by a high ridge on the west that runs sloping to the river. The soil of the plain is light and sandy, that along the creek probably far superior to that near the river. Further up in the hills are sugar maple trees, from which the creek takes its name. Here, on this creek and plain, the Delawares and Caddoes—now encamped near here with and as part of the Wichita tribe—had told me, before we commenced the journey from Fort Arbuckle, they desired to settle. The Wichitas and Kichais desired to settle in a similar small valley on the south side of the Canadian, about twenty miles to the northward. I have consented to these locations.

I have selected as the site for the Wichita agency that of the old Kichai village, on the south side of the river, near the mouth of the valley already mentioned; and there I propose to erect the permanent agency-house and out-buildings, as soon as I can close a contract for the same on reasonable terms, and in the meantime to erect a cheap, temporary cabin for the agent, to be afterwards used as a kitchen or other out-building, and a shed to protect from the weather the goods and articles in my hands to be furnished the Wichitas and affiliated bands; and the Texas Indians, I propose to place on the south side of the river, above and below the agency, allowing them to select the site for their respective towns, unless the Shawnees, Delawares, and the Caddoes among them desire to settle with, as they should do, the Delawares and Caddoes now here, on the north side of the river, and the Huecos and Ta-wa-ca-nos, who speak the same langauge as the Wichitas, with that people and the Kichais, on the Canadian; in which case, the wish of each should of course govern.

Of the country on the Canadian selected by the Wichitas and Kichais, I obtained accurate information from Se-kit-tu-ma-qua, my Delaware interpreter, who is thoroughly acquainted with it, and I therefore did not deem it necessary to examine it in person. The Wichitas and Kichais all desire to settle there; and as they have resided in this region from a time beyond anyone's memory, and have a better claim to it than any other tribe, they ought, I think, to have the privilege of selecting their home. Moreover, I desired, before coming to a final conclusion, to see the country on the Little Washita, west of the ninety-eighth parallel, which had been mentioned to me, and accordingly I returned by the way of the upper waters of that creek, but found no country there, beyond the ninety-eighth parallel, comparable to that on the main river. [Indian Affairs, 1859, pp. 305–309.]

The chart accompanying his report is shown in map 3, and a later chart locating the new reservation in map 4.

On his return to Fort Arbuckle on the 30th, he found Major Neighbors there and he continues:

After being fully informed by myself and Lieutenant Stanley, commander of the escort, Mr. Blain, and the other gentlemen who accompanied me, of the character of the several portions of the country explored by us, with which also some of the head men with him are familiar, Mr. Neighbors has entirely concurred with me in regard to the fitness of the place selected by me whereon to locate such of the Indians under his charge as may not readily affiliate with those now in my superintendency, and will proceed, at the end of three days from this time [the letter was dated July 2], to the reserves in Texas, and immediately carry out your instructions, by forthwith removing all the Indians there, with their cattle, horses, and all other moveable property, to the site selected for an agency, and there proceed to select the locations for the several bands. [Indian Affairs, 1859, pp. 309–310.]

The head men of the tribes concerned who had accompanied Neighbors to the Fort were then called in council and the plans that had been made for them explained whereupon "the Indians declared themselves entirely satisfied with the country selected for them, well known to many of them, and ready to remove at once" (Indian Affairs, 1859, p. 310). On the allotment of the land among its new settlers, Rector says:

It is the settled opinion of Mr. Neighbors and myself, that, beyond all possible doubt, it will be found wholly impracticable, for many years to come, to assign to any of these Indians distinct parcels of land, by metes and bounds, in severalty for each family, and to confine their right of occupancy and possession to only so much land as shall be thus covered by individual reservation. They need far more land for grazing than for cultivation. They are not prepared to become land-owners and individual proprietors of the soil. They are, and will long be, far in the rear of that point. If that system is tried, the whole plan of colonization will prove a disastrous and melancholy failure. In a few months the reserves would be abandoned. It has always been the habit of most of them to live in towns, each staking off and cultivating a portion of one comon tract, contained in a single inclosure. It has been found necessary to adopt this system on the Texas reserves.

It was the system of the Mexican Pueblos; and there can, it is certain beyond all peradventure, be no other pursued with profit in the case of any of these Indians.

Each band, to make the present experiment, in which the good faith and honor of the United States are so much concerned, successful, must be put in exclusive possession of a much larger tract of country than is needed for cultivation, and, when part of it has been inclosed, be left to subdivide that part among themselves each year, as the needs of each may require. This is always done among themselves equitably and justly. We have proceeded upon these principles in selecting the country to be occupied by these bands, and earnestly hope that our views and action may be approved by you and the Secretary of the Interior. The plan of assigning to each head of a family his forty or eighty acre lot, to be his own, would not succeed for a day or an hour.

As to the country around the Wichita mountains, it ought to be reserved as common hunting grounds, for which alone nearly the whole of it is fitted. [Indian Affairs, 1859, p. 311.]

The necessity of providing facilities for emigration and provision until the first crop could be garnered in the new country was also stressed. The unarmed Indians should be provided with rifles for defense against hostile tribes and to enable them to hunt. There should be a blacksmith shop and only one, carefully regulated, trading house. It was hoped that this experiment would prove successful and induce the remaining wild tribes to settle down.

On July 9th Neighbors arrived at the Brazos Agency and prepared to move his charges as soon as the promised military escort arrived. On the 25th he states that his transportation was arriving and that part of his escort had come so that he expected to leave within the next 4 days. He expresses annoyance at the action of state troops under Capt. John Henry Brown in preventing the Indians from gathering in their stock which happened to be beyond the limits of the reservation, and notes that the Comanche of the upper reserve and State troops had had a brush in which one on each side was killed. A Tawakoni Indian had also been killed by an unknown person. He was delayed a couple of days longer than he had anticipated so that it was August 1 before the movement began (Indian Affairs, 1859, pp. 318, 320, 328). His account of it is contained in his letter to the Commissioner dated at the Camp on the False Washita, August 18, 1859, which runs as follows:

Sir: I have the honor to report that I left Brazos agency, Texas, with Indians of that reserve, on the 1st instant, after having instructed Agent Leeper to move forward with the Comanches from Comanche agency, and form a junction with me at Red river.

Agent Leeper, with all the Comanches, marched on the 30th ultimo, under an escort of one company of infantry, under Captain Gilbert. Our escort consisted of one company of infantry and two companies of second cavalry, all under the command of Major G. H. Thomas [the later Federal general of Civil War fame].

Both parties arrived at the crossing of Red river on the evening of the 7th instant, where the parties were, on the 8th, crossed over.

We arrived at Major Steen's crossing of the False Washita on the 16th. Having communicated with Agent Blain, who was camped about five miles below, and finding that he had not designated the point for the Wichita agency, I, on the 17th, moved up the river about four miles [four miles northeast of the site of the present town of Fort Cobb], where I have established my camp, to await the arrival of Superintendent Rector, or his deputy, to whom I am to turn over the Indians now under my charge. I have this day issued to the Indians under my charge seven days' rations, which is the total amount of provisions brought with me from Texas. This issue was necessary, from the fact that no provision had been completed to furnish the Texas Indians on their arrival.

Previous to leaving the Brazos agency, I sold the whole stock of hogs belonging to the Indians, and placed Mr. Buttorff, a very respectable citizen, in charge of the agency buildings; and Captain Plummer left a small party of troops at the same point, to guard some supplies belonging to the troops. I also made an arrangement with Mr. Buttorff and several of the stock raisers in the vicinity, to gather up the Indian cattle, a large portion of which they were unable to collect, on account of the hostile attitude assumed by the State troops and a portion of the citizens, one Indian having already been killed in trying to gather his stock, as heretofore reported.

Agents Ross and Leeper are both with me. In addition to the necessity for Agent Ross's services on the trip, there was no government property left at the agency, except the buildings, and none of the employés were willing to remain; they were consequently employed for the trip, as teamsters, &c. I have also with me the blacksmith, with all his tools and material.

As soon as Mr. Rector arrives, I will forward invoices of all the property, both Indian and government, brought with me, as well as the census rolls, list of employés, &c.

There were but few incidents worthy of note on the trip. We had one birth and one death. On the 13th instant, a party sent by me to find Agent Blain's camp, were attacked by a party of nine Kiowas, near the head of Beaver creek. They drove off four of the horses, and wounded very severely one Caddo Indian. One of the Kiowas was killed, whose dead body we saw next day.

On the 14th, Major Thomas, having been ordered back to Camp Cooper by General Twiggs, returned. I am sorry to learn that all the escort are to return immediately, by General Twiggs' order, and Captain Plummer's command of infantry will leave to-morrow, which leaves the Indians here without a troop for their protection. It is hoped that you will, as early as practicable, have a military force sent to this country. Our movement has been very successful, and all concur in the opinion that we have made quick time, the distance from Brazos agency being 170 miles.

Hoping that my proceedings will meet your approval, I am, very respectfully, your obedient servant,

ROBERT S. NEIGHBORS,
Superintendent Indian Affairs, Texas.

HON. A. B. GREENWOOD,
Commissioner Indian Affairs, Washington, D. C.
[Indian Affairs, 1859, pp. 328-330; *see* Nye, 1937, p. 35.]

Having turned the Indians over to S. A. Blain, their new agent, who had been in charge of the Wichita, Neighbors and Leeper (former agent of the upper reserve) set out to return to Texas on September 6. The next day they were attacked by a party of hostile Indians who robbed them of three horses and inflicted three pretty severe wounds upon Leeper. On the 13th they reached Belknap, in Young County, Tex., and on the day following Neighbors was killed by a man named Ed Cornett, who was a stranger to him but no doubt inflamed by events leading up to the movement of the Indians. It would be interesting to speculate as to whether the decision of the Virginian General Thomas to remain on the Union side in our Civil War, which broke out 2 years later, was influenced in any manner by his experience on this occasion and the opposition in which Federal and State troops were placed. The military post of Fort Cobb was established on October 1 (Indian Affairs, 1859, pp. 333-334; Nye, 1937, p. 35).

In the report for the following year, 1860, the Caddo agent complains that these Indians

appear still to be pursued and threatened by the Texans; and to add to their misfortune the extraordinary drought which has visited this portion of [the] country has not only cut off everything attempted to be raised by them in the way of agriculture, but has destroyed the grass for many miles around. [He states that] the Caddoes have eighty-four and a half acres in cultivation, consisting of different small fields or patches, some of which have tolerably good fences. They have twenty-three picket houses covered with grass and eighteen with boards. The Anahdahkoes have seventy-six and a half acres inclosed, seventy-three and a half of which have been cultivated, and, like the Caddoes, it consists of small fields or patches, with tolerably good fences. They have thirty-three picket houses covered with grass and five with boards; also one loghouse covered with boards. [Indian Affairs, 1860, p. 156.]

In the late summer of 1860 Caddo Indians, along with Tonkawa, and Wichita, accompanied Texas Rangers, then stationed at Fort Cobb, in an expedition against the Kiowa and Comanche and in attacking a camp near the head of the Canadian River a Caddo killed a prominent Kiowa named Bird-Appearing. This occasioned trouble at a later time between the two tribes.

Next year, when the Civil War broke out, the greater part of the Caddo remained faithful to the Federal Government and fled to Kansas, but some sought refuge as far from home as Colorado. Those who remained are believed to have assisted in the destruction of Fort Cobb and the agency buildings on the night of October 23–24, 1862, although they laid the blame upon Osage, Shawnee, and Delaware Indians from the Kansas agency. Later these Indians attacked and almost exterminated the Tonkawa near the site of Anadarko, inflamed by the rumor that they had been seen cooking the body of a Caddo youth. In revenge for the death of Bird-Appearing, a war party of Kiowa killed a Caddo Indian near the Caddo settlement on Sugar Creek south of Anadarko in the summer of 1861, but attempts to repeat the success 2 years later resulted disastrously for the attackers (Nye, 1937, pp. 41–44).

In 1864, 370 Caddo and 150 "Jenies" (Hainai) were reported living in Kansas. They seem to have been settled near Le Roy in Coffee County (Indian Affairs, 1864, p. 319). Here they remained for more than 2 years after the war had come to an end, and the story of their restoration is told as follows by Henry Shanklin, U. S. Indian Agent in charge of the Wichita Agency in Kansas, in a communication dated September 1, 1867:

In April last I received instructions from the honorable Secretary of the Interior to remove the Indians in Kansas under my charge to their former home in the leased district, and funds were placed in my hands for their removal and subsistence en route. Supplies were purchased and arrangements made for transportation, but the unprecedented rainy season caused the Arkansas and all the streams south to remain bank-full until the latter part of June, when the first crossing was effected by means of a boat hauled here a distance of nearly 100 miles. In attempting this crossing one of the Indians was drowned. I then concluded not to make any further attempt until such times as the streams could be crossed with safety. Every effort was made on my part to comply with instructions, but poor progress was made in battling with the elements.

On the 26th June I received instruction from the Commissioner of Indian Affairs to report to Superintendent James Wortham the cause of delay in removal, and from whom I would receive further instructions, and under whose directions the removal of the Indians was placed.

The latter part of July preparations were again made for their removal, under the direction of Superintendent Wortham. A few days before the time of departure the cholera broke out with fearful violence among the Wichitas—eighteen deaths in five days. The Wacoes, Keechies, and Towacaries, although living in close proximity, were not affected for some days after this terrible disease made its appearance. The Absentee Shawnees, Caddoes, and Delawares, living on Dry creek, some ten miles distant, were in good health. A physician was sent for and directed to render all the aid he could to the afflicted. He reported the disease to be *cholera morbus*, caused by their eating green plums and melons, recommending their breaking up camp and moving immediately as the most effective means to restore them to health. The day following several of the Towacaires were sick, and it became apparent that a panic had spread among the bands afflicted—refusing to be moved at this time, giving as their reason, at this late hour, that the Great Spirit had given them strength to plant some corn in the spring, and if they neglected to gather it, would not give them strength to plant in the future. My impression was that undue influence had been used by some unprincipled persons, but am satisfied, upon inquiry with a number of the Indians, that they wished to remain a short time, to mourn over the graves of their departed friends. They now express a willingness to move at any time the superintendent may direct.

The Absentee Shawnees, Caddoes, and Delawares had broke camp and made every preparation for removal. Supplies and transportation being ready, it was thought advisable to move those bands that were not as yet afflicted with the disease.

On the 3d of August they left the south bank of the Arkansas, in apparent good health, for their new home. I learn from Captain C. F. Garrett, issuing commissary, who accompanied them, that the cholera broke out among the Shawnees at Buffalo Springs, and that over fifty deaths occurred before they reached the False Washita, also that forty-seven Caddoes had fallen victims to this terrible scourge. [Indian Affairs, 1867, p. 322.]

In 1868 the same agent writes:

Since my last annual report the Indians attached to this agency have all been removed from their temporary home on the Arkansas river to their old home on the Washita, in the vicinity of old Fort Cobb, where it was confidently expected they would be permitted to settle by themselves, open up their fields, build their villages, and live in peace the remainder of their days. [Indian Affairs, 1868, p. 287.]

The chief of the Caddo Indians at this time was Show-e-tat or Little Boy, known to the Whites by the distinguished epithet of George Washington (pl. 3). According to information contained in the Jackson Catalogue of Photographic Prints made in 1877 this chief was

born in Louisiana in 1816 [and] is probably the most progressive Indian on the reservation; has long since adopted the dress and customs of the whites; owns a trading-store, and has a well-cultivated farm of 113 acres, with good houses and improvements. He was captain during the Rebellion of a company of Indian scouts and rangers in the service of the Confederate States army, and engaged in three battles, one on Cache Creek, Indian Territory, with Kiowas and Apaches; one with the Cheyennes, in the Wichita Mountains; and one of the Little Washita, with renegade Caddos.

Unfortunately, George Washington's progress had not been entirely in salutary directions, since Nye informs us that the presence of a quantity of liquor found among the Kiowa and Comanche in 1868 was traced to him, and that the firearms with which those tribes were terrorizing the Texas border came from New Mexico via Mexican traders and Caddo George Washington. Two years later Show-e-tat was present at Fort Sill when the Kiowa chiefs Satanta and Big Tree were taken to Texas as prisoners, and he was father confessor to the third chief, old Satank, who was shot while attempting to kill his guards (Nye, 1937, pp. 66, 147, 167, 185–189).

The boundaries of the Caddo reservation were defined in 1872, and the same year Thomas C. Battey of the Society of Friends undertook missionary work among them (Hodge, 1907, *art.* Caddo).

On October 6, 1873, a council was held at Fort Sill to consider the terms under which the Kiowa chiefs Satanta and Big Tree should be released by the Governor of Texas, Edmund J. Davis, who had held them in custody. At this council speeches were made, not only by Kiowa Indians, but by chiefs of the Comanche, Kiowa Apache, Waco, and Caddo. The difference between the status of the Caddo and the other tribes is well exemplified in the address of Guadalupe, the Caddo chief (pl. 4, fig. 1) who said:

I do not belong to this agency but come to see and hear what occurs at this council. I have time and again advised these Indians for the sake of the Caddoes to cease going on the warpath, but I am sorry to say that it has not stopped. I used to live out on the Brazos, and I defy any man to say that I or my people have ever raided on any one. These very Kiowas and Comanches that are here today were the cause of my tribe being removed from Texas. I too am tired of trifling with these raiding Indians. If they won't quit let them say so. My tribe has been raising cattle and hogs and farming on the Washita, and these raiders interfere with us as much as they do with the whites. I am dressed in the hat, pants, and boots of a white man. I did not steal them, but bought them with money from my farm. I talk this way to my red brothers, for I feel it is for their own good. I have the white man by the hand and am bound to be his friend. I would like to see settled this trouble between the state of Texas and these Indians. I think that Satanta and Big Tree have been sufficiently punished, but that is not my affair. It is between the Texans and the Kiowas and Comanches. [Nye, 1937, pp. 222–223.]

Another prominent Caddo at this time was White Deer or Antelope, a delegate to Washington in 1872 (pl. 5.)

In 1876 we find the following report of Caddo conditions:

The Caddoes, numbering 467 persons, principally engaged as farmers and stock-raisers, are a quiet, inoffensive people, most of whom have adopted the habits of civilized life. They are much interested in the school at the agency, and co-operate in securing the punctual attendance of their children. . . . The remnant of 30 Iowans [Hainai], who left this reservation two years ago during the disturbance, have now become thoroughly incorporated with, and are, to all intents, Caddoes. [Indian Affairs, 1876, p. 64.]

In 1877 we read:

The *Caddoes* show an increase in numbers of 63, due in part to absentees (principally Ionies [Hainai]) returning from the Shawnee and other adjacent nations, and in part to actual increase by births.

Together with the *Ionies* and *Delawares*, they cultivate 1,400 acres of land, having added 80 acres the past year. They have added 25 new houses, and but a very few families are now living in the old grass houses. [Indian Affairs, 1877, p. 112.]

In September 1878, the Kiowa and Comanche Agency was consolidated with the Wichita Agency under P. H. Hunt, who had previously been at the head of the former (Indian Affairs, 1879, p. 62).

In 1881 a mission was opened in this tribe by the Protestant Episcopal Church (Hodge, 1907, *art.* Caddo).

In the Indian Office reports for 1880 and several succeeding years, complaint is common that the Caddo and Delaware were making little progress, and the Agent, James I. David, in his report for the year 1886, seeks to answer this:

The number of these people is about 521 Caddoes and 41 Delawares, with 125 of scholastic age. They have 924 acres in cultivation, 1,216 head of cattle, 631 horses, 518 hogs, and a large number of domestic fowls.

These Indians are said to have retrograded within the past fifteen or twenty years, or at least have made no progress beyond self-support or independence. This may be true, but it is not altogether their fault. Years ago it was thought by some of my predecessors that it would be a good idea, in order to more readily civilize the wild Indians fresh from the plains and war-path, to settle them among the Delawares and Caddoes, who at that time had farms and improvements all along the Washita Valley, that they might learn from the example of their more civilized brethren. The result was that the Kiowas and Apaches who were placed with the Caddoes and Delawares stole and ate their fat ponies and cattle to such an extent that they had to abandon their farms and move what was left of their live stock to the upper part of their reserve and commence new as far from their blanket brothers as possible.

The one great trouble with this people is they have no title to their lands further than an executive order placing them within the country they now occupy, and whenever this subject is debated in Congress these people become excited in anticipation of losing their lands, and I am convinced that if their titles were confirmed by law they would go to work with greater energy and will. However, they all want their fields enlarged, and by giving them seed-wheat this fall they will be in good condition for the future, should the season be favorable, though I have been unable to have the land broken that I expected on account of the drought. [Indian Affairs, 1886, pp. 128–129.]

Whether due to his encouragement or to other causes, the report for 1887 states that "the Caddoes especially seem to have taken new heart, and I am informed by those who are familiar with them that they have worked more and better this year than for many years past" (Indian Affairs, 1887, p. 82). This year witnessed the passage of the Severalty Act by the provisions of which the Caddo became citizens of the United States, and subject to the laws of Oklahoma, as soon as Oklahoma was organized (Hodge, 1907, *art.* Caddo).

Shortly after this move to assimilate Indian life to that of the white culture which had flowed around it, came the great messianic movement among the Plains tribes which we know as the Ghost Dance Religion. Mooney thus describes the manner in which it was introduced to the Caddo and its effects upon them. His account was written in 1893–94 after about 3 years of investigation.

A number of Caddo first attended the great Ghost Dance held by the Cheyenne and Arapaho on the South Canadian in the fall of 1890 on the occasion when Sitting Bull [an Arapaho, not the famous Sioux leader] came down from the north and inaugurated the trances. On returning to their homes they started the Ghost dance, which they kept up, singing the Arapaho songs as they had heard them on the Canadian, until Sitting Bull came down about December, 1890, to give them further instruction in the doctrine and to "give the feather" to the seven persons selected to lead the ceremony. From this time the Caddo had songs and trances of their own, the chief priest and hypnotist of the dance being Nĭshkû'ntŭ, "Moon Head," or John Wilson [pl. 4, fig. 2]. The Caddo and the Delaware usually danced together on Boggy creek. The Wichita and the Kichai, who took the doctrine from the Caddo, usually danced together on Sugar creek about 15 miles from the agency at Anadarko, but manifested less interest in the matter until Sitting Bull came down about the beginning of February, 1891, and "gave the feather" to the leaders. From this time all these tribes went into the dance heart and soul, on some occasions dancing for days and nights together from the middle of the afternoon until the sun was well up in the morning. The usual custom was to continue until about midnight. Cold weather had no deterrent effect, and they kept up the dance in the snow, the trance subjects sometimes lying unconscious in the snow for half an hour at a time. At this time it was confidently expected that the great change [reuniting of the whole Indian race, living and dead, on a regenerated earth] would occur in the spring, and as the time drew near the excitement became most intense. The return of the Kiowa delegate, Ä'piatañ, in the middle of February, 1891, with a report adverse to the messiah, produced no effect on the Caddo and their confederates, who refused to put any faith in his statements, claiming that he had not seen the real messiah or else had been bribed by the whites to make a false report.

About the time that Black Coyote and the others went out to see the messiah in the fall of 1891 the Caddo and their confederates sent out a delegation for the same purpose. The delegates were Billy Wilson and Squirrel (Caddo), Nashtowi and Lawrie Tatum (Wichita), and Jack Harry (Delaware). Tatum was a schoolboy and acted as interpreter for the party. Like the Arapaho they came back impressed with reverence for the messiah, and at once changed the time and method of the dancing, in accordance with his instructions, to periodical dances at intervals of six weeks, continuing for five consecutive days, the dance on the last night being kept up until daylight, when all the participants went down to bathe in the stream and then dispersed to their homes. They were dancing in this fashion when last visited in the fall of 1893.

The principal leader of the Ghost dance among the Caddo is Nĭshkŭ'ntŭ, "Moon Head," known to the whites as John Wilson. Although considered a Caddo, and speaking only that language, he is very much of a mixture, being half Delaware, one-fourth Caddo, and one-fourth French. One of his grandfathers was a Frenchman. As the Caddo lived originally in Louisiana, there is a considerable mixture of French blood among them, which manifests itself in his case in a fairly heavy beard. He is about 50 years of age, rather tall and well built, and wears his hair at full length flowing loosely over his shoulders. With a good head and strong, intelligent features, he presents the appearance of a natural leader. He is also prominent in the mescal rite, which has recently come to his tribe from the Kiowa and Comanche. He was one of the first Caddo to go into a trance, the occasion being the great Ghost dance held by the Arapaho and Cheyenne near Darlington agency, at which Sitting Bull presided, in the fall of 1890. On his return to consciousness he had wonderful things to tell of his experiences in the spirit world, composed a new song, and from that time became the high priest of the Caddo dance. Since then his trances have been frequent, both in and out of the Ghost dance, and in addition to his leadership in this connection he assumes the occult powers and authority of a great medicine-man, all the powers claimed by him being freely conceded by his people.

When Captain Scott was investigating the Ghost dance among the Caddo and other tribes of that section, at the period of greatest excitement, in the winter of 1890–91, he met Wilson, of whom he has this to say:

"John Wilson, a Caddo man of much prominence, was especially affected, performing a series of gyrations that were most remarkable. At all hours of the day and night his cry could be heard all over camp, and when found he would be dancing in the ring, possibly upon one foot, with his eyes closed and the forefinger of his right hand pointed upward, or in some other ridiculous posture. Upon being asked his reasons for assuming these attitudes he replied that he could not help it; that it came over him just like cramps."

Somewhat later Captain Scott says:

"John Wilson had progressed finely, and was now a full-fledged doctor, a healer of diseases, and a finder of stolen property through supernatural means. One day, while we were in his tent, a Wichita woman entered, led by the spirit. It was explained to us that she did not even know who lived there, but some force she could not account for brought her. Having stated her case to John, he went off into a fit of the jerks, in which his spirit went up and saw 'his father' (i. e., God), who directed him how to cure this woman. When he came to, he explained the cure to her, and sent her away rejoicing. Soon afterwards a Keechei man came in, who was blind of one eye, and who desired to have the vision restored. John again consulted his father, who informed him that nothing could be done for that eye because that man held aloof from the dance."

While the author was visiting the Caddo on Sugar creek in the fall of 1893, John Wilson came down from his own camp to explain his part in the Ghost dance. He wore a wide-brim hat, with his hair flowing down to his shoulders, and on his breast, suspended from a cord about his neck, was a curious amulet consisting of the polished end of a buffalo horn, surrounded by a circlet of downy red feathers, within another circle of badger and owl claws. He explained that this was the source of his prophetic and clairvoyant inspiration. The buffalo horn was "God's heart," the red feathers contained his own heart, and the circle of claws represented the world. When he prayed for help, his heart communed with "God's heart," and he learned what he wished to know. He had much to say also of the moon. Sometimes in his trances he went to the moon and the moon taught him secrets. It must be remembered that sun, moon, stars, and almost every other thing in nature are considered by the Indians as endowed with life and spirit. He claimed an intimate acquaintance with the other world and asserted positively that he could tell me "just what heaven is like." Another man who accompanied him had a yellow sun with green rays painted on his forehead, with an elaborate rayed crescent in green, red, and yellow on his chin, and wore a necklace from which depended a crucifix and a brass clock-wheel, the latter, as he stated, representing the sun.

On entering the room where I sat awaiting him, Nĭshkû'ntŭ approached and performed mystic passes in front of my face with his hands, after the manner of the hypnotist priests in the Ghost dance, blowing upon me the while, as he afterward explained to blow evil things away from me before beginning to talk on religious subjects. He was good enough to state also that he had prayed for light before coming, and had found that my heart was good. Laying one hand on my head, and grasping my own hand with the other, he prayed silently for some time with bowed head, and then lifting his hand from my head, he passed it over my face, down my shoulder and arm to the hand, which he grasped and pressed slightly, and then released the fingers with a graceful upward sweep, as in the minuet. The first part of this—the laying of the hands upon the head, afterward drawing them down along the face and chest or arms—is the regular Indian form of blessing, reverential gratitude, or prayerful entreaty, and is of frequent occurrence in connection with the Ghost dance, when the believers ask help of the priests or beg the prayers of the older people. The next day about twenty or more Caddo came by on their way to the agency, all dressed and painted for a dance that was to be held that night. They stopped awhile to see us, and on entering the room where we were the whole company, men, women, and children, went through the same ceremony, with each one of the inmates in turn, beginning with Wilson and myself, and ending with the members of the family. The ceremony occupied a considerable time, and was at once beautiful and impressive. Not a word was said by either party during the while, excepting as someone in excess of devotion would utter prayerful exclamations aloud like the undertone of a litany. Every face wore a look of reverent solemnity, from the old men and women down to little children of 6 and 8 years. Several of them, the women especially, trembled while praying, as under the excitement of the Ghost dance. The religious greeting being over, the women of the family, with those of the party, went out to prepare the dinner, while the rest remained to listen to the doctrinal discussion. [Mooney, 1896, pp. 903–905.]

After this time the Ghost dance religion faded away but left in its wake a more enduring cult connected with the use of the peyote. In the above quotation it will be remembered that Mooney says John Wilson was "also prominent in the mescal [i. e., in the peyote] rite," and he continued this prominence until his death. Petrullo gives a considerable account of his activities as leader of the "Big Moon cult," one of the two forms which the peyote ritual took among the Delaware, but he speaks of him as a member of the Black Beaver Band of Delaware, the one living with the Caddo, and seems to have failed to identify him with the John Wilson of Mooney's narrative. Since, according to Mooney, he was half Delaware, and only one-fourth Caddo, there is some excuse for this, but it is probable that he was considered by the Indians themselves as a Caddo. Presumably his mother was half Caddo; though this bit of information is omitted in the accounts we have of him (Mooney, 1896, p. 904; Petrullo, 1934, pp. 31–44, 78–86, 133–139).

At any rate, Weston La Barre in his monograph on The Peyote Cult (1938) devotes an Appendix to "John Wilson, the Revealer of Peyote," in which his identity with the John Wilson of the Ghost dance cult and his influence in spreading the Peyote religion are fully recognized. This Big Moon sect seems to represent the more liberal branch of the peyote movement, though when La Barre wrote, while still strong among the Osage and Quapaw, elsewhere, even among the Delaware and Caddo, it was "waning considerably" (La Barre, 1938, pp. 151–161).

It is interesting to remember that peyote was used by medicine men among the Hasinai at the beginning of the eighteenth century, and, recalling the elaborate ritualism of the Caddo, as well as their various contacts with Christian missionaries, including the presence among them of established missions for about three decades, one wonders whether such a background does not constitute part of the explanation of John Wilson. It may put the ancient fire cult of the Natchez and Caddo, Franciscan teachings, the Ghost dance religion, the peyote cult, and the North American churches founded on the last mentioned in one line of descent.

In 1894 a Roman Catholic mission was opened in this tribe after an intermission of 121 years (Hodge, 1907, *art.* Caddo).

Allotments were made to every Caddo man, woman, and child under the terms of the Severalty Act in the year 1902.

Besides the individuals whose likenesses have already been referred to (pls. 3–5), a few others are introduced. Plates 6 and 7 are from photographs made by Mooney in 1893 and plates 8, 9, and 10 from photographs taken at the Bureau of American Ethnology in 1898.

PHYSICAL, MENTAL, AND MORAL CHARACTERISTICS

Observations along these lines by early writers are very superficial but they have a certain interest because of the great changes which took place among our American Indians before more exact methods of approach could be used. The accompanying discussion involves some repetition, but it is believed justified.

Espinosa (1927, pp. 175, 177) remarks that "as to personal appearance [the Hasinai] are well built and robust, but, at the same time light and strong," and the "Texas Indian women are of good features and nearer white than red." Solís (1931, p. 60) says: "They are well formed and white. . . . The Indian women are pretty, being fair." Hidalgo notes that they had "good features and thin faces," and Morfi, who, however, is apt to copy Espinosa and Solís, discerns "regular features, whiter than the Mexicans, and other Indians of the south," and adds that they were "corpulent, light, robust" (Hidalgo, 1927, p. 55; Morfi, 1932, p. 40). At a much later date (1820) Padilla records these impressions:

They are strongly built, well developed, brave, and vigorous. They resist fatigue and the extremes of that changeable climate at all seasons; for they are accustomed to it. [Padilla, 1919, p. 53.]

The impression of size and fairness was perhaps due to comparison with Indians farther south, for Mooney considered them "rather smaller and darker than the neighboring prairie tribes," and, as has already been noted, the Omaha called them "Black Pawnee" (Mooney, 1896, p. 1094; Fletcher-La Flesche, 1911, p. 102).

By early writers, with one or two exceptions, the character of the Caddo is rated rather high. Joutel says that they were not thievish like some other peoples, but he visited them in 1687, and when Solís 80 years later calls them "great thieves" some of the responsibility for this apparent decline may have to be borne by Europeans (Joutel, 1878, pt. 3, p. 350; Solís, 1931, p. 62). Or is it possible that Europeans did not understand the native moral code? Solís, it should be stated, was not prepossessed in favor of the Indians north of the Rio Grande, describing them as "very dirty, foul-smelling and pestiferous" and adding that "they throw out such a bad odor from their bodies that it makes one sick" (Solís, 1931, p. 43).

They appealed to Casañas as " an industrious people" who "apply themselves to all kind of work," but it was necessary to make presents in order to obtain service from them in return. "So strong is this characteristic that only the person who gives them something is good while all others are bad" (Casañas, 1927, p. 40). Hidalgo and Espinosa call them "good humored and joyous," and the latter continues: "As a general rule, the Asinais Indians are naturally quick, intelligent, friendly, high minded, and without low thoughts." They were "always ready for war expeditions and of good courage. They preserve an inviolable peace, but they never form a truce or make friends with an enemy." They were well disposed toward both the French and Spaniards but, he thinks, more especially toward the latter.

It is not necessary to prove the friendship of these Indians by any proof save that of the experience of those who have lived among them for some time. For, up to this time, I have never seen anyone who has left the country of these poor Indians who does not speak of their kindness.

He proceeds to illustrate this by describing their welcome to Alarcon, yet in that there was as much of social custom as of spontaneous good will (Hidalgo, 1927, p. 55; Espinosa, 1927, pp. 152, 175, 179).

Morfi, as remarked above, is apt to lean heavily on the earlier missionaries. In his History he describes the Texas as "industrious," and says in the Memorias:

> The Texas are lively by nature, clear-sighted, sociable, proud and high minded . . . of great heart, and very quick in military activities. With their friends they keep unchangeable peace, and with their enemies they never, or very seldom, make peace . . . With all these good qualities [particularly hospitality which he has just enlarged upon] the Texas are still not lacking in defects. In the market at Natchitoches they provide themselves with skins, tallow, and cattle, with munitions and guns, for which they have such a love that they never go out without an *escopeta* on their shoulder. They also acquire an abundance of strong liquors, and with this facility, they give themselves much to intoxication. They are inclined by nature, as are all Indians, to robbery and suspicion. They are lascivious and too strongly attached to their customs; but their love for the Spaniards is very peculiar, as shall be seen by some examples given in this history. [Morfi, 1935, p. 83; 1932, pp. 40, 54.]

But of course devotion to ancient customs need not be a vice nor devotion to a particular foreign nation such as the Spaniards a virtue. One wonders to what extent the thievery with which later writers charge them might have come from the same source as the cause of intoxication. Solís says:

> They are great thieves and drunkards because whiskey and wine are furnished to them by the French of Nachitos with whom they have commerce, [yet he remarks elsewhere] all these nations [Nacogdoche, Nabedache, Kadohadacho, Hasinai, and Nasoni] are peaceful Indians, gentle, jovial, except now and then some are bad and preverse. [Solís, 1931, pp. 60, 69.]

De Mézières also commends them for their industry as exemplified particularly in the cultivation of the ground, but this was an ancient virtue among them and what proportion of virtue and what proportion of habit entered into it it would be impossible to say (Bolton, 1914, vol. 2, p. 173). Sanchez writing in 1828, for instance, expresses the opinion by inference that this was a virtue of the women, and particularly the old women, rather than the men. Like so many other Europeans he was impressed with the apparent over-burdening of the female sex and the laziness of the males (Sanchez, 1926, p. 282), yet in the countries of most of these critics peasant women not only labored in the fields but were sometimes yoked to the plow alongside of domestic animals.

One or two other writers vouchsafe information regarding the character of the separate Caddo tribes. Thus Sibley says of the Kadohadacho that they "are looked upon somewhat like Knights of

Malta, or some distinguished military order. They are brave, despise danger or death, and boast that they have never shed white men's blood," the last a vaunt rather too common to be altogether satisfying and paraded for obvious reasons. The Hainai "have a good character," and the Natchitoches Indians have been the "steady and faithful friends" of the French since that post was established. They helped them against the Natchez and "the French inhabitants have great respect for this nation, and a number of very decent families have a mixture of their blood in them" (Sibley, *in* Amer. State Pap., Indian Affairs, 1832, pp. 721, 722, 724). Sibley speaks of a Kadohadacho Indian—called the Grand Ozages because of his exploits against the Osage tribe—who accompanied Freeman in his expedition up Red River in 1806 and was called by the latter the best Indian he had ever seen (Sibley, 1922, p. 21). Sibley describes the Kadohadacho chief of his time as " a remarkably shrewd and sensible fellow," while Marcy in 1855 speaks of José Maria, under whom the removal from Texas took place, as " a very sensible old chief . . . who feels a deep interest in the welfare of his people; and is doing everything in his power to better their condition" (Sibley, 1922, p. 95; Schoolcraft, 1855, vol. 5, p. 712).

Padilla (1820) devotes considerable space to the morals of the Caddo tribes, or rather to his conception of their morals. He says of the Kadohadacho:

Considering the fact that they are heathens, the moral customs of these natives are good, since they are not ambitious like the Comanches nor deceitful like the Lipanes . . . They enjoy social intercourse, dislike theft, and treat Spaniards well, entertaining them in their houses and aiding them in every possible manner. They are faithful in keeping their contract; for the merchants of Natchitoches advance them munitions, trifles, and liquors at a good rate of exchange for furs. For all these they pay punctually, in spite of the fact that there are among them foreigners who come from Natchitoches and other points of the United States for the purpose of trading their wares to the said Indians for their products. Still, there are some swindlers and scoundrels who do not pay the debts they contract . . . Their knowledge is reduced to a small number of ideas so that they can barely judge of the present; and, although they remember the past, they scarcely ever provide for the future for the purpose of bettering their situation and of becoming more civilized. But due to their continuous trade with foreigners, it seems that they should not be called absolutely barbarous or savages. They, of all the Indians, perhaps, are the most civilized. [The Yuganís] are very sociable Indians and very docile and primitive [but these may have been the Yowani Choctaw who joined the Caddo for some years. The Nacogdochitos] are much more given to drunkenness than the Yuganís and consequently much poorer. [The San Pedro Indians (Nabedache)] have good inclinations and simple customs . . . They are but little addicted to firewater. They are liberal and generous with what they have. [The Texas (Hainai) resembled them. The Nadacos] are primitive and humane. They are given to the use of firewater because of their extreme trade with foreigners. [Padilla, 1919, pp. 47, 48, 49, 52.]

Notices bearing on the Adai and Eyeish have been omitted from the above discussion because of the fact that they stood somewhat aside from the true Caddo groups and had a much worse reputation. We have few references to the Adai except De Mézières' comment. In his time the tribe was almost extinct, "given extremely to the vice of drunkenness," and "cannot be useful or of any advantage" (Bolton, 1914, vol. 2, p. 173). It is evident whose advantage De Mézières was concerned about. The second of these two tribes is almost always represented as the black sheep of the Caddo flock. The first witness for the prosecution seems to be Solís:

> The Indians of this Ays Nation are the worst of this Province: drunkards, thieves, given to *mitotes* and dances, and to all kinds of vice, principally that of licentiousness. They are idle, overly audacious, shameless. They have lost respect for many of the Religious in word and deed, even laying their hands on them. They look with scorn on everything connected with our Holy Faith. There was an Indian of this Nation who sacrilegiously said that he loved and appreciated *Misuri* (who is the Devil), more than he did the Most Blessed among all those created, the Holy Mother Mary, Our Lady, and other scornful things about our Holy Faith; they also make jests about the Fathers. On account of this, I judge that there is no hope, not even a remote one, of their reduction and congregation, and that there is immanent and almost certain danger to the life of the ministers among these pagans. [Solís, 1931, pp. 67–68.]

From De Mézières: The mission was

> so unfruitful that all that the ministers gained were labor, sorrow, and expense; for these lazy, insolent and greedy people so satiated themselves with material food that they would not accept that [spiritual food] which was longed for by their [ministers'] apostolic zeal . . . their vices are without number; and the hatred which they have won from the natives and Europeans, general. [Bolton, 1914, vol. 2, p. 257.]

Morfi says that from the Ais mission there

> resulted very little fruit, owing to their particular aversion and total unappreciation for the sacred religion. One neophyte of this nation, after being well instructed in the catechism, had explained to him the perfection of the Queen of Angels, and when the missionary hoped, as a result of the attention with which he had listened, to receive some expression of devotion, was surprised to see him coldly say, "Well, I prefer *Misura* (meaning the Devil) to that woman which you praise."
> These Indians are the vilest of all the province, being drunkards, thieves, lascivious, very much given to celebrations, lazy, without shame, and childishly insolent, when their audacity is not checked by fear. Many times they offended their minister by word and act, traits, all of which, as De Mézières said, have made them not only hateful to the Europeans, but all the nations in their neighborhood. [Morfi, 1932, p. 4.]

In his Historia, Morfi comments briefly thus:

> They are given to all kinds of vices and to extreme drunkenness. They are generally hated both by the natives and the Europeans. In order to redeem them the mission of Nuestra Señora de los Dolores was founded, but, being obstinate and lazy, they merely ate everything the missionaries brought or

raised. They showed no inclination to work, nor did they ever give ear to the teachings of our doctrine, for which reason the mission was hopelessly abandoned. [Morfi, 1935, p. 81.]

Yet Padilla states that these Indians were "fond of the Spaniards" (Padilla, 1919, p. 49). As the Eyeish tribe has long been swallowed up in the Caddo population, it is impossible to review the case against them. It is quite certain, however, that the Eyeish idea of *Misura* or *Misuri* was not identical with the Spanish idea of the prince of devils. Part of the secret of their disreputable character is probably to be found in the circumstance that they were a small tribe with a peculiar dialect of Caddo and a relatively undeveloped culture. For this reason, without doubt, they were looked down upon by other Caddo before any mission was established among them. The salvation of the masses in any human group lies in social control and in the standards of leadership. But if a fragment of humanity is cut off from that social control because it is relegated to a lower level, the standards which might have saved the individuals belonging to it no longer operate. If people are precluded from rising to the social level of surrounding people with superior standards, they will probably not try to emulate them, and, unless saved by exceptional individuals within their own contracted group, their moral debacle is assured. But moral leadership in a small group, when even the leadership is shut off from the possibility of rising in the esteem of a wider social hierarchy, has to be maintained under the greatest disadvantages and discouragements. It must be supported by lofty standards internal to the leader, and while the history of the world proves that such direct dependence on the ideal without social encouragement is possible, it also shows that it is difficult in the extreme.

After the remnants of the Caddo had been moved to Oklahoma they impressed most of their agents, like the one who reported for them in 1876, as "a quiet, inoffensive people," most of whom by that time had "adopted the habits of civilized life." He adds that "they are much interested in the school at the agency, and co-operate in securing the punctual attendance of their children" (Indian Affairs, 1876, p. 64). A few years later we begin to hear complaints that they were making but little progress, but the explanation of this appears to be found in the report for the year 1886 which has been quoted but will bear quotation again:

These Indians are said to have retrograded within the past fifteen or twenty years, or at least have made no progress beyond self-support or independence. This may be true, but it is not altogether their fault. Years ago it was thought by some of my predecessors that it would be a good idea, in order to more readily civilize the wild Indians fresh from the plains and war-path, to settle them among the Delawares and Caddoes, who at that time had farms and improvements all along the Washita Valley, that they might learn from the example of their more civilized brethren. The result was that the Kiowas and Apaches who were placed with the Caddoes and Delawares stole and ate their fat ponies and cattle to such an extent that they had to abandon their farms and move what was left of their live stock to the upper part of their reserve and commence new as far from their blanket brothers as possible. [Indian Affairs, 1886, pp. 128–129.]

Another illustration of the truth that effort can only be looked for when its rewards are assured.

MATERIAL CULTURE

VEGETABLE FOODS [12]

The Caddo had reached a stage of development where they depended for their livelihood more upon the products of their fields than their gleanings from the wilderness. Joutel, the first European to record Caddo customs extensively, observes:

It is [the women] also who do the greater part of the [soil cultivation], although I noticed after a time a very good custom in this nation; they hold a kind of assembly when they wish to work the soil of one cabin where gather sometimes more than a hundred persons of both sexes, as is done in France, and notably in the country of Caux, when they wish to harvest a field of rapeseed, where each one goes to work, and the one who owns the field treats all the workers. They [the Hasinai] do the same thing: the day being appointed, all those who are informed come to work with a kind of mattock which some make of a buffalo bone (*palette de boeuf*) and others of a piece of wood fastened with cords made of tree bark. While all these laborers work, the women of the house for which it is done busy themselves in the preparation of food, and when they have labored for a certain time, that is, until about noon, they stop and are served of the best. If one comes back from the hunt with venison, it supplies the feast; if they have none, they cook corn in the ashes or boil it mixed with Brazil beans which doesn't make a too good mixture, but it is their way. They wrap what they have boiled in corn husks. After this repast most of them amuse themselves for the rest of the day; so that after they have worked for one cabin, they go another day to another. The women of the house have also to plant the *corn, beans,* and other things, the men not concerning themselves about it. [Margry, 1875–1886, vol. 3, pp. 363–364.]

Later, in the country of the Naordiche (Namidish), they passed through a region where they "found men and women cultivating their fields in order to sow corn, beans, and pumpkins." But they also had "corn well advanced, almost ready to eat, and a quantity of beans which they were already eating" (Margry, 1875–1886, vol. 3, p. 392). This advanced corn was evidently the "little" or early corn. Regarding their method of cultivation, Joutel says:

These savages have no utensil of iron, and so they can only scratch the earth, not being able to open it very deep; however things grow there wonderfully well. [Margry, 1875–1886, vol. 3, p. 364.]

In the autmn, according to the same writer, they were accustomed to burn over the prairies (pp. 345–346). His party was in the country

---

[12] There is mention of vegetable foods on pages 61, 74, and 86.

of the Assonis (Nasoni) in June, "the season during which they worked their fields, and in consequence feasts were common to which they then invited one another and rejoiced," and they frequently invited the Frenchmen (Margry, 1875–1886, vol. 3, p. 395).

During his 3 months' contact with the Caddo, Joutel did not have opportunities to observe all of the customs connected with planting, and these are given in more detail by the Spanish missionaries. Casañas may be quoted first:

Among the seed which the Indians plant at the proper season, is corn of two kinds, which they plant in abundance. One kind matures in a month and a half and the other in three months. There are five or six kinds of beans—all of them very good, also calabashes, watermelons, and sunflowers. The seed of all these, mixed with corn make very fine *tamales*. They also use another kind of seed like cabbage seed which, ground with corn, makes a kind of meal. But it is necessary to have water at hand, since it is like flour and, when eaten in a dry state, is liable to stick in one's throat. [Casañas, 1927, p. 211.]

On their method of working the fields:

At planting time, they come together and plant whatever each one has to plant, according to the size of the family—beginning first at the home of the grand *xinesí*. There they plant only a small spot in front of the house in order that he may have something green to enjoy. All of the Indians give him portions of what they have so as to dress and clothe him. Next they plant the corn and other crops for the *caddi*. Then they work for the other officials and the old men. In this way they continue working from the highest to the humblest until each has planted what he needs for the year. The *caddices* work like the rest, but the grand *xinesí* never goes out of the house for anything except to take a walk or to make certain visits . . . The Indians have one very wise custom, that is, the men do not work with the women, but apart from them. Those who hunt work steadily, for they are obliged to supply food until the planting is finished. [Casañas, 1927, p. 217.]

The following items are from Espinosa:

Before they begin their planting they inform all the women in order that they may provide food for the day designated. They all gather together, old women, girls, and children. They make two or three mats of little strips of cane which an old woman, who acts as supervisor, provides for them. These they turn over to a captain who makes an offering of them in the fire temple in order that they may have good crops that year. They end the ceremony by eating together all they have brought from their houses and then they adjourn the meeting. There is also a general meeting of men and women in the house of the captain where there is a small fire temple. Here they cut the wood to make their hoes of black walnut.

They clean a spot of ground about a stone's throw in circumference and collect a quantity of wood which they heap up in piles. With great joy they distribute dried deer meat, meal and other foods which have been provided and depart for their homes much pleased. A *tamma*, who is an official among them, goes around and very carefully collects the first fruits of the tobacco, which never fails to produce in season. This he delivers to his captain whose duty it is to ward off the tempests by his conjuring, to pray for rain, and to be the first to bless the first fruits for use. They respect him a great deal, and they are careful to get him to help them to plant their crops. [Espinosa, 1927, pp. 170–171.]

The crops which the Asinais plant are also community crops. They begin first at the house of the *chenesi*, who is their leading priest and the person who takes care of their fire temple, of which I shall speak later in the proper place. They then plant for the principal captain and afterwards for all the rest in their order as fixed by the captains in their assemblies. What the Indians do all together is to clear the land and dig it about the depth of a handbreadth. They do this first with wooden hoes of seasoned walnut, and then with iron hoes which they have acquired from the Spaniards and from the French who live in Natchitoches. This work is finished in two or three hours and the owners of the house give them an abundance of food. They then move to another spot to do the same thing. The planting of the corn and the beans and the other seed is the duty of the householders. Usually the old Indian women do this. They will not permit a woman who is pregnant to help them under any consideration because they say the crop will be spoiled. They plant two crops each year, the first at the end of April, for this is when the rain ceases. They then plant the small corn, the stalk of which is not more than a *vara* [2.78 feet] in height. However, it is covered from bottom to top with ears which are very small but covered with grain. This crop is gathered at the end of May. It is very helpful to them in case the season has been dry. Upon the same ground, after clearing it anew, they plant [the late corn].[13] This crop is gathered at the end of July, as I found from experience during the years that I lived at the mission. They plant their beans in an odd way. In order that the vines may run and be protected from small animals and from mildew, they stick a forked cane at each hill. Thus the vine bears *more abundantly* and it is no trouble for them to gather the crop because they pull up the cane and carry the whole thing home. In their houses they have large baskets made of heavy reeds, into which they put their shelled corn and beans. In order that the weevil may not get in they cover the grain with a thick layer of ashes and then cover the baskets to keep out the rats.

These Indians are so provident that they make a string of the best ears of grain, leaving the shucks on, and put it up on a forked stick at a point in the house where the smoke will reach it. For this purpose, they select the quantity they will need for two years' planting, so that, if the first year is dry, they will not lack seed for the second year. They will not touch a grain of this though all the other corn they had saved for their use is gone. On the contrary, they hurry out to hunt for corn, trading for it on other ranches where the crop was more abundant. [Espinosa, 1927, pp. 156–157.]

Espinosa's description of the first fruits ceremony will be given later. Hidalgo (1927, p. 56) also mentions the communal planting and use of wooden hoes.

Morfi's dependence on Espinosa is self-evident:

Before beginning to plant their fruits they advise the women of the day appointed, so that they can prepare the provisions. When the time arrives all the women, old and young, and girls, meet under the leadership of an old woman who takes care to see that thin reeds have been cut, with which they soon weave two or three mats, which, carefully finished, they offer to one of the old captains, who presents them to the Fire Temple, so that that year

---

[13] Lacuna in publication.

they shall be given abundant crops; and to end the function, they eat together the provisions brought by the women, with which the meeting is dissolved.

Tobacco is one of the plants they cultivate with most anxiety; but they never let it get perfectly ripe; when it is time to pick it, one of the *Tamas* goes from hut to hut, collecting the first crop of this fruit, which he faithfully delivers to the Captain whose duty it is to drive away the storms with his incantations, to pray that rains will not lack at the proper seasons, and to be the first in blessing the new fruits; he is much respected, and they dc his planting for him with special care. They also celebrate the construction of their hoes (*azadones*) holding a meeting of all the men and women of the nation, in the house of a captain where there is a Fire Temple, of the second order. There they cut the wood, which they use in constructing those instruments, which are of black walnut; clear the land in a circle, measuring one stone throw in diameter; they gather an abundance of wood which they place right there in piles, all of which is in preparation for the great festival. They also bring roasted venison, corn meal, and other eatables, which they have prepared. These they divide among themselves in very festive manner, and retire content. [Morfi, 1932, p. 31.]

Sowing is also done by the community. The first one to begin it is the *Chenesi* or Supreme Priest, in whose care is the Sacred Fire. That of the Principal Captain immediately follows, and then that of the other Indians, in the order assigned them by the captains at their meetings. This work is very light, because it is reduced to tilling the soil only one span deep, after having cleared it of undergrowth. This was very painful, however, when they did it with hoes of burned walnut; but today they have an abundance of iron instruments, which are supplied them by the missions of the province and by the Spaniards of Louisiana. This work is finished in two or three hours and the owners of the field then give them something to eat. They go to the other parts to do the same, leaving the sowing to the care of the old Indian women. These take particular care that no pregnant woman participates in this work, persuaded that the least lack of care in this regard would infallibly ruin the crop.

They sow two crops of corn per year; the first at the end of April, which is the time when the rains cease; they plant [the] little corn, whose stalks do not grow to be more than a *vara* [2.78 feet] high; but from the foot to the tassels they are covered with little ears, with much grain. At the end of May they raise this crop, which is a great alleviation to them, if the preceding year was a non-productive one. They clear the land again and plant in it what they call the big seed, which to ripen perfectly, takes only until the end of July. So that these Indians in only three months, usually gather two abundant crops. They plant beans with much care. So that they will rise from the ground and to keep them free from insects, they place at the foot of each plant a reed on which it climbs. By this means it gives more return and it is easier for them to gather, because they cut the plants off, stalk and all, and take them to their houses. Here they make large baskets with *otatillos*, a kind of very strong solid reed, in which they store the shelled corn and the beans, separately, mixing in some cupfuls of well sifted ashes as a preventive against worms, and carefully covering the baskets so that the rats can do no damage.

These Indians are so foresighted that they foretell the possibilities of time. The crop having been gathered, they then select the largest and fullest ears leaving on them the leaves which are immediately next to the grain. They make a long string with them which they hang up in their houses in a place where they will get smoked. This corn they keep for future planting. Fearing the ruin of the first crop, they save such an amount as they deem necessary for two years sowing. This is a sacred deposit which they only use when afflicted by very grave necessity. If they lack grain they resort to some other means but never take a grain of the reserve corn. [Morfi, 1932, p. 43.]

The two kinds of corn are those which the Louisiana French called "little corn," similar to our popcorn, and "flour corn." The wooden hoes were probably of hickory rather than black walnut. The original cultivated plants were corn, beans, pumpkins, sunflowers, and tobacco, but they had introduced watermelons before La Salle entered their country. Joutel did not, indeed, observe them until he reached the Quapaw villages at the mouth of Arkansas River, but he was not among the Hasinai when the crops were ripe, and La Salle brought some back to the coast after his earlier expedition (Margry, 1875–1886, vol. 3, p. 249). Casañas also mentions them only 4 years later. It is evident that they must have been introduced into the Mississippi River region through Texas.

Joutel thus describes how corn was treated:

The women sifted it (*grouler*) and then pounded it and made it into very fine flour. If these Indian women had mills, it would relieve them a great deal, since this is very laborious. They have big mortars which they make out of trunks of trees excavated by means of fire to a certain depth, after which they scrape them out and clean them. As many as four women may beat the corn. Each one has a big pestle about five feet long, and they preserve a cadence in the way the blacksmiths beat on their anvils. After they have pounded for a certain time, they take out the said meal and other women pass it through little sieves which they make very neatly out of large canes, and when they wish to have it very fine they use little winnowing baskets (*vannettes*) on which they shake the said flour, in which the finest remains caught on the bottom; the grits and the bran come out above. In this way they have as fine flour as can be made and as fine as I have seen in France and elsewhere. We paid them for their trouble with beads, needles, rings and other things. [Margry, 1875–1886, vol. 3, p. 367.]

The Cahinnio presented them with two loaves of bread, "the finest and the best we had so far seen; they seemed to have been baked in an oven, and yet we had not noticed any among them" (Margry, 1875–1886, vol. 3, p. 416).

The items contributed by our other authorities are few. Solís remarks that

They live on corn, which is abundant, since the land is so fertile that it yields two harvests a year, and every stalk at least three ears. But they do not have the forethought to grind it because there are no *metates*, and those which they get from the outside cost fifty dollars each; and so they cook it or toast it in order to eat it. *Cormaiz*, as the Tejas call it, is cooked with grease as is common in all the country. [Solís, 1931, pp. 60–61.]

He seems to have been strangely ignorant of, or oblivious to, the use of wooden mortars.

Joutel furnishes the following note regarding the cooking of beans:

These savages raise a good number because they grow very well in this canton; but they do not make much of a mystery in the preparation of them; they limit themselves to placing them in a big pot without removing the strings even, since they cover them with vine leaves, until they are almost cooked

and afterward they salted them by pouring warm water over them in which salt had been dissolved.

After being well cooked, the old woman (*chef*) took care to give each of us his portion in a bark apron (or small hamper), and we cleaned them as we ate. [Margry, 1875–1886, vol. 3, pp. 394–395.]

The use of sunflowers is noted by Espinosa:

They also plant quantities of sunflowers which grow to be quite large. The flower is also enormous. It has the seed in the center like the *piñon*. By mixing it with flour they make a roll of it which is quite savory and satisfying. [Espinosa, 1927, p. 152.]

And Morfi:

They . . . cultivate certain kinds of sunflowers from which, after enjoying their beauty, they use the seeds, which are like little pine-nuts, and which, ground, they mix with corn, and form a dough, which they make into small cakes or tamales of good taste, and much nutriment. [Morfi, 1932, p. 44.]

Hidalgo (1927, p. 55) comments thus: "The seed [of sunflowers] is like corn and this is what they eat in pottage which they make of corn and beans." Sunflowers are also mentioned by Joutel (Margry, 1875–1886, vol. 3, p. 348).

The cultivation of tobacco has been noted. In one place Espinosa (1927, p. 151) speaks of native "powdered tobacco."

In his Declaration, St. Denis says:

Their lands are all cultivated and there is no fruit in the world richer than that found here, nor more wonderful grapes of various kinds and colors in such quantities. The bunches are as large as twenty-eight and thirty-pound shot. [Castañeda, 1936, vol. 2, p. 221.]

This note is of particular interest because the subject of one of Catlin's sketches is "Caddo Indians gathering grapes," a rather unusual scene to associate with the red men.

Of a later period, Solís relates:

They have orchards of various kinds: peaches, plums, persimmons, fig trees, chestnuts, ash[?], pomegranates and other fruit. As in other places they make a paste of figs; they make it of persimmons also and keep it for gifts to present and sell to the Spaniards and the French. [Solís, 1931, p. 61.]

Morfi reproduces him thus:

Besides the land of the fields, they carefully cultivate orchards of which they possess many, and in which they have peaches, free stones, apricots, plums, figs, hazel-nuts, chestnuts, medlars (*nisperos*), Chinese pomegranates, strawberries, and other fruits. With the *nisperos*, after they are dried, they make cakes, which they keep for their provisions, and to sell or give to the Spaniards of Texas and Louisiana. [Morfi, 1932, p. 44.]

If Pénicaut may be trusted, peaches had reached the Natchitoches Indians when they were living with the Acolapissa on Lake Pontchartrain:

They have . . . peaches, in their season, which are very much bigger than those in France and also sweeter; strawberries, plums, and grapes which are a little dry and not at all as big as those in France. There are also nuts which they pound up into flour to make porridge in water for their children; they make of it also hominy (sagamité) or bread, mixing it with cornmeal. [Margry, 1875–1886, vol. 5, p. 468.]

The fruits and nuts anciently used by them were only such as nature supplied.

Casañas (1927, p. 210) remarks that there were "many species of acorns, all of them good, and some of them as sweet as chestnuts. From the other kinds the Indians make a kind of food which serves as bread, just as if it were corn." However, Joutel and his companions were served with "a kind of soup made of acorns which they had cooked in the juices of meat, but," he adds, "it did not seem to me very delicious" (Margry, 1875–1886, vol. 3, p. 369).

"They gather," says Hidalgo, "great quantities of nuts in the hulls and acorns for a year's supply" (Hidalgo, 1927, p. 55).

And Solís:

They eat many nuts which they grind in order to keep them, and the fruit of the medlar tree that is fiery, and other foods and warm drinks. [Solís, 1931, p. 70.]

But Espiñosa is more detailed:

They gather quantities of thick-shelled nuts and acorns to last a whole year. The entire country is filled with various kinds of trees, such as oaks, pines, cottonwoods, live-oaks, large nuts—which yield the thick-shelled nuts— and another kind of tree which yields small thin-shelled nuts. The Indians use all of these as food. In addition to the nut bearing trees, there are other fruit trees, like the medlar, the plum, and the large wild cherry. Among them there is found a white grape that looks like a muscatel. It only needs cultivation to make it as good as the domestic variety.

There are great quantities of red and white mulberries and large blackberries which are very sweet, a great abundance of pomegranates like those in China, and a quantity of chestnuts, although the fruit they yield is small, about like the white-oak acorns. The pastures and other portions of the land are very much like those in Florida—a country contiguous to Texas. Everything that is read about the beauty and fertility of the first named province can be applied to the latter with but little modification. [Espinosa, 1927, pp. 152–153.]

Again:

To make their pap, they grind a seed which the reed grass produces or more preferably the dry seed of the reed. When well cooked they are like grains of wheat and supply the place of corn in their foods. [Espinosa, 1927, p. 157.]

Solís:

> There is another kind [of meal] on which they live that is called *tuqui* that is like the *casave* of Havana. It is made of the roots of a certain tree. These roots are mashed and pounded up in wooden mortars, and they have to be used with grease or lard of the bear. They drink this preparation and it does them great harm in producing dysentery, bloody flux, and sudden fits. [Solís, 1931, p. 61.]

Morfi quotes both:

> When their crops fail them, they gather the seed of reeds, which is the same size as that of wheat, and when it is well parched, it contains much nourishment . . . The root of the *tuqui* tree is also of much aid to them. This they pound up in wooden mortars, pour some bear grease on it, and eat it, as it is, without anything else. [Morfi, 1932, pp. 43–44.]

Evidently many other productions of nature were drawn upon, and Casañas (1927, p. 211) refers to these in general terms as follows: "There are also many kinds of herbs, very good to eat. There are edible roots which, like sweet potatoes, grow under ground. They all grow wild." Along with beans and tamales, De Leon was given "ground nuts" (Bolton, 1916, p. 376).

The granaries on which food was stored have been mentioned already. Hidalgo says: "They put their corn away shelled. They keep their beans, acorns, and nuts in still other reed baskets" (Hidalgo, 1927, p. 56).

ANIMAL FOODS

Before their contact with Europeans the Caddo had no domestic animals except the dog, and that was eaten, if at all, only on ceremonial occasions and in times of famine. Horses reached them in advance of Europeans and the manner of their appearance along with the revolution in native economy which they effected will be considered later. Solís and Morfi speak of turkeys and domestic fowl among the Caddo but they were clearly introduced. Solís has an interesting note on dogs:

> They have . . . some dogs also which they call *jubines* because they are a mixture of dog and coyote or wolf. These dogs are very intelligent and cunning as well as great thieves; they have thin pointed snouts. [Solís, 1931, p. 61.]

Their reputed origin reflects a common belief and not a scientific fact. See Morfi's reference to these dogs on page 137. By 1820 the Caddo had acquired hogs and mules (Padilla, 1919, p. 48).

The basal position of agriculture in Caddo economy is shown by Espinosa's remark that "during the lean years they add to their supply of food by hunting animals and different kinds of birds and by catching fish in the rivers and lagoons" (Espinosa, 1927, p. 157). But this does not mean that they resorted to animal food only during times of want.

Casañas thus describes the animals of the Texas province:

This country contains various kinds of animals that are good to eat, such as wild hogs. They are quite large and savage like those in New Spain. There are many deer, prairie chickens, and wild ducks; but these are to be had only in the winter time. There are two other kinds of ducks, much smaller, but good to eat. There are likewise many kinds of fowls not so large as chickens in Spain. They come at the same time as the wild ducks. Rabbits are also to be had in great numbers and many kinds of birds that stay in the country the year round, such as partridges, quails, herons, and an endless number of birds that sing very melodiously in the spring. [Casañas, 1927, p. 211.]

Espinosa:

The animals that are most abundant in these woods are deer (*ciervos, ó venados*) from which the Indians secure their staple food, together with wild ducks. To these are added during the winter months many bustards and cranes, while partridges and quails are abundant during the entire year. [Espinosa, 1927, pp. 153–154.]

But by 1768 we learn through Solís that

in the woods they live on horses, mules, mares, deer, since there are many, bison which abound, bear, *berrendos* (a species of deer), wild boar, rabbits, hares, dormice, and other quadrupeds, with snakes, vipers, wild turkeys, geese, ducks, hens, partridges, cranes, quail and other birds that are on the beach or on the banks and margins of the rivers, with fish of all kinds, which abound.

He mentions also polecats (Solís, 1931, p. 43).

Aquatic birds were hunted by the Natchitoches on Lake Pontchartrain during the stay of that tribe with the Acolapissa Indians. Pénicaut thus speaks of his participation in this sport:

When the winter arrived we went upon the bayou (*canal*) and in the woods to kill bustards, ducks, and wild geese, which are much larger than those in France. There are during this season prodigious quantities attracted by Lake Pontchartrain on the shores of which they live. We brought some of them every day to be roasted at the cabins in which the savages made good fires on account of the cold, which, however, is not so long nor so severe as on the upper Mississippi. [Margry, 1875–1886, vol. 5, pp. 469.]

On the hunting of larger game, he says:

When they go to the chase, they dress in the skin of the deer with the horns on, and when they see one of these animals at a distance in the woods, they make the same motions as it does, which, as soon as it perceives them, runs up, and, when it is within good range, they shoot it. They kill many in this manner, and it must be admitted that they are more skilful than the French, as well in hunting wild cattle as in the chase of the bear and deer. [Margry, 1875–1886, vol. 5, p. 469.]

Joutel also noted this custom: The Indians, he says, "take the heads of deer which they tan and manipulate so well that on immitating [these animals] they often make them come within range. They hunt turkeys in the same manner" (Margry, 1875–1886, vol. 3, pp. 403–404).

Espinosa in his account of the usage supplies us with some of the rites that accompanied it:

Before they go out to hunt deer, they put on a post in their thatched huts the dry head of a deer including the neck and horns, while they pray to their *caddi ayo* that he will put the prey into their hands, while at intervals they throw pinches of the tobacco that has been provided into the fire. When they have performed this ceremony—which lasts more than an hour—they put its head at the door of the hut and with another just like it they go out in the woods to hunt, covering their naked bodies with white dirt. When they have killed a deer, they divide the animal. For some time they talk into its ear but I do not know the meaning of this puzzle. They load themselves with it for the return trip. They throw it down at the door and the cooks cut it up. They take pains to see that the one who killed it does not eat of it unless the others invite him and that he does not take anything else to satisfy his hunger. [Espinosa, 1927, p. 170.]

Morfi, as usual, parallels Espinosa:

When they want to go out on a deer hunt, they place on one of the beams of the hut, the neck and head of a buck, and pray to Caddi-Ayo to give an abundance of easy game. From time to time they throw ground tobacco into the fire. This being done, which lasts for more than an hour, they put the deer's head at the door of the hut; some boys paint or streak their bodies all over; and stript naked, and with another similar head, and their arms, go out to the wilds, in search of some of these animals. As soon as they find one and kill it, they whisper in its ear for a short while, and with much shouting, take it to the ceremonial hut, and throw it at the door. The owners of the house cut its head off, cut up the animal, cook it for all to eat, taking care that the one who killed it does not taste it, unless very hungry, in which case, invited by one of the guests, he can take all he wants. After such ceremonies they go out very contented to hunt, persuaded that they will return well provided for. [Morfi, 1932, p. 30.]

"Of meat," says Casañas, "they never have more than two kinds, one boiled and the other roasted" (Casañas, 1927, p. 212). He speaks as follows of the buffalo hunt (pl. 11), to which even the eastern Caddo tribes seem to have been much addicted as far back as the time of De Soto:

The Indian men have only one occupation, hunting. Although they are highly skilled in shooting arrows, they are not able to kill a sufficient amount of the game mentioned to supply their wants; and it therefore becomes necessary for them to make use of the buffalo. So, at various times in the year, the Indians come together for the purpose of going out to hunt buffalo. The nearest place they can be found is about four days' travel from this place. The reason for their going in bands to hunt the buffalo is fear of other Indians, their enemies. [Casañas, 1927, p. 211.]

Espinosa:

The buffalo is distant more than forty leagues from the Texas country, and to secure a supply of dried meat the Indians all go well armed because at this time if they fall in with the Apaches the two murder each other unmercifully. At this time, which is usually in the winter, they are accustomed to kill a great number of bears toward the north and they bring home a great deal of bear fat rolled up in moss and loaded on their horses. After rendering it out they keep it in pots for seasoning for the whole year. These bears live on nuts and acorns which abound in this country. They are not seen in the Texas country and the region thereabouts except when the crop of nuts and acorns to the northward has been short on account of the ice and the snow, as happened in the year [17]22, which was the first time I saw them alive so near the mission. Without boasting, I may say that, accompanied by a number of Indians who, with their dogs, had treed two bears, I killed them both with my own hands at one shot, and, from behind the protection of an oak, I succeeded in hitting another bear in the head when he was coming down a pathway alone. After taking their share of everything, the Indians left me enough bears' fat to supply me for many days. It is certainly true that they need nothing else for seasoning when they are supplied with this. [Espinosa, 1927, p. 157.]

Morfi:

With all of this, they do not forget the chase, for which they raise a certain kind of dog they call *Jubine*, with long, sharp-pointed snout, and as cunning as its master. In winter they go out on buffalo hunts, to provide for the kitchen. They also kill many bears at that time, which they quarter and wrap in hay to take home, where they fry them, keeping the grease in proper vessels for provisions for the whole year. There is no doubt that the fat and grease are an admirable supplement for garnishing their food, and even seasoning their salads. On these hunts they always go well armed and proceed with great caution, because, if, while on this trip, they meet the Apaches or other enemy nations, they engage in deadly combat. [Morfi, 1932, p. 44.]

Says Pénicaut:

They accompany all their meals with bear grease which is white in winter when it is congealed, like lard, and in summer like olive oil. It has no bad taste: they eat it with salads, making by means of it pastry, fried dishes, and all [the viands] in general that they prepare. [Margry, 1875–1886, vol. 5, p. 468.]

The following note was obtained by Parsons from the present-day Caddo Indians:

There is no restriction upon bear hunting—"Caddo, not like Kiowa who are afraid to kill a bear they think is a man." In fact, Caddo were great bear hunters (like Shawnee). They would go bear hunting in a party, choosing an honest man, not a liar, to build the camp fire and keep it up. This, in order that the bear would not get away, i. e., would stay near the camp. The party shared evenly in the game. The husband of a pregnant woman may not go hunting, he has to stay at home. Women eat bear meat, but a pregnant woman would probably not eat it. [Parsons, 1941, p. 43.]

Solís enlarges upon the care taken by hunters before crossing open ground where they might be met by enemies:

In securing their supplies they are very wise and cunning; when they have to cross a plain, they remain within the woods for some time, observing carefully to see if there is anything unusual, and if not, they cut a big branch from a tree in order to travel under cover so that those from a distance may not know that it is a man. In order to spy on the people who come in or go out of the woods, they climb a large tree which has a big high top and is near the road; from there they search out and see everything without being seen. [Solís, 1931, pp. 69-70.]

The essentially woodland character of the culture of these people is shown in the surprisingly large use made of fish. Let us quote Espinosa:

There are many lagoons in which an abundance of fish are found. These fish are not always found in the same spots, but the locations vary according to the rises in the rivers and *arroyos* during the winter. When warm weather comes the Indians go with their families to certain spots and stay for some days, living on fish. They carry home quantities of cooked fish. I ate some of these, among them the fish called *dorado* [*dorada?*]. [Espinosa, 1927, p. 153.]

In 1719 the Kadohadacho welcomed La Harpe with "a feast of smoke-dried fish" (Beaurain, 1831, p. 181), but they lived upon Red River where fish were presumably more abundant than with the Hasinai.

Pénicaut's account of fishing operations on Lake Pontchartrain may be added since the Natchitoches Indians took part in these but the Acolapissa, natives to the country, may have been their teachers:

After eating we went to look at their fishery. They drew their nets from the lake filled with fish of all sizes. These nets are actually only lines about six fathoms long. To these lines other little lines are fastened along the entire length about a foot apart. At the end of each line is a fish-hook upon which they put a little piece of hominy dough or a little piece of meat. With these they do not fail to catch fishes weighing more than fifteen to twenty pounds. The ends of the lines are tied to their canoes. They draw them in two or three times a day, and there are always many fish taken when they draw them. This fishery does not prevent them from working the ground, for it is accomplished in less than half an hour. When they had gotten all their fish, each one took theirs home, and, after they were cooked and prepared, as I have already described, with bear grease, they began to eat them, each one in front of his door, under and in the shade of the peach trees. [Margry, 1875–1886, vol. 5, p. 466.]

This kind of "net" is what is called a "trat line" or a "trot line." The eastern Caddo must formerly have depended very largely on fish and no doubt had a number of ways of catching them.

Most of our accounts of Caddo hunting come from the period after they had acquired guns and they adopted them very rapidly though, as late as 1806, Freeman calls the bow and arrow their "principal weapon" (Freeman-Custis, 1806, p. 28). At an earlier date the Kadohadacho country was famous for its bow wood, the Osage orange or bois d'arc. Joutel states that Indians came to their country to get it from distances of 50 or 60 leagues, and that two Caddo Indians joined his party on their way to the Quapaw to barter bows and arrows for products to be had along the Mississippi (Margry, 1875–1886, vol. 5, pp. 412, 424).

It would not be surprising if less savory articles entered into their diet from time to time such, for instance, as Morfi states were added to the menu of the coast tribes:

The coast tribes are unique in their gluttony. They eagerly eat locusts, lice and even human flesh. Their appetite does not require seasoning. They eat raw meat, tallow, bears' fat, and when they have them, are thankful. The best and most tasteful mouthful for them is that which costs them least work. With all of this they show a great passion for spoiled food. There arises from their bodies such a stench that it causes one who is little accustomed to them to become sick at the stomach. [Morfi, 1932, p. 49.]

It must be added in defense of the wretched coast people that the conditions of life in their country often permitted little choice between unsavory food and starvation.

For further notes regarding food used in times of scarcity or on war expeditions, see Morfi's statement in the section on War (p. 190).

SALT

Joutel's two Indian traders mentioned in the last section also had in their possession besides bows and arrows and for the same purpose, that is, barter, "little loaves of salt weighing about two or three pounds apiece." They stated that they had gotten these from the Tunica Indians, but we know that the eastern Caddo, particularly the Natchitoches, were also engaged in this traffic with the Mississippi River tribes (Margry, 1875–1886, vol. 3, p. 424). The salt industry here in De Soto's time seems to have been mainly in the hands of non-Caddo people, but the designation of one of the tribes which the Spaniards met is Naguatex, evidently the Nawidish or Namidish of later writers—which means "Place of Salt" (Robertson, 1933, pp. 238–248). Joutel says of that part of the Namidish tribe which he visited on leaving the Hasinai country:

They have a certain sand for which they go farther towards the hamlet we found last which is called Naouidiche, which signifies "salt," and, according to what I have remarked, the people of this hamlet have taken their name from this sand. They take a handful or two of it more or less, according to the things to be salted, they put in water to steep for a short time, after which they pour this water into the beans or meat which they wish to salt, and it is that which gives it the taste. [Margry, 1875–1886, vol. 3, p. 394.]

In his Declaration, St. Denis states that the Natchitoches had traded with the French since 1701, the chief article of exchange being salt, and he adds that "the salt secured from these Indians was whiter and purer than the salt that came from France" (Castañeda, 1936, vol. 2, p. 18).

Shortly after La Harpe had established himself among the Kadohadacho in the Nasoni town, he sent some of his men to obtain salt at a small stream 3 days' journey away. They returned with 200 pounds

(Margry, 1875–1886, vol. 6, p. 272).   About 15 leagues from the Adai Presidio there was a saline from which quantities of salt were obtained (Morfi, 1935, pt. 1, p. 219), and this is probably the one mentioned by Sibley "a few miles to the westward" of Bayou Pierre "towards Sabine . . . where the inhabitants go and make their salt" (*in* Amer. State Pap., Indian Affairs, 1832, p. 728).

CLOTHING AND PERSONAL ADORNMENT

Caddo clothing was similar to that of their neighbors and of the Southeastern Indians generally.   Most of their garments were made of deerskin or buffalo hide, the latter being used apparently in the main in winter or for the heavier outside coverings.   They were tanned by the use of buffalo, and evidently also deer brains.   In summer men wore little except the breechclout (*tapa-rabo* or *cendal*) which, it is to be assumed, was usually of deerskin.   In colder weather they added shirts, leggings, and moccasins made of buffalo hide— said to have been "beautifully painted and dressed"—and also of deerhide.   Around home they ordinarily went barefoot, moccasins being used in traveling.   At the harvest ceremony "they dress up," says Morfi, "in the best clothes they have such as *bayeta* (*baize*), soft *gamuzas* ["antelope skins" but probably intended for deerskins], with fringes of many little white nuts, black *gamuzas*, spotted at intervals with the same white nuts, bracelets, and necklaces of glass beads, ornaments all of which they use only on this day, or on others of unusual solemnity." (Morfi, 1935, p. 67; 1932, pp. 32, 46; Casañas, 1927, p. 213; Espinosa, 1927, pp. 171, 176–177.)   This, of course, represents the beginning of the adoption of European materials.   Later on in his description of this ceremony, however, Morfi states that some of the old men who took part had "their best clothes of buffalo hides curiously painted" (Morfi, 1932, p. 33).   Another garment was "made very skilfully of turkey feathers fastened by means of small strings" (Margry, 1875–1886, vol. 3, p. 353).

The women also wore breechclouts under their other clothing though the material of which they were made was different.   They put these on at an early age.   Morfi says, speaking of the girls:

From the time of their birth their mothers put breechclouts of grass or hay on them which modestly cover their nakedness and these they keep until death, renewing them when required to do so by necessity, without failing on this account to cover honestly the rest of the body.   [Morfi, 1932, p. 46, quoting from Solís, 1931, p. 42].

Their over-clothing is thus described by Espinosa:

They make their clothes from dressed deer skins, which cover them from head to foot.   These deer skins are very black and have a luster which these Indians alone know how to produce.   It looks like very fine cloth.   To make it more graceful they border all the edges with little white seeds which grow on certain plants. By skillfully piercing them they can easily sew them on. From another large skin, carefully dressed, and with an opening in the middle large enough for the head, they cover their shoulders and breast to the waist. They cut all the edges in fringe, so that the garment is very pretty. [Espinosa, 1927, pp. 176–177.]

Morfi's description which follows is evidently taken mainly from this:

> Their clothes are composed of two *gamuzas* [meaning evidently "deerskins"] : one covers them from the waist to the ankle; and the other with an opening in the center, through which they stick the head, . . . and so shiny that they look like the finest of cloth, and only these Indian women know how to keep them with such perfection. To make their skirts handsomer they border the edges with little white beads which are very small and are seeds of some herbs and are curiously pierced. In the same manner they sew them to the *gamuzas*. They put a little fringe on all edges of the upper garment, which makes it very pretty. [Morfi, 1932, p. 46.]

Solís says simply: "They dress in deerskins fringed and bordered with beads of various colors" (Solís, 1931, p. 60).

None of our Spanish writers, with one possible exception (see Manufactures, p. 158), mentions the use of textiles in the native costume aside from buffalo hair and materials of European origin, but Pénicaut, who professes to have spent the winter of 1706–1707 in the house of the Natchitoches chief when the Natchitoches were exiled from their own country and on the shores of Lake Pontchartrain, says that the chief's daughters wore skirts (*braguets*) made of cloth woven from nettles (Margry, 1875–1886, vol. 5, p. 465). This material, or mulberry bark, was commonly used for the clothing of women in the Southeast, and it may be assumed that the eastern Caddo were familiar with it though this happens to be our only reference.

Pénicaut states that both the Natchitoches, and the Acolapissa with whom they were living, removed all their body hair by the use of shell-lime and hot water (Margry, 1875–1886, vol. 3, p. 356). As to the general custom of removing this hair there can be no doubt and it is partly confirmed by Casañas (1927, p. 285), who says that they took "great pains to rid themselves of eyebrows and beard by the use of a shell." Other writers on the Southeastern Indians, however, speak of the use of shells as tweezers and one wonders whether Pénicaut is not mistaken as to the method.

Regarding their manner of dressing the hair, Joutel relates that most of the men had "their hair cut with the exception of some tresses which they fasten to or twist around a little piece of wood worn at one side, but all have a little scalplock on top of their head behind, like the Turks. However, some retain all their hair and do not cut any of it; [their hairs] are all straight, coarse, and as black as jet" (Margry, 1875–1886, vol. 3, p. 356). The men in the Kadohadacho province "cut their hair like the Capuchins; they grease it, and when they hold an assembly or have a feast they put upon it swan or duck down tinted red" (Margry, 1875–1886, vol. 3, p. 413).

The men [says Casañas] like to have nice long hair spread over their shoulders, and to have it well combed. Those who do not have hair of this kind, take great pains to scrape the head into the form of a tonsure, leaving in the middle of the head some long hair which reaches to the waist. [Casañas, 1927, p. 285.]

This last type is what Espinosa has in mind when he remarks:

They do not wear their hair long but cut close, leaving it about two finger lengths long, all very much alike and carefully combed. . . . They leave a thin lock of hair in the middle of the head like a Chinaman. To this they tie certain very beautiful feathers in a very curious manner. In this way each one looks like a sprout. When they see the feathers of the chickens from Spain which we raise they do not stop until they have collected the prettiest colored ones. They keep them in a chest to wear at their brightest. [Espinosa, 1927, p. 176.]

Morfi:

They cut their hair, leaving it about two fingers long, and they always wear it very much greased and even. In the middle of their head they let grow a thin, long lock, (like the Chinese) which they curiously adorn with rare and beautiful feathers. [Morfi, 1932, p. 45.]

A confirmative description comes from Sanchez:

They cut their hair in many different ways, but in every case the hairless spaces alternate with those with hair. The most striking of these hair cuts are those in which the wearer pulls all the hair out by the roots, leaving only a band or strip along the top of the head from the forehead to the base of the head [i. e., the back of the neck], imitating the comb of a rooster. [Sanchez, 1926, pp. 284–285.]

Joutel says of the Kadohadacho women: "Their hair is fastened behind, and they take much pains to part it in front" (Margry, 1875–1886, vol. 3, p. 413). Let us now quote Espinosa:

They always wear their hair tied, carefully combed, and dressed like a queue. After gathering it into a knot, they tie it into a curious knot at the neck with a red rabbit skin which they have colored for the purpose with an herb which grows throughout the whole region. [Espinosa, 1927, p. 177.]

He is partly paralleled again by Morfi:

Their hair, which is usually light, they wear always very well combed and braided, which they let hang, and tie it curiously at the head with a small cord of rabbit skin and dye it with the juice of certain herbs in which the country abounds. [Morfi, 1932, p. 46.]

Pénicaut asserts that, unlike the Indians with whom they were then living, the Natchitoches did not resort to tattooing (Margry, 1875–1886, vol. 5, p. 467), but it is evident that the custom was in vogue among most of the Caddo tribes though it is often difficult to tell whether tattooing is being described or painting. Joutel is, of course, describing the former when he says:

These savages have a singular usage: it is that of tattooing (*se piquer*) upon the body where they make all sorts of designs which remain marked permanently, since after they have made the punctures they force into them finely pounded charcoal which makes the marks permanent. The men make representations of birds and animals; the others tattoo on their breasts compartments very neatly made, and on their shoulders they have great flowers [or ornaments (*fleurons*)] which we call *du point d'Espagne* [a kind of pillow lace in which gold or silver threads were interwoven and popular in Spain]. Without doubt they suffer much pain when these are made; it is only once and for good. [Margry, 1875–1886, vol. 3, p. 349.]

One of his companions who had taken up his residence among the Indians "was tattooed like them and marked on the face so that he differed from them little" (Margry, 1875–1886, vol. 3, p. 353). Tonti describes the Kadohadacho of both sexes as "tattooed on the face and all over the body" (Cox, 1905, vol. 7, p. 48).

Bienville says of the Nakasa (perhaps part of the Yatasi) "all the savages here have a circle tattooed round the eyes and on the nose and three lines on the chin." Espinosa states that

none of these [Hasinai] Indian women have more than one line painted in the middle of the face, but they tattoo their arms and breast very curiously. This is done with a pointed instrument when they are children. [Margry, 1875–1886, vol. 4, p. 440.]

For "painted" in this quotation we should evidently read "tattooed," since the same subject is rendered by Morfi:

On the face they have a [single] streak from the root of the hair to the chin; but they paint their breasts and arms with a diversity of figures; a cruel operation which is performed on them while they are children. [Morfi, 1932, p. 440.]

If it were simply paint there would have been no cruelty. The same writer adds in another place:

These women streak their bodies with all kinds of figures, of animals, birds, or flowers, that is, the married women, or corrupt ones, of whom there is an abundance, do; but the girls have only one streak . . . which runs from the forehead to the point of the nose, and ends on the chin, so that nothing is as easy there, as to recognize the different kinds of women, for they themselves take care to increase the streaks when they in any way lose their virginity. [Morfi, 1932, pp. 46–47; Solis, 1931, p. 42.]

Part of what Joutel has to say on the subject of ornamentation, as already quoted, seems to apply to the women. He adds:

The women have very good busts, their features are beautiful enough, but they spoil them in different ways: some make a single line extending from the top of the forehead to the chin; others a kind of triangle at the corner of each eye, with those that they make on their breasts and shoulders; they also tattoo their lips all over, and when they are thus tattooed it is for life. I do not doubt that they suffer when these [marks] are made since it is necessary to draw the blood in order to let the charcoal enter. But the breast is a very sensitive part of the body. [Margry, 1875–1886, vol. 3, p. 363.]

He found that the women of the Kadohadacho province had also disfigured their breasts and faces "by making marks upon them in the way described already" (Margry, 1875–1886, vol. 3, p. 413).

Joutel has little to say regarding the use of paint apart from tattooing, but on one occasion he observes that a troop of women entered the cabin where he was, having their faces and their bodies daubed and painted (*matachez et barbouillez*) (Margry, 1875–1886, vol. 3, p. 375). In describing the Hasinai country the missionary Olivares says that it contained certain heavy green rocks used by the natives in making green paint (Castañeda, 1936, vol. 2, p. 72). Casañas remarks of the same region "there are also some mines [deposits] of *almagres* [red ocher] so fine and so much prized by certain distant tribes that they carry it away to their own country" (Casañas, 1927, p. 209), and adds that the women "like to paint themselves from the waist up to the shoulders in various colored streaks, particularly the breasts. They paint themselves with great care" (Casañas, 1927, p. 285). But, as he does not speak specifically of tattooing elsewhere, it is possible that tattooing is included in this statement. In connection with his account of native festivals and preparations for war, he considers the matter at greater length:

Their custom of painting themselves for their *mitotes* is ridiculous. They use paints of various colors and all gather together in one place whenever they are ready to set out on a war expedition. They claim that the paint serves to keep their enemies from recognizing them. They do the same thing for the same reason whenever they know that visitors are coming from some other tribe. [Casañas, 1927, p. 214.]

Speaking of the men, Espinosa (1927, p. 176) notes that "they paint their faces with vermilion and bears' grease so as to be redder and slicker," and Solís (1931, p. 60): "They are very much painted with vermilion and other colors." Morfi (1932, p. 46): "They paint their faces with vermilion and bear grease so as to make their complexions smooth and of high color. This mixture notably disfigures their natural beauty."

After Sanchez has described the manner in which Caddo men removed the hair from the sides of their heads, he continues:

On the artificially bald space they apply different colors in waving and snakelike stripes that reach to below the neck. They are all fond of making their faces show a vermilion red. The Indians thus give themselves the name of red men, establishing thereby a race group like the white or black races. Perhaps the predilection shown by the American Indians for vermilion is derived from a vain idea of race consciousness or lineage, for though they apply different colors to their faces they prefer red above all others. [Sanchez, 1926, p. 285.]

Padilla (1820) remarks that "they paint their faces with vermilion and charcoal," which at least adds the information that they used black paint as well as red (Padilla, 1919, p. 49).

Casañas has the following regarding ornaments:

Neither the men nor the women lack articles of adornment for their festivities, such as collars, ornaments, and pendants such as the Mexican Indians wore when they were heathens. These Indians knew neither gold nor silver. Many of their ornaments they have secured from other nations, such as glass beads, bells, and other things of a similar nature which are not to be found in this country. At their festivities some of the guests pride themselves on coming out as gallants, while others are of so hideous a form that they look like demons. They even go so far as to put deer horns on their heads, each conducting himself according to his own notion. [Casañas, 1927, p. 213.] . . . They are fond of bells . . . They also like hats, glass beads, and everything in the shape of ornaments; and things which make a noise. In lieu of these, they wear little white shells they find in the fields which are shaped like beads. They wear snake rattles, deer hoofs, and other similar things, all of which they fasten to their leather garments, so as to make a great deal of noise. The women also like these things very much . . . The men like fine feathers. [Casañas, 1927, p. 285.]

Ornamental feathers were preserved "with great care in hollow clean reeds" [Morfi, 1932, p. 46.]

Espinosa speaks of the Indian costumes of

very fine deer skins, with ruffles decorated with little white ornaments, some very black deer skins, decorated with the same ornaments, bracelets, and necklaces which they wear only on this and other feast days. [Espinosa, 1927, p. 171.] . . . The men love very much to wear certain curious ornaments in their ears and when they secure earrings, beads, or necklaces, they wear them around their necks, or on their ankles and knees in their *fiestas.* [Espinosa, 1927, p. 176.]

Solís says that "they wear numerous beads of many colors as well as many feathers of various colors," while the women had "some smooth long bones hanging from their ears" (Solís, 1931, p. 60). In an earlier description, inclusive of Coahuilteco, Karankawa, and Aranama Indians as well as the Caddo, he observes that "they make holes in the muscles of their noses and the tips of their ears in order to hang beads in them, also little shells, small conk shells from the sea, small stones of various colors" (Solís, 1931, p. 43). Morfi repeats about what the others have said: "They like very much to place some curious things in their ears, and when they acquire earrings, necklaces, or beads, they adorn their necks, wrists, and knees," but he also notes the use of buffalo wool in the manufacture of "belts, ribbons, and other dress ornaments" (Morfi, 1932, pp. 45, 46).

We notice the stress laid upon the European origin of many of their ornaments by Casañas, Espinosa, and Morfi, and this may explain why Joutel has so little to say regarding anything but paint, feathers, and tattoo marks. It is also singular that none of these early writers except Solís, whose remarks are general, mentions nose ornaments since in later times they were used so frequently that "the Caddo tribal sign [is] 'Pierced nose,' in allusion to their former custom of boring the nose for the insertion of a ring" (Mooney, 1896, p. 1092).

Nevertheless, Morfi, in speaking of the means of distinguishing one tribe from another makes this as his fifth point, that "they can be distinguished from one another by their ears, and noses, because some pierce the former, and others the latter, and some, both" (Morfi, 1932, pp. 20, 21). Nose ornaments also appear in Sanchez's report:

Some wear a bunch of silver earrings joined with lead and suspended from the nose, hanging over the mouth; others wear in like manner the figure of a small horse. On their ears they wear similar clusters or strings of small metal plates that fall as far as the breast. (See pl. 12.) The Caddos commonly wear a medal more than two inches in diameter, and they have the entire lobe of the ear pierced with holes for glass beads, or feathers. Others, instead of metal ornaments wear well-cured heads of birds. [Sanchez, 1926, p. 284.]

This description is not wholly confined to the Caddo, but Padilla (1820) states of them specifically: "They pierce their noses and wear pendant silver ornaments of different kinds" (Padilla, 1919, p. 49).

The dress of the medicine man was in many ways peculiar. Morfi says of him:

He has a costume becoming to his ministry, decorated with big bunches of feathers (grandes plumeros), adding necklaces made with skins of coral-colored snakes, which are very showy and of bright colors. [Morfi, 1932, p. 27.]

If these were skins of the serpent now known as the coral snake, it should have been sufficiently powerful medicine for any doctor, and it is to be suspected that the medicine men were not unaware of the potency of coral-snake poison.

Turkey tails were used as fans in dances.

In addition to his specific information, Morfi has considerable to say regarding the differences in dress between various tribes, one item of which has already been quoted. Tribes might also be distinguished "by the lines with which they paint their faces, which each nation does in a different way" (Morfi, 1932, p. 20), and

by the cut of the hair; some form a kind of ring or tonsure, as the Friars have; others cut off all their hair, leaving on the top of the head a large lock or braid in Tartar style, of natural length, which they care and esteem very much; and some of them do not cut their hair at all. [Morfi, 1932, p. 20.]

Although they were recorded at a relatively late date (1820), Padilla gives a number of interesting particulars bearing on distinctions between the Caddo tribes. The Kadohadacho "pierce their noses and wear pendant silver ornaments of different kinds. They shave a part of their heads with razors, and paint their faces with vermilion and charcoal." The "Yuganís," (perhaps a band of Yowani Choctaw rather than Caddo), living east of Nacogdoches, differed from the Kadohadacho "in being a little darker and in shaving their beards in streaks with lancets, using charcoal." The Nacogdochitos, on Neches River like the Yuganís, resembled them "except in the streaks they make on their faces." The Eyeish differed from the Kadohadacho "only in language and in the manner of shaving their heads . . . They pierce their noses and paint their faces with vermilion" (Padilla, 1919, p. 49). The San Pedro Indians (Nabedache) "do not shave their faces, although they cut their hair in such a way as to make them different from the Texas Indians [Hainai?]." These two tribes lived near each other "and the difference can scarcely be distinguished, except by the way they cut their hair and by the name." The Anadarko "are darker than the Kadohadacho and some of them shave their faces in streaks" (Padilla, 1919, p. 49).

For a good description of war paraphernalia we have to turn again to Pénicaut, who accompanied St. Denis to Mexico through the Hasinai country in 1714 and testifies as follows regarding these last mentioned people:

These savages make war very differently from those on the banks of the Mississipy, for they are all mounted, armed with quivers made of ox [buffalo] hide and filled with arrows, which hang slung over their shoulders behind the back; they have a bow and a little shield (*plastron*) also of rawhide, on the left arm with which they parry the arrows. They have no other bit to their bridle than a hair cord which passes into the horse's mouth; their stirrups are suspended by a cord also made of hair which is fastened to a doe skin doubled into four thicknesses and serving them as a saddle. The stirrup is merely a little piece of wood three inches wide and five long, on which they put the foot in order to mount and hold themselves in place. [Margry, 1873–1886, vol. 5, p. 502.]

Morfi says that saddles as well as shields were made of buffalo hide (Morfi, 1935, p. 67).

In 1805 Sibley tells us that the Natchitoches Indians still retained their Indian dress but he does not take the trouble to describe it (Sibley, in Amer. State Pap., Indian Affairs, 1832, p. 724). In 1820 Padilla notes that the men were wearing shirts made of "chintz or flowered goods" and indicates that the women were using the same material (Padilla, 1919, p. 53). According to Casañas, they liked European materials of a blue color more than any others (Casañas, 1927, p. 285). Head deformation seems a former custom (see p. 31 and Walker, 1935).

Photographs of Caddo Indians taken during the last half century show few vestiges of their ancient clothing, although we recognize moccasins of a common Plains type (see also pl. 13) and shirts which may be descended from aboriginal patterns appear with fringed margins. The edges of the leggings are also fringed. In one case the leggings appear to be tied just above the ankle. The hair is parted in the middle and brought into two braids, one on either side of the head, the ends being tied with hide or beaded cords. One shows a braided scalplock hanging over the forehead and several have a feather or two in the hair. One shows a headband, but this seems to belong rather to the tribes farther east and there are scanty references in the literature. The hair of the women, as was to have been expected, is parted in the middle and seems to be gathered into knots behind.

HOUSES

Our earliest descriptions of Caddo houses are from French explorers. Of the Nabedache houses, Father Anastasius says:

Their cabins are fine, forty or fifty feet high, of the shape of bee-hives. Trees are planted in the ground and united above by the branches, which are covered with grass. The beds are ranged around the cabin, three or four feet from the ground; the fire is in the middle, each cabin holding two families. [Cox, 1905, vol. 1, p. 232.]

Joutel is more liberal in his estimate of the number of families to a cabin but otherwise his description is much the same:

There are usually eight or ten families in these cabins which are very large, for they are some sixty feet in diameter; they are made in a different way from those we had seen before. They are round, in the shape of beehives or rather like big haystacks, being of the same material except that they are taller; they are covered with grass from bottom to top. They make the fire in the middle, the smoke escaping above through the grass. These savages make them in a manner different from the others; they cut down tall trees as big around as the thigh, they plant them erect in a circle and bring the ends together above, after which they lath them and cover them from bottom to top.

When we were inside of the said cabin, one of the largest in the canton, a place was indicated to us where we could put our property and lie down, for they are much more convenient than those which we had met before, in that the savages raise the beds on which they lie about three feet from the ground; they furnish them very neatly with large reeds, separating each bed by means of mats, of which they form a sort of arbor. [Margry, 1875–1886, vol. 3, p. 345.]

A little farther on he contributes a note regarding the houses of the "Assoni" (Nasoni):

The cabins of these savages are made like those of the Cenis [Hasinai], of which I have spoken already, except that they are not so lofty; there is a large platform above the door, made of pieces of wood planted upright with others across them, and rows of canes pressed very closely together, on which they put their ears of corn. There is another opposite on which they place tuns or casks which they make of canes and bark, in which they put their shelled corn, beans, and nuts, acorns and other things, and under that they put their pots. Each family has its own tuns; they have their beds to right and left, and of the kind I have already described. These [Indians] have besides a big platform in front of their cabins which is raised from ten to twelve feet, on which they put their ears of corn to dry, after they have gathered them, and which they take care to sweep every day. [Margry, 1875–1886, pp. 393–394.]

Joutel also speaks of an assembly house made when a war party was being collected and in which the warriors stayed until they were ready to march, after which it was burned (Margry, 1875–1886, pp. 345, 347, 357). It was probably made like the permanent houses but with less care.

Massanet thus describes the house of the Nabedache (Tejas) chief as it appeared in 1690:

The house is built of stakes [poles] thatched over with grass, it is about twenty *varas* high, is round, and has no windows, daylight entering through the door only; this door is like a room-door such as we have here. In the middle of the house is the fire, which is never extinguished by day or by night, and over [?] the door on the inner side there is a little mound of pebbles very prettily arranged. Ranged around one half of the house, inside, are ten beds, which consist of a rug made of reeds, laid on four forked sticks. Over the rug they spread buffalo skins, on which they sleep. At the head and foot of the bed is attached another carpet forming a sort of arch, which, lined with a very brilliantly colored piece of reed matting, makes what bears some resemblance to a very pretty alcove. In the other half of the house where there are no beds, there are some shelves about two *varas* [5.56 feet] high, and on them are ranged large round baskets made of reeds (in which they keep their corn, nuts, acorns, beans, etc.), a row of very large earthen pots like our earthen jars, these pots being used only to make the *atole* when there is a large crowd on the occasion of some ceremony, and six wooden mortars for pounding the corn in rainy weather, (for, when it is fair, they pound it in the courtyard).[14]

This was probably the same house as that described by Joutel 3 years earlier, but Massanet adds some details regarding out-houses attached to that of the chief.

Soon I noticed, outside the yard, opposite the door of the governor's house, another long building, in which no inmates could be seen. I asked who dwelt therein or what purpose it served, and was told that the captains were lodged in that house when the governor called them to a meeting. On the other side I saw yet another and smaller vacant house, and upon my inquiring about this one they answered that in the smaller house the pages of the captains were lodged, for there is a law providing that each captain shall bring his page when the governor assembles the captains, and they observe this custom. As soon as they arrive they are lodged in that house, and for each one is laid a large, brightly colored reed mat, on which they sleep, with a bolster made of painted reeds at the head; and when they return home, each one carries with him his mat and pillow. While they attend the meeting the governor provides them with food, until he sends them home. [Casis, 1899, p. 304; see also Bolton, 1916, p. 378.]

Two of our Spanish authorities give not merely descriptions of the Hasinai houses but the social and ceremonial customs accompanying their erection. The earlier of these is by Espinosa:

Their houses are built of wood with very long, flexible laths [poles]. Their manner of building them is as follows. Whenever the owners of a house de-

---

[14] Casis, 1899, pp. 303–304. The height is evidently exaggerated as 20 varas would be 55.6 feet. See also Bolton, 1916, pp. 377–378.

cide to build one, they advise the captains whom, in their language, they call *caddi*. The latter set the day and order the overseers whom they call *tammas* to go around to all the houses and give notice in order that all may aid in the building. These two messengers mount their horses—of which the Texas Indians have a great number since the first entry of the Spaniards. They carry in their hands a number of little sticks equal to the number of laths [poles] needed for the house. They go the rounds and leave at each ranch one of the little sticks so that he who receives it may take care to cut and clean a lath [pole] and bring it and put it in the hole designated for it. Another member of the household is placed in charge of a sufficient number of men to continue the work of lacing the laths [poles] together. These thongs, made of the bark of a tree, are so strong that they can not be broken between the hands however thin they may be. To the Indian women, one or two from each house, is given the duty of bringing a load of grass. This grass is coarser than the largest wheat and is used to cover the whole roof. These arrangements being made, the *tammas* go and sleep at the place where the building is to be done. When day breaks, they call the people designated together. At dawn, the captains arrive and take their places without putting their hands to the work other than to oversee it. At sunrise, upon the first call of the messenger, each comes running with his lath [pole] on his shoulder and puts it in the hole which he has previously dug. The laths [poles] are placed in a circle and in the middle they put up a very tall pole with knots on it for climbing. Two Indians are placed on top on a cross made of two pieces of wood. Each throws out a noose and seizes a lath [pole] by the top, working in unison. They continue to tie them until they have forced a figure like a half orange.

They then cover the laths [poles] with heavy timbers, all working at the same time and with such dexterity that, each working upward upon his own lath [pole], they do not take more than an hour to finish it from bottom to top. Others come in to relieve them and cover the house with grass to a thickness of three hand breadths. They work from the bottom to the top exactly opposite to the way the Spaniards thatch their houses. They work so dexterously that a little after midday they are finishing the hut, forming of carefully tied grass the figure which their imagination suggests to them. The building finished, they cut the middle post off at the bottom and the building is thus left standing. During all this time the overseer walks around with his rods made of two or three fresh, flexible branches for the purpose of hurrying the people. Even though they bring the materials they have been instructed to provide, he goes out to meet the man or woman who is late and who arrives after the work is begun. If the delinquent is a man, the overseer gives him four or five licks across the breast and, if it be a woman, he uncovers her shoulders and does the same thing. This is done without exception of persons, for even though it be his own wife or sister who is at fault, she receives her punishment. No one is offended at this but rather laughs at it. During all the time the people are working the householders are busy preparing food for everybody, having previously provided quantities of deer meat and many pots of ground corn, which in this section of the Indies is called *atole*. Then they serve the food from the captains down to the smallest, in order, abundantly, and carefully, because they have earthen vessels, some large and some small, in which to serve the old and the young. This done, the crowd scatters and each goes to his own home much pleased. The difference they make in building these houses is that they use more laths [poles] than usual for the captains and leading men. Consequently, their houses are very much larger. But no one, even though he be a leading captain, is excused from feeding all those who assemble. In fact, the feast is all the more abundant and more time is used in preparation so that everybody may be abundantly fed. [Espinosa, 1927, 154–155.]

He states that the temple common to the Neches and Hainai was "large, round, and thatched" (Espinosa, 1927, p. 160).

Morfi's description is, in the main, taken from Espinosa:

When the father of a family wishes to construct or move a house he advises the *Caddi* or principal captain of the tribe and with his consent, determines a day for the work. The captain calls the cryers or *Tammas* of the tribe and delivers to them as many little sticks as the number of poles thought necessary, commanding them to go to all the houses of the tribe so [that] their inmates will participate in the work. Immediately, the two *Tammas* get on horseback, and proceed to the different places. They leave one or more of these sticks at each *rancheria*, according to the number of poles they are to supply already trimmed and ready to be nailed in their respective places. To another man of the family he gives charge of a number of twigs which they use for weaving the walls between the poles, and the leash to bind them, which is the bark of a tree, so strong that though it is very thin, a strong man cannot break it in his hands. To one or two women of the same *rancheria* is entrusted the cutting and gathering of grass which is used to make the roof to cover the edifice. This grass is longer than entire wheat stalks and very suitable for the use. All of this having been arranged among the whole tribe, on the evening of the assigned day, the *Tammas* go to sleep at the place where the new habitation is to be constructed, and there the future owners give them splendid presents. At dawn of the following day, they begin to cry out, to call the people together. The captains arrive first, and take their seats, without otherwise participating in the work, which is authorized by their presence. As the sun rises, the first voice to be heard is that of the *Mandon* or Director of the work; each one runs with his pole on his shoulder and nails [sets] it in its corresponding place which is already prepared in a circle. In the center of this is placed a heavy log with notches from top to bottom, like a ladder. Two Indians climb this log pulling together the ends of the poles that form the circle, and tie them to the center, forming a sort of cupola, or dome. While this is being done the other workmen begin to weave the long twigs between the poles so skilfully that each workman carrying on his weaving along his post can complete the entire structure in less than an hour. Other Indians, after having partaken of refreshments, enter and cover the house with grass three spans long. They begin by placing it at the bottom and working upward in the opposite direction used by the Spaniards in the neighboring provinces, but with such velocity that by a little after midday they crown the work or little house, constructing at the tip, with the same grass, the figure they care to improvise. They then cut the great log from the center, and the house is finished.

During the work the Directors go about with some flexible green branches with two or three prongs, hurrying the people. If anyone arrives late, though he brings the material assigned to him, the Director goes out to receive him; if a man, he gives him four or five strokes across the breast; and if a woman, he bares her shoulder and gives her an equal number of strokes. This punishment is inflicted without exception to everyone, because even though it be the sister or wife of the Director himself, who is guilty of the offense, she must inevitably suffer the same punishment. There is never anyone, in consequence, who commits this offense[!]. During the work the owners of the house prepare the dinner, for which they have provided in advance, venison, ground corn, the latter being used by the Indians to make much *atole*, or *poteadas*, and they go around serving it abundantly and with order, from the captains to the last member present, offering it in little clay pans (*cajuetillas*), which are very curious. When the eating is finished the meeting breaks up. The houses of the captains and principal people contain more poles than those of the common people; but not one, not even the first chief of the nation, is exempt from giving this festival, but on the contrary, the abundance of the food increases in proportion to the rank of the owner of the house.

As soon as the hut is delivered to the owners they construct their beds, raised from the floor on four stakes, on which they fix some poles; they stretch on them some buffalo hides which make a good mattress, and they cover them with others. [Morfi, 1932, pp. 40–42.]

The same writer states that the temple was constructed like one of the private dwellings except that it was larger (Morfi, 1932, p. 24).

Brief notes from other writers serve mainly to confirm the descriptions already given. Hidalgo says:

Their houses are made of grass, some of them quite large and tall. Others are medium sized and others still smaller like half an orange. In each of these many families live. They keep their corn in lofts and garrets and in big reed baskets. [Hidalgo, 1927, p. 56.]

Elsewhere, however, he adds the interesting fact that they "have the doors of all their houses toward the east," and continues, "I heard them tell the soldiers . . . they did this because it never blows from that side, [but] I do not understand the mystery" (Hidalgo, 1927, p. 52).

Solís:

These Indians live in grass houses that are round and very well sheltered; since they are roofed from the ground, they look like domes. The beds are hung up high on thick poles in the woods. [Solís, 1931, p. 60.]

Some mistake has probably been made in translating the last sentence. Solís evidently meant to say that the thick poles were obtained in the woods or were made of wood.

Padilla: "The Caddo houses are of straw, some are of wood, but all are well built" (Padilla, 1919, pp. 47, 48). The San Pedro (Nabedache) Indians "build their houses of straw because it is easier [to handle] than wood. But their houses are large and usually neat" (Padilla, 1919, p. 52).

Parker (quoted by Schoolcraft): The Caddo, Hainai, Anadarko, Waco, and Tawakoni "live in houses built of a framework of poles, in a conical shape, thatched with long prairie grass, with low doors; the fires built in the centre of the lodge; the lodge, circular, about twenty-five feet in diameter and twenty high" (Schoolcraft, 1855, vol. 5, p. 682).

Mooney:

They formerly lived in conical grass houses like the Wichita, but are now in log houses and generally wear citizens' dress excepting in the dance [Mooney, 1896, p. 1094.]

See also page 181, and plates 14 and 15. The first of the two illustrations is from a negative made by Soulé between 1868 and 1872 and shows that Caddo architecture had become considerably modified at the time indicated. The second, from a sketch by Eastman dated March 2, 1849, the use of which was kindly furnished by the late David I. Bushnell, Jr., illustrates very well the manner in which Caddo hunting camps were distributed over the country before the tribe moved from Texas. Mr. Bushnell also suggested that the "sickle" shown in plate 16, figure 1, made from the lower jaw of a deer, was used in cutting grass for the thatch.

With the exception of the resort to cabins of white provenience in later times, all of these accounts indicate dwellings practically identical with the grass houses of the Wichita. There is, however, evidence that a different type was in use among the Kadohadacho. In the "map of the Cadodacho Indian settlements, near Texarkana," reproduced from the original in the Archivo General de Indias by Prof. H. E. Bolton as the frontispiece to his volume on Texas in the Middle of the Eighteenth Century (Bolton, 1915; pl. 1 in this bulletin), most of the houses seem to be grass houses of the conventional type or granaries, but a few, particularly one on a mound which is presumably a temple, have what look like wattle walls. And Casañas says:

Some have settlements better organized than others, such as the *Cadaudachos*, *Nasitow*, and others whose houses are located close together and are well plastered. [Casañas, 1927, p. 287.]

This variation may probably be attributed to influences from the Mississippi Valley.

The communal nature of house construction is emphasized by the writer last quoted:

As regards other features of their government, these Indians help each other in such a manner that if one's house and all his possessions are burned up, they all gather together, build him a new house, and furnish him whatever he needs for his subsistence and comfort. [Casañas, 1927, p. 217.]

We have one reference to a skin tent used during hunting trips. Shortly before reaching the village of the Petit Caddo, De Mézières

met the Indian chief in a field tent which they make of hides or skins of the deer which they kill. It was so small that there was scarcely room in it for a bench of reeds with a buffalo [hide], which was his bed. There was another little tent where he had the fire, which this people are never without. [Bolton, 1914, vol. 2, p. 76.]

It would be interesting to know whether this elementary affair had any features in common with the tipi but no details are forthcoming.

In later times the Caddo did not have the reputation of being a mound-building people. In the sketch reproduced by Bolton, however, one structure, probably a temple, is located upon a mound, and De Mézières states specifically that the temple of the Nabedache was built upon a mound "which their ancestors erected" (Bolton, vol 2, 1914, p. 263). This use of mounds for temples, even artificial mounds, does not prove that the Caddo erected them, but there is no good reason to doubt it since the erection of mounds was common to all the tribes of the lower Mississippi south of the Quapaw.

MANUFACTURES

Except for their descriptions of house building and some few notes on clothing already given, little is said by our authorities regarding native manufactures. In general they resembled those of the Southeastern cultural area to which the Caddo properly belonged, but their proximity to the Plains added some new features. They appear in the sixteenth century as buffalo hunters and their dependence on the buffalo for raw materials was particularly close, so that Morfi's remarks, although not restricted in application to the Caddo, certainly included them:

In addition to furnishing meat that deserves first rank for its flavor and healthfulness, its brains serve to soften leather; its horns to make spoons, cups, and ornaments for the head or the home; the shoulder blades to dig and cultivate the soil; the ligaments to string the bows; the hoofs to make glue used in tipping the arrows; the bristles to make rope; the wool to make belts, ribbons, and other dress ornaments; the skin to make saddles, rope, shields, tents, shirts, boots, and shoes [i. e., leggings and moccasins], and coverlets against the cold or rain. [Morfi, 1935, p. 67.]

As it happens, this contains the only reference bearing on the material of which spoons were made though such articles are mentioned by Casañas (1927, p. 212) and several were collected by Dr. Edward Palmer for the National Museum (pl. 16, fig. 2). As in the eastern woodlands generally, the deer was also a prime source of raw materials, its skin supplying clothing, its brains being used in tanning along with those of the buffalo, and its tendons being employed in all sorts of ways. Joutel's party carried along their provisions in deerskin bags, following probably the example of the natives (Margry, 1875–1886, vol. 3, p. 359). We have described the manner in which deer heads were used in stalking other deer. Joutel and his companions were seated upon bearskin rugs by the Cahinnio (Margry, 1875–1886, vol. 3, p. 515) and we may safely assume that bearskins were used as clothing though there is no mention of the fact.

Turning to wood as raw material and passing over the houses, besides the ordinary beds around the inside of them, we may note special seats of greater height used by the xinesí and the cadis.

These seats [says Casañas], are called *tapestles* and they are like tables. The high officials seat themselves thereon and place their feet on a high bench. . . . The leaders do not take their seats on this elevation except for a special ceremony. [Casañas, 1927, p. 213.]

Moreover, "in the home of each *caddi* and of the nobles there is a certain bench which nobody is allowed to approach except the grand *xinesí* himself when on a visit," and "in all of these houses there is also a high bed like an alcove where the *xinesí* may sleep and rest" (Casañas, 1927, p. 217). Casañas speaks of "benches of wood, all of one piece and not very high from the ground" used as chairs (Casañas, 1927, p. 212), and a "little square wooden bench, of one piece, with four feet, and slightly raised from the ground" which Espinosa (1927, p. 160) saw in the temple was evidently one of these. This is the wooden duho of the West Indies reported from several other places in the Southeast. We recall also benches brought out by the Nabedache chief for the accommodation of De Leon and his companions (Bolton, 1916, p. 378). Espinosa perceived in the temple "two little chests about three palm lengths long, and raised upon a wooden altar with four little forked poles with curious covers of painted reed" (Espinosa, 1927, pp. 160–161), but these were probably cane baskets although small wooden coffers are reported from several Southeastern tribes. Nevertheless, inside of these chests were

four or five little platters or vessels of black wood like circular shields, all curiously worked and having four feet. Some represented little ducks, having the head and tail of a duck. Others had the head and tail of an alligator or lizard. [Espinosa, 1927, p. 161.]

Morfi copies this description but likens the wooden vessels to soup plates (Morfi, 1932, p. 25). At the door of the temple, in the town of the Acolapissa and Natchitoches, Pénicaut saw figures of birds made of wood, and inside of this temple there were figures of "dragons," serpents, and toads enclosed in three coffers (Margry, 1875–1886, vol. 5, p. 467).

A coffin "as big as an ox cart," which figures in the narrative of Casañas, must have been a crude affair (Casañas, 1927, p. 299). Here, as throughout the Southeast, visitors were entertained at points remote from towns in quickly constructed brush arbors.

Fire was made in the common American way by means of two firesticks, but it is curious that, except for a bare mention by Espinosa (1927, p. 169), our only information regarding this comes from Pénicaut, whose account is not applicable merely to the Caddo:

They take a little piece of cedar wood of the diameter of the finger, and a little piece of wood of the mulberry (*muret*) which is very hard; they put the one against the side of the other between their hands, and by turning them together, as if one were trying to stir chocolate, there comes out of the piece of cedar wood a little piece of moss which takes fire. That is done in an instant. [Margry, 1875–1886, vol. 5, p. 469.]

The moss was, of course, placed next to or about the point of action.

Live coals were handled with wooden tongs, and the Nasoni when visited by Joutel were using cane torches in a way familiar to us among the tribes farther east (Casañas, 1927, p. 291; Margry, 1875–1886, vol. 3, p. 390).

Wood was also used in the manufacture of mortars and pestles for the reduction of corn to flour, and the former were probably excavated in the usual southern manner by means of fire.

Bows were made principally from the famous bois d'arc or Osage orange for which the Kadohadacho country was famous, as has already been noted. Not an item of information is supplied us regarding the method of manufacture of either the bow or the arrow except for the part buffalo glue played in the latter (see p. 154).

We are told that some hoes were made of seasoned walnut (Espinosa, 1927, p. 156) but it may be suspected that the wood was actually hickory.

Rattles made of gourds or calabashes filled with little stones are mentioned several times and a drum occasionally. At the ceremony held for Alarcon the Indians used "a drum made out of an old kettle partly filled with water and covered with a piece of wet rawhide" (Castañeda, 1936, vol. 2, p. 104). The following description by Espinosa seems to indicate a drum of a different type:

They then take hollow logs, covered on top with green branches, bury the ends of them, and select eight strong Indian women, who, seated at intervals with sticks in each hand, use each the hollow log as a drum, to the accompaniment of the calabash which the old men play, and the songs of the men and women singers to the number of more than twenty. [Espinosa, 1927, pp. 173–174.]

Natchitoches and Acolapissa Indians were observed by Pénicaut dancing to the sound of a small drum (Margry, 1875–1886, vol. 5, p. 466).

Flutes, or rather flageolets, of carved crane or heron bone are several times reported and others "of carved reeds with the necessary holes" (Espinosa, 1927, p. 161). A Caddo flageolet collected by James Mooney in 1896 is shown in plate 17, figure 1. These are said to have been used in the dances—in which case their customs differed from those of the more eastern tribes—and by doctors. Espinosa thus refers to another instrument, a rasp, in use by the last-named practitioners:

Their instruments are little polished sticks with slits like a snake's rattles. These rubbed on a hollow skin make a noise nothing less than infernal. [Espinosa, 1927, p. 165.]

There is frequent mention of reed mats and baskets. Casañas notes that they laid their meat "on very pretty little platters which

the women make of reeds" (Casañas, 1927, p. 212). In the house
of the *xinesi* were "two small boxes made of reeds," which were used
as contribution boxes (Casañas, 1927, p. 291). Visitors were often
seated on reed mats (Margry, 1875–1886, vol. 3, p. 389). Massanet
observed "very brilliantly colored" pieces of matting about the native
beds, and Hidalgo was pleased with their "very curious rugs of
reed of different colors which could be used in ladies' drawing
rooms." He also notes basket-work sifters employed in making
flour (Bolton, 1916, p. 378; Hidalgo, 1927, p. 56). "In their houses
they have large baskets made of heavy reeds, into which they put
their shelled corn and beans" (Espinosa, 1927, p. 156; Bolton, 1916,
p. 378). The altar in the temple described by Espinosa (1927, p. 160)
was made of reed mats, and numbers of mats of various sizes were
kept there. Among the Nasoni Joutel observed bark hampers in
which food was served (Margry, 1875–1886, vol. 3, p. 393), but this
is the only mention we have of a bark receptacle though there are
several notices of the use of bark ropes. Joutel's party found that
ropes made of bark from "little walnut trees," which the Indians
pointed out to them, made better halters for the horses than hides
because the dogs were wont to gnaw these latter in two, it being a
time of scarcity when the Frenchmen passed through the Hasinai
country (Margry, 1875–1886, vol. 3, p. 392).

Feather garments were much in use and they were adopted by
two of La Salle's Frenchmen when they turned Indian after his
assassination (Margry, 1875–1886, vol. 3, p. 353). In the temples
were observed "rolls of ornamental feathers, crowns made of skins
and feathers, [and] a bonnet of the same" (Espinosa, 1927, p. 161).
The medicine men had "particular insignia or feathers" on their
heads and feathers were used in some way in the ceremonies accompanying work over a patient, especially fans made of the tail feathers
of a turkey (Espinosa, 1927, p. 165). In the ceremonies accompanying the reception of Governor Martin de Alarcon "a very curious
feather" was placed upon his head (Espinosa, 1927, p. 180).

Caddo pottery is justly famous and there are many references
to it but no description of the method of manufacture. Casañas
merely says: "There are . . . many deposits of clay from which the
Indians make pretty pots" . . . and "the plates they use are round
earthen pans" (Casañas, 1927, p. 212). Massanet speaks of "very
large earthen pots like our water jars" used only in making *atole*
(Bolton, 1926, p. 378). Hidalgo: "They make large pots in which
to keep water, make *atole*, and to preserve other things they need
to carry. They make other jars for use" (Hidalgo, 1927, p. 56).
Espinosa mentions "earthen vessels, some large and some small, in
which to serve the old and the young," and notes that bear's fat
was kept in some of them (Espinosa, 1927, pp. 155, 157). Among the

furnishings of the temple were "earthen-ware vessels which are evidently incense burners in which they burn fat and tobacco" (Espinosa, 1927, p. 160). The importance of this industry to women is demonstrated by the same missionary when he says: "From clay, they make by hand all the utensils they need for their household use" (Espinosa, 1927, p. 177). Archeologists know well, and pot-hunters only too well, how many of these beautiful objects were laid away with the dead.

Although shell gorgets have been found on many Caddo sites, often beautifully carved, there is no mention of them by the early writers, and only one note of the use of shell ornaments, "little white shells they find in the fields which are shaped like beads" (Casañas, 1927, p. 285). Reference has already been made to the employment of shells in removing hair from the body. (See page 141.)

As noted in the chapter on Clothing, undoubtedly the Caddo were familiar with textiles such as other Southeastern tribes wove out of the inner bark of the mulberry and certain nettles or wild varieties of hemp, but I find only two references, one by Pénicaut who observed their use among Natchitoches women living side by side with the Acolapissa and some distance outside of the true Caddo country (Margry, 1875–1886, vol. 5, p. 465), and the other a somewhat obscure note by Espinosa. When he first entered the Hasinai country in 1715 with Ramón and they were met ceremonially by the Indians, the missionary says: "We began to take our seats on saddles that were tied and served as low chairs, while coarse cloth served us as carpets" (Espinosa, 1927, p. 151). The use of the word saddle suggests at once that the "coarse cloth" may have been trade material and the reference is, therefore, beclouded. The eastern Caddo undoubtedly were acquainted with those textiles but the western ones probably had less use for them and the substances entering into them might have been less easy to secure.

Pipes are spoken of several times but no intimation comes to us regarding the materials of which they were made (Castañeda, 1936, vol. 2, p. 55), though they were presumably of stone. The pipe presented to Ramón in 1716 "was adorned with white feathers, attached from one end of the stem to the other, the stem being more than one *vara* in length." Plate 17, figure 2, shows a tobacco pouch made of the skin of a skunk, collected for the National Museum by Dr. Edward Palmer. Dugout canoes were in use among the eastern Caddo. We have, however, not a single description specifically applicable to manufacture by these Indians. Aguayo, in order to cross the Trinity, asked some of the Hasinai Indians "to construct a raft after their own fashion of dry wood and canes" (Morfi,

1935, p. 236, footnote). Solís mentions crossing the Sabine River on a raft and such devices were necessarily common (Solís, 1931, p. 63).

As will be evident from the contents of the temples, a certain amount of carving was executed and we are told of painted mats, "a curiously and beautifully painted deerskin" (Espinosa, 1927, p. 151), representations of ducks, alligators or lizards, and other animals, and body paintings and tattooings (Espinosa, 1927, p. 161; Hidalgo, 1927, p. 56). While the designs of some of these are complimented by Spanish historians, none of them has come down to us, but that Caddo women at least had real artistic ability of a high order is witnessed by some of the exquisite ceramic remains that are constantly being dug up in the former territory of these people.

It appears, therefore, that little knowledge remains of the technical processes of the Caddo Indians, but it also appears that they conformed for the most part to those in vogue in better known territories to the east, and from these sources, as also in some measure from what we know of the arts and industries of the plains tribes, the picture may be filled in. The same is true of the esthetic processes outside of ceramics, but of this last we derive little from other sources. In Caddo ceramics the art of the Southeast easily reached its apex, for while there are specimens of pottery from the Middle Mississippi region and Moundville which show as high technical excellence, there are none that, upon the whole, exhibit equal artistic feeling.

SOCIAL USAGES

BIRTH AND INFANCY

Joutel informs us that, in conformity with the usual Southeastern custom, women occupied separate houses every month.

Regarding childbirth itself Solís and Morfi are our principal authorities, the account of the second being based largely on that of the first named. Solís says:

The women go through childbirth in this manner: on the bank of the river or creek where they are living, they make some huts in which to dwell; in the midst of one they put a low forked pole which is strong and well placed in the ground, and in the hour when they feel the birth pangs they go to that little hut and by helping themselves with the pole they bring forth the child and afterwards throw themselves into the water, bathe themselves and the child, and come as they are to the ranch where all the others are. All this I have observed in these lands. [Solís, 1931, p. 70.]

Morfi:

Being pregnant does not interfere with their work. When they recognize that the time for giving birth is growing near, they themselves construct on the banks of the river or creek nearest their *ranchería*, a little shelter, covered on top, and on three sides, in the center of which they firmly fix a big stake. When they feel the first pangs, they retire to this little hut, and without other aid, take hold of that stake, and give birth to their children. They immediately enter the water, though it be necessary to break the ice, with the infant in arms, gently bathe themselves and the infant, and return to the house of their husband, to continue their labors, as if nothing had happened to them. [Morfi, 1932, p. 47.]

As soon as the child is born [says Espinosa] the priests begin to go through various ceremonies with it, which seem to show a desire to represent baptism. When the new born child is six or eight days old, they inform one of their priests. He comes to the house and takes his particular seat and they place the young child in his arms. He caresses it and talks for a long time into its ear. Next he bathes it all over in a large vessel and asks its parents what name he is to give it. Usually the name they bestow upon it is the diminutive of the name of the parents. If it is a girl this same office is performed by a decrepit old woman who is also a quack. A great number of the rabble have been assigned to this particular person as parishoners. To conclude the ceremonies, gifts, in the form of remuneration, are made to those officiating and they that day feast sumptuously on what they secure. [Espinosa, 1927, p. 164.]

Morfi renders this as follows:

The naming of children is a ceremony which seems to or pretends to imitate our holy baptism. Six or eight days after the birth of the infant the parents advise one of the medicine men or priests. He enters the house of the newborn, takes his particular seat, and they place the infant in his arms. He caresses it very much, and whispers in its ear for a long time. He bathes all of the body in a big vessel. He asks the parents the name they wish to give it, which usually is a dimunitive of [one of] their own names; and from that day it is so called. If the baby is a girl the same thing is done by an old decrepit woman, who is also a medicine woman, of whom they also have an abundance, the whole country being divided among them, as into parishes. After the ceremony is concluded they offer the priest various presents, as gratuities and that day they eat splendidly, all that there is in the house. [Morfi, 1932, pp. 36–37.]

Not infrequently children were killed shortly after birth:

Mothers have killed their newborn children because the fathers did not want them. On one occasion they set fire to a house and left two little children to burn, declaring that they were good for nothing. [Casañas, 1927, pp. 302–303.]

According to the Caddo now living, "a child is suckled well past babyhood" and a five year old girl is described as "a suckling" (Parsons, 1941, p. 32). The name given in infancy might be bestowed by any relative and it might be retained through life or replaced by another, perhaps that of the guardian spirit or a nickname. There is said to have been no reluctance to mention the name of a dead person. (Parsons, 1941, p. 25, and consult pages 25–27 for further details regarding naming; also pp. 307–308 below.)

MARRIAGE

Solís offers some general remarks not very complimentary to the Indians:

Speaking of all of the Indians of this Province of Texas in common with all the nations that inhabit it, whether they are of the mission or live in the woods and sea-coast, they all marry: those of the mission who are taught, *Yn Facie*

Eclesie according to the order of Our Mother Church; those who are not, by natural contract, but it is with many abuses, and in order that there may not be any in the mission it is necessary to be very careful, and that the minister watch out for this. They exchange or barter their wives. If one of them likes the wife of another better, he gives him his and something of value besides, and they exchange one for the other and barter them. They lend them to their friends in order that they may use them, they sell them for a horse, for gunpowder, balls, beads of glass and other things which they esteem. [Solís, 1931, pp. 41-42.]

Casañas:

The custom they follow when a man takes a wife is not very commendable. In some ways the arrangement seems a good one; but I have found that it is not very binding. If a man wants a certain woman for his wife who he knows is a maiden, he takes her some of the very best things he has; and if her father and mother give their permission for her to receive the gift, the answer is that they consent to the marriage. But they do not allow him to take her away with him until they have first given notice to the *caddi*. If the woman is not a maiden, there is no other agreement necessary than that the man say to the woman that if she is willing to be his friend he will give her something. Sometimes this agreement is made for only a few days. At other times they declare the arrangement binding forever. There are but few of them who keep their word, because they soon separate from each other—especially if the woman finds a man who gives her things she likes better than those the first man gave her. Only the noblest families consider this kind of contract binding. Therefore, in *their* circles, no one dares to trouble another's wife. There is no punishment for this loose conduct. They feel no disgrace because of leaving one another; nor are they prevented from deserting each other because outsiders think they are married. This is why they have neither disputes nor quarrels. They first talk the matter over, the personal sentiments of each being expressed; then they arrange the matter between them. The woman usually starts by saying that the man she has gave her many things but what he gave her was little in comparison with what the new man offers her; therefore, the first one should bear the proposed change patiently and hunt him another wife, or he should go out and hunt something else to give her so that she will stay with him. She says other things of a similar nature which, on the one hand, make a person laugh, and, on the other hand, cause one to feel pity and compassion. There are but few men who remain married long before abandoning their wives. The thing I approve is that they have only one wife at a time. If a man wants to take a new wife, he makes a difference between them, never living with them both at the same time. If the first wife finds that he has another wife in view, she makes it a point of honor (a rare thing among them) to leave him at once and go away in search of another husband. The women have a very cruel custom, that is, if, when they give birth to a child, they know that the father does not like children they will kill it. These women are, indeed, not ashamed to confess their cruelty, but even openly boast of it. The Indian nobles seem to be much more humane, and seem to have some regard for reputation. [Casañas, 1927, pp. 283-284.]

Espinosa:

Marriage endures among these people only so long as it is not unsatisfactory to the contracting parties. In that case new mates are sought. The marriage is not celebrated with any particular ceremony although the man secures beforehand the good will of the fathers or brothers of his choice by bringing them some deer meat which he leaves at the door of the house without saying a word. If the inmates take the meat inside and eat it, it is an unmistakable sign that they consent to the arrangement. The man does not have to secure the consent of the woman for she always falls in with the wishes of her parents. They then live together as animals, as Father Acosta describes it, in speaking of the Indians of Peru. As to fidelity, some of them make much of it and punish their wives with a beating if they catch them at fault. Others make nothing of it or regard it as a joke. Ordinarily these Indians care little if their wives have intimate relations with other men of the tribe. It is nothing for them to speak freely with each other about it with jokes and suggestive remarks as [if] it were a fine jest. The great depth of immorality in which they live can be seen from this. [Espinosa, 1927, pp. 164–165.]

Morfi relies on Espinosa but he adds some particulars:

Polygamy is permitted with no other restriction than desire; though, or because of the same indolence which is natural to them, or because of the care the women give to winning the hearts of their husbands, it is unusual that an Indian has two wives. They inherit the wives of their brothers, whether or not they have children. Affinity is not an obstacle to matrimony; but consa[n]guinity is, very much so, and they scrupulously avoid it. When a youth intends to take a maiden for his wife, he is first nice to her parents or brothers, taking them some venison, throwing it before the door of their house, without saying a word. If they take it, and eat it, it is a sign that they approve the match. The will of the girl is not awaited, it being supposed that she has no other than that of her parents or guardians.

Matrimony lasts as long as they conform to it, and at the least misunderstanding, each one, if so desired, looks for another companion. Some husbands go into mourning if conjugal chastity is lacking, and punish the adulteress with lashes of the whip. Others, and they are the more numerous, either disregard or overlook it, without caring whether their women are too familiar with others of the same nation or whether they are too free in their actions and obscene language, all of which they regard as a joke. [Morfi, 1932, p. 44–45.]

Joutel also remarks on the looseness of the Hasinai women and says that the Kadohadacho women changed their husbands often (Margry, 1875–1886, vol. 3, pp. 363, 413.)

Morfi tells of the existence of "hermaphrodites," or berdaches, among the Karankawa but does not say whether they were to be found with the Caddo (Morfi, 1932, p. 55).

Dr. Parsons gives many details regarding marriage in modern times. Her data agree rather strikingly with that of the older writers in emphasizing the looseness of the marriage tie and the unfavorable social attitude toward sexual jealousy. Matrilocal residence is emphasized (Parsons, 1941, pp. 28–32).

DIVISION OF LABOR BETWEEN THE SEXES

Casañas gives this in a few words:

During [the winter] season they entertain themselves around the fire by making hand-work. The men make arrows, moccasins, and such other little things as are needed by those who till the soil. The women make reed mats, pots, earthen pans, and other clay utensils for domestic use. They also busy themselves in dressing deerskins and buffalo hides—the women as well as the men; for all of them know how to do this, as well as how to make many other little things that are needed around the house. [Casañas, 1927, p. 215.]

Speaking specifically of women's work, Espinosa remarks:

All the house work falls upon these poor women, for they are the ones who grind all the meal in the queer wooden mortars which they have for this purpose. They put the meat which their husbands have killed to cook in very large pots. From clay, they make by hand all the utensils they need for their household use. They gather the crops, clean the grain, and keep it very carefully. When it is cold they go into the woods to gather nuts and acorns for the year's supply. They are so provident that when a guest presents himself at the house, whatever the hour may be—they immediately put into his hand a large tray filled with food, an abundance of which they have prepared in the morning. [Espinosa, 1927, p. 177; cf. Morfi, 1932, p. 47.]

The industry of war—if such it may be called—was, of course, in the hands of the men and so was hunting, most of the ceremonial rites, and most of the gaming—again, if we may speak of it as an industry. Women brought in the animals their husbands had killed after they reached the neighborhood of their homes, and they had complete command of the cooking and the food supply. Joutel says that some one woman in each house had entire supervision over the latter (Margry, 1875–1886, vol. 3, p. 393). The fields were cultivated by men and women working together but planting was all done by the women, and the heavier part of farming seems to have fallen upon them. On the other hand the greater part of the house building operations was assumed by the men, the women's work being confined largely to providing prairie grass for the thatch.

It is the women [says Joutel] who perform almost all the house work, go after wood, pound corn and do almost everything else, even on the hunt. After the men have killed animals, it is ordinarily they who go to get the meat, and even in cultivating the fields they are the ones also who do the greater part of it.

Besides preparing food for workers during the communal field cultivation, "the women of the house also have the duty of planting corn, beans and other things; the men do not have anything to do with it" (Margry, 1875–1886, vol. 3, pp. 363–364).

CLANS

On entering the Hasinai country, Joutel observes that they came upon many cabins, "which formed hamlets, there being seven or eight, twelve or fifteen, together, at intervals, and the fields around the said cabins. . . . But there are considerable tracts of land where there is no one for more than a league" (Margry, 1875–1886, vol. 3, pp. 341, 344). On their way from the Hasinai towns to those of the Namidish and Nasoni they again found "from time to time cabins arranged in hamlets or cantons, for we sometimes made a league and a half without finding one." When they reached the frontier tribe, the Cahinnio, however, Joutel notes that unlike the other bands its houses were gathered into one compact settlement, evidently for protection against the Chickasaw and Osage (Margry, 1875–1886, vol. 3, pp. 387, 416).

Espinosa:

These natives do not live in settlements confined within the limits of a *pueblo*, but each division of the four principal tribes among whom the missions were located lives in *ranchos* some distance from each other. The principal reason for this is that each family seeks a place large enough for his crop and one where there is water at hand for household use and for bathing—which is very frequent among them all. [Espinosa, 1927, p. 154.]

Morfi, paraphrasing Espinosa:

Though they do not live in regular pueblos, but in scattered habitations, each remnant or tribe occupies a definite territory, and the families mutually assist one another. Each of them selects that place which is judged the most opportune for their sowing and where there is a permanent supply of water for drinking and bathing, which they frequently do in all seasons. [Morfi, 1932, p. 40.]

The only hint of a true clan system among the Hasinai is given by Morfi in his Memorias in these words:

They also say on some occasions that some of them are descended from bears, others from dogs, beavers, coyotes, etc. Their forefathers seeing the danger caused them by the Devil, to deceive his malice, transformed themselves into those brutes, without losing their minds, and retaining the faculty of restoring themselves to their primitive being when convenient to them. [Morfi, 1932, p. 26.]

But this involves a common animistic idea, which has no necessary connection with the institution of clans.

We know, however, that there were clans among some of the Caddo whether or not the institution extended to the western divisions. In a letter dated November 17, 1763, to Don Angel de Marto y Navarrette, the Governor of Texas, by Cavallero Macarti, Commandant of the Natchitoches post, quoted by Morfi in both his Historia and his Memorias, the writer says, speaking specifically of the Kadohadacho: "They are divided into four tribes or families, known by the names of beaver (*Castor*), otter (*Nutria*), wolf (*Lobo*), and lion (*León*)" (Morfi, 1932, p. 6; 1935, p. 88).

There is a resemblance between this list and one obtained by the present writer in 1910 from White Bread [15], though I do not know to which tribe that Indian belonged, and he enumerated five clans instead of four: Ta'naha, (Buffalo), Nawŏ'tsi (Bear), Ki'shi (Panther), Ta'sha (Wolf), and Ta'o (Beaver). White Bread added that the clans were graded in this order following the supposed relative powers of the several animals. If a man of a more powerful clan

---

[15] Swanton, 1931. The name given in this paper as White Bead should be White Bread.

married a woman of a clan less powerful, the boys were entered in the father's clan and the girls in the mother's. If, on the other hand, a woman of a more powerful clan married a man of a less powerful one, the children all belonged to the mother's clan. It goes without saying that marriages took place also within clans, for otherwise the "weaker" ones would presently have run out, and if clan intermarriage was at all frequent it is difficult to see how such a fate could have been avoided anyhow. Probably what we have here is an attenuated recollection of an institution, rather than a complete statement. My informant added that when a man of one clan married a woman of another, the immediate relatives on each side would make fun of each other. If a person saw such a relative on a good horse, he could tell him to get off and then mount it himself, leaving the one who was dispossessed to even the score at some future time. Such relatives could say to each other all sorts of things, even those of the most outrageous character. He added that each tribal name had a meaning—which is evident in many cases— and each had a clan story, all of which formed parts of a whole.

Still another list of clans was obtained by James Mooney when he was collecting the material for his volume on The Ghost Dance Religion. This is as follows: Na'wotsi (Bear), Ta'sha (Wolf), Ta'-năha (Buffalo), Ta'o (Beaver), Iwi (Eagle), Oăt (Raccoon), Ka'-g'aih (Crow), Ka'gähănĭn (Thunder), Ki'shi (Panther), Sûko (Sun). The Buffalo clan was sometimes called Koho' (Alligator) "because both animals bellow in the same way" (Mooney, 1896, p. 1093). He probably obtained his information from Caddo Jake, a Natchitoches Indian, who was also interviewed by me, and who not only confirmed the correctness of Mooney's list but said that there were formerly many more clans whose names he had forgotten. He did not know to which clan the children belonged nor is Mooney definite on that point. Taken in connection with the evidently nonexogamous character of the system described by White Bread and Spier's failure to discover exogamous groups (Spier, 1924, pp. 262–263), doubt is cast on the existence of a normal clan system. It is possible, however, that the Natchitoches Indians had a clan system more completely developed than the other Caddo though it is surprising that neither Sibley nor any of the other officials and explorers who were brought intimately into contact with these people mentions the fact.

Mooney was told that men of a particular clan would not kill the animal from which the clan was named, and that

no Caddo in the old times would kill either an eagle or a panther, although they were not afraid to kill the bear, as are so many of the western tribes. The eagle might be killed, however, for its feathers by a hunter regularly initiated and consecrated for that purpose. [Mooney, 1896, p. 1093.]

It will be noticed that all of the clans in Macarti's list except the Otter are represented in the others, and since the Buffalo was sometimes called the Alligator and the Alligator and Otter are both denizens of river margins, these clans may have been identical. By "lion," of course, the panther is meant.

Perhaps some of the remaining clans were actually introduced by the Quapaw, who lived for a few years in Kadohadacho territory, and contributed a minor band to the tribe. According to Dorsey they had Bear, Eagle, Thunder, and Sun clans or gentes. Our record of Quapaw organization is, however, incomplete, and we find Raccoon and Blackbird gentes among the related Omaha (Dorsey, J. O., 1897, pp. 226–230); therefore, the Quapaw tribe may have had them as well. Adoption of Thunder and Sun clans from Siouan people is particularly probable since these do not occur among other Southeastern tribes, unless we except the Sun caste of the Natchez. The Bear, Raccoon, and Eagle were in existence also among the Creeks and the Bear among the Chickasaw (Swanton, 1928, pp. 115–116; 1928 a, p. 196). It seems possible that clans were adopted by some of the eastern tribes subject to influences from the Muskhogeans and Siouans, but that the western representatives of the family were organized more after the pattern of the Natchez, whose ceremonial customs they so largely shared.

Parsons attempts to explain reference to clans on the ground that the supernatural helpers were actually intended, but a statement like that of Macarti must involve something more (Parsons, 1941, p. 12).

TERMS OF RELATIONSHIP

The following Caddo terms of relationship were collected by Leslie Spier from Bill Edwards, a Caddo of the "xasině" (Hasinai) band, meaning apparently the Nabedache because the "kadohadatc, hianaǐ, and anadark" are noted as separate. The author comments: "I lack confidence in the Caddo, particularly as the unusual separation of collateral from lineal relatives suggested would indicate misunderstanding."

The phonetics are as follows:

a as in father; ă as in hat; à like u in hut; e like a in fate; ě as in met; i as in pique; ǐ as in pin; o as in note; ŏ as in not; ö as in the German schön; u as in rule; ŭ as in put; ω as in law; d and t may be variants of a single intermediate; ' is a weak glottal stop, except after k where it is almost a fortis; ' is a breath.

ebŭ't, grandfather. [1] [16]
ikŭ", grandmother. [2]
à'à, father. [3]
àhàaiǐme', "big father"; father's older brother. [3]

---

[16] Numbers in brackets following terms of relationship indicate order given in Caddo relationship system shown in table 1, p. 169.

ăhătĭt, "little father"; father's younger brother; stepfather. [3]
ĭna'', mother. [4]
ĭnahaiĭmě, "big mother"; mother's older sister. [4]
ĭnatĭt, "little mother"; mother's younger sister. [4]
ĭkwě'ĭ, stepmother. [5]
ăhaĭ', father's sister. [6]
eba'', mother's brother. [7]
ebakĭn, father-in-law; [8] (real or conceptual) daughter's husband. [8]
ĭnka'an, mother-in-law. [9]
tcuhuănŭ, mother's brother's wife; (real or conceptual) son's wife. [10]
ĭne'tĭt, man speaking—older brother; [11] parents' sibling's son older than self. The final syllable *tĭt* is customarily dropped in this and the following terms.
tu'ĭtĭt, man speaking—younger brother [12]; parents' sibling's son younger than self. [12]
kĭ'nĭtĭt or *kĭnĭtsĭ,* woman speaking—brother; parents' sibling's son.
taĭ'ĭtĭt, man speaking—sister [13]; parents' sibling's daughter, woman speaking—younger sister [13]; daughter of parents' sibling younger than self. [13]
ĭe, woman speaking—older sister; parents' sibling's daughter older than self.
dahaĭ', spouse of (real or conceptual) sibling.
saĭĕtĕ, "old lady"; wife (nonvocatively). [14]
honĭstĭ, "old man": husband (nonvocatively).
nătsikwaĭ, spouse (nonvocatively). There seems to be no term [14] for spouse in direct address.
hanĭ', son [15]; daughter [15]; (real or conceptual) brother's child [15]; woman speaking—(real or conceptual) sister's child. [15]
pa''tsĭ, man speaking—sister's child [16] (also given for father's sister's daughter, but this seems to be an error).
bŭkkĭntc, man speaking—grandson [17]; greatgrandson. [17]
kahanĭtc, woman speaking—grandson; greatgrandson. This and the above term probably include the granddaughter and the greatgranddaughter.
The application of the following terms is by no means clear.
Cahŭ't was given first as meaning "cross-cousin" and even "parallel-cousin," but the final explanations were the following:
cahŭ't, father's father's brother's son's son or daughter, etc. [18] Presumably a cousin in the speaker's generation related through a grandparent.
sa'kĭn, father's father's brother's son's son's son or daughter [19], etc. Evidently the child of *cahŭ't.*
wahadĭn, father's father's brother's son's son's son's son or [20] daughter, etc., i. e., the child of *sa'kĭn.*
ĭne'tĭt, etc., The terms for siblings are applied to the children [11] of *wahadĭn.*

One cannot marry cross- or parallel-cousins, nor any *cahŭ't, sa'kĭn, wahadĭn,* or their children, *ĭne'tĭt,* etc. "One boy was at the river and he became deaf and dumb. The old men asked about him and found out his parents were *wahadĭn.*" If a man marries the oldest sister of several and she dies, a younger sister may take her place if it is agreeable. There are said to be no exogamous groups, but in conversation with my informant maternal affiliation seemed to be stressed.

Conversation is tabooed between parents-in-law and children-in-law except in cases of serious need. This is equally binding to all concerned. [Spier, 1924, pp. 261–263.]

The accompanying table shows the essential features of this scheme, which Spier classifies with the Mackenzie Basin Type. It is incomplete, since we should know the lines of descent from the mother's father's brother as well as the father's father's brother. From what is said regarding prohibition of marriage with descendants of the paternal grandfather's brother, and the prevailingly matrilineal character of the organization as noted by both Spier and myself, it is probable that the incest group included relatives through both parents and that there was an inner group including the direct ancestors and descendants of self, the parents, their brothers and sisters and their descendants, and an outer group including the paternal grandfather's brother's descendants and probably those of the maternal grandfather's brother. The system is not usually found in tribes with clans or gentes, the only exceptions, aside from the Caddo, being the Gros Ventre, Two Mountain Iroquois, the Zuñi, some of the southern California tribes, and perhaps the Munsi.

The terms of relationship used by a woman present few differences. She had distinct terms for brother and the parents' sibling's son, and for older sister and parents' sibling's daughter older than self, called her younger sister and parents' sibling's daughter younger than self by the same term that a man used for all of his sisters and his parents' sibling's daughters, called her husband "old man" as he called her "old woman," and had a different word for her grandchildren, and greatgrandchildren.

Lesser and Weltfish state that "Hainai kinship terms and usages . . . differ from those of Caddo proper [Kadohadacho]," and in all probability this difference existed between more bands than these two (Lesser and Weltfish, 1932, p. 14).

Since the above was written a more thorough investigation of Caddo kinship terms has been made by Dr. Parsons illustrated by references to specific cases. While the native terms are rendered by somewhat different phonetic symbols, it is surprising, in view of Spier's modest statement quoted above, how few changes are suggested. There is more information regarding the extension of the terms, some evidence adduced that cross- and parallel-cousins may have been differentiated, and a set of age-class terms recorded. While Parsons found that "the principle of grouping is that of the maternal family," her informants knew nothing of clans. One of them, White Moon, stated that "between relations by marriage within the same generation, i. e., between those who call each other *da'hai*', there is a joking relationship . . . as well as with one kind of cousin you call 'sister,' *dahai*'." Avoidance of parents-in-law seemed to be unknown but in their presence "a man may not swear or make sex jokes" (Parsons, pp. 11–25, 71–75).

TABLE 1.—*Caddo relationship system*

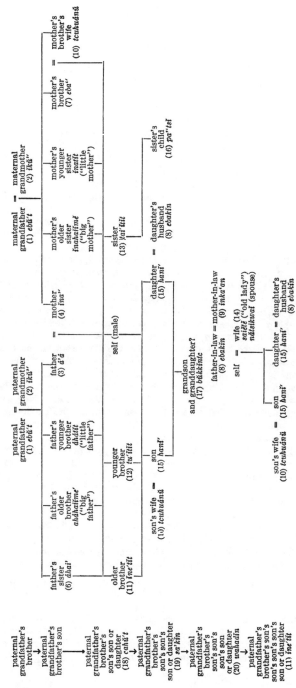

GOVERNMENT

We begin our consideration by citing some paragraphs by Casañas, the first missionary to the Hasinai:

These allied tribes do not have one person to govern them (as with us a kingdom is accustomed to have a ruler whom we call a king). They have only a *xinesi*. He usually has a subordinate who gathers together four or five tribes who consent to live together and to form a province or kingdom as it might be called—and a very large one, too, if all these tribes had one person to rule over them. But such a head they have not, and I, therefore, infer that this province which in New Spain is called "Tejias"—which really expresses just what they are because each tribe is a friend to all the others—cannot be called a kingdom. [Casañas, 1927, p. 286.]

In each tribe there is a *caddi*. He is like a governor ruling and commanding his people. The office of *caddi* also descends through the direct line of blood relationship. Each *caddi* rules within the section of country occupied by his tribe, no matter whether it be large or small. If large, they have certain officials called *canhas*. Of these, there are then seven or eight to aid in governing. If the tribe is small, there are only three or four. It is their duty to relieve the *caddi* and to publish his orders by reporting that the *caddi* commands this or that. They frighten the people by declaring that, if they do not obey orders, they will be whipped and otherwise punished. These *canahas*, in turn, have their subordinates called *chaya*. They do everything the *canahas* tell them to do. They have still other officials whom they call *tammas*. These are the officers who promptly execute orders. They whip all the idlers with rods, beating them on the legs and over the stomach. The *canaha* has to call the old men together to the home of the *caddi* for the discussion of any matter. When the Indians go out on the warpath or to hunt buffalo for meat, the *canaha* gives orders for fitting up the place where the *caddi* is to rest, to eat, and to sleep. Whenever the *caddi* wants to smoke the *canaha* brings a pouch filled with tobacco and puts the pipe of peace into the mouth of the *caddi*. The peace and harmony among the officials described is so great that during the year and three months [we have been among them] we have not seen any quarrels—either great or small. But the insolent and lazy are punished.

Now a word concerning the women. The wife of the *xinesi* and the wives of the *caddices*—and each official has only one wife—are designated by one general title, which is *aquidau*. When this name is used it is immediately understood that the person spoken of is either the wife of the grand *xinesi* or of some *caddi*. Each of the other women in the village has an individual name.

All the men who have achieved some victory in war are called *amayxoya* in addition to their own names. This means "great man." The arms and banners they must carry are the skins and the scalps of the enemies each one has killed. The grand *xinesi* has skulls hung up in a tree near his house. [Casañas, 1927, pp. 216–217.]

On an earlier page Casañas has the following regarding this grand *xinesi*:

By nature these Indians are tractable and obedient to the commands of the grand *xinesi* who is like a petty king over them. He holds office by the direct line of descent. If one dies, the nearest blood kin to him becomes his successor. To him are subject the nine tribes named below.

These have been considered elsewhere. They are the Nabadacho (Nabedache), Necha (Neches), Nechavi, Nacono, Nacachau, Nazadachotzi (Nacogdoches), Cachae (Hainai), Nabiti (Namidish), and Nasayaha (Nasoni?). "These nine tribes," he concludes, "occupy about thirty-five leagues and they are all subject to the grand *xinesi*" (Casañas, 1927, pp. 215, 216).

Hidalgo and Espinosa call this head chief or high priest of the Hasinai *chenesi*, which shows that the *x* of Casañas' form of the name was pronounced like English *sh*. The sound was evidently heard by some as *ch*, by others as *sh*.

Some items may now be added from Espinosa:

All of these people have their principal captains. The office of each is perpetual and one's sons or relatives inherit it when he dies. There is no controversy or litigation in this arrangement. If the chief captain dies, leaving only a small son, the Indians recognize him as their head and, during his minority, they furnish him a council composed of *caziques* who supply the place of chief and carry him to all the meetings of the *zagalejo*. They assign to him the highest seat. He usually sleeps or runs around while the older people are holding their conferences. In addition to these, the whole nation elects a person who serves them as a general during wars. When they get out on a campaign they obey him implicitly, without disregarding an order in the slightest degree. [Espinosa, 1927, pp. 175-176.]

As in so many other cases, Morfi copies Espinosa but he adds certain material:

In each of the Texas tribes there is a principal chief whom they respect and obey. This office is perpetual and hereditary in the oldest son, or, in his absence, in the next brother, or nearest of kin. In this succession they never cause any litigation or the least of misunderstanding. If the heir is a minor, they recognize and proclaim him superior and appoint one of the principal *caciques* to be his guardian and master, to assist him and instruct him during his minority. This guardian brings the boy to all of the meetings and congresses, seats him in the first place in order of precedence among those assembled, and though during the time they treat the most important matters of state, the boy is usually playing or sleeping, all resolutions are made in his name.

Besides this Superior Chief, each tribe elects a General, who, subordinate to the former, commands in matters of war. He is obeyed with great punctuality and without anyone contradicting his orders, When a victory is gained, he bids farewell to the people and goes to the battle field and with the other forces marches last, to cover the retreat.

The nations neighboring Texas and those of the North generally elect their captains by acclamation and solicit the Governor of Texas, or the Commandant of Natchitoches, to present him with the baton, and confirm the election . . .

The authority of these captains in all the nations is very limited, and they cannot force their people to follow them anywhere. They know very well that when there is no pay or recompense, there can be no obligation; but on the other hand the chiefs are not responsible for the results of those expeditions to those who do not follow them, but do as they themselves wish. With all of this there is never a lack of those who follow the chiefs. Sometimes they stimulate them with words, but most frequently they convince them with actions. If the captain wishes to leave for the chase, they celebrate a great festival, and those who attend to eat must accompany him. When he plans some action of war, he announces in the pueblos, that those who wish to accompany him must fast on a certain day and those who comply with this severity go with him. By this fast they do not contract an indissoluble obligation. To those who are present on the day of the march, or to those who remain, or turn back on the road, they tell with indifference, that they do well; thus they are enlisted, freed, or dismissed, without there resulting any gratitude or feeling whether they are deserving or infamous. In a word the chief's authority is in proportion to his eloquence, his fame for valor, or the love and esteem in which the nation holds him. [Morfi, 1932, pp. 47–49.]

Casañas lets us know something of Caddo councils and the manner in which they were conducted:

They are timid by nature; and, therefore, they have great respect for the grand *xinesi*, for the *caddices*, and for the leading men. If the *caddi* wants to do any thing, he calls the old men together, listens to each of their views, and then decides to do what he thinks best, explaining his views to some of the men and urging agreement. So all go away satisfied and of the same opinion. In these meetings it is not considered polite when one is speaking for the others to talk. Instead they all listen, only giving signs to indicate that they are listening attentively. When one speaker stops, another begins. In this manner each speaks in order, according to his age. This deference to age is observed not only in talking but in sitting down, and in all other courtesies that Christians are accustomed to observe. There is another custom followed in these meetings. No one is allowed to enter the room where the councillors are assembled. If something comes up, some one appears at the door, and by signs makes known his desire, whereupon the matter is soon decided. The old men severely reprimand the young men if they seat themselves or talk in their presence. It has happened on various occasions when I was sitting and talking with old men, and young men wanted to mingle with us, that the old men not only censured this action but, with their own hands, struck the offenders. The respect and obedience they show the grand *xinesi* is remarkable. Every one tries to keep him satisfied by giving him something of everything he has and by going out to hunt something for him to feast upon. Finally, in controlling them he has only to say, "I want this or that done."

All obey because they fear his frown. They agree that his proposition is very reasonable, and it will be best that nothing except what he says should be done. [Casañas, 1927, p. 218.]

In his letter to the Viceroy of Mexico, Casañas suggests that the Hasinai be controlled through their *xinesi:*

I should like very much, Your Excellency, to have this man honored in some way as he is the head chief of the whole province. He who has hitherto been honored by being made governor and presented with the staff of command is now no more than a *caddi*, and, as such, he together with the other eight *caddices* of these nine nations is subject to the grand *xinesi*, and however much he is honored it is impossible that he cease to recognize the *xinesi* as his lord. I know it will be of more value to honor the *xinesi* than the other. This done, all the other *caddices* will feel obliged to recognize him as their grand *xinesi*, since they have never known a higher authority than that of a *xinesi*. [Casañas, 1927, pp. 299–300.]

Solís found a woman in the Nabedache town who had great authority and enjoyed peculiar privileges:

> In this village there is an Indian woman of great authority and following, whom they call Santa Adíva which means "great lady" or "principal lady." Her house is very large and has many rooms. The rest of the Nation brings presents and gifts to her. She has many Indian men and women in her service called *tamas conas*, and these are like priests and captains among them. She is married to five Indian men. In short she is like a queen among them. [Solís, 1931, p. 46.]

In 1690, among the Kadohadacho, Tonti was visited by "a woman who governed this nation," and at the same time he seems to speak of a male chieftain (Cox, 1905, vol. 1, p. 46). These two references remind us very strongly of the position of the so-called White Woman among the Natchez, mother of the heir apparent to the Natchez head chief's position, but we have no intimation other than this that the Caddo had the same sort of privileged caste compelled to marry among commoners. It seems surprising that nothing is said about this institution by the earlier missionaries, Casañas and Espinosa. Morfi quotes Solís but adds no details.

The communal institutions of Hasinai society appealed very much to Casañas:

> As regards other features of their government, these Indians help each other in such a manner that if one's house and all his possessions are burned up, they all gather together, build him a new house, and furnish him whatever he needs for his subsistence and comfort. All these things they do together. At planting time, they come together and plant whatever each one has to plant, according to the size of the family—beginning first at the home of the grand *œinesi* . . . Next, they plant the corn and other crops for the *caddi*. Then they work for the other officials and the old men. In this way they continue working from the highest to the humblest until each has planted what he needs for the year . . . Those who hunt work steadily, for they are obliged to supply food until the planting is finished. During sickness, these Indians visit and aid each other with great kindness, trying to give to the sick all possible consolation by taking them something nice to eat. Some of them present the trinkets they own, others lend them. Among them there is no exchange, save by bartering. It seems that everything they own they do not hold as personal property but as common property. Therefore, there is no ambition, no envy to prevent peace and harmony among them. [Casañas, 1927, pp. 217–218.]

Each of the present Caddo divisions has its chief and the two must act together for the tribe. Before their elevation to the chieftainship they served as assistants. Heredity played no part in the selection. The place of the ancient *tamma* or crier is now taken by a son or son-in-law of the chief when a council is to be called (Parsons, 1941, pp. 10–11).

FEASTS

Casañas has considerable to say about these:

> They eat while seated on benches of wood, all of one piece and not very high from the ground. The ground, or their knees, serve as a table. For table

cloths and napkins, they make use of the very first things they can lay their hands upon. They wipe their fingers on whatever they find in this way, no matter whether it be a piece of wood or something else; while those who are not so nice will use their feet. But, in spite of all this, they lick their spoons—using for this purpose the two fingers of their right hands. The plates they use are round earthen pans; and, as the Indians always eat their meat boiled or roasted and without broth, they put it on very pretty little platters which the women make of reeds. When they are in the part of the country where they have none, they use leaves or the ground itself. While those who are not very polite use their own feet. The usual way of sitting is with one knee raised. The way they give thanks is to take a pipe with tobacco. Of the first four whiffs they take, they blow one into the air, one toward the ground, and the others towards the two sides. It seems that whenever they eat they try to finish up everything set before them. They take a long time to eat and while they are eating, they sing and talk, and, from time to time, whistle. Those who eat everything placed before them consider themselves great men. Sport is made of those who eat but little, while those who eat to surfeiting are detested. It is a habit with them whenever they arrive at a house, never to ask for anything to eat. For it is customary to set whatever a host may have before a visitor as soon as he arrives. After eating, the guests are supplied with the requisites for smoking. Before the meal, however, they take nothing until a portion of everything is first sent to the *caddi*. If the host is a chief, he invites the whole village to come to his house on a certain day. The *caddi* goes with all the rest and the feast begins. The *caddi* takes something of everything and throws a portion into the fire, a portion upon the ground, and a portion to each side. Then he retires to a corner; and while all the others form ready to dance, he speaks—first to the corn, asking that it allow itself to be eaten. In the same way he talks to the other things they use. He tells the snakes not to bite, the deer not to be bitten. He then consecrates the whole harvest of the house to God and ends by declaring that God has said that they may now eat and that if they do not they ought to die of hunger. Everybody falls to and they eat until they are gorged—for their way of eating always comes to this.

If the host is an Indian who cannot afford the expense of arranging such a feast, he takes something to the *caddi* who is highest in rank before the others begin eating. As soon as he returns, he throws food into the fire and to the four winds, saying that he is now going away and that they may begin eating. The privilege of seating themselves on an elevated seat is granted only to the grand *xinesi* and to the *caddices*. None save these officials have high seats in their houses. These seats are called *tapestles* and are like tables. The high officials seat themselves thereon and place their feet on a high bench. Whatever this official says or does is carefully heeded, just as the Catholics obey the Holy Gospels. If he issues a command it is more strictly obeyed by these Indians than the ten commandments are observed by the Christians. Therefore, the leaders do not take their seats on this elevation except for a special ceremony. [Casañas, 1927, pp. 212–213.]

Speaking of the Natchitoches and Acolapissa Indians without distinction, Pénicaut says: "They are neat enough in their manner of eating: they have separate pots for each thing they cook, that is to say, the pot which is for meat is not used for fish" (Margry, 1875–1886, vol. 5, p. 468). He places their morning meal at about 8 a. m., but this was after part of their work had been done, not before work as with us (Margry, 1875–1886, vol. 5, p. 467).

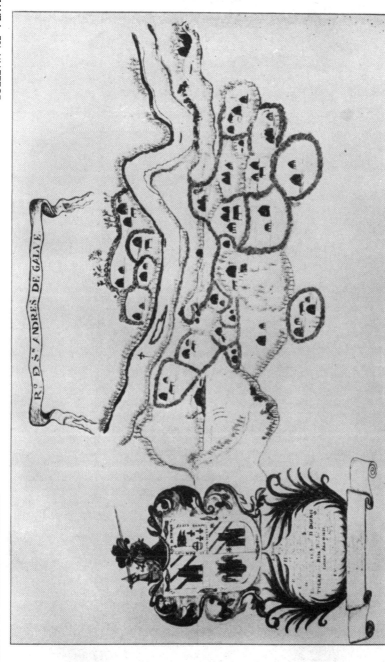

MAP OF THE KADOHADACHO SETTLEMENTS, BASED ON TERAN'S EXPLORATION OF 1691 AND SHOWING THE TERAN COAT OF ARMS.

The original is in the Archivo General de Indias, 61–6–2, and is on parchment 60 by 38 cmm.   Reproduced from Texas in the Middle Eighteenth Century (frontispiece), by Herbert E. Bolton.

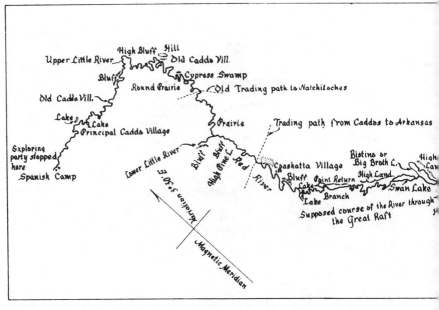

Nicholas King's Map of the Red River in Louisiana, *drawn up from the survey notes of the Freeman-Custis Expedition of 1806, definitively mapped the lower 615 miles of the Red and was widely adopted. It appears here redrawn from the original.*

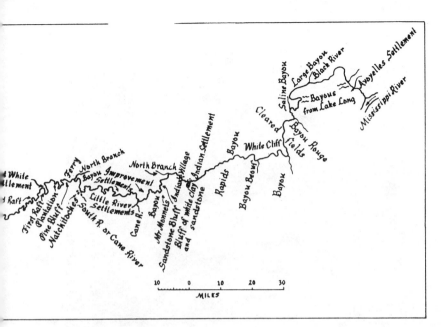

White
Settlement

First Raft

Plantation

Pine Bluff

Natchitoches

South R. or Cane River

Little River
Settlements

Bayou Improvement
Settlements

North Branch

Ferry

North Branch

Cane R.

Bayou

Mr Monnet's

Sandstone Bluff

Bluff of white clay
and sandstone

Indian Village

Indian Settlement

Rapids

Bayou Boeuf

Bayou

White Cliff

Bayou

Cleared
fields

Bayou Rouge

Saline Bayou

Large Bayou

Black River

Bayous
from Lake Long

Avoyelles Settlement

Mississippi River

10   0   10   20   30

MILES

2. Show-e-tat, from photograph by Alex. Gardner, 1872. (Bur. Amer. Ethnol., No. 1366–a.)

1. Show-e-tat, from photograph by Soulé, between 1868 and 1872. (Bur. Amer. Ethnol., No. 1373–b.)

THE CADDO CHIEF SHOW-E-TAT, OR LITTLE BOY, KNOWN TO THE WHITES AS GEORGE WASHINGTON.

2. JOHN WILSON (SEATED), LEADER IN THE GHOST DANCE AND IN THE PEYOTE RITUAL AMONG THE CADDO INDIANS; WITH A CADDO INDIAN OR A DELAWARE (STANDING).

From photograph by Mooney, 1893. (Bur. Amer. Ethnol., No. 1372.)

1. THE CADDO CHIEF NAH-AH-SA-NAH, KNOWN TO THE WHITES AS GUADALUPE ("WARLOUPE").

Born in 1825 near Natchitoches, La.   From photograph by Alex. Gardner, 1872.   (Bur. Amer. Ethnol., No. 1365-b.)

2. White Deer, from photograph by Alex. Gardner, 1872.   (Bur. Amer. Ethnol., No. 1364–b.)

1. White Deer, from photograph by Alex. Gardner, 1872.   (Bur. Amer. Ethnol., No. 1364–a.)

WHITE DEER, OR ANTELOPE, CADDO DELEGATE TO WASHINGTON IN 1872.   HE DIED THE SAME YEAR.

1. GEORGE PARTON, JUDGE OF CADDO INDIAN COURT.
From photograph by Mooney, 1893.   (Bur. Amer. Ethnol., No. 1371–b.)

2. HOME OF GEORGE PARTON, CADDO INDIAN JUDGE.
From photograph by Mooney, 1893.   (Bur. Amer. Ethnol., No. 1371–c.)

2. CADDO MAN WITH HIS HORSE.

From photograph by Mooney, 1893. (Bur. Amer. Ethnol., No. 1373-a.)

1. MINNIE AND CHARLIE PARTON, CADDO INDIANS.

From photograph by Mooney, 1893. (Bur. Amer. Ethnol., No. 1371-a.)

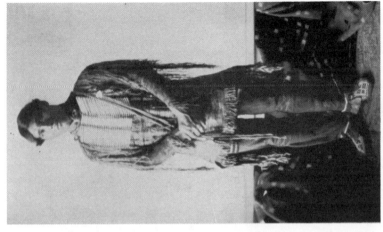

2. STANLEY EDGE, A CADDO INDIAN, BORN IN 1874.

From photograph in collection of Bur. Amer. Ethnol. (No. 1367-b.)

1. SAM HOUSTON, A CADDO INDIAN, BORN IN 1838.

From photograph by Sawyer, 1898. (Bur. Amer. Ethnol. No. 1370-a.)

2. Thomas Wisler, from photograph in collection of Bur. Amer. Ethnol. (No. 1368-a.)

1. Thomas Wisler, from photograph in collection of Bur. Amer. Ethnol. (No. 1368-c.)

THOMAS WISLER, A CADDO INDIAN, BORN IN 1862.

2. Bar-zin-debar, from photograph by Sawyer, 1898.   (Bur. Amer. Ethnol., No. 1369–b.)

1. Bar-zin-debar, from photograph by Sawyer, 1898.   (Bur. Amer. Ethnol., No. 1369–a.)

BAR-ZIN-DEBAR, OR TALL MAN.

"CADDOE INDIANS CHASING BUFFALOE; CROSS TIMBERS, TEXAS."

From the painting by George Catlin, listed as above in his London catalog of 1848. Original now in the Division of Ethnology of the United States National Museum.

CADDO ORNAMENTS.

a, b, c, d, silver ear pendants (entire length 1¾ in., length of pendant 1 in.), collected in Arizona in 1868; *c,* silver Caddo earring, presumably collected at same time as *a; f, g,* silver rings rudely engraved, worn by Caddo Indians (length of disks 1⅝ in. and 2⅛ in.; diameter of rings ⅞ in. and ¾ in.), collected in New Mexico in 1868. All above collected by Dr. Edward Palmer.   (U. S. N. M. Nos. 6946, 6948, 6949.)

CADDO MOCCASINS, UNDECORATED.

Diameter, 5¼ in.; width, 4½ in.; length, 9½ in.   Collected by Dr. Edward Palmer in 1858.
(U. S. N. M. No. 6986.)

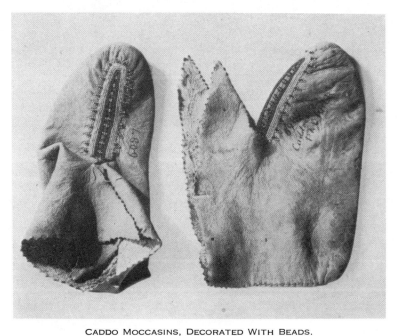

CADDO MOCCASINS, DECORATED WITH BEADS.

Length, 10 in.; diameter, 7 in.   Collected by Dr. Edward Palmer in 1858.   (U. S. N. M. No. 6987.)

A CADDO CAMP.

From a volume of prints made by Soulé between 1868 and 1872. (Bur. Amer. Ethnol., No. 1373-c.)

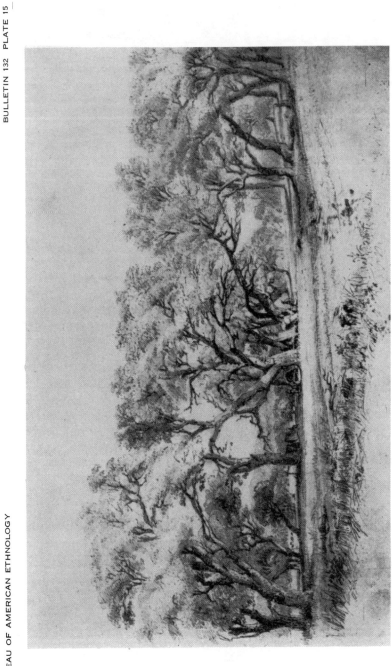

"ENCAMPMENT OF CADDO INDIANS," AT LIVE OAKS, 2 MILES FROM FREDERICKSBURG, TEXAS.

From a sketch by Seth Eastman, March 2, 1849, in the collection of the late D. I. Bushnell, Jr.

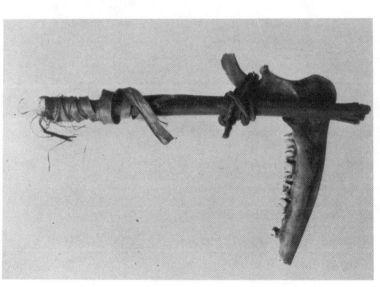

2. CADDO BISON HORN SPOONS.

Collected by Dr. Edward Palmer.   (U. S. N. M. No. 6883–5.)

1. SICKLE MADE OUT OF THE LOWER JAW OF A DEER.

Collected by Dr. Edward Palmer.   (U. S. N. M. No. 6880.)

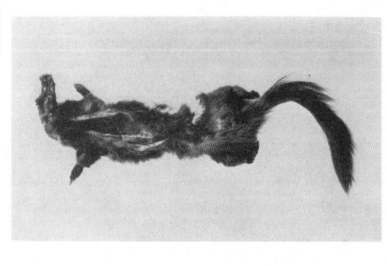

2. CADDO TOBACCO POUCH MADE OF THE SKIN OF A SKUNK.

Collected by Dr. Edward Palmer. (U. S. N. M. No. 6924.)

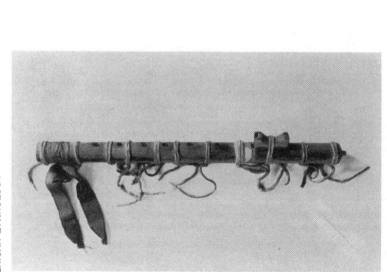

1. CADDO FLAGEOLET.

Collected by Mooney in February 1896. Length, 15⅜ in.; diam., 1 in.; bore, ¾ in. It has six finger holes, the uppermost one 1⅝ in. below the lip of the reed.

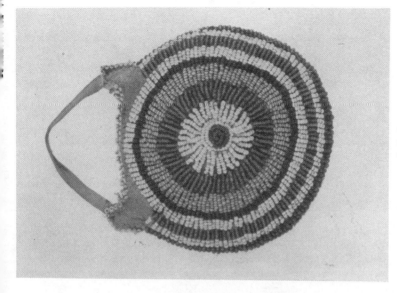

2. Back.

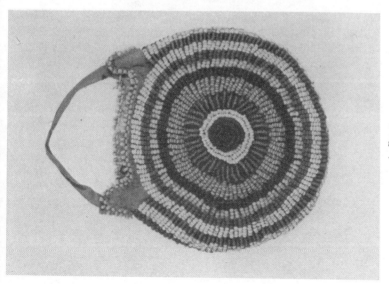

1. Front.

CADDO BEADED SKIN CHARM BAG.
Diameter, 3⅜ in.   (U. S. N. M. No. 362328.)

PAINTED WOODEN FIGURINE WITH A HUMAN SCALP-LOCK WIG.
Attributed to the Caddo.   Height, 6½ in.; width, 2¼ in.; depth, 3⅛ in.   (U. S. N. M. No. 378577.)

GAMES

The Caddo were fond of foot races and wrestling. Their principal game in the old days was a kind of hockey. They also played a game in which four split canes were used. The concave sides of three of these were red and one black. They were all thrown down together on a square block. If they then lay with their convex sides or their concave sides all up, it counted 4. If the black one lay concave side up and the others convex it counted 2. If any of the red ones lay with the red showing it counted nothing. Illustrations of several sets of these "dice" in the Field Museum of Natural History are given by Culin (1907, pp. 98–99).

They also played a guessing game with a long white ivory bead. Two sides were formed with a leader for each. The leader of one side took the bead and gave it to one of his men. This man then shuffled it about and the leader of the opposite side had to guess where it was. The side scoring eight points first won. No gambling was connected with this game. The participants sang constantly and the victorious party ended with a grand song of triumph.

Another game was played by two persons on a board having nine holes. Three pins were placed in a row in front of each on opposite sides. The object was to get the three pins in a row again and a player could move to any vacant hole on the board, each player watching carefully so as to block his opponent.

Still another game was played with grains of corn laid in a certain way. All the grains but one were eliminated by jumping one grain over another.[17]

The Caddo also played the hoop and pole game described in the following myth:

In the story of the "Brothers Who Became Lightning and Thunder," Doctor Dorsey tells of two brothers, the elder of whom made two arrows for his younger brother; one he painted black and the other he painted blue. They then made a small wheel out of the bark of the elm tree. One of the boys would stand about fifty yards away from the other and they would roll this little wheel to each other and would shoot the wheel with the arrows. They played with the wheel every day until finally the younger brother failed to hit the wheel, when the wheel kept on rolling and did not stop. They followed its traces and, after a series of adventures, recovered the wheel from an old man, whom they killed. Later they ascended to the sky and became the Lightning and Thunder. [Culin, 1907, pp. 462–463.]

The "guessing game" is the "hand-game" described in more detail by Parsons. According to her informants the players used two little bones and played for six points. Her account of the foot races shows that interest in this ancient Caddo sport has been perpetuated to the present day (Parsons, 1941, pp. 40–42).

---

[17] Notes I obtained in 1912.

CEREMONIES USED ON MEETING STRANGERS

The Caddo and some neighboring peoples were in the habit of meeting strangers with loud wails. This was first observed by De Soto's followers in the case of a messenger from the Tula chief who came "weeping bitterly" (Robertson, 1933, pp. 197, 198). When Joutel was among the Hasinai he was much alarmed by the entrance into the house where he was staying of several wailing women, since he had been informed by La Salle that such actions pointed to the death of some person, either accomplished or meditated (Margry, 1875–1886, vol. 3, p. 374). Later, when Tonti accused the Namidish of having slain some Frenchmen, the women present confirmed his suspicions by beginning to cry, but he did not ascertain actually whether or not his fears were justified (Cox, 1905, vol. 1, p. 49). However, the meaning of this usage does not seem to have been the same invariably. Many years ago Mr. Mooney informed me that Plains Indians of his acquaintance met him with tears when he revisited them, on the ground, they said, that he reminded them of those who had died since last they met.

The dialect of the Kadohadacho seems to have been the common medium of communication among all Caddo, but there was little difference between it and the dialects spoken by the other Caddo tribes except those of the Adai and Eyeish. The sign language was in use among them as early as the end of the seventeenth century and is mentioned by Joutel (Margry, 1875–1886, vol. 3, p. 389), Massanet (Casis, 1899, p. 302), and Casañas (1927, p. 286), and described rather definitely by Morfi. After some words on the diversity of speech among East Texas Indians generally, the last mentioned says:

> But all of them find it convenient to use another kind of language, in which it is not necessary to use the tongue, and that is the sign language with which they are exceedingly clever. They send ambassadors to one another and they are days at a time in conversation treating on subjects of lasting importance, explaining and making each other understand the most hidden thoughts, without need of words. [Morfi, 1932, p. 20.]

Joutel observed that they, along with members of other tribes, indicated surprise by placing their hands over their mouths (Margry, vol. 3, p. 430).

Amenities between the tribes are thus described by Espinosa:

> The way in which they most clearly show their civilization is in the embassies which they send to various settlements, especially when they wish to call them together for war. The captains receive the person who goes as an ambassador with great honor. They assign him the principal seat and, following their custom, give him a great many presents while preparing the reply they are to give him. They are so strict in the observance of their pledges that they do not fail, even a day, in gathering together to go in search of the enemy, the most outspoken of whom are the Apaches. Upon the occasions on which the Caddo-

aches, who live toward the north, come forty leagues to the Texas country, they send a messenger in advance to give information of their coming. Hostages are immediately exchanged and information furnished all the houses in the settlement so that the necessary provisions may be prepared. Each gives liberally and all the *caziques* come out with their captains to receive them several leagues before they reach the settlement. They all dress in gala attire according to their custom. After they arrive at the houses they give dances and festivals and exchange gifts of whatever the country yields in abundance. Thus they renew their friendship and make treaties to defend each other against their enemies.

They observe the same custom with the tribes that lie to the south who live near the shores of the Mexican Gulf. They are in the habit of coming to the aid of the Texas Indians. To keep them well disposed in times of war, the Texas Indians entertain them every year after the crops are gathered which is the time when many families, men and women, come to visit the Asinais. This is also the time at which they trade with each other for all the things they lack in their own settlements. They preserve close friendship with all the Indians who are subject to the French and when one party visits the other, the exchange of courtsies is very marked. The preparations for receptions are very great. These Indians have been thus carefully trained in politeness by the French and our Indians try not to be outdone by them in politeness and courtesies. They do not yield a point in proving themselves equally as warlike and valiant. [Espinosa, 1927, pp. 178–179.]

Morfi covers this ground in the following excerpts:

They are very attentive and civil to the ambassadors who are sent them. The captains go out to receive them. They give them a principal seat, and bestow many honors on them at their meetings. They grant them hospitality in a comfortable house and give them presents, and splendid ones, when they give them the reply they desire. And the pacts drawn up on these occasions are so punctiliously observed, that if they resolve to form a campaign together, they never fail to comply with the terms agreed upon, unless something occurs to make it impossible. [Morfi, 1932, p. 53.]

When the Cadodachos . . . go to visit them [the Texas] they send a messenger ahead, to advise them of their arrival. They immediately extend the due hospitality, and command the publication of this notice to the pueblo, so each family will contribute to its respective part of the provisions, which they all do with pleasure. The principal captain with the *Caciques*, elders, and officers, all in ceremonial attire, go out beyond the pueblo to receive the guests, festively take them to their houses, supply them in profusion, and exchange presents and renew former confederations. They show the same attentions to the Nations of the South, immediately on the coast of the Gulf of Mexico, who in matters of warfare are accustomed to ally themselves with the Texas; to thank them for this friendship they receive them with love every year after the crops, which is the regular season in which the men and women visit the Asinais, and exchange those things they respectively want in their pueblos. With those Indians who are subjects of French domination they also have friendly relations and when they receive their visits though they pay them the highest respect, they are outdone by the visitors, who are very vain with their great civilities, and do not want the Texas to get the better of them in this regard. [Morfi, 1932, pp. 53–54.]

With these accounts may be compared the descriptions of the manner in which they welcomed the Spaniards and French, as given on pages 30, 38–39, 43, 57, and 60.   A few others deserve reproduction at this place.

When Joutel's party came within half a league of the Kadohadacho (really the Nasoni) town—

one of our savages went to inform them. They came out before us, the chief mounted on a fine gray steed.

This chief showed us many signs of friendship on his arrival. We informed him that we harmed no one, at least unless they attacked us first; we had him smoke, after which he made a sign to us to follow him, and we came with him to the bank of a river, where this chief motioned to us to wait until he had informed the old men.

A short time afterward a troop of them arrived and, having reached us, gave us to understand that they came to carry us to their village. Our savages indicated that this was the custom of the country, and it was necessary to submit and let them do it. As soon as we had agreed to this ceremony, seven of the most distinguished presented their backs or shoulders. M. Cavelier, as chief, was the first to mount, and the others did so likewise.

As to myself, who am rather tall and who was besides burdened with clothing, a gun, two pistols, lead, powder, a kettle, and various togs, I weighed as much assuredly as my bearer could support; and because I was taller than he and my legs would have touched the ground, two other savages supported them. Thus I had three bearers. The other savages took our horses in order to lead them, and we arrived with this ridiculous train at the village. Our bearers, who had covered more than a quarter of a league, had need of rest, and we need to be delivered from our mounts in order to laugh in private, for it was necessary to avoid carefully doing it before them.

As soon as we had arrived at the chief's cabin, where we found that more than two hundred persons had come to see us, and when our horses were un-loaded, the old men gave us to understand that it was customary to bathe strangers on their arrival, but that, as we were dressed, they would bathe only our faces, which an old man did with clear water from a kind of earthen pan, and he washed only our foreheads.

After this second ceremony, the chief made a sign to have us seated on some-thing like a small scaffold, raised about four feet from the earth, made of wood and canes, and thither the chiefs of the four villages came to harangue us one after the other. We listened to them with patience, although we understood nothing of what they said, and were much wearied on account of their length and still more from the heat of the sun which beat directly upon us.

These harangues finished, which were for no other purpose than to assure us that we were welcome, we gave them to understand that we were going to our own country intending to return soon in order to bring them merchandise and all things they had need of.

We then made them the customary presents of axes, knives, beads and needles and pins for their women, telling them that when we returned we would give them much more.

We informed them besides that if they would give us some corn or flour, we would give them something else in exchange, which they consented to. They did this after having fed us on hominy (sagamité), bread, beans, pumpkins and other things of which we had great need, we having eaten almost nothing during the day, some from necessity, others from devotion like M. Cavelier, who had wished to observe the fast of the Eve of St. John whose name he bore. [Margry, 1875–1886, vol. 3, pp. 404–406.]

After leaving the Red River towns, in July 1687, Joutel and his comrades came into the territory of the Cahinnio Indians, the frontier tribe of Caddo.

Having stopped to eat on the banks of a river, we heard the noise of some hawkbells or house bells, which made us look around when we perceived a savage with a naked sword in his hand, ornamented with feathers of different colors, and two hawkbells which were making the noise that we had heard.

He signed to us to approach and informed us that he had been delegated by the old men of the village whither we were going to come to us. He made many friendly gestures. I observed that this sword was Spanish and that it gave him pleasure to makes the bells ring.

Having gone on half a league or about that with him, we saw a dozen more savages coming toward us who made many endearing gentures and conducted us to the village, into the cabin of the chief, where we found dressed bear skins laid down on which they had us sit. They gave us food and the old men who attended us thither were served afterwards; and the women came in a crowd to look at us . . .

On the 7th [the next day] the old men came to visit us and they brought us two buffalo skins, four otter skins, one white deer skin, all very well dressed, and four bows, and all that in acknowledgment of the present we had made them previously. The chief and another man returned some time afterward and brought us two loaves of bread, the finest and best we had yet seen; they seemed to have been cooked in an oven, and nevertheless we had not noticed any such among them. This chief remained with us some hours; he seemed to have much intelligence and prudence and understood readily our signs, which constituted our common language. He retired after having directed a little boy to bring us everything we might want. [Margry, 1875–1886, vol. 3, pp. 415–416.]

The same day they experienced the calumet ceremony for the first time among Caddo people.[18]

That evening, we took part in a ceremony which we had not seen before. A troop of old men, followed by some young men and some women, came near our cabin in a body and singing at the top of their lungs. The one who marched at their head carried a calumet ornamented with different kinds of feathers. After having sung for some time in front of our cabin, they entered and continued to sing for about a quarter of an hour. After that, they took M. Cavelier, the priest, as being our chief, and led him ceremoniously outside of the cabin, holding him up [by grasping him] under his arms. When they had reached a place prepared for the purpose, one of them put a great handful of grass under his feet, two others brought clear water in an earthen dish and washed his face; after that they seated him on a skin prepared for the purpose.

When M. Cavelier was seated, the old men arranged themselves around him also seated, and the master of ceremonies stuck up two forked sticks, on which having laid a crosspiece, all painted red, he spread over it a dressed buffalo skin, and then another of a deer dressed white, and then put the calumet upon them.

---

[18] When La Salle visited the Hasinai in 1686, Father Anastasius says that the Frenchmen were met by several chiefs followed by warriors finely attired and "bearing the calumet ceremoniously," but this did not involve the performance of the regular calumet ceremony to which Joutel refers, nor was this "calumet" the regular peace pipe.

The singing began again; the women joined in this music, and the concert was accompanied by means of hollow gourds in which were some large bits of gravel to make a noise, which the savages beat, keeping time with the music of the choir, and, what was most pleasant, one of them placed himself behind M. Cavelier to hold him up while making him move with a swinging motion from side to side with movements regulated to the same cadence.

This concert was not yet finished when the master of ceremonies led forward two girls, one wearing a kind of necklace, and the other the skin of an otter, which they placed on the forks side of the calumet. After that, he seated them side of M. Cavelier so that they faced each other, their legs extended and interlaced, upon which the same master of ceremonies placed those of M. Cavelier so that his legs were above and crosswise of those of the two girls.

While he was occupied in this way, an old man fixed a painted feather back of M. Cavelier's head, tying it by means of his hair. The singing, however, kept on continually, so that M. Cavelier, wearied at its length, and besides, ashamed to find himself in this posture between two girls without knowing the reason, made a sign to us to inform the chief that he felt sick. Immediately two of them seized him under the arms and brought him back into the cabin and made signs to him to rest. This was about nine o'clock in the evening, and the savages passed the entire night singing until they could do so no longer.

Day having arrived, they came to get M. Cavelier, brought him outside of the cabin with the same ceremony, and seated him, singing all the time; then the leader of the ceremonies took the calumet, filled it with tobacco, lighted it, and presented it to M. Cavelier, but withdrew it and advanced it without giving it to him as many as ten times. Having finally placed it between his hands, M. Cavelier made a pretense of smoking it and returned it to them. They had us all smoke afterwards and then all smoked in their turn, the music still continuing.

About nine o'clock in the morning, the sun becoming very hot, M. Cavelier, his head being bare, exhibited signs of great discomfort. They then stopped their singing, conducted him back into the cabin, took the calumet, placed it in a deerskin case along with the two forks and the crosspiece of red wood, and one of the old men offered it to M. Cavelier, assuring him that with this sign of peace he would be able to pass through all the nations that were allied to them, and that we would be well received everywhere; and this was where we saw for the first time the calumet of peace, the others not having had any knowledge of it as some have maintained. [Margry, 1875–1886, vol. 3, pp. 416–419.]

And here is Espinosa's description of the way in which the Hasinai welcomed Governor Martin de Alarcon when he assumed the government of the Texas Province in 1718:

[The Indians] came out to meet the governor who was all ready to receive them after the Indian custom. A gunshot distance from the mission [of Purissima Concepción], the captains appeared on horseback. One took his spurs, another his sword, another his cane. They then placed him on the shoulders of the principal *cacique*, while still another supported his feet. One of the Indians led his horse by the bridle and, thus laden, they came to the mission. They had already prepared a throne with curious buffalo robes which serve as carpets. Before setting him down, they washed his face very clean and carefully gave him a pipe of peace containing tobacco. This is the ceremony by which they declare anyone a captain-general among them. Afterwards they had a speech made in the name of the whole nation in which they told him that two days later all the people would come to that place to render obedience. On the third day a great number of persons from the four missions, men and women, gathered, together with their captains. When night came on, they lighted a great many fires and placed a very artistically cushioned seat in a doorway to give to the governor for investiture. They put on his head a very curious feather and, sitting down, they began to sing to the accompaniment of fifes and drums, the men and women being in separate ranks. Then one after another, in the name of the various settlements, each made a speech in his own language and began to make offerings to him of beautifully dressed skins and many jars of eatables. This ceremony lasted about half the night. They enjoyed it so much that the Indians wanted to keep on until morning, but, at my request, they consented to finish in their own *fiesta*. They permitted us to rest—which we did. I made a speech in the name of the governor, thanking them in their own language for their politeness and promising that the Spaniards would always favor them. They were very much pleased thereat and discontinued their songs until the following day. [Espinosa, 1927, p. 180.]

The account of this given by Castañeda is drawn from documents unavailable to the writer and is as follows:

When he approached Concepción Mission on the Angelina River he was met by Captain Ramón, Father Espinosa, a number of soldiers, and the mission Indians drawn up in line to welcome him. Father Espinosa had left the main expedition four days before and hurried to Concepción Mission to arrange for the reception of the governor. A salute was fired, the bells rang merrily, and all the Indians cheered and presented their gifts. Then followed a curious ceremony. The Asinay Indians adopted the new governor as a member of their tribe and initiated him with great solemnity. This evening Alarcón rode his horse to a large straw hut which had been built specially for the occasion by the Indians. When he arrived, several chiefs came out to receive him. He was first helped down from his horse, then a chief took his sword and pistols, another took him up on his back, and a third held his feet. In this manner they carried him into the hut. At the door they gently washed his face and hands and dried them with a piece of cloth. With a chief on each side, their hands on his shoulders, Alarcón was escorted to a seat prepared for him. After he sat down, the principal chief gave him the peace pipe which he smoked and then passed to the others. After they had all smoked, several Indians rose and with expressive gestures made known to the governor their great pleasure at his coming, to which he replied by explaining to them the pious zeal of His Majesty, who had sent him and all the missionaries to help them and instruct them in our holy faith and defend them against their enemies.

The governor decided to make Concepción Mission his headquarters while in East Texas and asked the Indians to build a shelter for him, which they did promptly. This was a circular structure with walls made of branches and the roof covered with grass, in the shape of a rounded dome. To celebrate the completion of the house and to honor Alarcón the Indians held a native dance. At this celebration the initiation of the governor was completed. The Indians came decked in bright feathers and dressed in skins. They built a large fire in front of the hut, placed a special seat near it, and spread a number of buffalo skins on the ground in place of rugs. The principal chiefs then entered the house, where the governor was and adorned him carefully with white feathers plucked from the breasts of geese, which they placed on his head after their own fashion. They then painted a broad black stripe upon his forehead, which came down each side of his face to about the middle of his cheeks. He was now taken before the fire, made to sit down on the buffalo skins and to lean back on one of the chiefs who sat on the specially prepared seat and placed his hands upon the governor's shoulders. The ceremony had thus far been conducted in silence. Now they began to beat on a big drum made out of an old kettle partly filled with water and covered with a piece of wet rawhide. The beating of the drum was accompanied by the swish of rattles. The Indians all sat on the ground and arranged themselves in groups, the men, women, and children seated separately. When the drum began to beat and the rattles to swish, they all began to sing in unison. Four additional large fires were now built and the leaders, who held lighted torches made out of bamboo [cane], diligently went about the crowd to keep order. From time to time the din ceased and one chief or another would stand before the governor and make a long talk with forceful gestures. They declared they were glad the Spaniards had come back, that they considered the new governor one of their own, that he was their *Caddi*, or chief, that they would always be friendly to him and his people and that they wanted him to help and to protect the Indians against their enemies. Alarcón replied to these manifestations of attachment by declaring he would help and protect them, but they must swear allegiance to the king to whom they should always be grateful for all he had done, for it was he who had sent the soldiers to shield them, and the missionaries to instruct them in our holy religion. The ceremony lasted until three o'clock in the morning, according to the chronicler. [Castañeda, 1936, vol. 2, pp. 103–104.]

In 1716 Ramón and the missionaries sent into the Province of Texas were received in this manner:

On June 27th we met thirty-four Indians, five of them being captains. They all embraced us and showed the joy with which they received us in their country. On the next day after we had traveled nine leagues ninety-six persons came out to meet us, with all their captains and leading men. We went to meet them carrying a standard upon which was engraved the images of the Crucified Christ and Our Lady of Guadalupe whom they all adored, all kneeling and kissing the images.

We marched on in a procession singing the *Te Deum Laudamus* until we came to a very large arbor that had been provided for the occasion and our songs ended in tears of rejoicing. We began to take our seats on saddles that were tied and served as low chairs, while coarse cloth served us as carpets. Each captain took a hatful of the powdered tobacco they used and placed it upon a curious and beautifully painted deerskin. They all stirred it around to show their union of wills. They then put some of the tobacco in a pipe adorned with many white feathers as a sign of peace among them. One of the principal Indians lighted it and, after taking a whiff, he passed it to the priests and other Spaniards, for this is their most usual ceremony when receiving friends. We made on our part presents of chocolate to all the *caziques* while, in the name of His Majesty, the captains divided among all the Indians hats, little blankets, tobacco, and other trinkets. The Indians returned the favor with young corn, muskmelons, tamales (which are rolls of corn), beans cooked with corn, and nuts. [Espinosa, 1927, pp. 151–152.]

Describing the same ceremony, Ramón says that the Indians

brought out a large pipe, used only to make peace. Each one took a portion of tobacco, which they have in abundance, and, filling the bowl [with it], they lighted it and began smoking. The captains smoked first in this manner: the first puff of smoke was blown to the sky, the second to the East, the third to the West, the fourth to the North, the fifth to the South, and the sixth to the ground, these being the signs of lasting peace.

The chief smoked first and passed the pipe to Ramón who then passed it on until every man and woman present had smoked it. Afterward "the chiefs took out more tobacco from their pouches, piled it in the center, and invited Ramón to take some," and Ramón reciprocated (Castañeda, 1936, vol. 2, p. 55).

It may be remarked that this order in placating the powers of the cardinal points is unusual, the commoner method being to continue on and generally in a counter clockwise direction.

In oratory Caddo speakers were evidently no whit behind other Indians as may be gathered from the comments of Pierce M. Butler, Agent for the Cherokee, on the bearing and speech of the Caddo spokesman at a convention held in 1845 (see p. 97).

PUNISHMENTS

Some of these have been touched upon in connection with house building (pp. 150–151). Casañas adds the following:

The punishments they use and inflict upon the delinquents consist of whippings, according to the crimes. For murder, they give the criminal so many licks that he rarely recovers his senses. If he has shot someone with an arrow, or if he has committed a personal offense, dealing, perhaps, a mortal blow to the *caddí* or to one of the family of this official—such as his father, mother, sons, or relatives,—he receives the death sentence. I have not seen the punishment myself, but it is such a common thing among them that even the children know about it. If a person shoots another with an arrow or does something else like it, one can be sure that the punishment will be inflicted and that it will result as described above. [Casañas, 1927, p. 283.]

Theft both within and without the tribe is dealt with by Espinosa:

The Texas Indians maintain an inviolable peace with the surrounding nations and they all preserve their own customs without any occasion being furnished for trouble; for, if it happens that a private individual does any damage or steals any of the many horses they possess, the aggrieved tribe sends to that band one of their principal men with a notice for the *caziques* to gather together, have the delinquent brought into their presence, force him to return the stolen property, and give him a sharp reprimand, threatening that if he repeats the offense, they will expel him or make an example of him. They observe strict justice in their dealings with each other. When one takes anything from another, the aggrieved person does not make a complaint, but presents the case to the principal captain. After consultation with the other captains and the old men, he makes the delinquent give satisfaction. He leaves the parties so well satisfied that there is no cause for future trouble. [Espinosa, 1927, p. 178.]

Morfi parallels this as follows:

When any one steals a horse from his neighbor, or commits another robbery, the offended nation sends a complaint to the offensive nation by one of its principal tribesmen. A meeting of *Casiques* is immediately held; they have the offender brought into their presence for trial, and oblige him to restore what he stole, keenly reprimanding him, intimating to him that if he should again be guilty of the same offense, they will either perpetually banish him from the tribe, or so punish him as to serve as a public warning. Among themselves they also so observe the administration of justice, and when one has a case against another, they do not settle it between them, but take their complaint to the principal captain of the tribe, who with the opinion (*dictamen*) of the other captains, and elders, corrects the guilty party, leaving both parties satisfied, without cause for future dissension. [Morfi, 1932, p. 53.]

WAR

Their idea of valor [says Morfi] is very distinct from ours. To show their valor they suffer by exposing themselves naked to the great heat of the sun, without even covering their heads or seeking shade, or wanting to; and they endure the cold of winter without looking for shelter, though at that season they commonly use buffalo hides; to show that they know how to scorn it they leave their huts at dawn when the frost is heaviest, break the ice on the river and bathe themselves. Flight at the sight of an enemy is not a dishonor. The warrior who brings any spoils from battle, though he got them through treason, or bad faith, is a hero. [Morfi, 1932, p. 52–53.]

Joutel supplies us with some notes regarding war customs which have the virtue of being based on direct observation. In March 1687, he was entertained in the cabin of one of the chiefs and was conducted from it by some old men to their assembly cabin so called

because they make such cabins when they are preparing for war and have feasts there in order to excite the young men to go. We found mats spread out on which they made us sit and had us smoke but they did not make as much ceremony over us as had those of the first town.

The white men slept, however, in the house of the chief. Joutel learned from a Frenchman who had been longer among them "that these savages did not reenter their own cabins after the assembly cabin had been made, that the women took care to bring them food, and the young people to wait upon them." The Caddo were already going to war on horseback (Margry, 1875–1886, vol. 3, pp. 354, 374). Joutel continues:

They make war . . . after the Turkish manner, giving no quarter, and bringing back scalps as trophies, so that one can tell the cabins of the warriors and brave men by the number of scalps there, for they tan them very neatly and display them in one of the most conspicuous places in the cabin. When there are many to share one scalp, they take it and separate the hairs, that is, the ones that are long; they make of them little tresses which they attach to the side of a reed which is placed in the row of scalps.

I have said already that the men had a big assembly cabin where they prepared for war with feasts and rejoicings, so that they do not ever retire into their own cabins. The women then bring food to that place for them, where the young men serve them and eat afterwards, and, when they have eaten and smoked, they train the youths in racing. I had the pleasure of seeing them go through with their exercises many times, since the cabin I lived in was very near that in which they were, so that I saw all that they did. Two of the most active chiefs ranged all the young men in a row and after they were all in order, they started off the instant a signal was given, and struggled to see who would win. They then planted two posts some distance apart, and a number started to run to see who could excel in rapidity in greater or fewer turns, after which they exercised themselves in shooting with the bow. They spent their days in this manner. [Margry, 1875–1886, vol. 3, pp. 354–355.]

Before setting out they "set fire to their assembly cabin in order to burn it down, as if it had been made and dedicated merely to serve on this occasion during a limited space of time" (Margry, 1875–1886, vol. 3, pp. 357–358).

During the absence of the warriors we saw only the old men who came to see us from time to time and related news which we had difficulty in understanding. Since I was able to interpret only by means of signs, I was often very much embarrassed. What disturbed me more than anything else was the fact that sometimes the women began to weep and I was unable to guess the reason; and as I had learned from M. de La Salle that they wept when they desired to play some rascally trick, as if they were weeping on account of the death of those they desired to kill, therefore that did not please me any too well, since I saw these sorts of faces often. I learned afterward that these wailings were caused by the remembrance of some of their friends or relatives who had been killed on these war parties like the one that had just been undertaken. As I was ignorant of this, that action often alarmed me . . .

We were in the midst of all this disquietude until the 18th of the same month [May], when to, our great surprise we saw at daybreak a troop of women enter our cabin with their faces and bodies daubed and painted. When they were all inside, they began to sing different songs in their language and at the top of their lungs, after which they began a kind of round dance holding one another by the hand. For what reason did they undertake that ceremony which lasted for perhaps two or three hours? We learned that it was because their people had returned victorious over their enemies, and because, as soon as the village had been informed, they had assembled in the manner I have described. Their dance ended in some presents of tobacco which those in the house made to the women who had come. I noticed during the dance of these latter that some of them took from time to time one of the scalps which were in the said cabin, and that they made with it gestures, presenting it sometimes in one direction, sometimes in another, as if to mock the nations from which the said scalp might have come. About midday one of the warriors also arrived at our cabin who was apparently the one who had brought news of the defeat of the enemies. The said savage told us that the people of his village had killed perhaps forty persons and that the others had fled, at which each one showed signs of great joy. But what displeased me was to see that however joyous these women were they began to weep. I kept apprehending some evil plot against us, on account of what I had heard said in the past. After all these ceremonies, all the women began to work, to pound up Indian corn, some to make porridge and others to make bread; they prepared to carry food to the warriors.

They set out next day, the 19th, to meet them . . . and toward evening all arrived. We learned then what had happened; they had met, surprised, and terrified their enemies through some gunshots by our people, who, having killed some, caused the others to take to flight. And, in fact, before any had been

killed, the enemy held their ground firmly and showed no sign of fear; but at
the gunshots, which they had not expected, they had fled as rapidly as possible:
so that our savages killed or took forty-eight persons, as well men and women
as children. They killed many women who had climbed into the trees, in which
they were concealed, having foreseen that they could not run away, and not
having enough time to get to their feet with the others. Few men were taken
in this defeat but the women remained as victims, for it is not customary for
the savages to give quarter, unless it be to infants. They took off the scalp of
a living woman after which they asked for a charge of powder and a ball from
our people, which they gave to the said woman and sent her back to her nation,
having told her to give that to her people and inform them that they might
expect in future to be treated in the same way.

I think I have spoken elsewhere of scalping, which consists in cutting the
skin completely around the head, as far down as the ears and forehead; they then
pull off the entire skin, which they take pains to tan and taw [dress] in order
to keep it and exhibit it in their cabins. They thus leave the victim with the
skull exposed, as they did the above-mentioned woman whom they sent back
to carry the news to her nation. They led the other [captive woman] along until
the women and girls had joined them with the provisions they were bringing.
Then they gave the unhappy woman to be sacrificed to their rage and passion,
according to what the men of our party told me, who were witnesses of it.
When the said women had arrived and were informed that there was a slave,
they all armed themselves, some with sticks, others with wooden skewers which
they sharpened, and each one struck her according as desire or caprice seized
one or another. This unfortunate woman only awaited the final blow, suffering
martyrdom that is to say, for one pulled out of her head a fistful of hair, another
cut off a finger, another gouged out an eye, so that each one of them studied
how to make her suffer some evil; and finally there was one who gave her a
heavy blow on the head with a club, and another buried a skewer many times
in her body; after which she expired. Then they cut her body into many pieces
which the conquerors divided among themselves, and which they forced several
slaves they had taken in the past to eat. They returned then in triumph from
their war, and of the forty-eight persons they had taken they gave quarter only
to some young children, bringing back all the scalps, and many of the women
even who had gone to the war with the others came back loaded with
heads . . .

The next day twenty savages assembled and went to the cabin of the chief
whither all the scalps were brought as trophies, as well as the heads. They
then began to rejoice greatly, and it lasted all that day at the aforementioned
cabin; but the ceremony lasted three days, since they went then to the cabins
of the most noted among them, whom they call *cadis*, which signifies chiefs or
captains. They invited the six Frenchmen who had gone with them to take
part in their rejoicings since they had taken part in their victory: so that,
as we were in a cabin belonging to one of the most distinguished men, they
came there after having finished at the cabin of the head chief.

I wondered at the way in which they behaved.

After all had arrived, the old men and the most esteemed took their places
on the mats, on which they seated themselves. Then one of the aforesaid
ancients, who had not been with these, and who appeared to be the orator,
and acted as chief of the ceremonies, made for them a kind of eulogium or
discourse of which I understood nothing A short time afterward the warriors
who had slain enemies in battle and had taken scalps, marched, preceded by a
woman carrying a great reed and a deer skin; then followed the wife of the

said warrior bearing the scalp, and the said warrior followed with his bow and two arrows, and, when they reached the place where was the orator or chief of ceremonies, the said warrior took the scalp and put it in the hands of the said orator, who, having received it, presented it toward the four quarters of the earth saying many things which I did not understand; after which he laid the scalp on the ground, or rather on a mat spread out for this purpose. Another then approached until each one had brought his scalp as a trophy. When all that was completed, the orator delivered a kind of discourse, and food was served, the women of the aforesaid cabin having taken care to cook hominy in many big pots, knowing that the crowd was going to come. After they had eaten and smoked they began a dance, in the nature of a round dance, but which they did not close up. They kept a kind of cadence which they marked with their feet and with fans made of turkey feathers: in such a way that they accompanied all with their songs which seemed to me too long since I did not understand them.

Their ceremony ended with some presents of tobacco, which the occupants of the aforementioned cabin made to the old men and warriors. I ought to mention also that the chief of the ceremonies had brought to the scalps hominy and tobacco as if they had been able to eat and smoke. They also had two young boys whom they had taken and whom they had spared. One of them was wounded and was unable to walk; they had in consequence placed him on a horse, and, as they had brought along pieces of the flesh of the woman whom they had tortured, they made these two young boys eat some as well as some other slaves whom they had taken at other times. I did not notice that they themselves ate of them. After they were through, they went to still other cabins, and this ceremony lasted three days in these cantons . . .

The 22d of May there arrived among these savages one of their warriors whom they believed to have been killed, he having remained wounded on the field of battle and left for dead. He stated that for six days he had eaten only some little uncooked roots; five or six arrow wounds, three of them in the body, had caused him to lose much blood. The fast, the fatigue, added to the fear he had experienced, which cannot have been slight on seeing himself abandoned, all that had contributed to enfeeble him, so that they made a little cabin for his sole use in order that he might have more complete rest, where they treated him after their manner, by cleaning the wounds well. Some persons among them sucked these, spitting out the blood and matter which they drew from them. They also gave him some simples to staunch the wounds. As this warrior had been a long time without eating, they made him take some very weak hominy and gave him a very little of it at a time. The other savages were very much rejoiced at his return. He related the manner in which he had come away from the battlefield, after he had recovered from his wounds, and how he had seen a band of the enemy who, luckily for him, had not discovered him for it is not to be believed that they would have spared him. [Margry, 1875–1886, vol. 3, pp. 374–382.]

Arrived at the Nasoni town of the Kadohadacho, the Frenchmen observed another token of the barbarity of Indian warfare in the person of a young man who had escaped from the "Chepoussa, their enemies," perhaps the Chickasaw, after having had his nose and ears cut off. There they were constantly visited by "women accompanied by some warriors with their bows and arrows" who

came into our cabin to sing with a doleful air, weeping the while, which would have caused us pain if we had not seen this ceremony before and learned that these women came thus into the cabin of the chief to beg him, with songs and tears, to take vengeance on those who had killed their husbands or relatives in past wars, as I have already said. [Margry, 1875–1886, vol. 3, pp. 409–411.]

Pénicaut, who accompanied St. Denis across the Hasinai country in 1714, gives another picture of warfare among these people in which none of the gruesome details are spared, though, from his tendency not to overwork truth where a good story is to be extracted, it should be treated with some caution.

These savages make war in a very different manner from those on the bank of the Mississippi, for they are all mounted, armed with a quiver made of buffalo skin filled with arrows, which they wear slung over the shoulders behind the back. They have a bow and a little shield also of buffalo hide, on the left arm, with which they parry arrows. They have no other bit to their bridle than a hair cord which passes through the mouth of the horse. Their stirrups are suspended by means of cords also made of hair which are fastened to a doeskin doubled into four thicknesses and serving them as a saddle. The stirrup is merely a little piece of wood three inches wide and five long, on which they put the foot to mount the horse and to hold themselves there. [Margry, 1875–1886, vol. 5, p. 507.]

Most of the men of the town St. Denis was then visiting were on a war expedition against the Kichai. Pénicaut continues:

They returned from the war the day after we arrived at their village. They numbered a hundred and fifty men armed and mounted, as I have just said. They carry themselves perfectly on horseback. They brought with them two prisoners out of six which they had taken; they had eaten four on the way back. These two prisoners were placed in the town square in the midst of a guard of twelve savages for fear that they might enter one of their cabins, for it is the custom of these savages that, if a prisoner, escaping by force or craft, enters one of their cabins, his life is spared and he is thenceforth reputed to belong to their nation. One hour later two "frames" (cadres) were prepared in the prairie which is at the end of the village. These frames are merely two posts planted in the earth four feet apart and nine feet high, on top of which is a bar which crosses from one to the other, to which they bind the prisoners with a cord by both hands and suspended in the air. Underneath there is a stake planted in the earth through which is a hole. Through this hole a cord is passed which is fastened to the ankles of these poor wretches, which they stretch as tight as they can in order to keep them well extended in the air, the feet reaching only within fifteen inches of the ground. They keep them thus during a half hour evening and morning, in the morning with their faces turned toward the rising sun and in the evening toward the setting sun, without giving them food the first day. They also make the victim dance in spite of himself, and the second day in the morning they fasten him again in the same manner, with his face toward the rising sun. All the men and women in the village assemble round the frames where these poor fainting persons are tied. Each family lights its fire before which they place a pot full of hot water, and, when the sun has arisen, four of the oldest savages, each one with a knife in his hand, make incisions in the arms, thighs, and lower legs of the ones hung up whose blood runs from their bodies to the extremities of their feet where four old men receive it in vessels. They carry this blood to two other old men whose duty it is to have it cooked in two kettles, and when this blood is cooked, they give it to their women and children to eat. After they have consumed this blood, the two dead men are detached from the frame and placed on a table where they are cut up. The pieces are distributed to the entire assembly of the village, and each family cooks some of it in its pot. While this meat is being cooked they begin to dance. Then they return to their places, take this meat from their pots and eat it.

I was so heart-sick at the sight of this horrible feast that I was sick for three days and my comrades like myself were unable to eat until after we had left these cruel cannibals. [Margry, 1875–1886, vol. 5, pp. 502–504.]

Except for brief mention by Casañas, other writers spare us such gruesome details in connection with their narratives of the Caddo but Morfi fully makes up for it in his account of the Karankawa Indians of the Texas coast (Morfi, 1932, p. 51), and Solís makes his atrocity stories general. Although speaking more specifically of the eastern and southern Texas Indians, he states that his remarks are of very wide application:

They are cruel, inhuman and ferocious. When one nation makes war with another, the one that conquers puts all of the old men and old women to the knife and carries off the little children for food to eat on the way; the other children are sold; the vagabonds and grown women and young girls are carried off to serve them, with the exception of some whom they reserve to sacrifice in the dance before their god and saints. This is done in the following manner: they set a nailed stake in the ground in the place where they are to dance the *mitote;* they light a big fire, tying the victim who is to be danced about or sacrificed to that stake. All assemble together and when the harsh instrument, the *caymán,* begins to play they begin to dance and to leap, making many gestures and very fierce grimaces with funereal and discordant cries, dancing with well sharpened knives in their hands. As they jump around they approach the victim and cut a piece of flesh off of his body, going to the fire and half roasting it in sight of the victim, they eat it with great relish, and so they go on cutting off pieces and quartering him until they take off all of the flesh and he dies. They take off his hair with the scalp and put it all on a pole in order to bring it to the dance as a trophy. They do not throw the bones away but distribute them, and each one whose turn it is to get one walks along sucking it until he is thus finished. They do the same thing with the priests and Spaniards if they catch any. Others they hang up by the feet and put fire underneath them and so go on roasting them and eat them up. For others they make long poles of the thickness of an inch of resinous pine, of which there is a great deal, and set fire to them and torture the victim with them, and afterwards they set fire to him and half roast him and eat him up. For others they do not use a knife to cut them to pieces but they tear them to pieces with their teeth and eat them raw. [Solís, 1931, pp. 42–43.]

The institution of berdaches is also pinned upon the coast Indians, probably to an unreasonable extent, and we hear that, as with the Florida Indians, berdaches accompanied war parties of the same people (Morfi, 1932, p. 55).

Morfi describes the equipment of warriors as follows:

All of the nations of the province [of Texas], and up to its borders, manage a gun, dagger, sword, lance and hatchet with particular skill, and most of them have not forgotten the bow and arrow. For defensive arms they have oval shields of leather (*adarga*), leather jackets (*cuera*), and helmets, which are a kind of cap (*montera*) made of skins, which they adorn with a diversity of plumage, and well painted buffalo horns. [Morfi, 1932, p. 53.]

According to the same writer they differed from the tribes farther east in carrying no food with them:

When they go out on campaigns, they never carry with them other provisions than those provided by their rifles or arrows. They rely upon the prodigal riches of the entire province for wild cattle and game. When these are lacking they do not decline to eat foxes, rats and snakes; and when the dearth is so bad that even these are not found, the temperance and fortitude with which they stand it is as admirable as the voracity exhibited when there is an abundance of food. [Morfi, 1932, p. 49.]

They put on paint when going to war—and also when expecting visitors so that they would not be inconveniently recognized by seekers for vengeance (Casañas, 1927, p. 214).

When on the march

they always have scouts ahead, flankers and rear-guards, who with inexpressible anxiety examine the territory. To encamp they always select advantageous sites, and post sentinels at opportune places; they are ever on the alert evening and morning, so that they get little sleep, and that, light. They arise at dawn, take a bath, if there is an opportunity to, regardless of the weather; on the march they never separate themselves at any considerable distance beyond the main body of the troops. These precautions, which are never omitted under any pretext, protect them from surprises and facilitate their making an advantageous attack. [Morfi, 1932, p. 50.]

Morfi has the following regarding smoke signals:

Anything new which occurs in the province which interests them, they communicate from one tribe to another, by means of smoke signals which they instantly give, and they know whether they are called, whether they are to flee, or whether they are told to take any special care. These are such speedy communications that by them they are instructed in a few hours at the greatest distance as to what happens in Béjar, and in the other presidios. This is the reason that we are generally unsuccessful in the most of our expeditions; one will never accomplish what one desires if everything is not done with inviolable secrecy so that not even our soldiers know where they are going. [Morfi, 1932, pp. 50–51; Solfs, 1931, p. 42.]

The most of the time [says Hidalgo] the men spend in visiting and in planning their wars, which usally occur during the winter time. For the two functions mentioned above [planting and war] the Indians choose a leader, but in all other matters they are their own bosses. They wear the scalps of their enemies at their belts as trophies and hang them from reeds at the entry to their doors as signs of triumph. [Hidalgo, 1927, p. 57.]

Two paragraphs follow from Casañas:

Before going to war, they dance and sing for seven or eight days, offering to God meat, corn, bows, arrows, tobacco, *acoxo* [cf. *acoxio*, an herb], and fat from buffalo hearts, praying for the death of their enemies. They pray also for strength to fight, for fleetness to run, and for valor to resist. There is plenty to eat. In front of those who are dancing there is a pole and on it hangs a portion of everything they are offering to God. In front of the pole a fire is burning. Near by is a person who looks like a demon. He is the person who offers the incense to God, throwing tobacco and buffalo fat into the fire. All of the men assemble around the blaze; each one takes a handful of smoke and rubs his whole body with it. Each believes that, because of this ceremony, God will grant whatever he may ask—whether it be the death of his enemy or swiftness to run. On other occasions the incense is not offered by burning in this way. In this case a kind of burned pole is taken and set up by the fire. This pole and the fat for the incense—which has already been burned—they offer to God. Every time a dance begins, a man steps forward as a preacher does and tells the people what they are to ask God for in the next dance. In these gatherings there are many abuses. They pray also to the fire, to the air, to the water, to the corn, to the buffalo, to the deer, and to many other similar things, asking some of them to permit themselves to be killed for eating. To others they pray for vengeance. They ask the water to drown their enemies, the fire to burn them, the arrows to kill them, and the winds to blow them away. On the last day of such a meeting the *caddi* comes forward and encourages the men by saying, "Well, now, if you really are men, think of your wives, your parents, or your children, but I charge you not to let them be a hindrance to our victory." I trust in the Lord that when their language is learned, we can garner in a great harvest because many tribes are gathered together in these meetings. [Casañas, 1927, pp. 214–215.]

All the men who have achieved some victory in war are called *amayxoya* in addition to their own names. This means "great man." The arms and banners they must carry are the skins and the scalps of the enemies each one has killed. The grand *xinesi* has skulls hung up in a tree near his house. In conclusion it may be said that these Indians practice no greater cruelty than their enemies do. They tie a captive's feet and hands to a post, like a cross. Here they tear him to pieces, drinking the blood and eating the flesh, half roasted. [Casañas, 1927, p. 217.]

A few items are supplied by Espinosa:

In addition to these [officers], the whole nation elects a person who serves them as a general during wars. When they set out on a campaign they obey him implicitly, without disregarding an order in the slightest degree. Even though they may have traveled all day without taking food, they do not even moisten their tongues from the water holes they pass until the leader makes camp—after exploration has been made to see that no enemy is near. After they have gained a victory over their adversaries, the leader sends out a number of the Indians he has with him, others remaining to guard the camp and the rear. These Indians formerly used bows and arrows and shields in their wars with other Indians. But at this time, they have secured so many guns, due to their proximity to the French, that they know how to manage them skillfully and use them for war, for hunting when at home, and always carry them when traveling. [Espinosa, 1927, pp. 175–176.]

Upon occasions when these Indians gain a victory over their adversaries they bring back the skulls of their enemies as trophies and keep them hanging in a tree until in the course of time they decide to bury them. For this ceremony, they gather on an appointed night, men and women, at the place where the skulls are hanging. They build a number of bonfires and, having provided their sad and mournful instruments, they arrange their singers and their bands of musicians, painted black. Seated upon the ground, covered from head to foot with buffalo robes, and with bowed heads, they all sing together. The rest dance without moving from the spot, the women in one file and the men to one side. This dance lasts the greater part of the night. Then a decrepit old Indian with certain young men surround the tree where the skulls are, each with an arrow pointed in the same direction. They all give a shout or cry. They then turn in another direction and do the same thing. From time to time they discharge a gun towards the skulls and raise a confused cry in unison. When the morning comes they cover their faces and arms with white dirt and carry the skulls and inter them in the cemetery which is near the fire temple where they spend the rest of the day in celebration. The whole thing seems to be the work of hell, the songs as well as the ceremonies connected with it. They offer to these skulls ground *pinole* and other foods which the living instead of the dead consume, after they have said their prayers and gone through with their superstitious ceremonies. [Espinosa, 1927, p. 174.]

Parsons has the following note regarding the war dance as recalled by modern Caddo informants:

In the war dance . . . the men bunch around the drum and move dancing around the dance floor. They carry a tomahawk or a scalp on a stick, and wear the typical war bonnet of eagle feathers fastened to a strip of cloth. On the face is painted the characteristic mark of the dancer's supernatural partner— Coon, Fox, Lightning (shown in an accompanying illustration). The women, wearing their buckskin dress, stand together, on the outside, moving slightly.

If a feather falls out of the bonnet of a dancer or off the decorations of his person, some senior with war experience has to pick up the feather and "tell an old story of some place where they had a fight and won it." At the end of the story everybody who has a drumstick beats once on the drum, then the dance goes on. [Parsons, 1941, pp. 53–55.]

Consult the same writer also on eagle hunting (p. 43).

See also the chapter on burials (pp. 203–210).

TRADE

Trade between Indian tribes was much more extensive in pre-Columbian times than is often supposed, and we have several significant notes regarding Caddo participation in this. In 1542, when De Soto's followers visited the Guasco, a Hasinai tribe, they found there "turquoises and cotton blankets, which the Indians gave them to understand, by signs, were brought from the west" (Robertson, 1933, p. 256). We are not informed what the Hasinai paid in exchange for these things but may suspect that wood of the bois d'arc, or Osage orange, for use as bows was one of the commodities since the Tewa Indians are known to have obtained this material from the east, and in 1687 Joutel informs us that the Kadohadacho country was famous for it. Indians came to get it from distances of 50 or 60 leagues, and when the Frenchmen left on their way to the Mississippi two Indians joined them with bows which they proposed to sell to the Quapaw at the mouth of the Arkansas (Margry, 1875–1886, vol. 3, p. 412). Three years later Tonti found them "making very fine bows" which they traded to distant nations (Cox, 1905, vol. 1, p. 48).

The eastern Caddo also carried on a trade in salt. The two Indians just mentioned who accompanied Joutel were taking along besides bows "salt in little loaves of about two or three pounds each" to barter with the same people (Margry, 1875–1886, vol. 3, p. 424). They were said to have obtained these from the Tunica Indians, and we know that both the Tunica and the related Koroa were much involved in the salt industry, but it also extended to the Caddo. The Taensa with Tonti in 1690 remained some days in the Natchitoches town to traffic for salt (Cox, 1905, vol. 1, p. 45). In 1700 Bienville met Koroa Indians bringing salt to the Taensa on the Mississippi but later he came upon six Natchitoches who were taking salt to the Koroa, so that the latter were to some extent middle men (Margry, vol. 4, pp. 432, 435). The reference to salt contained in one of the prominent Hasinai tribal names has already been commented upon.

The trading routes already established, especially those toward the west, were quickly utilized for the introduction of European commodities as soon as white settlements came sufficiently close. Before 1680 some of the Coahuilteco Indians and, in particular, the Jumano under a noted chief called Juan Sabeata, were resorting to the Hasinai annually to barter European goods for whatever the Indians of that confederation had to offer. There "each year the Indians held a fair in which the plunder obtained from the Spanish outposts along the whole northern frontier of New Spain was bartered and traded" (Castañeda, vol. 1, p. 326). By 1686, therefore, when La Salle first entered the Hasinai country, European objects, including European horses, were by no means rarities in that region. Father Anastasius reports:

We found among the Cœnis many things which undoubtedly came from the Spaniards, such as dollars and other pieces of money, silver spoons, lace of every kind, clothes and horses. We saw, among other things, a bull from Rome exempting the Spaniards in Mexico from fasting during summer. Horses are common. They gave them to us for an axe; one Cœnis offered me one for our cowl, to which he took a fancy. [Cox, 1905, vol. 1, pp. 232–233.]

The distribution of intangibles is interestingly demonstrated in a later paragraph:

There were then some Choüman ambassadors among them, who came to visit us. I was agreeably surprised to see them make the sign of the cross, kneel, clasp their hands, raise them from time to time to heaven. They also kissed my habit, and gave me to understand that men dressed like us instructed tribes in their vicinity, who were only two days' march from the Spaniards, where our religious had large churches in which all assembled to pray. They expressed very naturally the ceremonies of mass; one of them sketched me a painting that he had seen of a great lady, who was weeping because her son was upon a cross. He told us . . . that if we would go with them, or give them guns, they could easily conquer them, because they were a cowardly race, who had no courage, and made people walk before them with a fan to refresh them in hot weather. [Cox, 1905, vol. 1, pp. 234–235.]

This information came not from the Hasinai directly but from the Jumano or Chouman. There is, however, no reason to suppose that the latter would have refrained from communicating the remarkable things they had seen to the other tribes.

When he returned to his fort on the Texas coast, La Salle brought with him five horses laden with corn, beans, pumpkin seeds, and watermelons (Margry, 1875–1886, vol. 3, p. 249).

On approaching the first Hasinai village the year following, Joutel was met by three Indians, one on horseback, and one dressed in the Spanish manner, "having a little doublet or jacket the body of which was blue and the sleeves white, as if worked on a kind of fustian; he had very well fitted breeches, stockings of white worsted, woolen garters, and a Spanish hat, flat and wide in shape." He also claimed to have visited the Spaniards in person (Margry, 1875–1886, vol. 3, pp. 338, 341).

There were seven or eight who had sword-blades, with big bunches of feathers on the handles. These blades were squared like those of the Spaniards; they also had many big hawkbells, which made a noise like those on mules . . . Some also had some pieces of blue stuff which they had gotten from the Spaniards [Margry, 1875–1886, vol. 3, pp. 341, 342.]

For a very fine horse Joutel gave a knife and an axe. He continues:

What I understood very well was their taste for knives and axes, which they love very much, [and] of which they have great need, not having any at all, although they have been to visit the Spaniards, which enables one to see that the latter do not give them much. Except that the women have some pieces of very coarse blue cloth of which they make a sort of small coat, which they wear in front and behind, but there are few of them [Margry, 1875–1886, vol. 3, pp. 347, 349].

The word *capitan* had already been adopted into their language from Spanish in the form *capita* and *caballo* (horse) with a pronunciation which the French rendered "*cahouaille*" (Margry, 1875–1886, vol. 3, p. 353).

On reaching the Kadohadacho they were able to report that those Indians and all of the tribes to the west of them had horses while those to the east did not, but noted an exception in the case of the Cahinnio on Ouachita River who had two very fine gray horses. The source of supply was plainly shown by the horses which they themselves secured. "Some were marked on the thighs, which must have been done by farriers, and two of them even were geldings" (Margry, 1875–1886, pp. 410, 423).

Besides scalps and the accompanying honors, the main motive behind the expeditions which the Hasinai undertook against the "Canoatinno" was horses (Margry, 1875–1886, vol 3, pp. 348, 353).

In order to obtain food and horses with which to pursue their journey toward the northeast, Joutel and his companions dispensed among the Indians in the Hasinai, Nasoni, Kadohadacho, and Cahinnio towns considerable quantities of axes, knives, beads, needles, and pins (Margry, 1875–1886, vol. 3, pp. 339, 344, 347, 348, 353, 360, 365, 390, 392, 393, 395, 401, 406, 412, 419). They also gave in trade copper rings. Father Anastasius had in his possession some chaplets made of red and white beads which they unstrung and made into bracelets and necklaces for trade with the Indians, and they used in the same manner some necklaces of false amber brought along by the same priest (Margry, 1875–1886, vol. 3, pp. 347, 353, 365, 390, 392, 393, 395, 401, 406, 412, 419). Iron hoes were also in demand and the Frenchmen promised that they would bring some when they came back but these seem to have been omitted from their original outfit (Margry, 1875–1886, vol. 3, pp. 290, 391). On approaching the Cahinnio town they were met, as we have seen, by an Indian carrying a sword and two hawkbells, and a saber in Joutel's possession was so much desired by the chief of this tribe that the owner parted with it in exchange for guides (Margry, 1875–1886, vol. 3, p. 421).

While nearly all articles of European origin found among the Caddo clearly came from Mexico, Joutel was informed that a few beads were from the northeast, perhaps having filtered in from the French descending from Canada (Margry, 1875–1886, vol. 3, p. 357).

Three years after Joutel's passage through the Caddo country Tonti penetrated it nearly to the Namidish town and there, in exchange for "seven hatchets and a string of large glass beads," he obtained four Spanish horses "two of which were marked on the haunch with an R and a crown (*couronne fermée*) and another with an N." "Horses," he adds, "are very common among them. There is not a cabin which has not four or five" (Cox, 1905, vol. 1, p. 49).

In 1716 Ramón found among the Hasinai 18 or 20 long French arquebuses, many beads of various colors, numerous trinkets, large knives, pocket knives, pieces of cloth of good grade, particularly blue, and hatchets, and "upon being asked where they secured all these things they said the French from Natchitoches brought them in square boats on the river and gave them to the Indians for horses and skins of animals" (Castañeda, 1936, vol. 2, pp. 19, 29, 66). According to St. Denis, who ought to have known since he was so much engaged in it himself, trade between the French and Natchitoches Indians had begun in 1701 and it must have extended to the Hasinai almost immediately.

Casañas has considerable to say regarding the Hasinai appetite for European goods:

> They are fond of bells, knives, and everything made of iron—such as axes and mattocks; for, as they are a people who build houses to live in and plant crops for food, they need these things most of all. Therefore, when things of this kind are given them—say woolen garments and especially blue, the color of the sky,—they appreciate them more than if they were heaps of gold and silver. They also like hats, glass beads, and everything in the shape of ornaments; and things which make a noise. [Casañas, 1927, p. 285.]

This missionary wishes that he might have "some bells, some small clasp knives, some glass beads, and some blue cloth—which they greatly prize—some blankets, and other little things to exchange with these Indians," by trading with which he "could have started a convent with the articles it would have been possible to make from the best materials that are abundant here" (Casañas, 1927, p. 301).

If Casañas' preaching was as effective as he seems to have thought, the following quotation adds to the list of European intangibles transmitted to the Indians. He says that his argument that God caused death by pestilence instead of malevolent human beings "made such an impression upon them that nobody disputed me. On the contrary, all who were present went away and told others. All were amazed and the captain went to see other tribes to tell them what I had said" (Casañas, 1927, p. 295).

Like Joutel, Hidalgo found that the Hasinai greatly appreciated iron hoes. They had "axes of different kinds which they secure from the French" (Hidalgo, 1927, pp. 56, 57). In fact, trade between the Caddo and French through Natchitoches which sprang up as soon as that post was established by Saint Denis in 1714 flourished much more vigorously than the legitimate trade with Spanish settlements. When he visited the Hasinai in November of that year, he bartered guns, beads, knives, and cloth for cattle and buffalo hides. It is only fair to state that the greater partiality of these Indians for French trade was due very considerably to the tolerance of the French in supplying them with firearms and liquor. The truth would not be strained greatly if we said that they stole from the Spaniards in order to trade with the French.

In 1767–68 Solís found all the Hasinai "armed with guns, and," he continues, "they manage them with great skill; one is rarely found with a bow and arrow." They were receiving guns, ammunition, cloth, and whiskey from the French. They were also in possession of domestic fowl, presumably from the same source (Solís, 1931, p. 61). In speaking of the stock at the Mission of Nuestra Señora de los Dolores de Benavente de los Ays, he says:

The Indians steal as many as they can; the bulls, cows, and calves for eating, the horses, mules and mares (of which there is a drove) for their commerce and traffic with the French to get whiskey, sugar-cane whiskey, vermilion, beads, cloth, powder, balls, guns, tobacco and other things. [Solís, 1931, p. 67.]

The Natchitoches trade as it existed toward the end of the eighteenth century is thus described by Morfi:

In each of the friendly pueblos or tribes of the Texas and tribes of the North, there resides a merchant from Louisiana, who is always instructed in the language of the nation where he is; who knows how to read and write, and is very prudent to make himself loved by the natives. He has to maintain commercial relations and peace between the nations, [and] the friendship which they have for us, watch their movements with care, and give notice of the least news he learns, in his own pueblo and in the surrounding ones as well as in the country of the enemy nations. This is a most useful Providence, if executed as ordered, but many serious and dangerous abuses have been introduced through the bad choice of the subjects. [Morfi, 1932, p. 56.]

In 1820 Padilla found the Kadohadacho exchanging "furs from the bear, the deer, the beaver, the otter, and other animals" at Natchitoches for "carbines, munitions, merchandise, tobacco, and firewater." He adds:

They are faithful in keeping their contracts; for the merchants of Natchitoches advance them munitions, trifles, and liquors at a good rate of exchange for furs. For all these they pay punctually, in spite of the fact that there are among them foreigners who come from Natchitoches and other points of the United States for the purpose of trading their wares to the said Indians for their products. [Padilla, 1919, p. 48.]

Eight years later Sanchez found that the Caddo and numbers of other Indians continually entered Nacogdoches to trade "but they are all peaceful and carry on their trade in the city with skins, corn, pumpkins, and beans" (Sanchez, 1926, p. 283).

The unequal effect of European influences upon peoples of differing environment is well illustrated by the following observation of Espinosa about 1722:

Although the Natchitoches have a greater number of guns than the Texas Indians, the number of horses they have is limited. The latter thus travel on foot while the Texas Indians ride on horseback with great skill, their feet hanging loose and, traveling at a great rate, they guide their horses with only a slender cord which they use in place of a bridle. This the herdsmen call a barbequejo. [Espinosa, 1927, p. 179.]

We have here an indication of the same process which acted so rapidly to build up a Plains culture associated with the horse. Horses were introduced from the Southwest to a region where they rapidly attained a cardinal position in war and in the communal buffalo hunt. In the woodlands to the east they were practically useless for both purposes. In woodland warfare they would have been a hindrance rather than a help.   At an earlier period, it is true, De Soto's only salvation was in his cavalry, but to this was added the advantages of armor for man and horse and, more important still, between his period and the end of the eighteenth century firearms had been developed from cumbersome implements into weapons of deadly effectiveness.   On the open plains they added to the power of the horseman but where there was plenty of cover the horse was a mere encumbrance.   In the woodlands, too, the scarcity of buffalo and the nature of the country limited collective hunting very considerably.   And so it happened that tribes like the Cheyenne and Arapaho were sheared off from their woodland relatives and became typical Plains Indians.   It was this tendency evidently which helped differentiate the Crow from the Hidatsa, the Teton Dakota from the Santee, and probably the Ponca from the Omaha and the Kansa from the Osage, and tended to split the Osage themselves.

The Hasinai were prevented from becoming fully fledged Plains Indians by their devotion to agriculture and the pressure of more northern tribes, and on the other hand the Natchitoches and Kadohadacho were uprooted from the woodlands and impelled to unite with their western relatives and so to adopt a marginal Plains complex. It is evident, none the less, that all of the Caddo originally possessed a woodlands culture, and we may say that in reality they never became anything other than woodland people though part of them took on for a while a Plains veneer.

Besides the pure trading motives—an exchange of goods for goods or goods for services—a political motive must be added, presents given to the Indians to "retain their good will" or "bribe them" into compliance with the will of the givers, as you may choose to call it. The potency of "presents" was remarked upon by Casañas in paragraphs already quoted.   The political motive is particularly apparent in the "presents" which Aguayo distributed so lavishly in 1716 immediately after St. Denis' successful trading operations among the Hasinai.   On July 31 Aguayo was so "deeply impressed" by the kindness of the Nacono tribe in sending him provisions "though in a moderate amount" that he distributed "many pocket- and butcher-knives, scissors, combs, and sundry trinkets . . . To the chief he gave a silver-mounted cane and a complete suit of Spanish clothes, and to his wife twice the number of presents given the others." (Buckley, 1911, p. 44; Morfi, 1932, pt. 1, p. 206.)   To the Indians attending on the refounding of the mission of San Francisco de los Neches he distributed "clothing and gifts" in a manner "more lavish than had ever before been witnessed by the Indians." (Buckley, 1911, p. 46; Morfi, 1932, pt. 1, p. 209.)   August 8 Aguayo made a similar distribution "to gain the good will of Cheocas, the Aynay

[Hainai] chief, seeing that he had a large following." (Buckley, 1911, p. 47; Morfi, 1932, pt. 1, p. 211.) He also entrusted to 80 Kadohadacho who were present "clothes and trinkets" for their people at home "hoping thereby to gain their good will in advance of his arrival" (Buckley, 1911, p. 47).

This effort on the part of Spain appears, as is evident from the preceding paragraphs, to have been a failure. All occasion for it came to an end with the annexation of Louisiana to Spain in 1762. Similar competitions east of the Mississippi involving particularly the Creeks, Cherokee, Choctaw, and Chickasaw were much more serious and served to debauch all parties to the competition.

De Mézières supplies several lists of goods to be given to the Caddo tribes along Red River and a contract covering the disposition of them. We copy these from Bolton's "Athanase de Mézières and the Louisiana-Texas Frontier, 1768–1780."

List of the effects which should be given to the three Indian nations of the Post of Natchitoches, copied from the Instruction drawn by the Most Excellent Señor Conde de Orreilli, to-wit:

To the Nation of the Grandes Cados, for their annual present

A hat trimmed with galloons	Forty-eight awls
An ornamented shirt	Forty-eight worm-screws
Two fusils	Two hundred flints
Two blankets of two and one-half points	Twenty-four steels
Three ells of cloth	Forty-eight hawksbells
Two ordinary shirts	Two hundred needles
A copper kettle	Ninety ells of tape
Twenty pounds of powder	Ten rolls of tobacco
Forty pounds of balls	Two jugs of brandy
One pound of vermillion	Six mirrors
Two pounds of glass beads	Two pounds of wire
One pound of thread	One flag
One ax	Half a piece of cord
Two adzes	Twenty-five pounds of salt
Twenty-four large knives	Two hatchets
Forty small knives	One ell of ribbon for the medal

To the Nachitos Nation

One hat with feathers	Twelve awls
One laced shirt	Twelve worm-screws
One staple fusil	Fifty flints
Four pounds of powder	Thirty ells of tape
Eight pounds of fine shot and balls	Two jugs of brandy
One pound of vermillion	Two mirrors
One pound of glass beads	Fifty needles
Half a pound of thread	Six steels
Twelve large knives	Twelve hawksbells
Twelve small knives	One pound of wire

To the Nation of the Pequeños Cados

One hat with plumes
One laced shirt
One staple fusil
One copper kettle
Ten pounds of powder
Two blankets of two and one-half points
Two ells of cloth
Two staple shirts
Twenty pounds of fine shot and balls
One pound of vermillion
Two pounds of glass beads
One pound of thread
One ax
One adz
Twenty-four large knives
Twenty-four small knives

Twenty-four awls
Twenty worm-screws
One hundred flints
Twelve steels
Twenty-four hawksbells
One hundred needles
Sixty ells of tape
Five rolls of tobacco
Two jugs of brandy
Four mirrors
One and one-half pounds of wire
One flag
Half a piece of cord
Twenty-five pounds of salt
Two hatchets
One ell of ribbon for the medal

To the Yatasse Nation

One fusil
One blanket of two and one-half points
One ell of cloth
One shirt
One copper kettle
Six pounds of powder
Twelve pounds of fine shot and balls
One pound of vermillion
Half a pound of thread
One ax
One adz
Twelve large knives
Twelve small knives

Twelve awls
Twelve worm-screws
Fifty flints
Six steels
Twelve hawksbells
Fifty needles
Thirty ells of tape
Five rolls of tobacco
Two jugs of brandy
Two mirrors
One pound of wire
Two hatchets
Twenty pounds of salt

[Endorsement] I certify that this is a copy of the original. JOSEPH DE ORUE [rubic]. [Bolton, 1914, vol. 1, pp. 132–134.]

CONTRACT OF JUAN PISEROS WITH DE MÉZIÈRES, NATCHITOCHES, FEBRUARY 3, 1770

List of Goods necessary for the annual Supply of the Village of the Grand Cadaux

No 10 [Enclosure].

Forty staple fusils of good caliber
Sixty ells of Limbourg, red and blue
Thirty woolen blankets, twenty of two and one-half points and ten of three points
Four hundred pounds of French gun powder
Nine hundred pounds of bullets, caliber thirty to thirty-two
Thirty pickaxes ⎫
Thirty hatchets ⎬ of good quality and well turned
Thirty tomahawks ⎭
Fifty shirts, half gingham and half white
One gross of hunters' knives with three nails

One gross of pocket knives with horn or dog's head handles
Six dozen large boxwood combs
Six dozen pairs of scissors
Sixty pounds of small glass beads, sky blue, white, and black
One thousand flints
Six dozen large steels
Six dozen awls
Six pounds of pure vermilion
Six dozen mirrors of pliant copper
Six pieces of scarlet *tavelle*
Twelve pounds of copper wire suitable for bracelets and worm-screws

List of Goods necessary for the annual Supply of the Village of the Petit Cados

Thirty staple fusils of good caliber
Forty ells of red and blue Limbourg
Forty fine blankets, half three points and half two and one-half points
Two hundred pounds of French gun powder
Four hundred and fifty pounds of balls, caliber thirty to thirty-two
Twenty pickaxes
Twenty hatchets
Twenty tomahawks
Thirty pounds of glass beads, sky blue, white, and black
Four pounds of pure vermillion
Half a gross of hunter's knives
Id. of pocket-knives with horn or dog's head handles
Half a gross of boxwood combs
Four dozen steels
Four dozen wormscrews
Five hundred flints
Two dozen mirrors
Six pounds of copper wire, coarse and fine
Twenty-four shirts

List of Goods necessary for the annual Supply of the Village of the Hiatassés

Fifteen staple fusils
Thirty ells of red and blue Limbourg
Twenty fine blankets, of two grades
Thirty shirts
Two hundred pounds of French gun powder
Four hundred and fifty pounds of balls
Ten pickaxes
Ten hatchets
Ten tomahawks
Thirty pounds of small glass beads, sky blue, white, and black
Four pounds of vermillion
Half a gross of large hunter's knives
Half a gross of pocket knives
Id. of combs
Id. of awls
Id. of wormscrews

Id. of steels
Five hundred flints
Four pieces of *tavelle*
Three dozen mirrors
Six pounds of copper wire, coarse and fine

I the undersigned, resident and merchant in this post, certify that I have agreed with M. de Mezieres to purchase, bring up, and put at the disposition of the Sieurs Alesis Grappe, Dupin and Fazende Moriere, the merchandise mentioned above, of good quality, marketable, and well chosen, to serve and to be distributed by them to the nations of the Cados d'Acquioux and Hiatassés, our allies, in conformity with the intentions of his Excellency, which delivery I obligate myself to make to the above-named persons, payable in the stipulated term of a year from the following spring on condition of their paying fifty per cent profit on the purchase price in New Orleans, according to the certified invoices which I shall exhibit. I agree to accept deer skins of good quality and marketable at thirty-five sous apiece; bear's fat at twenty-five sous a pot; buffalo hides, good and marketable, at ten livres, I reserving, in view of my advances and the length of the term of credit, the choice of goods which may please me best, until I am completely paid.

Natchitoches, Feb. 3, 1770.

(Signed) PISEROS.

[Endorsement]   Copy compared with the original.
Natchitoches, Feb. 3, 1770.   DE MÉZIÈRES [rubric]
[Bolton, 1914, vol. 1, pp. 143–146.]

To this may be added the

INSTRUCTIONS FOR THE TRADERS OF THE CADAUX D'ACQUIOUX AND HIATASSÉS NATIONS, FEBRUARY 4, 1770

His Excellency the Captain-general of this province, having by his orders of the 24th of November, 1769, enjoined me to choose persons known for their good habits and their zeal for the service of the king, that they might be sent to the Indian villages to encourage the savages more and more to work, and not to permit them to remain in an idleness dangerous not only to their own interests but to those of his Majesty as well, I have chosen the Sieurs Alexis Grappe, Dupin, and Fazende Moriere, to reside in the villages of our good friends and faithful allies, the Hiatassés and the Cadaux da Kioux, where they shall strictly observe the following instructions:

1st. The merchandise customary in the trade with the savages shall be furnished them to their satisfaction, they paying the ordinary trade price.

2d. No English merchandise shall be introduced among the Indians, under the penalty inflicted upon contraband traders, nor any kind of intoxicating drink, under pain of arrest and confiscation of goods.

3d. These goods shall be sold and distributed only to those Nations which are friendly to ours; thus the Naytanes, Taoüaiaches, Touacanas, Yscanes, Quitseys, and Tancaoüeys, who are all enemies, shall have no part in it, either directly or indirectly, until new orders are issued, under the penalties inflicted upon traitors to the king and the country.

4th. The said traders shall arrest all French or Spanish wanderers or vagabonds and confiscate their effects, demanding if necessary, the forcible aid of the Indians. I will forewarn the chiefs in this particular in order that these rovers may be brought to this post.

5th. They are enjoined to watch carefully that no Englishman shall introduce himself into the villages within the district of this post to trade with the Indians or for any other purpose whatsoever. In case one does, they shall do their best to have his goods pillaged and him arrested, and even killed if he gives any resistance.

6th. The said traders are pledged to send me couriers whenever they learn any news of interest to the service of his Majesty.

7th. They are likewise pledged to maintain peace and entire harmony among the people allied with us; and if any quarrel should occur between the families or individuals of the villages where they reside, or even among the neighboring tribes, they are pledged to stifle it and to conciliate the parties.

8th. The said traders are expressly ordered to explain daily to the Indians the inestimable advantage which they enjoy of being under the happy dominion of his Majesty; that all the French are charmed to live under the laws of so august a monarch; that his protection is assured to all natives who comport themselves as becomes men; that this great king considers them as his dearest subjects; and that in return he very properly expects them to submit to his will, but with no other purpose than their own happiness.

9th. The said traders likewise shall make forcible [harangues], whenever occasion arises, to the Indians of hostile nations who may come near them, concerning the unpardonable offense of which they are guilty toward the grandest, the most just, and the best of all masters, telling them that if they do not desist from their pride and their violence they will see fall upon them the weight of a vengeance which they will not be able to escape; that the French, united to-day with the Spaniards by indissoluble bonds, far from giving them any assistance, will treat them as their cruel enemies; but that if, on the contrary, they give true signs of repentance by promptly making an enduring peace, they will be received and added to the number of the children and subjects of this worthy sovereign.

10. As the service of God and the good of the religion ought to be kept in mind by all Christians, it is recommended to these traders that they take care that no adult or infant Indian in danger of death shall be without the blessing of holy baptism. They ought to feel the importance of this article; the recompense of a work so meritorious is to them well known.

At the government headquarters, February 4, 1770.

Copy   DE MÉZIÈRES [rubric].

[Bolton, 1914, vol. 1, pp. 149–150]

Containing, it is to be seen, the usual amount of political wing-flapping indulged in when reason is at a discount. No doubt many Frenchmen would have enjoyed testifying in private to the beneficence of Governor O'Reilly's regime. As we have already seen, the Grappe family was to play a considerable part in the liquidation of the Natchitoches Indians.

BURIAL AND BELIEFS REGARDING THE FATE OF THE SOUL

There are references to burial customs by Hidalgo, Espinosa, Morfi, and Solís, as follows:

Hidalgo:

They bury their dead, after bathing them, interring with them the trophies they have captured with the deer skins they possess, and with all the gifts their relatives supply. They place there something of everything they have to eat as well as buffalo hides. They bury the scalps so that their enemies may go along to serve them in the other life. They place there provisions for the journey and other possessions to serve for clothing. [Hidalgo, 1927, p. 57.]

Those who die, [says Solís] are buried in a sitting position, with their guns, powder, balls, meat, and provisions, with their jug of water and all of their feathers and beads. [Solís, 1931, p. 61.]

The longest and best account is that of Espinosa who has been copied by Morfi. Espinosa says:

These Indians understand well and confess a belief in the immortality of the soul. This is evidenced by the burials and the funeral honors they pay as follows. They prepare the dead body for burial, after first bathing it, by clothing it in the best clothes they have or in fresh deer skins. With great lamentations, they keep it for several hours in the home. They provide great quantities of *pinole*, corn, and other eatables. If it be a man, they collect his bows and arrows, his knife, and the other things needed in life and, if it be a woman, all her domestic utensils, canisters, grinding instruments, and earthen-ware vessels, because they say the dead will have need of them where they are going. When asked where the souls of those who die go, they answered, that, as soon as the souls leave the body they travel towards the west and from there they rise once more into the air and go close to the presence of the great captain whom they call *caddi ayo*. From thence they go to wait in a house located towards the south, called the House of Death. And being asked what death was and if it was not eternal, [they said] that they believe or persuade the old people to believe that everybody is very happy there and that there is no hunger, nor sickness, nor suffering, and that all remain in the condition in which they were when death overtook them, so that if a woman dies when she is pregnant she will continue to be in this condition, while if she dies with a child at her breast, she will continue to nurse it—and other errors of a similar nature. But they do not say a man and his wife will be remarried after death. By chance, I asked them if anybody went to this place without punishment. They said, yes, except those who were wicked—and they consider such, only those who are their enemies. They say that these enemies go to the house of *texino* who is the devil, and that he punishes them very severely. They do not consider adulterers, sodomites, concubines, or thieves even worthy of punishment and they conceive of suffering as applying only to physical pain. So when they bury a person, they go through all the prayers or forms of their saints. They say that the dead are going to rest and that they will cease from any wrong thing they did, but that, if they do not pray, the devil will take them to his house. In any case it amounts to the same thing.

The honors or funeral ceremonies for those who die in war or when absent from their homes are celebrated in the following manner. All the people are invited for the appointed day and sufficient quantities of the foods available at the season are provided. Almost a gunshot from the house, they build a pile of small wood. All gather together, the mourners, men and women stretched upon their beds. A leader among their holy men appears and speaks a few words to them. They set up a weeping, or it might better be called a howling, in which the mourning women join. About seven men leave the house, turn their faces toward the east and say their prayers. In front of them they have a very small vase in which there is moist cornmeal. After the leader of the old men finishes a prayer they take part of the ground corn from the little vessel and scatter it to the four winds. Three of them, who serve as patrons of the funeral, eat the rest of it. They then reenter the house and the mourners renew their clamor. All the captains sit down in their order. The patrons seat themselves near the mourners and tobacco and meal is then offered to the old saint. He takes it and walks around the fire which is in the center of the .house. He repeats the formula, throws some of the meal and tobacco into the fire, and then turns and presents it to the patrons. This done, two or three Indians come forward and present bows and arrows to the wife or the mother of the deceased. Then, one after another, the captains step forward and offer one, six, or eight arrows to the bereaved, according to the condition of each. The women then express their condolence and present their gifts of beads, a knife, or clothing. This is all collected and all the ornaments of the deceased are added to it. The Indians roll this up, add some fine deer skins, and cover with a mat woven of reeds. In the meantime an old man and a young man unite in singing a very mournful song. One of the patrons takes the roll on his shoulders and carries it to the fire. Another carries a handful of dry grass and another fire. When they reach the pile of wood, they set fire to it on all sides, throw the mat and all the arrows and clothing on top of it, and burn them to ashes. The confusion is increased by the mournful cries of the mourners and friends. In the meanwhile some of those in the circle laugh and joke. The whole ceremony is crowned by a feast which is divided among all those present. This ended, the company disbands. All this, so they say, is in order that the soul of the deceased may go to the house of rest and when it returns to view its body it will find what has been done with it. [Espinosa, 1927, pp. 162–164.]

Morfi's version is as follows:

As soon as one dies they wash the corpse carefully and dress it in the best clothes the deceased had, or make new curious deerskin clothes. They keep the corpse in the house for some hours, during which time the laments do not cease. They provide a great amount of *pinole*, corn, and whatever they have to eat. This done they take the body to the grave which is already dug, with sufficient depth and size, and set it up in it, with much propriety. On each side of the corpse they place the provisions, without forgetting the water; if it is a man's body, they also put [with it] bow and arrows, knife, gun, and some munitions; if it is a woman's body, they put the objects becoming to her sex, as little baskets, mortars, and clay vessels, with the supposition that all of these will be needed in the other life. If asked where the souls of the deceased go, they reply, that as soon as they depart from their bodies they go a long way to the west; from there they direct themselves through the air to meet at the habitation of the Caddi-Ayo, from whence they go to stop at a house situated in the south, which they call House of Death. They imagine, or the elders persuade them to, that there, all live in perpetual joy, that there is no hunger, illness, nor any of the other penalties of our present life; but that they will remain eternally in that state or situation which is chosen for them by the last illness, so that if a woman dies pregnant, she will always remain so; if giving birth, she will carry the infant in her arms, etc. From this place of delights they exclude the wicked (*reprobos*), but they only look upon their enemies as such. These, they say, go to the house of the *Texino*, or *Demonio*, who cruelly punishes them. As regards their own nation or their allies, there is one guilt which is inexpiable. Adulterers, sodomites, concubines and thieves, are not subject to any punishment provided they are buried with the proper ceremonies and prayers of their ritual, because in such a case they are purified and go to the house of pleasure; but those who are buried without that ceremony, the Devil takes as his own. In this regard they are not as sensual as the Mahomedans, because among the delights of their imaginary paradise, they do not include those sensual pleasures which Mahomet, in great detail, promised to his subjects. Thus, though husband and wife live together in the House of Death, and are happy, they are not as man and wife.

When a *Texa* dies away from his family either in war or peace, they give him a different funeral. The day for the ceremony being chosen, this being when they have provided sufficient provision at the house in mourning, all the members of the tribe assemble, care having been taken to notify them opportunely. A stone-throw from the house a pyre of wood is arranged. All gathered, the mourning men and dishevelled women lie in their beds, *sin aveo*. One of the principal priests enters to see them; and briefly consoles them. That moment they all begin to cry and howl. This is taken up by all the women in the crowd who are outside. Then from the deceased's house seven men come out and, facing east, offer up certain prayers, having before them a little vessel of ground wet corn. As soon as the principal elder finishes his prayer, they take some of the corn from the vessel and throw it to the four winds. Three of the seven eat what remains for they are the ones who are to be the pallbearers at the funeral. The seven return to the house and renew their sorrowful howling. Then all of the captains sit down, according to their rank, and the pallbearers place themselves among the principal mourners, whether man or woman, and all present offer to an old priest tobacco and cornmeal. The offering received, they get up, go around a bonfire which is kindled in the center of the house, throw into it a part of the offering, pronouncing in a murmur, some prayers, and deliver the rest to the pallbearers. When these ceremonies are ended two or three Indians go out and offer a bow and some arrows to the wife, daughters or mother of the deceased, and then the captains [follow], one by one, giving to the mourners, four, six, or more arrows, according to the obligation, and generosity of the donors. Then the women present, at the same time that they offer condolences, offer strings of beads, knives, and some clothes. To all of this they add all of the personal effects of the deceased, and the best deerskins they have, wrapping them up in a mat. During the ceremony of the offering two Indians, one old and another youthful, do not cease to sing or beat time and in a mournful tone, until the offering is ended. Then one of the pallbearers takes the bundle, another a lighted stick of wood from the fire, and the third, a bundle of dried herbs. They all leave the house in a procession, arrive at the pyre, set fire to it all over, and throw the wrapped bundle into the bonfire. The friends and relatives of the deceased increase their cries while some of those present laugh loudly. They return to the house and this ceremony ends, like all the others, with a great feast for those invited. They execute all of this, according to what they say, so that the soul of the deceased shall go to the house of pleasure and so that when it comes to find its body, it may see what has been done in its honor. [Morfi, 1932, pp. 37–39.]

Joutel was made cognizant of certain mortuary customs during a night spent in one of the Hasinai houses.

About half past three I heard people marching around the house and muttering something. I went out to see what it was and then perceived savages to the number of five, some old men whom we had seen when we arrived, who were circling the cabin. I learned from the Provençal that they did that from time to time because the chief of the aforesaid cabin had died not long since. What they had in mind in performing these ceremonies I was unable to learn, not knowing their language. [Margry, 1875–1886, vol. 3, p. 346.]

In the Kadohadacho country one of Joutel's companions was drowned and it was observed that every morning while the Frenchmen were there the chief's wife carried a little hamper or basket of ground corn to place it on the grave (Margry, 1875–1886, vol. 3, p. 408).

Casañas goes into the mortuary ceremonies at considerable length, beginning with those performed on the death of one of the leading men:

For this function, there are two Indians who serve as priests. They say their duties are to talk to God and that He speaks to them. These two Indians order a coffin for the dead man. Their order is promptly obeyed. When the coffin is finished, the two Indians put into it some tobacco and some of the herb which they call *acaxio*, and also a bow and arrows. All these things they move about over the coffin from one place to another while they walk to and fro around about the coffin. They keep talking in a low voice as if they were praying. Their mode of speaking is so strenuous that they perspire even though it be cold. During this ceremony, the two wear skins. The ceremonies around the coffin being finished, the Indians go to the place of interment which is always near the house. There they talk again to themselves; but the grave is not opened until, with an axe, they have made a stroke at the place where the head of the dead man is to rest and another where the feet are to lie. While the grave is being dug, the two return to the house and give directions for placing the dead man in the coffin. Thereupon, they talk to the dead man again as if they were speaking to a living person. After finishing the talk they retire a little, saying that they are going to talk to God. After a while they bring back to the corpse the answer to what they have said to God and what God has said to them. Then another man comes out who has the same office, but, as he is old, he does not serve like the others but stands in the midst of all those who are present; i. e., the old men and the most distinguished men. He comes out with a weapon in his hand—one of the best they have.

The person I saw on two occasions had a sword without a scabbard. He spoke for nearly an hour, talking very loudly and earnestly, telling them how much they have all lost by the death of Mr. So-and-so who has always been fortunate both in war and in killing a great number of buffaloes and that he had been strong for work. He tells them that they must weep a great deal for him. He tells them all these things as well as many others of a similar nature. When he has finished the sermon, he goes to the dead person and sits close beside him, repeating to him, as if he were alive, all the things that he had said in his sermon, ending by saying to him that everybody loves him dearly; that everybody is weeping for him; that he must go in peace; that he must work in that other house with the others who have gone before, until those who have begun to work shall have assembled; that he must take up his hatchet and all the rest of the things that are wrapped with him . . . All these ceremonies being ended, they carried the dead body outside as fast as they could, shooting a great many arrows into the air. Then they put whatever clothes he had into the grave, placed the body on top of them, and closed the grave. The two men who served as priests talked earnestly and in a low voice, while the others stood round weeping. When all was finished they went home; and the first thing they did was to carry him some thing of the very best things they had, placing it on top of the grave. Then they put some tobacco and some fire there and left a pot full of water. Then they all went away to eat.

Such ceremonies as I have described are performed when the deceased is one of the chiefs. If he is an ordinary individual, the ceremonies are about the same, only there is not so much pomp. If it is the funeral of the grand *xinesi*, they do not bury him until two days after his death because all of the nine tribes must perform the ceremonies. After the interment they go through other similar ceremonies and certain other superstitious customs, such as placing the world in front of his door. This is done by setting up a very high pole with a large globe of grass on top. They indicate the moons by putting up some large sticks in the shape of the moon. Before these they dance ten days and nights and then each goes home.

I have not myself witnessed all these things, but I have seen all these tribes assembled for these ceremonies, and I saw all these symbols. I saw a coffin which was as big as an ox cart. [Casañas, 1927, pp. 297–299.]

The ideational background of their treatment of the corpse has been given in the descriptions of Espinosa and Morfi, and it appears again in the following paragraph from Casañas:

They have not only the impostures described, but still others, such as saying that, when a person dies, his soul—of which they are not ignorant and which in their idiom they call *Cayo*—goes to another house where a man guards all who are there until all are gathered together. That man they say has some very big keys, bigger than the oxen we have here. When all the souls are gathered together they will enter another world to live anew. For this reason, they bury their dead with all the arms and utensils which each possesses and for several days they carry something to eat to the place where they have buried a person. There are certain men whose duty it is to go up on the graves and talk there alone. I have frequently asked them what they were talking about and they always say that they are talking to God, asking Him to permit the dead to eat in order that they may have strength to reach the house because when they died they were without strength because they had died of hunger. They shoot arrows into the air to inform the master of the said house—who receives everybody—saying "Here he comes! Make him work until we are all united." These Indians are such barbarians that on several occasions they tried to make me believe that they had seen the dead eat what they had carried and that they heard them cry. [Casañas, 1927, p. 294.]

Pénicaut's description of burials in the Acolapissa-Natchitoches town on Lake Pontchartrain may be appended:

When a savage dies, they prepare a kind of tomb or rather a scaffold raised two feet from the ground and place the dead upon it. They cover this well with rich earth and place over that the bark of trees to guard it against animals and birds of prey; then underneath they place a little jar full of water with a plate full of flour. Every evening and morning they light a fire at the side of it and go there to weep. The richest people pay women to perform this last office. After six moons they unwrap the body of the deceased; if it has decayed away, they put the bones into a hamper and carry them to their temple; if it is not decayed away, they remove the bones and bury the flesh. [Margry, 1875–1886, vol. 5, pp. 467–468.]

This recalls Choctaw customs rather than those of the western Caddo.

Short-Man, one of G. A. Dorsey's informants, included in a myth the following account of Caddo burial customs:

When a person dies they dig a hole in the ground about four or five feet long and about three or four feet wide—according to the size of the person—and the body is laid head toward the west and feet toward the east. One of the family builds a fire at the feet of the person, and this fire should be kept up for six days and nights. Very often the person forgets to keep up the fire and lets it go out before the end of the sixth day, and when this happens they find that the grave is open and tracks are seen leading toward the east. They follow the tracks sometimes and overtake the dead person, but generally he gets away from them when they do overtake him. They build the fire all around the dead person; the wood for that purpose is of cedar and mulberry trees, and the sparks from the fire get on the person. At first the dead person pays no attention, but the people keep on building up the fire until the dead person begins to look around and try to escape the sparks from the fire. Then they know the dead person is coming to life again, for he is beginning to feel, and then they take hold of him and bring him back home, where he is kept for six days and nights. At the sixth day, in the early evening, some one of the family would bathe him, and then he would live again. When the dead person is not caught he becomes something like a very large monkey, and lives in the thickets and timber. Whenever the people meet a dead person he talks to them, and so the people think that dead people are crazy people. They do not know where their homes are or who their relatives are, and so they go off and stay in the woods or among the wild animals. That is the reason that large monkeys are called "the last people in the thickets." When any one or two people go out to hunt in the thickets or woods they always meet these monkeys, and the monkeys always ask for a wrestling match. They are very strong little men, and if the people do not pay any attention to them, they bother them all night long. These creatures are still living, but they do not talk as they did when the world was new. [G. A. Dorsey, 1905, p. 65; see also pp. 307–308 below.]

Dr. Parsons' informants stated that:

Before the corpse is taken out from the house, those present pass their hands over it, from head to feet, and then over their own person. Messages are sent through the deceased to other dead relatives. Anybody arriving too late to see the deceased will go to the grave, to the east side, and, making a pass over the grave, will pass his hands down his own person. This rite is repeated at the other sides of the grave, south, west, north. Graves are made near dwelling houses, nowadays on your own land . . . The head of the grave must be at the west, facing the rising sun. The grave diggers stand at the east end of the grave and one shoots to the west, into the grave. Then they let down the blanket-wrapped body. They put into the grave whatever they think the deceased should take with her or him; for a woman, cooking utensils, plates, etc., clothing; and for a man, besides clothes and blankets, bow and arrows "to defend himself on his road if anything bother him," since "evil things try to get the soul before reaching heaven." As such "evil things" are abroad at night the bow and arrows for the deceased should be made in the daytime. A woman will protect herself with her knife. If the deceased *is* interfered with, he will linger about until the shaman sets him on the right road again According to Ingkanish the besetting evil things are bad *ka^ayu* (ghosts) or *tsaki'u* (*ki'u*, horn), "devils" with horns. They are on both sides of the road which is "awful hard" to travel. It is narrow. There is a big river crossed by a small log. After you pass over that foot log you are safe, and you go on to *naawantikuki'das* (our father all home) or, as it is also called, *kiwat'hae'me* (home big) or *kiwat'hae'me kuki'das*, which is above, to the west.

The spirit stays six days before starting on its way. During these six days a fire must be kept up at the east end of the grave. Anybody in the family, man or women, old or young, may keep up this fire. All the possessions of the deceased, clothes, etc., are kept by this fire, hung on a pole. At the close of the six days things which are unfit for further use are burned, other things are smoked, and may then be given away to friends or relatives. Members of the household of the deceased who have been staying at home are smoked at this time, after which they take a bath in the creek. Now at noon there is a meal at the grave. The pots are set in a circle, and with a spoon a man, any one may be chosen, takes some food into his hand from each pot and puts this food on the middle of the grave, it is for the journey.

Recurrently, at the same time of year, for two, three, or four years a feast for the deceased person is made, . . . and food is taken to the grave, or, as Ingkanish puts it, a beef is killed and a piece taken to the grave which is encircled clockwise four times. There is much visiting about in connection with these characteristically Southeastern feasts, as acquaintances as well as relatives are entertained. It has become customary to hold a peyote meeting the night before a death feast. At the feast the next Ghost dance will be announced.

Of the dead it is said, *Ganiha^ada'* (R), he passed away, or *hayuna* . . . , "he has gone home" is White Moon's free translation. At death people go up to the sky. Deceased relatives and others are seen in the Ghost dance trance, in fact the entire "village of the dead" may be seen.

There is or was a ceremony to bring back the dead. Kanoshtsi' (Kanosh, French), a doctor who died in 1908, had four sisters, long since dead, who were also doctors and practiced bringing back the dead, with success if they began to work soon after the death. They sent their supernatural partners after the deceased. They could catch up with the deceased and bring him back to the body providing he had not passed beyond certain clouds in the sky. These women doctors conducted their ceremony "to catch up with the dead" in a large permanent "grass house." Their brother has been heard to say that had he only paid more attention to his sisters' methods he would have been as good in practice as they. [Parsons, 1941, pp. 36–39.]

This material has been included practically entire because burial customs are of particular interest to archeologists.

When I visited the Caddo in 1912, I was given to understand that they buried their dead at full length, feet to the west, so that the bodies faced west, the way the soul goes. This may have been an error but not certainly so, as the custom of laying bodies head to the west came in with Christianity, and in aboriginal times the soul was supposed to travel west, not east as Short-Man seems to have told Dorsey.

RELATIONS TO THE COSMOS

RELIGIOUS BELIEFS

It is clear that a supreme heaven god was recognized by the Caddo similar in attributes, no doubt, to the heaven god which we encounter throughout the Southeast generally:

They are not ignorant of God. Indeed, all of them know there is only one God whom they call in their language *Ayo-Caddi-Aymay*. They try, in all their affairs, to keep him in a good humor in every way possible. They never in any manner venture to speak of him in jest, because they say that, when he punishes them for anything, he does it well and that whatever he does is best. They also believe that he punishes those who are angry with him. [Casañas, 1927, p. 288.]

The most complete account of this belief and the myth connected with it is given, however, by Espinosa:

Throughout the whole Asinais nation, which is composed of more than four-teen or fifteen divisions which speak the same dialect, the belief prevails that there is a great captain up in the sky whom they call *caddi ayo*, which means "the captain up above." They say that he created everything; and in order that it may be shown how disconnectedly they reason, they tell a story as follows: They say that in the beginning of the world there was one woman only who had two daughters, one a maiden, the other not, without there being designated any man by whom either the mother or daughter would have been able to pro-duce. One day the two sisters were alone, away from the mother . . . They were attacked from the rear and this is what happened.

Suddenly there appeared a huge, misshapen serpent, of ferocious aspect and with horns, whose ends could not be seen. They call him *caddaja*, devil, or demon. He attacked the pregnant sister, tore her with his claws, chewed her up, and swal-lowed every bit of her, while the maiden climbed to the top of a very tall tree. When the devil had finished eating her sister, he raised his eyes in search of the maiden to do the same with her. He tried to climb the tree but, not being able to do so, he began to try to cut down the tree with his teeth and claws . . . See-ing the danger in which she was placed, the maiden dropped down into a deep hole of water which was at the foot of the tree and, diving down into it, came up at a distant spot and escaped to where her mother was. The ugly giant began to suck up the water to drain it away and make a prisoner of the maiden; but she had fooled him and had left the place. The maiden told her mother everything that had happened and together they went to the spot where he had murdered the sister. They searched among the drops of blood which the demon had scattered when he was eating her and they found a tiny drop of blood in a little acorn shell. They covered it with another half shell, the mother put it in her bosom and car-ried it home. She put it in a little jar, covered the mouth well and put it in the corner. At night she heard a noise as if the little jar were being gnawed. Upon going to examine it she found that the drop of blood had turned into a boy as small as one's finger. She covered it again and the next night, hearing the same sound, she found that he had grown to the stature of a man. She was very much pleased and at once made him a bow and arrows. He asked for his mother. They told him how the devil had eaten her and he set out to seek him. When he found him he hit him so hard with the point of his arrow [lit. bow] that the devil never appeared again. He returned then to his grandmother and his aunt and told them that it was not good to stay on earth and he ascended with them to *cachao ayo*, as they call the sky. And there he has been ever since, governing the world. This is the first god they recognize and worship. They believe that he will reward or punish them for the good or evil they have done. [Espinosa, 1927, pp. 158–160.]

The following note by Casañas seems to show that the *caddi ayo* lacked something of the omnipotence attributed to him in the passages just quoted. His aunt or grandmother appears to have shared his attributes.

Another gross superstition they have, in which all of them believe implicitly, is that the old men made Heaven and that a woman, who sprang from an acorn, first gave them its outlines; and that it was done by placing timbers in the form of a circle and that Heaven was formed in this way. They further declare that the woman is in Heaven and that she is the one who daily gives birth to the sun, the moon, the water when it rains, the frost, the snow, the corn, the thunder, and the lightning; and many similar absurdities, such as when one of the leading men dies they go through many ceremonies. [Casañas, 1927, pp. 296–297.]

However, according to the cosmogonic myth as related by Espinosa, it was the *caddi ayo* who sprang from the acorn and not a woman, and Casañas may have misunderstood his informant.

Morfi has rendered this myth with few changes:

In all of the nation of the Asinais, or Texas, as has already been said, there are of the one language more than 14 or 15 tribes who believe in the existence of a great captain who lives in heaven, whom they call *Caddi-Ayo*, which means "Captain of the Above," or "on high," (*de arriba ó de lo alto*). To this god they attribute the creation of all beings, though (their tradition filled with contradictions) they suppose them pre-existent to the origin of their creator, which they relate in this way.

In the beginning of the world, there was a single woman who had two daughters; one of these was a virgin and the other pregnant. (They are not embarrassed in not finding the man by whom the mother and the daughter became pregnant.) One day when the two girls were alone, and the pregnant one was lying down on the lap of the virgin, they cruelly took her away by a strange event. It happened that unexpectedly there appeared before them the *Caddaja* or *Demonio* in the form of a gigantic man, of ferocious appearance, and with his forehead decorated with horns, which were so enormous that their tips were lost from sight. The moment he appeared he snatched the pregnant girl, and tore her to pieces with his claws, and soon devoured her. The virgin, fearing the same misfortune, took advantage of this interval, and climbed to the top of a big tree. The Devil's appetite not being satisfied with the pregnant one, he looked for the other to devour her as well. Seeing her among the branches, he tried to climb up to her, but could not; and without knowing that he could get her down with his horns, he applied his claws and teeth to cutting down the tree at its roots, to capture her. The virgin seeing herself in this sad plight, and there being no other way to avoid it, she quickly flung herself into a deep creek which ran nearby. This did not cause the *Caddaja* to give up hopes of getting her, and to accomplish this, he set out to drink the water so as to drain the stream and have it dry, in order to offer to his greediness this second victim; but by swimming under water, she deceived his cunning and escaped from the danger, going away from that place, to where her mother was, to whom she told the tragic end of her sister. The two together departed immediately for the place where the incident occurred. The mother looking for the tracks of blood of her daughter, found a drop inside an acorn shell. She took it up with care, covered it with another half shell of the same fruit, placed it in her bosom, and went back to the hut where she lived. She put the acorn and drop of blood in a large earthen jar, covered it well, and placed it in a protected corner of the room where she slept. That night she heard something making a slight noise within the vessel, a sort of nibbling or scratching. When day dawned she investigated, and found that the drop of blood had turned into a very well proportioned and beautiful child; but so small that its size did not exceed the length of a finger on one's hand. She was filled with joy at such a remarkable recovery, and, to assure her good fortune, again covered the jar with the same care. The noise was repeated that night, and, investigating it the following day, she found that the child had grown up to be a man of regular size. The grandmother's joy increased upon seeing such a handsome grandson, and, without losing time, she made a bow and a sufficient number of arrows which she gave him, before taking him out of the jar. The newborn, who already spoke the language with perfection, immediately asked for his mother. The grandmother told him about her tragic end, without keeping secret the cruel author of that barbarous act. Worried, the youth went out to seek him, to avenge such an unheard of offense. He found him without much trouble, and wounded his body badly with the point of his bow [with his arrows?], and flung him so far, that up to the present he has not been seen again. Having avenged the infamous death of his mother, he returned to his grandmother and aunt. He made them see how painful it would be to all of them to live in a land where they had before their eyes a thousand objects to remind them of the sad end of his mother, and that this memory would spoil for them all joys; he persuaded them by his reasoning to accompany him gladly to heaven, or, as they say, to *Cachao-Ayo*, where they all live, the youth having the duty of governing the universe. Thus those Indians tell the history of the origin of the first of their divinities; whom they adore, and worship, attributing to him the distribution of rewards and punishments for the good and bad works of each of us; though they never attribute to the latter, so much malice that pardon cannot be obtained through the practise of certain ceremonies. [Morfi, 1932, pp. 21–23; quoted in Amer. Anthrop., n. s., vol. 1, pp. 593–594.]

Connected with the cult of this being were several temples and priests. Reverting to Espinosa:

They have especial superstitions in connection with fire and they worship it. There is a house set apart for this purpose where there is always a fire. They have appointed an old man whose duty it is to keep it up always. He is their *chenesi* or chief priest. They say that if it goes out everybody will die. This house, which was rebuilt in December, 1716, is half way between the Naichas and the Ainas and is common to both people. They say it is the house of the great captain. It is large, round, and thatched, and has within it an altar made of reed mats. On the bed are three finer mats, two of them very small. To one side of the door, upon benches, are other reed mats folded into a roll. In the front of the bed is a little square wooden bench, of one piece, with four feet, and slightly raised from the ground. Upon this bench there is usually tobacco and a pipe with feathers and earthen-ware vessels which are evidently incense burners in which they burn fat and tobacco. Their fire or bonfire is always made of four very large, heavy logs which point toward the four principal directions. The wood is brought in small and kept in a pile outside. Here the old men gather for their consultations and war dances and when they need rain for their crops. Ordinarily their prayers are vain and mere fables. The ashes from their fire continue to accumulate outside and when they bring any bones of the enemy whom they have killed, they bury them in these ashes. Near this house there are two other small houses about a gunshot distant. They call them the houses of the two *cononicis*. These, they say, are two boys or small children whom their great captain sent from the *cachao ayo*, or the sky, for the purpose of discussing their problems with them. They pretend that these children were in these houses until a little more than two years ago according to some (this was the time when two priests of the Cross were in Mexico trying to arrange for the entry into the Texas country), or, until the time their enemies, the Yojuanes, burned these houses, according to the Indian interpreter. This was when, so he says, they saw the children ascend in smoke and they have not come down again. In these houses there are two little chests about three palm lengths long, and raised upon a wooden altar with four little forked poles with curious covers of plaited reed.

In company with another priest, I found that inside these chests there were four or five little platters or vessels of black wood like circular shields, all curiously worked and having four feet. Some represented little ducks, having the head and tail of a duck. Others had the head and tail of an alligator or lizard. In addition to these there were many feathers of various shapes and colors, handfulls of feathers of wild birds, a white breast knot, some rolls of ornamental feathers, crowns made of skins and feathers, a bonnet of the same, many little carved crane bones which serve them as flutes or fifes, others of carved reeds with the necessary holes, and many other little instruments which they use in their *mitotes* or dances. One of these little houses in which the two little chests are located is very clean and well swept. The fire temple is like a parish house or cathedral for the Assinais. There is another among the Naichas, still another among the Nacocdoches and the Nazonis. They carry fire from this temple to those houses. Usually the Naichas and Ainais gather for their special feasts of the year in one temple and the Nacocdoches and the Nazonis in the other temple which is located among the Nacocdoches. All of the houses, or most of them, are supplied with fire from the principal temple—not that it is carried every day, but they are supplied therefrom when the houses are built, and they keep it burning. If it goes out at any time, they consider it a sign that all that family will die and they bring new fire from the fire temple with great ceremony which I will describe in the proper place. They are very much afraid of angering the fire and they offer up to it the first tobacco and the first fruits of their corn, a portion of the game they kill, and a part of all their crops. They claim that fire created all of these things for them. However, some of the deluded people claim that men came up from the sea and spread all over the earth. They call these fire and water creatures *nicaddi* but they always include fire in their ceremonies. They say that in the beginning there were many demons in the land who killed them and caused them great damage. They say these demons were giants, big and horrible. Some claim to be descendants of bears, others of dogs, others of otters, and others of coyotes and foxes. When I asked them why, they said:

"Seeing the damages these evil spirits or demons inflicted, their ancestors transformed themselves into these animals, but they were rational men, women and children at the same time." [Espinosa, 1927, pp. 160–162.]

Morfi:

They also offer their adoration to fire. For this they have a house or temple where they perpetually keep a fire, and the care of this is entrusted solely to the Chenesi, or High Priest, who himself and with the assistance of his subjects (*subalternos*) watches it with such zeal that it never goes out, as they are persuaded that if through any fatal accident this unfortunate event should occur, all the members of the nation would be immediately and irredeemably lost.

This house which was rebuilt in December of 1716, is situated in the immediate vicinity of the Netchas, and Ainais; it is common to the two tribes, and they say that the chief from on high lives in it. Its construction does not differ from that of the other houses of the community, except that it is larger. The Rev. Father Fr. Isidro Felix de Espinosa who attentively investigated it says that in this temple one sees a canopy formed with rush mats (*esteras*); in the place where the bed is, three mats (*petates*), one large, and two very small ones; and to one side of the door on small beds or cots (*tapertles ó camillas*), various rolled-up mats. In front of the bed there is located a little square stool (*banquillo quadrado*), with four legs, made of one single piece, and somewhat raised from the common floor. On this stool it was customary to have tobacco, a pipe, and some feathers, little pots of clay, which seemed to serve as incense burners, where they burned tobacco and grease. The sacred fire is in the middle of the temple, and they always keep it burning with four very long, thick, and heavy logs, which they constantly attend, arranging them in the direction of the four principal winds; the little wood with which they light them they keep out of the house, alongside the walls, piled in pyramids. Here the captains and elders meet to celebrate their council, not only in the deliberations of peace, and war, but in public necessities, and matters of importance to the state, as when there is a scarcity of rain, any menace for the destruction of the crops, etc. They exercise great care in taking out of the temple the ashes of the sacred fire, which they keep to make large mounds.

When they celebrate the removal of the bones of their enemies, killed in battle, they bury them in these ashes.

At the distance of a short gun-shot from the large temple, they constructed two other little ones, which they call the houses of the two *Coninicis*. These, they say, are two children who were sent from heaven by their Great Captain, to be consulted when in doubt. They visibly dwelt there for many long years, up to the middle of the present century, according to some, and were still there according to what the Indian interpreter said, until the Yojuanes Indians burned these houses, and then, they assert, they saw them ascend in smoke to heaven, whence they will never again descend.

In these little houses Father Espinosa found two chests made of reeds, and curiously painted, with their lids, and measuring about three spans square. They are located on a little altar-like platform of wood, on four little upright poles (*horconcillos*). In these chests were four or five vessels of black wood, each in the form of a soup plate (*escudilla*), well worked, and each with four legs, which represented in a reasonable manner, the figures of ducks, alligators and lizards; many feathers of all sizes and colors, some turkey skins (*pieles de pavo*), some white breast feathers, head dresses, also of feathers, but very beautiful; helmets (*morriones*) of the same; many small heron bones which serve them as flutes; others of carved reeds and a multitude of instruments which they enjoy at their dances or *mitotes*.

This great fire house of which I spoke in [paragraph] number four, is like the *Metropoli* of the whole province; in addition to this one, there is a second, at the Netches, and a third among the Nacogdoches and Nasonis, to which fire was taken from the first. Generally the Ainais and Netchas meet in the principal one; and the Nacogdoches and Nasonis in the last. Both the former and the latter fear that the fire will get angry with them, and to satisfy it, they make offerings to it of their first corn, tobacco, meat from the chase, and in a word, of all their crops. Of little consequence in their traditions, they give assurance that the fire produced them. And at other times they say that the first men who populated the earth came forth from the sea. Recognizing both fire and water as their creators, they call both by the name *Niacadi*, but in spite of their belief, when in need they always appeal to the fire, without heeding the water. They also say on some occasions that some of them are descended from bears, others from dogs, beavers, coyotes, etc. Their forefathers seeing the danger caused them by the Devil, to deceive his malice, transformed themselves into those brutes, without losing their minds, and retaining the faculty of restoring themselves to their primitive being when convenient to them. [Morfi, 1932, pp. 23–26.]

According to the same authority, the Nabedache also had a temple, unless we can suppose that in the following quotation he is attributing the Hainai and Neches temple to them:

The Navedachos are reduced to less than 40 families and inhabit the region of the head waters of the Neches. A short distance from their pueblo is a little hill on the top of which is a temple, raised by their forefathers, in which they practice a cult to their false divinities. But after their primitive fervor was extinguished, they did not carry out what they had planned. [Morfi, 1932, p. 5.]

Probably Morfi derived his information from De Mézières whose words are:

On one of the banks of the second [river], which flows near the village of the Navedachos, one sees a little mound, which their ancestors erected in order to build on its summit a temple, which commanded the nearby village, and in which they worshipped their gods. It is rather a monument to the multitude than to the industry of its individuals. [Bolton, 1914, vol. 2, p. 263.]

Tonti mentions a temple in the village of the Kadohadacho (Cox, 1905, vol. 1, p. 46), the same probably as that shown in the illustration already mentioned. He found another in the town of the Natchitoches, Ouachita, and "Capiché," evidently the one which Bienville observed in the village of the Natchitoches, Doustioni, and Yatasi, "a temple full of many 'pagodas' which have shapes of toads and many other creatures (insectes)." (Cox, 1905, vol. 1, p. 45; Bienville ms.) A few years later Pénicaut describes still another in the town occupied jointly by the Acolapissa and Natchitoches Indians:

They have [he says] a round temple before which they present themselves evening and morning, rubbing their bodies with white earth and raising their arms on high; they mutter some words in a very low voice during a quarter of an hour. There are at the portal of the temple figures of birds made of wood; in the temple are a quantity of little idols, both of wood and stone, which represent dragons, serpents, and creatures like toads, which they keep shut up in three coffers in the temple and of which the Grand Chief has the key. [Margry, 1875–1886, vol. 5, p. 467.]

De Batz has supplied us with a drawing of the temple which the Acolapissa Indians erected after they moved to the Mississippi River a few years later (Bushnell, 1927, p. 4, pl. 1). Although the one Pénicaut describes belonged properly to the Acolapissa, it was evidently similar to that which formerly existed in the Natchitoches town and may have furnished temporary lodgment to some of the Natchitoches sacred objects.

The reverence in which fire was held is indicated in several other places. Hidalgo says, in line with what has gone before: "They do not wish fire to be taken from their houses because [if that happens] they believe that someone in the house will die" (Hidalgo, 1927, p. 56).

There is another superstition, [says Casañas] viz., if they throw ice on the fire they say the cold does not have to go and must be angry. If someone dies or a house burns up they say that death is angry. Therefore, they make an offering of something by hanging it on a pole in front of the house. When a house burns, they also say that the ground on which they lived, or the hill near the house, has been angered and burned the house; so they do not rebuild the home there but in another spot. [Casañas, 1927, p. 296.]

The functions and activities of the *xinesi* or *chenesi* are dwelt upon at considerable length by Casañas some years earlier than the time of which Espinosa speaks:

The grand *xinesi* of this province has deceived all his vassals by telling them that, whenever he wants to, he talks to two children whom he has in his house and who came from the other side of Heaven. He says that these children eat and drink and that, whenever he wants to talk to God, he does so through them. On certain occasions, when he feels that his people do not bring him corn and other things they have, he reports that the two children are angry and are not willing to talk about questions of the general welfare of the tribe.

In addition, the *xinesi* tells his people that these two children have informed him that the people will not have good crops; that their enemies are going to kill them; that God is not going to help them, all because they have not given their captain a portion of all their supplies. And they not only give portions of everything to him, but I have been told that they even go hungry because he tells them these things. He calls all the tribes to his house and gives orders to all the *caddices* and the old men to come into the house where he keeps the two children. This house is very much larger than the one where he lives. They all seat themselves around the fire which the *xinesi* keeps burning both day and night. He always takes the greatest possible pains to see that it never goes out. He keeps a number of sacristans to feed the holy sacramental fire. The first thing he does in the view of the assembled men is to take some live coals with a pair of tongs. He then mixes fat from the heart of a buffalo with tobacco and offers the incense to the two children whom he has put upon a tall *tapestle*, two square *varas* in size. At the sides are two small boxes made of reeds into which he always puts a portion of the things the people bring him during the year. He now tells those assembled that the boxes are now empty. As soon as he is through offering the incense, he puts out the fire and shuts the door so that nothing can be seen distinctly. Thus all the men within are in darkness. Those outside sing and dance while those within are perfectly silent, listening to the *xinesi* who speaks in two assumed voices—one that of a child, the other somewhat like his own voice. In the latter voice, he speaks to the children, asking them to tell God that the *Asinai* are now going to reform and to beg of Him in the future to give them a great deal of corn, good health, fleetness in chasing the deer and the buffalo, great strength for fighting their enemies, and many women to serve them all. The petitions which he offers to God consist of these and many similar things.

After finishing the prayer he takes a small calabash in his hand. Inside this are usually some things which rattle. He throws this little calabash upon the ground. He makes them all believe that, if it falls upon the ground (without making any sound), God is angry and that he does not wish to speak to them. Then all are frightened when they see the calabash is on the floor not making any noise. They cry out in loud voices that they promise the great captain *Ayo Aymay* to bring something of every kind of food they may have to the two *caninisi*, i. e., the two children, and to their *xinesi*. As soon as the *xinesi* hears the promise made to God to furnish him with everything and to provide him with whatever he may need, he suddenly picks up the little calabash and begins to make a noise, imitating the voice of a child, and says that God is now speaking and says to tell all the rest that, if the tribe fulfills the promise which those present have given, He will give them everything which they ask for—and they must ask through their *xinesi*. Then the *xinesi* in his natural voice repeats what the children have said to him. He then tells the Indians to go out and search for meat and everything else they can find in order that neither God nor the two children may be angry again, promising them that the two children will always keep God satisfied. He sometimes tells them this in an angry voice and sometimes in a kind voice. He then opens the door and tells them to go home and not forget what they have promised God. They all go out in great haste without giving place to one another, making a noise like goats when running out of their corral. I have not yet been able to find out what this means.

The *xinesi* is left inside, stirring the fire and pulverizing meal for the children in a mortar which he has in the house. When he finds that all the others have gone to their own houses, he comes out and goes home, about a hundred paces away. In addition it may be noted that as long as these functions last, no one is ever permitted to see these two children. The *xinesi* threatens them with instant death, and then cites the example of a man who once saw them and immediately fell down dead. Those who enter must disrobe. [Casañas, 1927, pp. 290–292.]

Casañas at one time forced his way into this building without having obeyed the last injunction. He continues:

When I asked him about the two children and where they were, he was at once frightened and put in my hands a round piece of wood like the cover of a sweetmeat box. This was covered with skin like parchhment. Around the little box he had placed some crumbs from the bread which the Indians brought him as an offering. In the middle of the box was a hole into which tobacco is put. He told me that it was for tobacco for the two children to smoke. I saw that there was no trace of the children, and, having heard the nonsense he had spoken, I reprimanded him in such a way that he would not be angered. [Casañas wished to burn this box] but he would not agree that I should burn his children because he and all the *Asinai* loved them very much. He declared that the reason I did not see them was because it had not been possible to see them since [the period] just after the time when they had first come from Heaven. Then they were visible; but, now, the house that had been built for them when they came had burned down and they had perished in the flames. Only what I saw was left. I knew that all this was a lie of his, and I wanted to throw them in the fire. But when I was on the point of pitching them in, he became very furious. I, therefore, desisted in order not to stir up trouble . . . I left him thus; but I am of the same opinion that everything was a fraud invented by the *xinesi* himself for the purpose of deceiving his vassals. [Casañas, 1927, pp. 292–293.]

Hidalgo had heard of these "children":

I have heard it said on many occasions that the fire the Tejas Indians have in their houses was brought from the house of their high priest, whom they call *chenesi*. If the fire goes out they start immediately for the house of the priest to get new fire. It never goes out in the house of sacrifice. The Indians say they have two children from God whom they call in their language *coneneses* "the little ones." . . . The Indians go at night to say their prayers. Their priest assumes the voices of the two children and asks for what he needs for their use. He threatens that if the worshipers do not do as they are told they will be punished suddenly with snake bites. They make many prayers in their language to the two *coneneses* and when they have finished and start out at the door they bleat like goats that are following close after the herd. Once Father Fray Antonio Bordoi went into the house of sacrifice to see the *coneneses* to find out what they were. The priest objected and declared that he would certainly die. But the father went in and found a little box with packages. But he did not see any children. Into the fire which the Indians keep burning in their houses they throw a great amount of fat, offering it to the "Great Captain." [Hidalgo, 1927, pp. 50–52.]

When they kill a deer they never cut it up until the priest of the pueblo arrives. He cuts it up. The Indians had rather lose it than cut it open before their priest arrives. He cuts it up, selects the portion belonging to his priestly office, and it is sent to him. The same thing is done in the case of their crops of corn and beans. Each one and each family gives a portion of everything to the high priest. [Hidalgo, 1927, p. 52.]

Hidalgo does not exhibit the caution of Casañas in ascribing idolatry to the Hasinai:

The whole nation is idolatrous—as is at present recognized. They have houses of worship and a perpetual fire which they never let die out. They are very much perverted and in their dances they have Indian braves or Indian women who get drunk on *peyote* or *frixolillo*, which they make for the occasion, and the people believe everything these persons tell them they have seen. They have idols large and small. They believe in the devil and offer sacrifices to him believing that he is the true god. In the pictures they make of him they paint him with horns and a face of fire and with other features that prove their great deception. [Hidalgo, 1927, pp. 55–56.]

According to Espinosa, the Indians had "as gods, lions, bears, monkeys, and other unnatural representations of the devil." By "lions" he, of course, means panthers, but what he intends by "monkeys" we can only guess (Espiñosa, 1927, p. 158).

For further myth materials, see the publications of G. A. Dorsey and E. C. Parsons cited in Bibliography.

MEDICINE MEN AND MEDICAL PRACTICES

These are treated by Casañas and at still greater length by Espinosa. As often happened to missionaries, Casañas experienced most of the opposition to his work from these men.

All of them are liars and guilty of a thousand deceptions, while some of them are enchanters. Once one of them by his tricks tried to prevent me from baptizing a woman. I hurled an exorcism against him, and, all at once, he ran away as if I had tried to kill him. There was another Indian along who tried by certain ceremonies to throw fat and tobacco into the fire in order to do me some harm. I hurled an exorcism at him in the presence of more than thirty persons. So great was his fright that he was not able to hold the bow and arrow which they always carry in their hands; but he ran away from me and the others assembled there. Next morning they went in search of him to get him to cure the sick; but they found him dead in a valley. Since that time all the medicine men, whom they call *conna*, are afraid of me and give me a free path, praising what I do. They tell the sick that it is very good for them to permit themselves to have the water applied. [Casañas, 1927, pp. 295–296.]

He claims to have converted no less than five of these native practitioners. He continues:

Their treatment is nothing more than to suck the particular spot where the pain is and to drive the disease out of the house. At other times they claim that they drive the disease into the fire and burn it; and, because these poor people are so gullible and have such implicit faith, they promise to give everything they have to the physician if he will only cure them of their diseases. The physicians do nothing without mixing it up with some kind of superstition. Sometimes it happens that one of them will have poor luck curing diseases and many of his patients die. Some of the Indians take cudgels and kill him. [Casañas, 1927, p. 296.]

And now to turn to Espinosa:

The whole country is cursed with the pest of doctors or medicine men. They [operate by] a mixture of superstitions and lies, with a great admixture of trickery, which I do not yet know to be real witchcraft. These much bepainted medicine men have their own particular insignia of feathers which they wear upon their heads and curious necklaces of serpents' skins, and seats in the houses which are higher than the seats for the captains. To cure a patient, they build a big bonfire and provide an abundance of fifes and an abundance of feathers. Their instruments are little polished sticks with slits like a snake's rattles. These rubbed on a hollow skin make a noise nothing less than infernal. Before playing they drink their brewed herbs, covered with foam. They then, without moving at all, begin to dance to this infernal music and the songs of the condemned, for to this alone can the chanted jargon of the medicine men be likened. The ceremony lasts from the middle of the afternoon until near dawn. The medicine man stops his singing at intervals to apply his cruel treatment to the patient whom they have sweating on a grate over many coals that are kept burning under the bed . . . In the midst of the piteous complaints, the medicine man explains that the treatment he is giving is very mild. The doctors continue to suck and to spit. They put into their mouths a worm or blood which they have previously provided and declare that they took it from the body of the patient. It is certain that they devour whatever physical possessions the patient may have for their pay (whether the sick person lives or dies), for their cruel treatment lasts as long as there is anything they can eat or take. With other patients they scarify the side with flints and really suck their blood. They do the same thing for snake bites, spitting the poison from between their open lips. This is reasonable because the effect follows naturally. They declare they can divine whether or not the patient will die. If it is a prominent person there is a meeting of medicine men and each one tries out his own prescription. Naturally a cure sometimes follows because of these remedies for they apply the herbs with which this country abounds.

The great quantities of bitter drinks which the medicine men drink under the pretense that it is for the benefit of the patient [are taken under] a fantastic illusion, for this method of healing is reserved for the Divine Physician who himself took the bitter potion of gall and vinegar to heal our iniquities. And,

Christ being the patient, we are the ones who gain life eternal. It sometimes happens that the pain or sickness is caused by a tumor or swelling. For this they apply the treatment of the stone and sucking with the lips. They make the whole nation believe that sickness has its origin in the evil deeds committed by the neighboring nations of the Bidais, Ays, and Yacdo[c]as, who have many witch doctors.[19] These, so the Asinais say, come in secret or send the disease which they call *aguain* from their country because they are wicked and witches. In explanation of the etymology of this word it must be said that *aguain* means a thing that has a sharp point like an arrow, that it is shot from a bow of one whom they call *texino* and we call the devil, and that it strikes the patient. To remove this point or arrow, which they say is like a big white needle, they have their dances, songs, and the treatments above mentioned. Before undertaking them, they call to their aid the Bidais medicine men. They declare that the Bidais come to aid them in the shape of owls or *tecolotes* which the devil brings to them on these occasions. There are three kinds of owls on earth and when the Indians hear the sound of the hoot of an owl they raise a shout of joy as if they had won a victory. To this superstition they add another to the effect that the false god whom they call *ynici* comes to their aid because he is moved by their songs and prayers. These medicine men are the instigators of all the deceptions and foolishness of the Indians. They recite or mutter disjointed phrases through their teeth, with their faces turned toward the wall or toward a post in the house. They then take tobacco and throw it in the fire. They take a little of the meat which they procure from the buffalo and throw it also into the fire. Other little bits they throw to the four winds which they worship in all their functions. When they smoke they throw a handful of smoke in each of the main directions, first toward the captain above, who is none other then the one who fell into the abyss.

It is the duty of these medicine men to take the measure for building the houses, to be present at the blessing of the new building, and to be first at the function of feasting. The number of these medicine men is so great that even when one of the heads of this hydra is cut off by death, additional heads in the persons of new ministers of lies rise up at every step. These are certain young fellows who have scarcely reached the age of twenty years and, because each wishes to excel, they take great pride in becoming expert. A great number of the old fakirs or saints, with a bunch of medicine men, gather together, dressed for a feast in all the finery they have. They offer drinks to the prospective medicine men. The latter consume great quantities of tobacco. This, with their drinks, causes them to lose their senses, to make faces, and to fall upon the ground like drunken men. Here they remain either really senseless or pretending to be, for twenty-four hours, as if dead, until they decide to come to and begin to breathe. They then relate what they have dreamed or whatever their imaginations suggest to them. They say that their souls were far from them. The candidate then begins his song and this discordant music continues for eight days, the novices relieving each other and the assembled women adding their discordant cries. During these songs the Indians attack the pots which they do not cease stirring on the fire and they fill their stomachs while the candidates entertain the crowd with their songs and dances. These

[19] Two of these tribes, the Bidai and Yacdocas, were unrelated to the Caddo, while the third, the Ays or Haish, spoke, as we have seen, a divergent dialect. It is usual to find medicine men and wizards of such foreign or aberrant tribes clothed with imaginary powers of peculiar potency. And it is, therefore, not surprising to find Adai doctors regarded in the same way. This tribe, says La Harpe, was reputed to have the most famous sorcerers. (Margry, 1875–1886, vol. 6, p. 304.)

medicine men are very much respected and highly regarded by everybody. They are, in the general estimation, the oracles of all their deceptions. In truth, the devil, who is the instigator of all this foolishness, could not have left them a better patrimony than this trade to enable them to secure from the Asinais the best meat, and the first fruits of their crops. The greatest happiness to which they aspire is to be the ones selected to help them build their houses and gather their crops. Among the Nacocdoches, who are also Asinais, the medicine man usually receives death if he does not effect a cure or if his reputation as a healer becomes poor. In this case, the relatives of the man who dies as the result of the unsuccessful treatment, seize him with their claws, and beat him in the temples with sticks until he can not get well. In short, these medicine men are the greatest obstacles to the conversion of many who would receive holy baptism if they were not afraid of their threats.

They persuade the patients that life is destroyed by holy baptism; and when, in spite of them, certain persons have been baptized, the medicine men usually abandon them under the pretense that the waters of baptism have caused the disease to take such a form that all their skill can not avail to cure it. Many of these abandoned creatures have sought help among the Spaniards; and, through the mercies of God, after being abandoned by their own people, we have seen them recover and regain perfect health. The devil inspires all this. Among these medicine men or doctors, there are some who are graduates in astrology. [Espinosa, 1927, pp. 165–168.]

Here follows the February forecasting ceremony after which Espinosa proceeds as follows:

They forecast future events from many things that happen naturally. When the men are off on a buffalo hunt or in quest of their enemies in war, and it happens that a number of little birds come, they take it as a sign that the absent ones are near. They call these birds *banit*. When they go out to war they have a general meeting in the house of their captain and give drinks to the one whom they consider most valiant until he loses or pretends to lose his senses. After a day and a night he declares that he saw where the enemy were and reports whether or not they were prepared. From this they forecast victory. They do the same thing on the road when they go on a journey. With the tail of a fox they make an astrolabe to see future events. All their dances, prayers, and ceremonies around the fire are accustomed to have such good effect that last year when the prognostication was that they would conquer the Yojuanes, their enemies, the poor Naicha were whipped and lost many who were left captives. They consider it a sure sign if they fan the fire in winter with a fan or wing that such a snow or cold spell will soon come that everything will be killed. Often when they see us fanning the flames with these things they want to take them out of our hands. They say that we are fools or crazy to do such a thing and that we are not afraid because we are covered with clothes. When we reproach them with their foolishness, they declare that our fire is different because it is made with a rock and iron while that of the Asinais is made with sticks rubbed one on another. A little time ago they were asked why they did not, like all the Indians at the missions of the Asinais and the Naichai, leave their houses during buffalo time, when all the Nazonis and Nacocdoches left? A fakir answered that it was so the fire would not go out if wood failed, that the Nazonis and Nacocdoches had a different kind of fire which they made by rubbing two little sticks together. In this way they could leave their fire hanging up in their houses while the Ainais and Naichas had fire from their forefathers. The tradition is still preserved. [Espinosa, 1927, pp. 168–169.]

Morfi may now be quoted:

The multitude of medicine men (*curanderos*) with which the nation is flooded, contribute powerfully to the maintenance of faith in these delights, little cunning being necessary to deceive a superstitious people, who, instructed in advance in their favor, believe without examination, whatever these impostors propose to them. The method of becoming adept in this faculty is as impertinent and laughable as their traditions. Those who are destined for this profession, when they arrive at about 20 years of age, are assigned a day for the ceremony. When this arrives a considerable part of the priests and a greater number of medicine men meet, all in their official costumes, and give the candidate an infusion of herbs to drink, obliging him at intervals, to smoke much tobacco; the tobacco and drink soon make him lose his mind, and drunk, he falls to the ground, making many faces, and contortions, remaining in a faint, or pretending to, for a period of 24 hours, those surrounding, supposing him dead. After this time he comes to, with a sigh; with a languid voice, he tells everybody all he dreamed or what his fancy dictates, adding that his soul during that time visited in very remote countries. His song and music begin immediately, and last for eight days, being helped by one of the old teachers, the confused howling of women present, mixing in from time to time. These take care to supply plenty of food for presentation to the spectators, while the new doctor, with his dance and songs gives them enjoyment. These charlatans are very well looked out for and venerated by the others who out of respect for the profession, always offer them the first fruits of their hunts, and crops; they build them their houses, and sow their fields for them with a diligence which is the greatest happiness to which one can aspire among those miserable beings.

Each has a costume becoming to his ministry, decorated with big bunches of feathers (*grandes plumeros*), adding necklaces made with skins of coral-colored snakes, which are very showy and of bright colors. When they go to any house to exercise their impositions, there is prepared for them a very distinguished seat, even more ornate than that of the Captains themselves. If there is any cure to be made, they have a big bonfire lighted from which they take live coals to put under the bed of the patient, frequently renewing the fire. They are supplied with a feather fan, a whistle (*pito*), and the base (*bajo*) which is a small stick carved in the form of the rattle of a snake, which they tap over a stretched hollow skin, producing an infernal music, capable of giving any one a headache. Before beginning the music, they drink an infusion of certain herbs, and, stimulated by this potion, begin to play and sing in a furious manner. The singing comes in from time to time to torment the patient, who, suffering with fever from within and from the hot coals which they apply externally under and around the body, feels as if the impious medicine man (*medico*) were sucking his entrails. Applying skillfully their lips to the bare skin over the stomach, they suck violently and quickly, bringing pressure to bear with their heads in such a manner that it seems they reach the very spine. For these cases the charlatan comes well provided with blood, worms, and other small insects, which, putting in his mouth with skill, he spits out with opportunity, persuading the lookers on that he took them from the body of the patient; an error in which many Spaniards also frequently participate, and those not of low order. These treatments customarily last from mid-afternoon (*media tarde*) until daybreak of the following day. On some occasions they cut that part of the patient, near the liver, with a flint, and really suck the blood. They do the same with snake bites, cutting the body at the same place as the bite, which generally produces good results. They prognosticate the period of suffering, in which they usually deceive. When the patient is a Captain, or one of the principal ones, they hold meetings of professors, and in these cases, each one exerts himself to produce and effect some new nonsense. They drink many bitter infusions, persuading the patient that their secret advices are then more useful. When the illness is caused by any tumor, or swelling, they apply to the ripened part, a knife or flint, and empty it with the lips. One must concede that, in spite of so much error and extravagance, they do sometimes succeed in very singular cures because the land has an abundance of medical herbs, and, knowing many of them, they probably apply them with skill, especially in the healing of wounds, in which they have the greatest practice. They clearly believe that all internal maladies are caused by some witchcraft, which they attribute to the nearby Bidai, Ays, and Yacdocas, who also have an abundance of medicine men. These, say our Asinais, are wizards or charmers and secretly bring or send the illness, which they call *Aguaian*, which means "something sharp and penetrating," in the shape of an arrow, which, discharged from the bow of the *Texino*, or Devil, comes directly to the sick one. To extract from the body of the patient this point, which they say is like a thick small needle, white in color, they execute various dances, songs and ceremonies. They prepare themselves for these by invoking the Bidais medicine men, who they say come to their help, personally, disguised as owls (*Buhos ó Tecolotes*). As there are many of these birds in the country (as many as three species), the least sound of their mournful song suffices to make the Indians let out a shout of joy, as if they had secured a victory. They also add that the god *Ynici*, moved by their singing, and prayers, offers them his aid as well. Before finishing the cure they recite in a low voice some orations which they address to one of the beams supporting the roof of the house of the patient. They throw on the fire a portion of tobacco. From the buffalo meat given them, they cut a piece which is also offered to the fire, and some small pieces to the four winds, whom they salute in all their functions, with tobacco smoke, which they offer to each one, precedence always being given the Capitan Grande (their God). With these ceremonies they are sure of success, whether the patient lives or dies.

They do not fare so happily among the Nacogdoches, who, in spite of their affinity with the Asinais, and the fact that they share almost the same customs, make these impostors pay with their lives sometimes, for their deceits. When the patient dies after all their ridiculous doings, public opinion attributes the misfortune to the malice of the doctor, and then the relatives of the deceased do not let the charlatan get by without vengeance, for the effects of his ignorance or malice. Anyway, they are always the greatest obstacle to the conversion of the Indians to our holy religion, owing to the threats with which they intimidate them. They persuade them, as in many other parts of both the Americas, that the holy baptism infallibly takes their life; when either, because these impostors do not prevent it, or because the fear they inspire is destroyed by reason, some Texas Indian is baptized, they abandon him in his illness, refusing to give him any medicine, saying that the water which was placed on his head made his illness incurable, nor is the repeated experience that many of these already disillusioned (who resorted to the Spaniards for remedy), were cured and reestablished to good health (in spite of the fatal prognostications of their medicine men), sufficient to disillusion these unfortunates.

The functions of these impostors are not limited to the practice of medicine; it is also within their superintendence to take measures for the construction of houses, to bless them after they are finished, to name the newly born, provide the crops, to be the first in all festivals, so that to the character of a medicine man they unite that of a Priest.

Before they begin eating new corn, they call from each house one of these priests; who leaning against a post of the house mumbles his prayers, the other Indians gather some of the new fruits, part of which is shelled and the other ground, to parch, or to make *atole*. When the prayer is finished they offer some of the delicacy to the minister, who throwing some of his part into the fire eats the rest; the friends of the family customarily attend, as do the assistants of the priest, to eat, and celebrate these ceremonies. When this is over, the owners can eat and gather the crops without risk, which they would never do under any circumstances before this precaution is taken as they are persuaded that if any one of them should have the audacity to cut a single cob or ear of corn unless it were preceded by the prayers of the minister, he would be infallibly bitten by a snake. This excommunication extends even to animals, so that in order to save their dogs from this misfortune, they tie their fore-feet to their snouts, which prevents their eating fresh corn, of which they are exceedingly fond.

One single coincidence, not rare in a country where snakes abound and everybody goes barefooted, suffices to confirm them in the belief of this chimerical superstition. Whenever an accident of this sort occurs, the priests do not fail to attribute it to an infraction of this rule, even though the patient might not have thought about it. [Morfi, 1932, pp. 26–30.]

When there are many ticks on the mountainside, they take it as an omen that there will be an abundant crop of beans. If rains are frequent in March and April, they are sure of a notable scarcity in June, July and August. If at the time when the Indians are on a buffalo hunt, or on a campaign against their enemies, many little birds, which they call *banit*, pass over the province in transit, they believe that the absent are already near their houses. When they have decided to go out on a campaign, they call a general meeting at the house of the *Capitan Maior*, appoint one who is most accredited with valor, and give him his infusions to drink, until he loses or pretends to lose his senses. He remains in this real or apparent state of unconsciousness for one day, and one night, and then his memory returns, and he says that he saw where the enemies were, and whether they were prepared or not. And from this fantastical narration they foretell their victory or conquest. If they are on the road, they also make their divinations, using a fox tail; but ordinarily they are deceived. At the middle of the present century, they foretold a complete victory over their enemies the Yojuanes Indians, and their prophesies turned out so false that the *Netcha* Indians were defeated and destroyed, with death to many and a greater number held captive. They hold as infallible that if in summer they blow the fire with a blower or feather fan so much snow will fall that the whole nation will come to an end; and often, seeing the missionaries use those instruments to make a fire, wanted to take them from their hands, reprimanding them in fear of what they apparently exposed them to; to the Father's correct reply that they had experienced no danger as a result of that way of fanning the fire, they replied, that this was due, without doubt, to the fact that the fire of the religious was of another kind, produced with steel and flint. One time Father Espinosa, asking them why all the tribes of the Ainais and Nechas did not go out together on buffalo hunts, as did the Nasonis and Nacogdoches, a priest replied, that it was a prudent caution, so that the sacred fire would not go out on account of the absence of those who cared for it; that the Nacogdoches and the Nasonis had a different fire, which they lighted by rubbing two little sticks and leaving these in the temple, were sure of finding their fire when returning to their houses, and this was why they did not perish, but that the Ainais and *Netchas* kept their fire burning without interruption, from the time they received it from their forefathers, a tradition which they hold with the greatest tenacity. [Morfi, 1932, pp. 35–36.]

Our missionaries furnish us with some notes regarding actual diseases among the Caddo as well as the medical science of the time was able to diagnose them. In March 1691, there was a terrible epidemic among the east Texas Indians which destroyed from 300 to 400 in the immediate neighborhood of Casañas' mission and "about three thousand persons among all the friendly tribes of the *Tejias*" (Casañas, 1927, pp. 294, 303). Smallpox seems to be indicated but the identity of the disease is not disclosed. Solís is more specific:

The ills and diseases from which all the Indians frequently suffer, men as well as women, are smallpox, measles, typhoid fever, fevers, blisters, *onanahui-ates*, which makes them horrible to the sight and filthy, like many that I saw. In short these diseases, which are vices of the blood and are propagated in the blood and frequently suffered, are, I think, caused and induced by drinking whiskey and sugar cane wine with the bear grease that is drunk as if it were water because it is drinkable and does not curdle. They eat many nuts which they grind in order to keep them, and the fruit of the medlar tree that is fiery, and other foods and warm drinks. All these cause them to suffer many blood dysenteries. [Solís, 1931, p. 70.]

Morfi evidently copies Solís:

The maladies which are most frequently suffered by all of the nations of Texas, and which annually consume thousands of all ages and sexes, are small-pox, measles, fever and pustules or buboes, (*managuases*), which make the afflicted horribly filthy, and in a word, those maladies which originate from some defect in the blood as a whole, and which mostly result from the excessive use of strong liquors, and all suffer from the use of bear grease for which they have such a passionate desire that they drink it as though it were water, the latter always being kept in a liquid state. To this can be attributed princi-pally the cause of dysentery of blood, from which they die. [Morfi, 1932, p. 55.]

Native belief in the efficiency of their doctors and the malignant powers of their wizards was so great that much of it has persisted to the present day (see Parsons, 1941, pp. 32–36).

RELIGIOUS CEREMONIES

Some of these have been mentioned under other heads. Casañas makes the following general remarks:

At different times of the year, these infidels arrange certain feasts honoring the *caddices* and the grand *xinesi*, in celebration of the victories their ancestors have had. Some of the tribes invite other tribes to these feasts, the captains paying homage to the great captain, or *xinesi*, by presenting him with bows and arrows and with other things which they value highly. For three days and nights the feast goes on with dancing, eating, and fun; all those who have come feast but the *xinesi*. He goes without eating for three days and without sleeping for three nights. They do not let him sleep or eat. He does not even drink or rest, but he is continually stirring about from place to place as if making the sound of dancing. At these meetings and feasts certain superstitions are usually noted. The crowd that gathers is very large for men, women, and children come to the feast because they are given plenty to eat.

I trust in the Lord that when the evangelical ministers learn the language they will reap great fruit from these meetings where various tribes assemble together; for they gather in one place and only for these meetings at which the feast is celebrated, no matter whether it be in this nation of the *Asinai* or in a contiguous province. . . [The *caddis* or *xinesi*] like to have somebody at their side whose importance they recognize, so that all the other Indians may see and know the estimation in which they, themselves, are held. [Casañas, 1927, pp. 301–302.]

Joutel is the earliest writer to leave a record of the first-fruits ceremony; observed by him when he was staying in the town of the Assonis (Nasoni) :

When the corn was beginning to mature, I observed a ceremony which took place at the aforementioned cabin on account of one of the old men who arrived there. After his arrival, the women went to gather a great number of ears of corn. They boiled them and then put them into a hamper which they placed upon the ceremonial stool, which is used only for that purpose and on which no one sits; for one day I wanted to sit down upon it, and the good old woman told me that I must get up or I would die. To return to the ceremony, when all was so disposed, the said old man approached the above-mentioned stool, accompanied by the chief of the cabin, and there they remained for perhaps an hour or an hour and a half, muttering over the said ears of corn, after which they distributed them among the women who gave them to the young people, and to us also. But the aforesaid old man or the chief of the said cabin ate none of it. I asked the chief the reason for that. He indicated that he would eat of it after the sun had passed the earth eight times. As I had no knowledge of their language, I was not able to get any other explanation. I noticed that, after the said ceremony, the women went every day to gather corn to eat. This food did not fail us but since the corn was not yet in condition to be made into flour they then boiled the ears in order to eat them, and the savages did not begrudge us. I noticed also at this time the precautions they took regarding their dogs, for fear lest they eat the new corn; they bound their jaws and tied one paw in front under the throat, so that they might not be able to get at the stalk of the corn. [Margry, 1875–1886, vol. 3, pp. 400–401.]

The first-fruits ceremony is thus described by Espinosa :

To begin eating their new corn, they summon one of the shamans from each of the houses. While he stands by one of the posts and mutters his prayers between his teeth, a portion of the new crop is cut. Part of it is toasted and part of it is ground in the mortars to make *atole*. When the prayers are ended they present some of the food to the old man who throws part of this pittance into the fire and puts the rest in his bosom. He usually has to stop to do this as it is a considerable portion. Neither acquaintances nor friends are lacking at these functions, both of the old man and of the family. When they are all gathered together and the first fruits are eaten, the Indians are given permission to take and eat whatever they like. These shamans have fixed very firmly in the minds of these Indians the belief that if any part of the crop, large or small, either ears or stalks, is cut before these prayers are made, the guilty one will certainly be bitten by a snake. Even the dogs share in this threat or interdict; so, in order that a dog may not eat of the corn, the

Indians tie one of his legs or paws to his neck so that he goes around hungry on three legs and can not eat the corn, for dogs are extremely fond of it. And when by chance a snake bites anyone who has eaten of the corn before the ceremony described, they are confirmed in the belief in this superstition. [Espinosa, 1927, pp. 169–170.]

After considering the ceremonies connected with hunting and planting, which have been given elsewhere, Espinosa proceeds to describe the harvest feast:

After the crop has been gathered they hold their most notable feast, the one which the greatest number of people attend. Then only one or two stay in each house to take care of the aged and infirm. Notice is given through the messengers some days beforehand so that each may send his offering for the feast. Six days prior to this time, the men meet at the house of the captain (where there is a small temple and where a spot has previously been cleaned). The old men pray and distribute the warm drinks of foamy laurel tea. The old man who acts as *chenesi* orders the young men to go out in all directions to hunt deer, charging them to return soon and declaring that, in the meantime, with the old men, he will continue to make supplications to the *caddi-ayo*. If two or three are hunting, they all return to this house. This they repeat on the second day and all the meat, with the exception of the head and the intestines [of the animals], is prepared and cooked for the function. When the day arrives they take the best woolen clothing they have—which they carefully preserve for this purpose—also very fine deer skins, with ruffles decorated with little white ornaments, some very black deer skins, decorated with the same ornaments, bracelets, and necklaces which they wear only on this and other feast days. They all gather at the house designated where, on the previous day, they have prepared the things needed for the feast.

It is at night during the new moon in September. The first night the crowd of old conjurers, medicine men, captains, and the necessary officials and servants spend within doors. The rest who come lodge outside by families where they build a fire for light as well as because the cold is already beginning to be felt. After two of the old men say their prayers between their teeth, they stand for more than an hour, take tobacco—as well as bits of meat—and throw it on the fire which is in the middle of the house. Then they sit down on their benches and all the old men and captains are given the rest of the meat. They mix with it their drink of brewed wild olives which is served them three or four times in an earthenware vase. They take pipes of tobacco which they pass around to everybody. They draw from time to time and blow the smoke, first upward, then toward the ground, and then to the four winds, while all the people gather together as midnight approaches. At midnight a crier begins to call all the families in their order. They come in by threes, one woman from each house, and each presents a pot or small vessel of very fine meal and some rolls which they call *bajan* made of a thick paste of roasted corn and the seed of sunflowers. The majordomos then deposit these in two big receptacles of their own. In this way the criers continue to call and all the houses and families make their gifts. This finished, the offering is divided among the old men, the captains, and officials of the settlement. The celebration halts for some time while some of the young medicine men sleep. Others sing together accompanied by their instruments for the purpose of driving away sleep because there is great effort made not to sleep that night.

From midnight on one of the Indians is stationed as a watchman or sentinel. He watches to see when the Pleiades are perpendicular—from the house. They call these stars *las sanates*, i. e., "the women," because the devil has made them believe that these stars are people.   He then informs the chief conjurer who goes in company with another conjurer to a circle made of green canes stuck in the ground where there is a big bonfire which three or four novices feed continually.   The two men seated on an elevation serve as masters of ceremony. The Indians are formed, to their left, as follows, the old women in the first row or file, behind them the married women and the young girls, and, at the end the younger girls.   The little girls are in front of this file.   To the right there is an arbor with a bonfire under it.   Three old men, dressed in the best they have, consisting of curious buffalo robes, go to this fire, each following in the footsteps of the one in front, while the women and children in the ranks begin singing.   After a considerable pause, the old men again approach the circle, dancing as they come.   When they rejoin it, the singing stops and they deliver a harangue of pure jargon in a hasty, high-pitched voice without saying a single intelligible word.   As they arrive in front of each woman, she presents them, without rising, with a little pot of meal and rolls made of various grains. Each presents her own gift.   The songs of those in the circle continue and the old men go away in silence.   In the meantime, the novices, each in his turn, carries the offering to the front.   This continues for an hour, more or less. The song of the old men and women is continued longer although some time elapses before dawn.   Then all of them become more active to the music of the gourd or calabash filled with little stones.   This makes the noise which they accompany with their voices.   As day breaks, they stop singing and five old men divide the offering which has been collected.   After the song, they all await the rising of the sun.   Certain young men and boys are sent out into the nearby woods as if calling or speaking to the sun for the purpose of hastening its coming.   Just as it begins to rise they run about joyously and gaily and it seems as if they were giving thanks for their past crop or were beseeching the sun to aid them in the projects they are beginning.   All of one size or age are in one line; and, after giving the signal for starting, they all run as fast as they can to a tree which is about a gun shot's distance and then return to the starting point.   They make this turn two or three times until they give out.   Then the girls and boys in their turn, do the same thing.

All the relatives are intent upon seeing who gains the advantage and this person is the one that carries off the laurels of the occasion.   The wives and female relatives of the man who is left behind or becomes tired out without finishing the race, set up a terrible weeping, because they say that when this person goes out to war, he will be left behind either as a captive or dead, because of his lack of speed.   This ceremony lasts about an hour.   They then take hollow logs, covered on top with green branches, bury the ends of them, and select eight strong Indian women, who, seated at intervals with sticks in each hand, use each the hollow log as a drum, to the accompaniment of the calabash which the old men play, and the songs of the men and women singers to the number of more than twenty.   This music is for the dance in which they all engage, old women and girls, old men and boys, and little children.   They dance in a circle, the men facing the women, keep time, moving only their feet.   In this cherished frivolity they spend the time until midday, when tired and sleepy, each goes home to rest from his strenuous exercise. [Espinosa, 1927, pp. 171–174.]

Morfi:

The most celebrated festival of the Province is that which they celebrate after the crops, as an occasion of rendering thanks, at which all the families take part, the old and sick only remaining to care for the houses, who owing to their weakness cannot move about. The whole nation is advised some days before, through the *Tamas*, so that no one will fail to present his offering. The six days immediately preceding the fete all the men meet in the house of the Captain where they celebrated the ceremony of the hoes, and where the ground was left clear. The elders enter the house with only those servants whose duty it is to minister to them the drink which they call *cazina*, which they take warm and covered with foam, like our chocolate. The elder who performs the function of Chenisí, or High Priest, commands that all the armed people go out in squads to the four winds and hunt the deer, assured that they shall find many in a short time, for he with the other old men remains behind imploring Caddi Ayo. When they get anything they punctually bring it to the house, and throw away the entrails and head, preparing the rest for the coming feast. When this day arrives they dress up in the best clothes they have, such as *bayeta* (baize), soft deerskins, with fringes of many little white nuts, black deerskins, spotted at intervals with the same white nuts, bracelets, and necklaces of glass beads, ornaments all of which they use only on this day, or on others of unusual solemnity. With these adornments both men and women arrive at the house of the Captain, where from the evening before they are all well prepared for the ceremony. The principal fete is held during the full moon of September. After sundown on that evening, the priests, medicine men and Captains of the tribe, with the servants necessary to them for the ceremony, shut themselves up in the house of the Captain. The rest of the company accomodate themselves in family groups (*se ranchea por familias*) as they arrive, in the immediate vicinity of the house. Each one makes his bonfire as much for light as for protection from the cold, which already at this time begins to make itself felt. Among those shut in the house two elders stand up and for more than an hour say prayers in a low voice, throwing into the fire some handfuls of tobacco, and little particles of roasted meat. When this prayer is finished, out of respect for the same fire, which burns in the center of the room, they eat the rest, mixing with the goods, the drink which is a concoction of *asebuehe* leaves then given to them in a clay cup, three or four times. After supper they sit around on benches, smoking a pipe which they pass to one another, and which they fill with frequency. The first puff is blown toward heaven, the second, to the earth, and the next four to the four principal winds. At about midnight one of the *Tammas* or criers goes to the door of the hut and calls all of the families in turn. At his command they enter the meeting hall, three and three, one woman from each house, and each one of them offers to the congress a little pot or little basket of ground corn, and some balls, which they call *bajan* and which are made of parched corn, and sunflower seeds like hard taffy. The *maiordomos* collect these offerings and keep them separated in two big baskets, and with the same ceremony all of the families of the nation enter and offer. This offering over, it is immediately distributed among the priests, medicine men and captains. The festivities cease for a while, while some sleep, and others, to drive away sleep, sing and play on their instruments, doing all they can to observe that great night. After midnight one of the *Tamas* acts as a sentinel to see when the Pleiades (*Cabrillas*), which they call *Sanates*, which means "women," (because they believe they [the seven stars] are living creatures) are directly over the house of the meeting. He then advises the principal priest who, accompanied by the oldest of the congress, comes out of the house. They make their way to a large circle marked out in the cleared ground by green reeds stuck thereon. In the center there is a big bonfire which is constantly fed by three or four warriors appointed for the purpose. The two priests whose duty it is to perform the functions of Masters of Chapel, sit down; there follow in order, to the left, the old women in the first row; in the second, in back of the latter, the married young women, and unmarried ones. The maids are in the third row; and in front of this circle are the little girls. To the east of this theater is constructed a shed of branches with a bonfire in it, from whence come three elders, one behind another, highly decorated with their best clothes of buffalo hides curiously painted. At this time the two priests of the great circle begin to sing, accompanied by all the women. To the accompaniment of this music the three elders of the shed dance, and with much poise and majesty they approach the singers. When they enter the circle, there is a pause in the singing; and the one of the three who is in front delivers an oration in a loud voice with hastened disconnected words. Each of the women in the circle without changing her position, places on the ground a small pot of corn meal, and cakes made of various grains. The singing continues, and the three elders retire in the same order in which they came. Some assistants (*mozetonas*) collect the offering with much haste, like some one stealing, and take it to the shed. After an hour this same act is repeated. Only the singing of the two priests and women is continued any longer; though to rest they cease at intervals. At the approach of dawn, others join in the noise with gourds (*guajes* or *calabazas*) filled with pebbles which they shake in accompaniment to the voices. As dawn approaches the music ceases and the offerings are distributed among the priests of the circle, and the elders of the shed. They immediately send some young men and boys to the nearest woods in order that with repeated howling, they may call the sun, entreating it to hurry its rising. As soon as the sun appears they all begin to run with great shouting, and very festively as if to thank it for the past crop, and inviting it to celebrate with its presence their races which begin very shortly.

All of the same age and height place themselves in a row, and when the signal is given to start they run as fast as they can toward a tree about a gun-shot away; they go around it and with equal speed they return to the starting point and continue this exercise two or three times, until they are overcome. The boys follow, and even the girls do the same afterwards. While they are running the parents and relatives look on with great attention to see who is winning, and the winner receives the glory of being the strongest. For those who are left behind or who get tired before the conclusion of the races, their wives, relatives and friends raise a very sorrowful cry, foretelling speedy death or captivity. These races last for more than an hour; and then, having a hollow pole driven into the ground covered with branches, they select eight robust young women, who [seated] with other sticks in their [both] hands, make a drum of the large timber, accompanied by the *guajes* and *calabazas* shaken by the elders, to beat the rhythm of the singing [by over twenty male and female voices], and the dance begins. In this everyone present participates without exclusion of age or sex. They form two circles, one of men and the other of women, one facing the other. Jumping in unison they keep up this frivolous exercise until midday, when the great function terminates. They then return to their houses, very tired, and with no little desire to sleep. [Morfi, 1932, p. 31–34.]

Hidalgo makes brief mention of the harvest ceremony:

After their crops are matured all the Indians gather in the house and *patio* of their captain to hold their feasts. Those who are to dance come out of a house near the captain's. It is a little straw hut they build for the occasion. Twelve old men come out of it to dance, all having tufts or plumes. They advance singing in a strange tongue which the people do not understand. These twelve old men stay in the little straw hut as long as the feast lasts. There they go through their ceremonies, say their prayers, and drink a tea [*cacina*] like that commonly used in Florida. This I saw. Every evening these same twelve old men come to the *patio* of the captain's house, singing these same songs in a strange tongue. One follows exactly behind another and they immediately form a circle. There they hold three dances during these days and there are no more during the rest of the year. [Hidalgo, 1927, p. 52.]

What might be called a forecasting ceremony was held in winter:

In the month or moon of February, which they call *sacabbi*, there is a mass meeting of all the people. Having previously hunted rabbits, wild cats, wild birds, and badgers, having provided dry meat—which they have all the year round—and secured ground meal and other edibles which the country produces, of which the Indian women bring each a portion, they begin the celebration in the morning in the house where all the doctors and wise old men assemble. Two or three of them spend the morning in brewing tea from the laurel leaves while the old men drink the potion. Then, with their faces turned toward the wall, they pray to the captain on high. They take the wing of an eagle, which they call *ygui*, they use it in their dances and songs, and they carefully preserve it. In the meantime they salute the fire by throwing ground tobacco on it and continuously pass the pipe of tobacco from hand to hand. They then go through motions to show that the eagle whose feathers they are using has risen on high to consult with the captain who is there in regard to the weather for the year. When the old men have made their almanacs in private while muttering between their teeth, they come out and make it known or manifest to the public, saying, for instance, that this year—as they told me of 1718—will be abundant in nuts and acorns but not in corn for the water will fail at the best season. The years when there are many ticks (and they have them every year) they say they will have an abundance of beans. If it rains a great deal in March and April they say there will be but little water in June, July, and August. And their prognostications are so foolish that they usually lose their crops from an excess of rain. [Espinosa, 1927, p. 168.]

Morfi:

They also practice astrology and forecast the events of the year in another solemn festival. The men provide rabbits, mountain cats, deer, turkeys, badgers, and dried buffalo meat; and the women provide corn meal, fruit, roots, and other products of the earth. A general meeting of the tribe is held during the new moon of February, which they call *Sacabbi*. All the captains, with the oldest and most venerable medicine men, enter the principal house. These begin the ceremony at break of day by drinking *casina* or a concoction of laurel, in which they spend the whole morning, offering drinks of it from time to time to the captains. Turning then to some beam of the hut they say their prayers, addressed, according to what they say, to the Caddi-Ayo. They take an elaborately decorated eagle wing which they have prepared, and which they call Ygui, and with it in their hands they begin to dance and sing. Without interrupting this amusement they salute the fire, offering it some ground tobacco; and the pipe is passed around from mouth to mouth. They afterwards demonstrate that the eagle whose feathers they have in hand, ascends to heaven to consult with the *Capitan Grande*, for the coming events of the year. In the meanwhile the elders alone with much reserve, form their almanac, and the ceremony finished, leave the house to communicate it to the people, announcing for example, that the year will be abundant in nuts and acorns; but with a scarcity of corn, etc. Those Indians receive these decisions as infallible and usually pay for it with a lack of grain. [Morfi, 1932, p. 35.]

Festivals to train youths in preparation for war were held in spring. Joutel describes this training as he observed it in April 1687, as follows:

I had the pleasure of seeing their exercises since the cabin in which I lived was very near that where they were so that I saw all that they were doing. Two of the most active chiefs ranged all of the young people in a row and, after they were all so ordered, they set out instantly at a given signal and endeavored to see who could gain the advantage. They then planted two posts some distance apart and a number of them started running to see who would excel in fleetness by the greater or less number of turns, after which they made them exercise with the bow and arrow. They passed their days in that manner. [Margry, 1875–1886, vol. 3, pp. 354–355.]

Espinosa places this somewhat later but evidently is describing the same ceremony:

At the beginning of May these Indians have a feast very much like those observed in certain villages in Europe, for, from a reference to the *Thesoro de la Lengua Castellana*, it is seen that the Zagáles youths are accustomed on the first day of May to place in the plaza or in some other spot an elm, stripped except for a bunch of leaves at the top. Here they hold a celebration with various games and contests, saying that they are celebrating the May Day. In this same way, the Texas Indians celebrate the May festival by securing a very tall, straight, slender pine. After cutting off the branches—leaving only the top—they put it up in a level space. They make two very wide paths, cleaning off the surface so that they can run faster. These paths come together behind the tree and thus form a circle. Innumerable Indians gather together at the rising of the sun and begin to run along these paths, one after the other. They choose the strongest and the lightest. The one who runs around the May tree the greatest number of times without pausing is the victor and he is the one who receives the most applause. After they are tired out they generally have refreshments which the Indian women have provided. This is the day most celebrated among them, because it is a test for teaching them how to run when they fight their enemies. [Espinosa, 1927, pp. 174–175.]

Morfi:

At the beginning of May they hold other public races which they call corn races. For these they provide a very tall, slender, straight pine tree which they trim, leaving only the top branches. They fix it in the ground, in the middle of a well cleared space. They form two wide and ample paths which they clean with care, in order to run more freely and with more surety. These form a circle around the pine. At sunrise they begin to run, one behind the other, along the two paths, selecting for this exercise, the most robust and quickest men. They declare as victor the one who can make the greatest number of courses around the pine without rest. After they are very tired, they eat what the women bring for them, and retire. They look upon this as one of the most solemn days, and these races are the most celebrated, because they are held as training for war. [Morfi, 1932, pp. 34–35.]

In 1912 the Caddo remembered that they had had a scalp dance, a war dance, a duck dance, and a skunk dance. The scalp dance was later called the turkey dance because it was thought that the turkeys began it and that they still wear the scalps and dance this dance around trees. It was a women's dance. The war dance, on the other hand, was for men only. The duck dance was said to be a peculiar and a pretty dance. The Caddo were then said to have about four dancing places but one of these was cared for by a Seminole Indian.[20]

Material from the living Caddo Indians regarding exorcisms, prayers, offerings, feasting, tobacco rites, ceremonial orientation, and various other ceremonies as well as dances is given by Parsons (1941, pp. 43–57). Two objects of religious significance are shown in plates 18 and 19.

CONCLUSIONS

The most marked distinction between the Caddo and their neighbors to the east seems to have been in their language, and by this one feature they are connected more closely with some of the tribes of the Great Plains where all the other members of the linguistic family to which they have given their name belonged. Their exact position with reference to the Muskhogean, Siouan, and other groups will not be known, however, until much more work has been done upon the dialects of the several families. But, however widely they may be found to differ from other tribes in the Southeastern cultural province in this particular, their speech as yet lends no color to the theory that their origin must be sought in the direction of Old or New Mexico or any point to the west. Insofar as their origin myths cast light upon their past history, they indicate the east rather than the west. Their only connecting link with the west or southwest seems to have been the Jumano or Shuman Indians, and these, the latest investigations appear to indicate, were not originally Caddoans.

Physically, the Caddo are described as somewhat smaller and darker than the tribes to the north and perhaps this would apply also to the tribes east of them but the difference was not sufficiently great to be used as a basis for the theory of a recent origin outside of the country in which they lived at the dawn of written history. They probably belonged to the brachycephalic peoples like the Wichita and Pawnee, but so did most of the Choctaw and the other Indian groups on the lower Mississippi.

Like the rest of the Southeastern Indians, they cultivated corn, beans, squashes, sunflowers, and tobacco. Like them corn was their main means of subsistence, and its cultivation was central to their economic, social, and ceremonial life. Like them, they broke up their land and undertook the initial cultivation of their

---

[20] Personal notes.

fields in a body, town by town. We are not certain that they had town granaries distinct from those owned by each family but know nothing to disprove it. Like the Natchez, they cultivated first the fields of the chiefs and nobility, and like the Creeks, the field of the high priest among the very first.

Like the other Southeastern tribes, they made persimmon bread, and extracted oil from acorns and nuts, and they appear to have "farmed the wilderness" in a similar manner. In both sections it was usual to burn the fields over in the spring. Corn was reduced to flour similarly by the use of wooden mortars and a series of sifters made of cane. As a detail we may note that they provided their beans with poles instead of allowing them to grow up on the cornstalks, but our data are so meager that both systems may well have been employed throughout.

The buffalo here played a greater part in the domestic economy than among the tribes farther east but this was evidently due to nothing more fundamental than the near presence of vastly greater numbers of the animals. Along with the hunting of buffalo came the communal hunt and for the same reason, but even the western Caddo tribes continued to use deer and, like the tribes to the eastward, they stalked these animals by means of stuffed deer heads. Dogs played about the same part in the domestic economy as among the more eastern tribes, but there is no reference to a travois though the Indians to the west and north had them. Like the eastern tribes, they depended much upon bear fat to season their other food. Their eastern cultural connections are emphasized once more in the extensive part which fish played in their economy, and this was true, not only of the tribes near Red River but of the western Caddo also. We do not have the slightest intimation of any repugnance toward fish as food such as one meets on the western plains.

Besides the communal hunt, attributed in part to dread of meeting enemies on the buffalo plains, the only change traceable to the hunting of buffalo that is apparent is the use of lances in the chase and in war.

Their garments resembled those of the Indians to the east except that there appears to have been greater use of buffalo skins and less use of textiles. We notice also more mention of fringing on the edges of their skin clothing, and adjustment of the woman's upper garment by means of a hole poncho-fashion, instead of the eastern style of tying the two edges together over one shoulder. We get the impression that tribal differences were often apparent in ornamentation and in methods of treating the hair, but these were of such a minor character that it is impossible, from the data supplied us, to set off the Caddo in this way from other peoples. Pénicaut, indeed, states that the Natchitoches tattooed less than the Acolapissa of the lower Mississippi, but our other authorities speak of tattooing as being so general and elaborate, at least among the western Caddo, that his remarks must be largely discounted. The Caddo were noted for their nasal ornaments but these were in vogue also among the Chickasaw and Creeks. By the end of the seventeenth century the Caddo were not seemingly resorting to head deformation, but Garcilaso de la Vega affirms that the custom in the early part of the sixteenth century was flourishing among the supposedly Caddo Tula, and skulls showing frontal deformation have been dug up in the old Caddo country.

Caddo houses were identical with those of the Wichita and were somewhat divergent from the commonest types on the lower Mississippi, but in general plan they were merely a variant of the winter house of the Southeast minus the wattle work and mat covering. Except that Natchez houses were more often square than round, the method of construction given by Du Pratz coincides very closely with that described by the missionaries among the Hasinai. We miss the distinct summer and winter houses, but it is doubtful whether summer houses were in use along the lower Mississippi or anything corresponding to them except a rude arbor under which cooking went on in the hot season. House building was a communal enterprise both among the Caddo and the tribes east of them. In both sections the occupants of these houses slept on a bed or shelf around the inside next to the wall, and the fire was in the center. In both sections there were wooden seats like the West Indian duhos, wooden chests, and cane mats, hampers, and baskets of all kinds, besides the sieves, as already mentioned, used in making flour. The usual simple type of fire drill was employed, and cane torches to illuminate the ceremonial grounds at night. Hoes, rattles, flageolets, and drums appear to have been made in much the same way but our descriptions of them are not very full. We are told that flageolets were used in dances and if so that is at variance with general Southeastern usage. Caddo pottery has already been mentioned. Superior as it is, it conforms to Southeastern patterns. Dugout canoes were used by the eastern Caddo and cane rafts by all of them.

During their monthly periods and at the birth of a child, the women resorted to separate houses, a universal Southeastern custom. Adultery was not punished severely as a rule except apparently in the case of a noble. Otherwise the greatest looseness prevailed and in this particular we are reminded of the Natchez rather than the Chickasaw, Choctaw, or Creeks. Division of labor between the sexes was practically the same as in the Southeast generally. The social organization reminds us of the Natchez in that a marked class distinction existed, though it did not reach the same proportions, and also in the theocratic tendency of the state in which the Caddo seen to have gone somewhat beyond. The Kadohadacho, at least, remind us of the Chickasaw and Creeks in the presence of animal-named divisions. Although we seem to detect tendencies toward matri-lineal descent, the system certainly was not of that rigorous character which it reached in the tribes first mentioned. This difference is reflected in the terms of relationship which belonged apparently to the Mackenzie Basin Type instead of the Crow Type so generally exhibited in the Southeast. Chieftainships were transmitted patrilineally.

According to the Spanish missionaries the most powerful indi-vidual among the Hasinai was a kind of high priest who would seem to have corresponded to the Natchez guardian of the sacred fire, but we are unable to determine whether he was a high priest who had become king or a king who had become high priest. Under him were a number of town or regional chiefs and under these still other grades of officials. In brief, the government recalls that of the Natchez and Timucua most closely but somewhat more remotely that of the Creeks. Otherwise, like most other primitive groups, the Caddo tribes were so many mutual-aid societies, the individuals assisting one another in all the major activities and misfortunes of life.

The great ball game of the Southeast was not certainly known to the Caddo, and their greatest game was said to have been a kind of hockey, which may have taken its place. A form of the hoop-and-pole game was known to them but we do not hear of the employment of chunk stones in this. On the other hand they played the common dice game with short sections of cane, and they had a form of the moccasin game. Foot races and contests in shooting arrows are mentioned among the Caddo more than the tribes to the east of them.

A smoking ceremony was held on the arrival of strangers by all the Caddo when Joutel passed through their country, but the specific calumet dance had reached only the Cahinnio, the border tribe to the northeast. The washing of strangers as part of the ceremony of welcome was a somewhat peculiar Caddo trait, but we get something of the kind a hundred years earlier among the Indians of North Car-olina. They were peculiar also in the ceremony of greeting by wail-ing, though one type of this was noted by the French in Florida a hundred years before, and it existed among some of the tribes farther west. Like the more eastern tribes they punished by means of flag-ellations or, in cases of murder, with death. Their war customs present few points of difference from those in vogue on the Missis-sippi, but the burning of the house in which their assembly had been held after they were prepared to march and the absence of the rite of "striking the post" and accompanying self-glorification of each warrior in turn seem to set them off.

Even in aboriginal times the Caddo apparently resorted to trade more than many of the neighboring people. They were active in sending salt to the tribes along the Mississippi River and bow wood in all directions, as far west even as the Pueblos, but these enterprises cannot be said to differentiate them from their neighbors. They did, however, make it easy for them to open up trade with the Spaniards and French.

The Caddo did not place their dead on scaffolds but buried them in the earth. Pénicaut describes the former custom as if it were shared by the Natchitoches but it was not the ordinary Caddo usage. In both regions quantities of utensils were placed with the corpse, and the Caddo lighted fires at the grave for six nights, six being the sacred number. One of the most striking differences between their burial usages and those of the other Southeastern people was in the fact that they cremated the bodies of men who had died on war expeditions.

Everything that we are enabled to learn of the religious beliefs of these people allies them in general with the other tribes of the Southeastern province, but specifically and strikingly with the Natchez. They reverenced a supreme god called the "great chief above," or "chief above," whose birth and early adventures are preserved to us in what proves to be a version of the "thrown away" myth. Devoted to the cult of this deity were several temples in one of which, at least, there was a perpetual fire, and what is told us of the ceremonies connected with them ally the Caddo in a striking manner with their eastern neighbors, the Natchez and the Taensa. As in the case of the Creeks and Natchez, domestic fires were obtained from the fire in one of these temples. The two "children" believed to act as intermediaries between the supreme being and the chief priest are not paralleled along the Mississippi, but our knowledge of the beliefs of the river tribes is by no means complete. Their connection with the Pawnee and Wichita appears in strong traces of a star cult. The practices of the medicine men resemble those to which we are accustomed in descriptions of similar practitioners farther east. Herbs were administered, formulae repeated to the accompaniment of various instruments, and scarification and sucking of the affected part indulged in, and medicine men performed essential functions in the first-fruits ceremonies, house building, and the cultivation of the ground. The Caddo placed the same stress on their first-fruits ceremony as did the Natchez and Creeks, but seem to have had a more elaborate harvest ritual. As in the case of the surrounding tribes, they had hunting and planting ceremonies. The "forecasting ceremony" in February and the one held in May to train young men for warfare were different from anything mentioned along the Mississippi.

In spite of a number of minor differences between the culture of the Caddo and the culture of the other Southeastern tribes, the resemblances are much more in evidence, and the picture we get of their social organization and religious rituals allies them strikingly with the Natchez and Taensa. Their most marked divergencies were in their apparent failure to have developed the same strongly marked matrilineal system that is characteristic of the Southeastern province, and in their language. In these two particulars and the prominent position given to star lore in their myths, as well as the elaboration of their rituals, they are allied with the other tribes of the Caddoan stock, but they belong distinctly to the Southeastern cultural area and more particularly to the lower Mississippi manifestation of it. Upon the whole, their cultural position may have been slightly inferior to that of the Natchez but the difference was certainly small and in one detail at least, the ceramic art, they had no superiors short of the Pueblo country.

In brief, the connection of the Caddo with the Southeastern tribes is evident in every aspect of their lives—material, social, and ceremonial—such differences as existed being in matters of detail and never in fundamentals.

LETTER AND REPORT OF FRAY FRANCISCO CASAÑAS DE JESUS MARIA
TO THE VICEROY OF MEXICO, DATED AUGUST 15, 1691[1]

Exmo S^r:

Por las muchas noticias que tengo del fuego que arde en el pecho
Christiano y Chatolico de Vé me muebe a escriuir estos brebes renglones
que por no hauer tenido por las muchas ocupaciones tienpo en concluir
con una relacion larga que yba escriuiendo para que Vé supiera por
menudo lo poco que en este año he visto experimentado y conocido. Yó,
y tambien por las noticias que me an dado algunos Yndios principales
de esta prouincia de los Tejas y por otro nombre llamamos, Áçenay, y
juntam^{te} algunas de la probincia de los Cadodachos, me motiuo, á
escriuir a Vé. esta carta junto con esta breue relacion de las cosas
que mas é conocido ser necessarias al presente noticiar a Vé, para el
fomento de la conbersion de estas Almas de el Señor para que su
Santisimo Nombre sea ensalzado, y juntamente el de su Santisima
Madre en todas estas Naciones.

RELACIÓN

Exmo S^{r.,} En premier lugar doy á Vé mill parabienes de tan grande
empreza y de direcion tan justa a la Diuina Mag^d que es conquistar
las almas que estan en poderio del enemigo de los mortales en estos
reynos, y prouincias, y lo que se me ofreze en segundo lugar referir á
Vé son las noticias siguientes: Esta prouincia de los Asenay, es muy
fertil para qualquier cosa que en ella se quisiere hazer tanto; y aun
me atrebo a decir mas que la de España. Solo tiene una falta que es
ser tan montuosa de diferencia de arboles, y las llanadas son muy
pocas. Hay en tres parajes de esta prouincia que se pudieran fundar,
no digo pueblos, sino ciudades. Otros parajes hay no tan grandes,
pero muy buenos donde ellos estan poblados que se conponen de
cañadas y lomas. Las lomas son muchas y no mui altas. No llegara
ninguna de ellas a mill varas de alto. En muchas de ellas hay mucha
piedra y toda ella es muy blanda. Creo aunque yó no lo entiendo
es tierra de minas subiendo yó una loma en el medio de ella vi unas
piedras mui pesadas. Y dentro de unos ójitos estauan á modo de

---

[1] I have attempted to reproduce the lettering of the original correctly but have taken
liberties with the punctuation which in the MS is highly eclectic.

unos cabellos reluciendo como oro, que por hauer visto algunas en la Nueba España jugue seria lo mismo. En muchas partes de la prouincia creo sera lo mismo. Por cierta experiencia que hizo uno que hauia trabajado en minas; y dijo que hauia oro y plata. Tambien hay muchas minas de barro, que los Yndios hazen lindas óllas de el, y creo que asi como hazen óllas se pudieran hazer Tejas; y ladrillos. Tanbien hay algunas minas de almagre que por ser tan fino es a-lauado de algunas naciones distantes de estas, y lo lleuan a sus tierras. El panino de la tierra en lo que yo é reconoçido y visto en esta prouincia es tierra la mas parte de negra, y de suyo fofa que en tiempo de llubias haze much lodo. Que por tener algo del arenisco no detiene mucho el agua.

En toda esta prouincia no hay mas que tres rios el uno nombrado el de la Santisima Trinidad que esta, como doçe leguas antes de llegar a lo poblado de esta probincia, el otro llamado el de el Adchangel San Miguel que esta como tres leguas dentro de lo poblado, a orillas del qual se ha fundado la Mision de Vé., y por ponerse la primera cruz en el dia que la iglesia haze memorias de la Victoria de Viena, se puso por titulo a la Mision el Sanctisimo Nombre de Maria. Es puesto muy acomodado para todo. El tercero rio esta distante de este como diez leguas, y le he puesto yó por hallarme el dia de la Pasqua de Espiritu Santo el mesmo nombre. Arroyos en toda esta prouincia abra como treinta que siempre corre el agua. En algunos de ellos se an puestos nombres, y uno de entre ellos se llama el de la Venerable Madre de Jesus de Agreda. Hay tambien una infinidad dedos de agua que por ser muchos yó no los he podido numerar. Lagunas en la mayor parte de los llanos las hay, y algunas son grandes, otras pequeñas. En las grandes hay pescado de diferentes generos, como en los rios.

Las diferencias de arboles son de nogales la mayor parte de diferentes generos de nuezes. Hay tambien muchos morales. Hay otros arboles de diferentes generos de frutas, como son castaños pero la castaña no es tan grande, como la de España. Los demas son de frutas no conocidas en esa tierra pero muy buenas como son asses y ziruelas, no como las de España pero creo serian tan buenas si sé cultiuaran. Los demas no sé sus nombres, si sé que son muy buenas sus frutas por hauer comido de todas ellas. Hay tambien muchos generos de vellotas, todas muy buenas en particular unas que son tan dulzes como castañas. De las demas hazen las Indias un modo de comida que les sirue de pan, como el maiz. En toda la prouincia hay muchos pinos y mui altos. Hay otros arboles de diferentes generos que no sirben de otra cossa sino de recrear la bista por la dibersidad de las flores que tienen. Los demas arboles son de muy lindas maderas para fabricar de ella todo quanto se

quisiere hazer. Hay tambien diferentes generos de plantas como
son sanza mora, y una ynfinidad de parras, unas enrredadas en
los arboles, otras a modo de zepas por los campos, y son tantas que
pareze que a mano las an plantado. Unas y otras son de muy
lindas ubas. Solo les falta no estar cultibadas. Hay tanbien mucha
granadilla que en la Nueba España llaman del Peru.

Hay tambien otros generos de yerbesitas muy buenas para comer.
Hai unas raizes a modo de batatas que seden debajo de la tierra muy
buenas. Esto hasta aqui es lo que dandesi la tierra. Las semillas, que a
su tiempo siembran los Yndios son maiz en abundancia. Hay de dos
generos, uno que sedá, en mes y medio y otro que en tres meses sedá.
Tiene cinco ó seis generos de frixoles todos muy buenos, calabazas mui
buenas, sandias y mirasoles que la semilla mesclada con el maiz hazen
muy lindos tamales, como tambien de otra semilla semejante a la
semilla de coles que molida con maiz hazen polbos para comer que es
menester tener el agua cerca que por ser, como harina, y comerse,
enjuta se sueles pegar en el gasnate:

Es tierra de diferentes generos de animales muy buenos para comer,
como son jabalies, y estos bien corpulentos y brabos, como los de
españa, muchos venados, gallinas de la tierra patos reales y estos solo
en tiempo de ybierno los hay, otros dos generos de patos mas pequeños
pero mui buenos. Otras abes no tan grandes, como las gallinas de
castilla hay y muy buenas que juntamente bienen con los patos reales.
Hay muchos conejos, y otros generos de pajaros que todo el año estan
en la tierra, como son perdizes, codornizes, garzas, y vna infinidad de
pajaros que dan mucha melodia en tiempo de primauera.

Solo tienen vn trabajo que aunque diestros en desparar las flechas
no alcanzan a matar lo bastante de la sobredicha caza y por eso bes,
es neçesario balerse de la sibola que en diferentes tiempos de el año se
juntan para buscarla que lo mas cerca de esta prouincia suele estar
como quatro dias de camino. Y la causa de hir juntos a buscarla es
por algun peligro que tienen de sus enemigos.

Las comidas ordinarias que estos pobres miserables tienen para
su sustento es maiz, frixoles y lo demas que ariua tengo referido. De
la carne nunca hazen mas que dos guizados cocido y azado. El modo
de comer y estar asentados en vnos bancos que hazen de madera todos
de una pieza no mui altos. La mesa es el suelo o sus rodillas. Por
manteles y serbilletas se siruen de lo que hallan mas a mano con
aquello se enjugan los dedos, aora sea palo ó qualquier traste, y
los que no son tan politicos con su proprio pié. Mas con todo esto
son mas amigos de lamber la cuchara que serben por ella los dos dedos
de la mano diestra. Los platos con que se seruen son vnas cazuelas
redondas; y como comen siempre la carne coçida y assada sin caldo.
La ponen encima de unas espuerteçitas mui bonitas que las Yndias

hazen de otate, y quando estan en parte que no las tienen se siruen de unas ójas ó el santo suelo, y los no muy politicos su propio piés. Que hordinariamente el modo de asentarse es teniendo vna rodilla lebantada. Las graçias que dan es tomar vn chacuaco con tabaco, y las primeras quatro tomadas las hazen, vna en el ayre, y otra en la tierra, y las otras dos por los lados. Pareze que siempre que comen hazen enpero de acabar lo que les ponen delante. Comen muy de espacio, y estando comiendo cantan, hablan, y de quando en quando silban, y se tienen por hombres los que acaban todo lo que les dan. Hazen burla de los que comen poco, y aborrecen a los que comen hasta que les causa bomitos. Es estilo en ellos quando llegan a una casa nunca pedir de comer por que es costumbre en ellos luego que llegan a vna casa ponerles de lo que tienen, y acauado de comer luego les dan para que chupen tabaco. Antes de comer nada de lo cojen primero lleban al *caddi*, y si es alguno de los principales conbida a todo el pueblo para que vayan a su casa tal dia. Va el caddi y todo los demas y se empieza a hazer grande fiesta. El caddi toma de lo que se ha de comer y el a vn poco en la lumbre, y luego en el aire, en la tierra y em ambos lados. Solo se ba a un rincon, y mientras todos los demas empiezan a formar vn baile, el esta, ablando solo al maiz que se deje comer, y asi de las demas cosas que ellos usan. Habla a las culebras que no muerdan. Habla a los venados que no se las coman. Ofreze a Dios toda la cosecha de aquella cassa y con esto acaba que Dios le ha dicho que se lo coman, que sino se an de morir de hambre. Todos empiezan a comer hasta artarse que su comer siempre llega hasta aqui.

Quando es alguno que no puede hazer toda esta fiesta por el mucho gasto lleba al *caddi* algo primera antes que empieze a comer de lo sobredicho, y luego vaja, y hecha con poco en la lumbre y en las quatro partes, y le dize que se baya que ya puede comer lo. Esta seremonia de asentarse en alto solo lo haze el gran *xinesi* y los *caddiçes*, y tanpoco nadie tiene semejantes altos en su casa mas que ellos. Los altos son unos tapestles a modo de mesas. A el se asientan pomendo los pies aun banco. Lo que alli se haze y se habla lo obseruan, como los Catholicos el Santo Evangelis, y si es algun mandato lo guardan mejor que los christianos los diez mandamientos. Por esso no sea sientan en este alto sino por cosa muy particular.

El vestir de estos pobres ordinariamente solo ussan de unas gamuças, y cueros de sibolas muy bien aderezados. En tiempo de muchas calores, en sus casas los hombres hordinariamente andan desnudos, pero las mugeres aun que se an mui pequeñas siempre andan cubiertas de la cintura abajo. A hombres y mugeres no les falta con que con ponerse en sus fiestas de diferentes trastes, ó perendengues, como los que vsaban los Mexicanos en su gentilidad. Solo el oro y la plata que estos no lo canozen. Muchas de estas cossas han adquirido destras naciones, como son abalorios, cazcabeles, y otras cossas semejantes que la tierra no tiene. En estas fiestas vnos se precian de salir galanes, y otros de tan horrenda figura que parecen demonios hasta ponerse las llabes de benado en la cabeza, y assi cada uno se rige segun su ydea. El modo de embijarse en sus mitotes es ridiculo. Para yr a la guerra se juntan todos en un lugar pintados de diferentes colores. Esto dizen que lo hazen por no ser conocidos de sus enemigos. Lo mismo hazen quando saben ha benido algun huespede de otras naciones por la misma razon.

Antes de partir a la guerra estan baylando y cantando siete ó ocho dias ofreciendo a Dios carne, mais, arcos, flechas, tabaco, acoxo manteca del corazon de las sibolas, pidiendo a Dios muchas muertes de sus enemigos. Le piden fuerzas para pelear, ligeresa para correr, y valor para resistir. En todas estas juntas se da mucho que comer. Vnos baylan, y otros comen. Delante de los que estan baylando esta vn palo, y en el colgado algo de lo que ofrezen a Dios. Delante del palo tienen fuego encendido, alli esta a sentado vno que pareze vn demonio. Este es el que da el yncienço á Dios que es echar manteca de sibola y tabaco en la lumbre. Todos se acercan alrededor del fuego, y de el humo coge cada uno vn peinado y se refriego con el por todo el cuerpo, pensando en esto que Dios le conzede, lo que le pide, sea muerto de sus enemigos, ó ligeresa para correr. En otras ocassiones no le hecha este genero de yncienso a la lumbre, sino que toma vn palo encendido, y lo pone alli, y con el palo y la manteca que le hecha ynciensa todo lo que ofrezen a Dios, y cada vez que se acaua vn baile sale uno, ablando como quien predica, y dice lo que an de pedir a Dios el siguiente baile. En estas juntas tienen muchas abassiones por que tambien piden a el fuego, a el ayre, a el agua, a el mais, a las sibolas, a los venados, otras cosas semejantes a estas a unas que se deje matar para comer, a otras vengansa, pidiendo a el agua que ahogue á sus enemigos a el fuego que la queme, á las fllechas que los mate á el biento que se los lleue, y finalmente todo esto lo dirigen a la bengaza. El vltimo dia de esta junta sale el *caddi* y los alienta diciendo, ea hombres si lo sois no hay que acordarse de mugeres de padres madres, ni de hijos que parese acuerdo no sea estorbo de nuestra victoria. En estas juntas con fio en el Señor que entendiendo los min[ros] evangelicos la lengua se puede hazer mucho fruto por estar juntas muchas naciones.

El natural y ynclinacion que todos los ymfieles de estas naciones tienen segun he esperimentado en muchas ocasiones es mui bueno en muchas cossas como en darse maña a trabajar para tener algo de sustento para algunos tiempos de el año que por ser tierra de muchos frios y aguas no los deja salir de sus cassas. Y tambien por falta de ropa que lomas que suelen tener es vna pobre gamusa, ó cuero de sibola. En este tiempo se entretienen cerca de la lumbre en hazer algo de manos los hombres flechas zapatos de gamuza y otras cositas necesarias, como las que se ofrezen aun labrador del campo, las mugeres en hazer petates de otate, ollas, cazuelas, y otras cossas de barro para sus exisiceo. Tambien se ocupan en aderezar pellejos de venados y de sibolas hombres y mugeres que todos los saben hazer, y otros muchos trastitos necesarios del seruicio de la casa.

Son de natural apaçibles obedientes a los mandatos de el gran *xinesi*, que es como Reyesuelo de ellos, y este tiene el oficio por linea recta de su linaje que muerto vno entra el que es mas propinquo en sanguinidad á el. A este estan sujetos estas nuebe naciones: *Nabadacho* que por otro nombre se llama *Yneci*. En esta nacion esta fundada la mision de Nʳᵒ Padre Franᵒ, y la que yó he fundado en nombre de Vé. que del Santismo Nombre de Maria. La segunda nacion es de los *Necha*. Esta se diuide de estotra en el Rio del Archangel Sⁿ Miguel. Ambas estan entre el norte y lebante aun lado de estas dos mirando a el medio dia entre el sur y lebante esta la nacion de los *Nechaui;* y otra que esta media legua cercana de estotra llamada *Nacono*. Hazia la parte de el norte donde da fin la nacion sobredicha llamada *Necha* esta la nacion llamada *Nacachau*. Entre esta nacion y otra llamada *Nazadachotzi* que esta hazia el lebante tomando, el rumbo de la casa de el gran *xinesi* que esta, como al medio dia y en el medio de las dos naciones caé otra nacion que empieza de la casa de el gran *xinesi*, entre el norte, y lebante y se llama *Cachaé*. A el fin de esta nacion mirando hazia al norte está otra nacion llamada *Nabiti* y á la parte de esta mirando hazia el lebante esta otra nacion llamada *Nasayaha*. Estas nuebe naciones cogeran de largo, como treinta y cinco leguas, y todas estan sujeta a este gran *xinesi*.

En cada una de estas nuebe naciones hay vn *caddi* que biene a ser como gouernador que los gobierna y manda. Este *caddi* es tambien por linea recta de el parentezco de sanguinidad. Estos *caddizes* cada uno en su distrito segun la nacion si es grande ó pequeña. Si grande tienen algunos óficiales que se llaman *canaha* de estos tiene siete, ó, ócho para ayuda de su gouierno, que si la nacion es chiquita no tiene mas que tres o quatro. El oficio de estos es tomar labor de el *caddi* y publicarla diciendo que el *caddi* manda que se haga esto ó aquello. Les pone miedo diciendo que si no obedezen á el mandato los han de azotar y castigar. Estos tienen tambien sus oficiales que les llaman *chaya*. Estos hazen todo lo que el *canaha* les manda. Tambien tienen ótros que les llaman *tanma*. Estos son los que dan prisa a la cosa. A los floxos los azotan dando les con unas baxas a las piernas, y varrigas. El *canaha* tiene de oficio tambien llamar quando se ofreze los viejos que se juntan en casa de el *caddi* para tratar algun negocio, y quando van a la guerra y a matar carne manda conponer el puesto donde el *caddi* descanse para dormir y comer, y siempre que quieze chupar le trahe el chaquaco con tabaco, y se lo pone en la boca. Con estos óficios sobredichos estan con tanta paz y union que en todo un año y tres meses, no habemos visto riña chica ni grande. Antes si castigar a los floxos y atreuidos.

En algo todas las mugeres, la del gran *xinesi* y las de los *caddises* que ordinariamente no tienen mas que una, estas todas tienen un mesmo nombre que es *Aquidau*. Con este nombre ya se entiende que es muger del gran *xinesi*, ó de algun *caddi*. Todas las demas cada una tiene su diferente nombre.

Los hombres que an tenido alguna victoria en la guerra mas de el sobre nombre que tienen se llaman ay *Mayxoya* que quiere deçir grande hombre. Las armas y vanderas que estos tienen son tener los pellejos y cabellos de los enemigos que cada uno ha matado. Las calaberas las tiene el gran *xinesi* cerca de su casa colgadas en un arbol. Finalm^te en esto ellos no ussan demas rigor de lo que ussan sus enemigos. Que es atarlos de pies y manos en un palo a modo de cruz: Alli hazen pedasos bebiendoles la sangre y comiendoles la carne medio azada.

En lo demas deue gouierno es ayudarse vnos á otros de tal suerte que si a unos se les quema la casa y lo que tiene, todos se juntan y le hazen casa nueba, y le lleuan de lo que ellos usan para sustento y seruicio. Todos en comunidad en tiempo de sembrar se juntan y siembran lo que cada uno tiene que sembrar segun la familia de la casa empesando primero en casa de el gran *xinesi*. A este solo siembran un poquito delante de su casa para que tenga algo del verde para su recreo, por que todos le dan de todo quanto tienen para vesterse y sustentarse, y luego prosiguen en sembrar las milpas y sembrados de el *caddi;* y ban prosiguiendo por los demas oficiales y viejos, y de esta manera van prosiguiendo de el mayor hasta el menor hasta que cada uno tiene lo neçecario para el año. Tanbien trabaja el *caddi* con los demas, pero *el* gran *xinesi* nunca sale de su casa para nada solo para pasearse, y hazer algunas visitas. Para esto en todas las cassas, de los *caddises* y de los mas nobles se tiene a señalado un banco que nadie se asenta sino el, quando va, y una cama alta a modo de un nicho para que duerma y descanse. Una politica tienen muy buena que los hombres quando trabajan no trabajan juntos con las mugeres sino apartados unos de otras y los de la casa donde trabajan no los dejan trabajar obligacion si tienen hasta que se acaba el sembrado de aliñarles de comer. En las enformedades se visitan y seruen unos á otros con mucha charidad. Procuran a dar a el enfermo todo consuelo llebandoles alguns regalos. Unos á otros se prestan las

alaja que tienen, como entre ellos no hay trato alguno. Son camba-
lacheros. Pareze que en todo lo que tienen no lo tienen como cosa
propia sino comun. Por eso no hay ámbicion ni embidias para que
les ympidan la paz y union.

Todos de natural son timidos. Por eso tienen mucho respecto a
el gran *xinesi*, *caddises*, y mayores. Quando el *caddi* pretende alguna
cosa particular llama á todos los viejos, toma al sentir de cada uno,
y el resuelbe lo que mas conuiene, dando sus razones a unos y á
otros de lo que mas conuiene hazerse y determinarse de esa suerte.
Salen todos contentos y vniformes de el consejo. En estas juntas
tienen de politica no hablar los demas quando uno abla. Estan todos
atentos. Solo dan señas que oyen con atencion lo que se abla.
Acabado el uno empieza el otro, y de esa suerte cada uno se sigue por
su antiguedad; y esta politica de antiguedades no solo es en hablar
sino en los asientos y en lo demas que los xptianos suelen guardar.
Esta politica en las juntas que hazen. Nadie se junta con los sobredichos consejeros. Si alguno se le ofreze, algo se asoma a la puerta
y con señas lo pide. Luego lo despachan. Los viejos reprehenden,
mucho a los mossos si se assentan o hablan delante de ellos. A mi
me ha acontecido en algunas ocassiones hablar y estar asentado con
ellos y quererse mesclar algun moso, y no solo lo reprehendian sino
tambien le daban con las manos algun golpe. El respecto y obediencia
que tienen a el gran *xinesi* es grande. Todos procuran tenerle contento en darle de lo que tienen, y en salir a cazar alguna cosa para
que se regale. Finalmente en su gouierno no es mas que decir quiero
que esto, ó aquello se hagan. Todos siguen por el temor que le tienen
su parezer, diciendo que es cosa muy azertada, y sera bien no se haga
otra cosa mas de la que dize.

Los castigos que tienen y dan a los delinquentes es de azotes segun el
delicto. Si es de muerte le dan tantos que hordinariamente no pueden
bolber mas en si. Si ha flechado ó, ha hecho algun, agrauio personal
dando algun golpe mortal a el *caddi*, ó alguno de su familia, como son
Padre y Madre, hijos, y propinquos a su linaje, tiene sentencia de
muerte. Esto no lo he visto pero es cosa tan comun en ellos que hasta
los niños lo saben. Si ha flechado o ha hecho de esta suerte se puede,
ynferir que habra sucedido y sera como dicen.

El trato que tienen de tomar el varon a la muger no es con mui buena
politica. En algun modo pareçe que el trato es bueno, pero he visto y
reconocido que no es muy permanente. Si alguno quiere por su muger
a la que se saue es doncella, le lleua alguna cosa de lo mejor que tienen,
y si su padre y madre dan permiso que la hija lo reciua, esta es la respuesta que bienen bien en el contrato. Pero no se la dejan llebar que es
primero no se dé noticia al *caddi*. Si no son doncellas, no hay mas contrato que decir el hombre a la muger si quiera ser su amiga le dá algo.

Algunas vezes se haze este contrato solo por algunos dias. Otras vezes disen que ha de ser para siempre. Estos son pocos que obserban la palabra porque en poco se apartan unos de otros, en particular, si la muger halla alguno que le dá muchas cossas mas de su estimacion que el otro solo suele tener permanencia. Este modo de contrato, en los mas nobles, por no hauer quien se atreba a ynquietar sus mugeres por falta de no tener justicia ni castigos para esto. Por eso no tienen verguensa en dejarse unos á otros ni tanpoco temor que le ympida aunque unos, y ótros se bean juntos. No por eso tienen contiendos ni peleas. Solo se procura entre ellos, si antes se querian bien hablarse dando cada uno su sentim^to. La muger le suele responder diciendo que el que tiene le ha dado muchas cossas, y lo que el le dio fue mui poco, en conparación de lo que el otro le ha dado, y asi que tenga paciencia que mientras busca ótra, ó que baya a buscar algo que darla, y de esa suerte boluera con el, y otras cossas semejantes, á estas que de una parte son para reir y de otra parte tenerles lastima, y conpasion. Pocos son los que biben juntas sin dejar la primer muger. Lo que alabo es, que nunca tienen mas que una, y si tienen ótra no la tienen como la primera biuiendo junto con las dos, ni la que con el biue lo sepa porque si lo biene a saber la que tiene algun puntito de honrra (que son mui pocas) luego se ápartan, y ban en buzca de otro. Una crueldad grande usan las mugeres que pariendo, y conoze que su padre no quiere a sus hijos los matan. No tienen verguenza encontar sus picardias alabandose de estos en-redos. Solo los nobles que pareze que en todo son mas cautelosos, y tienen algo de reputaçion. Lo que en esta materia pudiera deçir no hauia de caber en todo el papel de esta relaçion. El remedio de todo ello lo dejo a Dios y a sus miñ^ros evangelicos que con su buen exemplo dotrina enseñanza y consejos, en sauiendo la lengua, sera facil apartar-los de estos enredos; y assi a lentemonos todos en el Señor que en poniendo les en el berdadero conocimiento todo sera façil para que de todas estas cosas se desengañen.

Para conoçer yó en ellos mucho docilidad, tambien doy esta breue noticia que puede ser que ahora en los principios sea algo de prouecho.

Son mui amigos de cascabeles, cuchillos y qualquier cosa de hierro, como hachas y azadones que como son todos gente que hazen cassas para biuir y siembran para su sustento son de las cosas mas necessarias que por qualquier cossa de estas dieran aunque tubieran mortes, de oro y plata, estiman mucho algo de ropa de lana, en particular la que es de color azul solo por tener, esta circunstancia que es tener el color de el cielo, y tambien sombreros abalorios; y qualquier cosa de peren-dengues, y cosas que hagan ruido que por falta de ello trahen colgado unas quentecitas blancas que se dan en el campo a modo de abalorios, cazcabeles de biboras, pesuñas de venado, y otros trastitos que todos se lo cuelgan a la gamuza para que todo haga mucho ruido. Las mugeres se aprecian mucho de todo lo dicho, y tambien de rayarse de la çinta hasta los hombros con dibujos diferentes en particular los pechos, que en eso tienen todo cuidado. Los hombres se aprecian mucho de buenos plumajes, de tener buena cabellera y bien peinada, y los que no la tienen tienen todo su conato en raparse la cabeza en forma de cerquillo dejando en medio de la cabeza unos cabellos largos que les llega hasta la cinta, y tambien ponen mucho cuidado en quitarse con una concha los pelos de las cejas y de las barbas.

Ó, que açertado seria probeer a estos pobres de las cosas sobredichas. Creo seria mui façil que se reducieran a biuir juntos porque lo que ellos an de sentir mas es hazer de nuebo biuiendas y abrir tierra nueba para sembrar; y teniendo estos ynstrumentos no tengo duda que junto con el amparo de los Españoles y la ensenanza buena de los miñ[ros] se an de poblar pueblos que sera gloria para ambas magestades para la de el cielo y tierra gloria de sus almas y de la Mag[d] de n[ro] Rey Catholico, aumento de su R[l] Corona y regosijo de sus Vassallos. Grande consuelo pueden tener las que su Mag[d] ynbiare a estas tierras por ser la lengua de estas naçiones mui comun y creo corra mas de cient leguas encontorno, y mas façil que a prender que la Mexicana. El modo de entenderse en señas no tengo notiçias de el fin de ellas. El Señor deje entenderlas a los miñ[ros] e evangelicos, para que con ellos se alabe el nombre de Dios y de su santisima Madre. Amen.

Adbierto que este nombre de *Texias* son todas las naçiones amigas. Este nombre es comun en todas ellas aun que la lengua sea diferente. Y siendo á si que este nombre es comun no es por otra cosa que por la amistad antigua que tienen. Y asi *Texias* quiere deçir amigos en todas estas naçiones. Todos estos amigos no tienen uno como suele tener un reino que los gobierne que nosotros llamamos rey, solo un *xinesi*, y este suele hauer uno que cogera en su gobierno quatro y cinco naçiones que bendra a ser todas juntas prouincias; reyno se pudiera deçir y mui grande, si todas estas naçiones amigas tubieran una cabeza que las gobernara. Á todas, esta no la tienen, y asi infiero que ni reyno se puede nombrar esta prouincia que en la Nueba España llaman *Texias* diçen mui bien que lo son, esto por ser amigos de todos los demas.

El propio nombre que tiene esta prouincia es *Aseney*. Esta prouincia se conpone de las nuebe naçiones ya nombradas y una naçion sola de estas nuebe no es Aseney, sino juntas con las ocho que quedan. Las naçiones amigas que por otro nombre se nombran Texias son las siguientes: *Nazonis Nacau, Nabaydacho, Nesta, Guasco, Cataye, Neticatzi, Nasayaya, Nauiti, Caxo, Dostone, Nadaou, Tadiuas, Nabeyxa, Nacoz, Caynigua, Cadaudachos; Quizi, Natzoos, Nasitox, Bidey.* Estas cinco ultimas es una prouincia muy grande que esta hazia el norte que dista de la prouincia, como cinquenta y cinco leguas, y las demas nombradas entre el norte: y lebante: *Guaza, Yaduza, Bata, Cojo, Datana, Chuman, Cagaya, Asseney.* Estos son ótros *Aseney* que estan de estos, entre el poniente y sur, como ochenta leguas de esta prouincia. El deçir que son unos que se diuidieron de estos es mentira. *Caquiza, Quiutcanuaha, Caai, Canu, Tiniba, Vidix, Sico, Toaha, Cantouhaona, y Mepayaya,* estos estan entre sur y poniente. *Canonidiba, Casiba, Dico, Xanna, Vinta, Tobo, Caquixadaquix, Canonizochitoui, Zonomi,* estos estan entre el sur y lebante, y todos los nombrados has aqui son amigos. Los enemigos de esta Prouincia de los *Áseney* son los siguientes: *Anao, Tanico, Quibaga, Canze, Áyx, Nauydix, Nabiti, Nondacau, Quitxix, Zauanito, Tanquaay, Canabatinu, Quiguaya, Diujuan, Sadammo.* Esta es una naçion muy grande. Ótros le llaman *Apaches, Caaucozi, Mani.* Estos son los enemigos. Solo tre ó quatro de estas naçiones que estan entre lebante y sur. Todas las demas estan hazia el poniente. Esto se entiende desta Prouincia de los *Áseney* noticias, y saben que unos son amigos y otros, enemigos. Todos los que estan hazia el norte y lebante todos estan poblados, y siembras de la misma manera que estos *Aseney.* Y hay algunas naçiones de estas que su poblacion esta con mejor forma que estas, como son los *Cadaudachos, Nasitox* &c. que tienen las casas unas cerca de otras y mui bien embarradas. La nacion de los Sadammo es mui grande. Las cassas todas estan cubiertas de *cibola.* Tienen mucha caballada mulada ropa: y muchos instrumentos de hierro. Dizen estas naçiones que de todo esto es en mucha abundancia. Estos no son rayadas, y dizen que la mayor parte de ellas ban bestidos. Son enemigos de todas las naçiones amigas de estos *Áseney.*

Confio que con la gracia de el Altisimo, y proteccion de su sanctisima Madre junto con el deseo que su Mag[d]. Catholica y amparo de Vé. todas estas naçiones se an de conquistar. Eso sera si los que binieren a esta tierra para que darse fueren de buen exemplo. Esto y con el expiritu de los miñ[ros] evangelicos cierto es que se podra esperar mucho fructo y gloria para ambas magestades.

Aora al presente conosco seria mui conbeniente para que esto tuuiera estabilidad, se pusiera un buen presidio y se poblara esta tierra con algunas familias repartidas en los parajes donde estubieren las misiones. De esta suerte no pongo duda sera façil que se redugan á pueblo juntandose con los Españoles que estubieren cerca de la mision. El presidio en qualquier parte que se ponga (yá se entiende que ha de ser con sus mugeres) de esta prouincia hasta los *Cadaudachos,* ha de estar mui bueno, y confio con la gracia de el Altisimo con el buen exemplo de todos se an de reducir todas estas naçiones á pueblos, y mas espero con el fabor diuino que los enemigos de todas estas naçiones an de querer ser amigos y se an de juntar

unos con otros. Lo que conbendria para todo esto seria mui bueno
que aora en los principios se pusiera una cabeza que tubiera zela de
la honrra de Dios que con su buen exemplo, prudencia y discrecion
lo mirara, como cosa tan de el agrado de el Señor y desseos de su
Mag^d. Catholica y de Vé. que no son ótros mas que poderle dar a
su Diuina Mag^d. muchas almas. No seria malo, tanbien digo, que
si por estar ausente el remedio que es el amparo de Vé. tubiera la
mano en algun modo algun miñ^{ro} evangelico para que se castigara
lo que se conociere tener necessidad de castigo y echar fuera desta
tierra al que con su mal exemplo causara, alguna rebolucion. De esta
suerte los ynfieles berian el castigo y no conocieran juntam^{te} que
supuesto se castiga es por ser cosa contra Dios que ellos no lo ignoran
que todos saben que ayun solo Dios que en su ydioma llaman *Ayo
Caddi Aymay* y procuran todos en sus cossas tenerle grato, y no se
atreuen de ninguna de las maneras hazer burla porque dizen, quando
los castigan en alguna cossa que esta bien hecho, supuesto que lo
haze, que el saue lo que mas conbilene, y dizen tambien que los que
se enojan con el los castiga.

Grande es el sentimiento que tienen todos que queden con ellos
hombres sin sus mugeres, y si posible fuera, tambien digo yá, que
seria menos conbeniente que no que dara ninguno sin su muger. Por
lo que tengo experimentado de otra parte veo no es posible por tener
quenta de lo poco que en estas misiones hay para que oro se las haga
daño a sus milpas. Una carta me escriuieron antes de partir de la
mision de Santiago, dando noticia de la gente que venia, y de los
ganados que se trahian. Fui a leer la carta delante de los capitanes,
y mas nobles que los halle estauan todos juntos en una junta; y lo
primero que repararon en la carta fue que binieran hombres sin
mugeres, sabiendo que era necessario que de los que benian quedaron
algunos para guardar el ganado. Si destos pocos hazen reparo quanto
mas lo haran siendo muchos los que binieron para que dar ex^{mo}
S^r. Todos los dias me estan preguntando otra bez se vengan los Españoles si bendran con sus mugeres, y yó les digo que si, y con todo
esto no me dan mucho credito y me dizen que able a Vé. que es el gran
capitan de ellos y por escrito le diga que ellos quieren ser amigos, pero
si an debiuir con ellos ha de ser de suerte que no se les haga perjuicio a
ellos viniendo sin mugeres, y biniendo con ellas estaran mui contentos.

Yó digo que en lo que piden es cosa muy ajustada a la razon
asentado yá esto. Lo que yó conozco conbendria mui mucho por la
experiencia que tengo de dos vezes que la santa obediencia me ha
embiado a conbersiones y por reguardo dejar tres o quatro hombres
solteros sin mugeres. He tenido muchas pesadumbres y peligro de
perder todo el fructo que se pudiera hazer, y asi suplico a Vé. postrado

a sus pies que lo mire esto como a tan del agrado del S^r. no se pierda. Esto por embiar delinquente sacandolos de las carzeles gente soltera y vagamunda que si aqui afuera entre Christianos hazian maldades, aca, han de hazer atrocidades ympidiendo a los miñ^{ros} del Señor con su deprabada vida y mal exemplo el fructo de estas almas. Este modo de gentes seria mejor embiados a otra parte donde les tubieran oprimidos con el azote en las manos que dessa suerte pudiera ser, y no destra manera ganar sus almas. O mi Dios que no an de procurar la salbacion de las almas que no se acuerda de la suya, y quien no se acuerda de la justicia de los hombres, como se acordara de la justicia de Dios. Grande lastima, pero con mucha confianza pueden estar los miñ^{ros} evangelicos que teniendo el amparo de Vé. (que todos sabemos) lo mira con mas encendido amor y desseos que nosotros propios. El altissimo si lo conserbe con este fuego diuino (amen).

Mas de todo lo dicho hasta aqui me ha parecido ser bueno relatar algo de los engaños y abussiones que estos miserables ciegos de luz de la feé tienen. Son tantos ex^{mo}SS^r., que es para llorar y tener les lastimaæ Adbierto que todas las naçiones cercanas a esta tienen los mismos engaños abusiones y ceremonias, no digo cultos falsos por que seria dar a entender que tienen ydolos, y hasta ahora vendito sea el S^r. no he descubierto que los tengan ni que otra naçion que estan comarcanas.

El gran *xinesi* de esta prouincia tiene engañados a todos sus vassallos diciendo les que el hablar siempre que quiere con dos niños que tiene en su cassa que binieron de la otra parte del cielo, y que estos dos niños comen y beben, y que siempre que quiere hablar con Dios se bale dellos, y en algunas ocassiones que Veé que no le lleban mais y de lo que ellos ussan dize que los dos niños estan enojados que no quiren hablar con el en cossas del bien de todos.

Antes si dize que los niños le han dicho que no han detener buena cosecha que los enemigos los han de matar, y que Dios no los ha de asistir, que esta mui enojado con todos por que no dan de todo lo que tienen a su capitan, y no solo le dan a el sino tambien me han dicho que ellos estan padeciendo al hambre por decirles estas cossas. Los llama a todos á su cassa, y juntos manda que todos los *caddises* y mas viejos entren dentro de la cassa donde tienen los dos niños, que es una casa muy grande mas que la suya donde biue; y alli se azientan todos arimados a la lumbre que siempre tiene el *xinesi* encendida de dia y de noche y mas cuidado tiene que no se apage, que muchos sacristanes en atisar las lamparas de el sanctisimo Sacramento. Lo primero que haze delante de todos es tomar unas brasas con un tapalcate. Alli le hecha manteca de el corazon de la cibola y tabaco; y da yncienso a los dos niños que los tiene puestos en un tapestle alto, como dos varas. A los lados estan dos cofrecitos de otate donde siempre pone

algo de lo que ofrezen a el entre año, y les diçe a todos los que estan
alli que los cofrecitos estan vaçios. Luego que acuaado de ynsensar
apaga la lumbre toda, cierra la puerta de tal suerte que no se vea nada
de claridad, que dan todos a escuras adentro. Los que estan afuera
estan vaylando y cantando. Los de adentro estan con mucho silencio
escuchando a el *xinesi* que forma dos vozes fingidas, una como de
niño, la otra aspera algo propia a el natural. Con esta habla a los dos
niños diciendoles que digan a Dios que todos los *Aseney* ya se enmen-
daran de aqui adelante, que les de mucho mais, que les de mucha
salud, ligeresa para correr tras de los venados y cibolas, que les dé
mucho esfuerzo para pelear contra sus enemigos, y muchas mugeres
para que todos se sirban de ellas. Estas, y otras muchas cossas semejantes a estas es la peticion que el haze.

Hecha esta peticion toma un calabacito en las manos que dentro hay
unas quentas que hazen ruido algunas vezes. Echa el calabacito en el
suelo y les tiene énganados a todos que siempre que el calabacito cae
en el suelo que Dios esta enojado, que no quiere hablar. Todos es-
pantados biendo que el calabaçito esta en el suelo que no haze ruido.
Dizen a voz alta que dan palabra a el gran capitan, *Ayo Aymay* de
lleuar que comer y de todo q^{to} tubieren a los dos *Coninisi*, que son los
dos niños, y a su *xinesi*. Luego que el *xinesi* oyé de todos la palabra
que dan a Dios de asistirle en todo, y probeele de todo quanto huuiere
menester de repente lebanta el calabacito, y buelbe a hazer ruido hasta
que el mismo finxe la voz, como de niño, y dize con ella que Dios dize
que diga a todos los demas que se cumplen la palabra que le andado
que todo quanto le pidieren por el *xinesi* se les conzedera, y representa
esta razon el *xinesi* con la voz natural que tiene diciendoles lo que le
an dicho los dos niños. Luego les dize que vayan ábuscar carne y de
todo quanto tienen para que ótra vez no se enoje Dios, ni los dos niños,
que siempre que los tubieren contentos a el. Y a los dos niños tendran
contento á Dios. Algunas ocassiones les dize esto con algo de asperesa,
otras vezes con algun modo de suauidad. Luego abren la puerta,
y el *xinesi* les dize que vayan a sus cassas que se acuerden de lo que an
prometido a Dios. Todos salen mucha prissa andarse lugar unos a
ótros haciendo un modo de ruido como los chibatos quando salen del
corral. Hasta aora no he podido sauer que peude ser aquello.

El *xinesi* que da adentro solo atisando la lumbre, y moliendo en
un mortero que tiene adentro para moler la comida á los dos niños,
y en sauiendo que todos se han ydo a sus cassas sale el y seba a la
suya que esta como cient passos de esta. Se aduierte mas de todo
lo dicho que siempre que se haze estas funçiones, ninguno permite
que vea los dos niños amenazandoles que se han de morir, luego
poniendoles por exenplo que uno que lo veo luego se murio, y que
todos han de entrar desnudos, de tal suerte es esto que yendo yó para

ber lo que heran esos dos niños llegue a la puerta con dos niños
que yo tengo mui hermosos, y lo primero que medijo antes que
entrara me hauia de desnudar. El sequito la gamuza y la puso
arimada a la puerta. Yó le dije, que no ymportaua nada que
entrara vestido. Respondiome me hauia de morir. Luego le dixo
que no moriria que antes si temiera algo si entrara desnudo. Riose,
como haciendo reirla de mi respuesta. No queria que entrara.
Yó luego entre de golpe, El me seguio por detras. Preguntele por
los dos niños que adonde estauan. El espantado fue luego y me
dio en las manos un palo redondo a modo de una cubierta de caxita
de dulze, y esta dentro de una cubierta de pellejo, como pergamino.
Por rededor de la caxita tenia puesto algunas migagitas de lo
que los yndios le lleban a ofrezer. Al medio esta honda aqui pone
tabaco, y me dijo que hera para que los dos niños chuparan. Visto
que ni rastro de niños hauia y oido los desparates que decia, lo
reprehendí de manera que el no se enfureciese. Dixele con prudencia
lo que el Señor me Ynspiro. Me escuchaua todo quanto decia sin
alborotarse. Le dije que tubiera por bien que yo echara aquello
a la lumbre, y que los dos niños que yo trahia en las manos quedasen
alli y yo juntamente en guardia de ellos, y lo que ofrecian en aquello
que dize que son dos niños lo ofrecieran a los dos que yó dejaua
alli, que bien veia el que todo hera disparate y engaño manifiesto, y
que todo hera mentira, y que no hera mas que por engañar a su
gente para que le trujeran muchas cossas. Bino vien que yó dejara
los dos niños álli y me quedara, pero que no hauia de quemar los
suyos porque el y todos los *Áseney* los querian mucho, que aunque
yó no los veia hera porque no las podia ver antes quando, recien
benidos de la otra parte del cielo si se veian y que ahora por hauerse
hechado fuego a la cassa que les hizieron quando vinieron se quemaron
junto con la casa, y que solo hauia quedado aquello que veia. Todo
esto conoci yó ser émbustes de el. Quise con esto echarles a la
lumbre, y quando estaua para echarlos se enfureçio muchissimo.
Dejelo de hazer porque no se mouiera algun motin. Apaciguele,
como pude, diciendole que a lo menos hauia de venir bien que los
dos niños mios y yó quedaramos álli. Dejome que ssi boluio en
ssi, y nos salimos mui alegres de la cassa, yó con determinacion de
fundar alli una mision. Dio noticia el a dos viejas que tenia en
su cassa. Una benia bien en todo, pero la otra le dijo tantas cossas
que lo conbençio y le disuadio de su parezer. Fui yó despues para
que mandara a seis ó a siete hombres. Binieran conmigo a ayudarme
a llebar los trastes. Me dijo que no queria, que quando antes dijo
aquello no sabia lo que decia. Dexelo en esto, y hasta ahora estoy
que todo aquello son engaños formados de si mismo para en gañar
a todos sus vassallos.

No me atrebo á afirmar hasta aora ser ydolatria, que si yó la conociera lo remediara aun que me costara la vida.

Conosco todo sera façil hauiendo freno de Españoles. Y no solo todos estos en velecos, sino tambien otros, como decir que quando uno muere se ba su alma que no la ygnoran que en su ydioma llaman *cayo* va a otra cassa donde los aguarda un hombre que esten todos juntos, y este es uno que diçen tiene unas grandes llabes, y dizen que son mas grandes que los bueyes que tenemos aca, y estando todos juntos han de yr a otra tierra a poblar de nuebo. Por esto los en tierran con todos los trastes que cada uno tiene, le lleban de comer donde le enterraron algunos dias, y ay unos que tienen por oficio de yr encima de la sepultura poniendose a hablar alli solos. Les he preguntado muchas vezes que es lo que ablan. Todos me diçen que ablan a Dios que les deje comer para que tengan fuerza de allegar a la cassa que quando murieron estauan sin fuerzas por estar muertos de hambre. Disparan flechas a el aire abisando a el dicho Dueño de la cassa que recuir a todos: "ay vá esse que lo hagas trabajar hasta que estemos todos juntos." Son tan barbaros que en algunas ocasiones me an querido dar a entender de lo que les lleban les han visto comer que dixeran, los oyen llorar.

Cierto es que del todo no dirian mentira de creer es que las miserables de sus almas lloraran en el ynfierno por estas abusiones. No ha sido posible nos dejaran lleuar los cuerpos de los bauptisados a la yglesia. En una ocassion el conpañero que el Sr. se llebo para si llamado Fray Miguel Font Cuberta, quizo con en peno llebar a uno que murio en cassa de el *caddi*. No fue posible, y les causo tanto enojo que pensabamos se hauia de lebantar algun motin. Quisso el Sr. que se apasiguase. Les paso el Demonio en la cabeza que nosotros hauiamos trahido la enfermedad a esta tierra, y quando bieron que con la enfermedad que el Sr. les embio en este año de 1691 en todo el mes de Março que murieron en toda esta prouincia, como trecientas personas poco mas o menos, se afirmaron mas en deçir que los hauiamos muerto yntentaron. Algunos querernos matar. Quando yó lo supe fuy en cassa del gouernador. Hallele que estaua con todos los viejos. Lo primero que me representaron todos fue lo dicho. Yó les respondi si ellos hauian muerto a el Padre Fray Miguel Font Cuberta y al soldado que hauia muerto, recien benido de su tierra, respondieron que todos que no. Yó les dixe que decian muy bien y que tenian mucha razon, que Dios los hauia muerto, y que Dios quando el quiere nos mata el porque yó ni nadie lo saue, que ha bemos de morir todos esso si el como quando y de que suerte ni el gran capitan de los Españoles lo saue ni yó sauia, si puesto el sol llegaria mi hora, y si algunos de los presentes llegaria âmanezer y que assi todos los que queremos a Dios habemos de conformarnos con su Sanctisima

Voluntad, que quando el quiere tambien mata los Españoles, de la misma suerte que ahora a ellos, y asi todo lo que Dios haze lo habemos de retener por bien hecho.

Estas y otras razones les dixe, y les hizo tanta fuerza que nadie respondio, en contra. Antes todos los que estauan alli fueron dibulgandolo a todos los demas. Todos se admiraron. El capitan fue a otras naçiones a avisar de lo que yo les hauia dicho que cierto es no sabian lo que decian y que todo hera embuste. Lo que hasta aqui hauian pensado que nosotros fueramos causa de su emfermedad y muerte los que fueron caussa de esta cisma no fueron todos, que hay algunos de mui buen juicio. Todos los mas heran los medicos que ellos tienen que todos son unos embusteros, cargados de mill abussiones y algunos algo de hechizeros. Uno con sus trampas quizo ympedirme no bauptizara a una muger. Le heche un conjuro. Luego se huyó, como si yó lo quisiera matar. Con el otro yntentaua con algunas ceremonias de echar manteca y tabaco en la lumbre hazerme algun daño. Echele un conjuro delante demas de treinta. Fue tanto el miedo que tubo que no azerto a tomar el arco y las flechas que siempre ellos trahen en la mano. Se fue huyendo de mi y de todos. A la mañana fueron en busca de el para curar los enfermos, y lo hallaron muerto en una cañada. Dende entonzes todos estos medicos que ellos llaman *conna* me temen, y me dan puerta abierta abonando y alabando lo que hago diciendo a los enfermos que es muy bueno que se dejen echar agua.

Antes que no sucediera esto se heria por ymposible que ninguno de estos embusteros se dejara bauptizar por alguna enfermedad que tubieran, y a sido el S^r. seruido que entre los que he bauptizado que son setenta y seis ha hauido cinco de estos y para echarles el agua no ha sido necessario balerme de exsorcismos. De los que tienen este officio han muerto muchos. Todos los demas se an llebado los diablos pareciendoles que solo sus conas heran buenas y que todo lo que nosotros haciamos hera falso. El curar de estos no es otra cossa mas que chupar a la parte donde le duele y echar la emfermedad fuera de la cassas. Otras vezes dizen que la hechan a la lumbre y la queman, y como los pobres son tan faciles en creer les tienen tanta fee que les prometen todo quanto tienen si los saca de la enfer. Estos no hazen cossa que no baya mesclada con alguna abussion. Sucede en algunas ocassiones que si alguno de ellos tiene mala mano para curar los enfermos, y mueren muchos toman unos garrotes, y matan al medico.

Tienen ótra abusion que si hechan el yelo a la lumbre, no se ha de yr el frio, y se ha de enojar. Quando muere alguno, ó se les quema alguna cassa, dizen que la muerte se ha enojado, y por esso le ofrezen alguna cossa colgandosela delante de la cassa en un palo. Dizen tambien que el solar que ellos biven, ó la loma que esta cerca de su cassa se ha enojado quemando les la cassa, y assi no la hazen alli sino en otra parte.

Ótra abussion tienen muy grande que todos estan mui en ella que es deçir que los viejos hicieron el cielo y que una muger que nacio de una vellota, les dio la trasa que fue poniendo unos palos en modo de circulo y de esa suerte fueron formando el cielo, y dizen que alli esta esa muger, y que esa muger es la que todos los dias pare el sol, la luna, el agua quando lluebe, el frio, la niebe, el maiz, los truenos, los rayos, y otros desparates, como estos quando muere alguno de los mas principales hazen muchas ceremonias.

Y para esta funcion hay dos yndios que seruen como curas que dizen tienen por oficio hablar a Dios, y que Dios les habla estos. Mandan que se haga vn ataud para el muerto. Luego lo obedezen con prestesa. Luego de hecho los dos ponen tabaco, y de la yerba que llaman *acoxio*, y arco y flechas. Todo esto lo ban mudando de una parte a otra por encima del ataud. Ellos ban dando bueltas por el ataud y solos estan hablando vajo como quien reza, y el modo de hablar es con tanta eficazia que los haze sudar aun que haga frio. Para esta funcion ándan en cueros los dos. Acauada esta del ataud ban adonde lo han de enterrar que siempre es cerca de su cassa. Alli tambien hablan solos, y no se abre la sepoltura que primero no den ellos con el azadon un golpe donde ha de tener la cabeza, y otro donde ha detener los pies. Mientras se abre la sepoltura buelben a la cassa, y mandan poner el muerto en el ataud. Luego hablan a el muerto, como si hablaran a un bibo. Acauado de hablarle se retiran un poco diciendo que van a hablar a Dios. Luego buelben la respuesta a el muerto de lo que an dicho á Dios, y lo que Dios les ha dicho a ellos. Luego sale otro de el mesmo óficio que por biejo no lo exercita. Este se pone en medio de todos los que estan alli presentes que son los mas principales y viejos. Sale con un harma en las manos de las mejores que tienen.

El que yo vi en dos ocasiones salio con una espada sin guarnicion. Alli predica cerca de una hora hablando muy alto y con mucha eficazia diciendoles lo mucho que an perdido todos que se hayga muerto fulano que siempre ha sido dichoso asi en las guerras como en matar mucha cibola y mui fuerte en el trabajo. Les dize que an de llorar mucho por el, estas y otras cossas semejantes a estas. Acauado de predicar va a el muerto y se asienta cerca de el, y le habla, como si fuera biuo de lo que ha dicho en su sermon, y acaua con decirle que todos lo quieren mucho, y que todos lloran por el que baya consolado y que les aguarde con los demas que estan alli en la ótra casa hasta que esten juntos todos, que empiezen a trabajar, que se lleue la hacha, y todo lo demas que tiene enbuelto consigo.

Estando yo en medio destas funciones qui se probar si el muerto hera xptiano, si me darian lugar para cantar un responso y entres ocassiones puse la mano en la voca de el predicador diciendole que callara un poquito que yo queria hablar a Dios, que todo lo que el decia no hera cossa de prouecho, y solo lo que yo diria a Dios hauia de aprouechar a el muerto. Nunca me ympidieron lo que yó queria, y es mucho de ponderar que lo que muchas vezes estos curas ó embusteros hazen les causa rissa a ellos mismos, y cantando yó el responso todos estauan con grande silencio, y en algunos les causaua tanta admiracion que despues estauan rato que no hablauan, Yó procuraua siempre a notar todas sus acciones, y me parecio que no solo se alegraban, sino que agradecian lo que yo hazia y dos vezes me hicieron que fuera a cantar, como antes. Acabadas todas estas ceremonias cargaron con el muerto acarrera abierta disparando muchas flechas en el aire. Luego le pusieron todos quantos trastes tenia suios en la sepoltura, y su cuerpo en cima de todo y cerrandola. Estauan los dos que seruian como curas hablando bajo con mucha eficazia, y todos los demas estauan llorando. Acauado todo esto buelben a la cassa, y lo primero que hazen es lleuarle de comer encima de la sepoltura de lo mejor que tienen. Luego le ponen alli tauaco y lumbre. y dejan alli una ólla llena de agua, y se ban todos a comer. Estas son las ceremonias que hazen quando muere uno si es de los mas principales es como lo dicho. Si es algun particular es lo mismo solo que no es con tanta pompa. Si es el entierro por el gran *xinesi* no lo entierran hasta despues de dos dias que ha muerto, porque todas las nuebe naçiones que tiene todas hazen estas ceremonias, y enterrado hazen otras ceremonias semejantes a estas, y otras, como ponerle el mundo delante de la puerta que lo forman plantando un asta mui alta, y en la punta una bola grande de zacate. Le ponen las lunas, a señalandolas con unos palos altos formando una, ó delante de todo esto vailan diez dias y diez noches, y luego se ban cada uno a su cassa.

Esto no lo he visto todo, pero e visto que yá estauan juntas todas las naçiones para hazer estas ceremonias, y vi todas estas ynsignias. Vi el ataud, tan grande como un carro. Quizo la diuina prouidencia que estando para morir pidiera el ser xptiano. Hizele confesar los misterios de nra Santa Feé, Bauptizele en su cama delante de muchos Yndios y delante de quien hauia de quedar por *xinesi*. Todos quedaron muy contentos y se admiraron muy mucho que se huuiera dejado bauptizar por algunas cismas que el demonio tenia lebantados que nosotros matauamos la gente con el agua que les echabamos en la cabeza. Boluio el Sr. por su causa dando le entera salud con manifestar la eficazia del santo sacramento de el bauptismo.

El hauer cobrado el gran *xinesi* entera salud ha sido confusion para todos, y bien para sus miñros para que no les ynpidieran el fructo que se puede hazer. En ellos el gran *xinesi* todos los dias esta alabando el santo secramento, diciendo que no solo cabró salud sino que luego que lo reciuio se sintio mejor, y ahora con mas fuerzas de las que antes de caer enfermo. Tenia el S^r. se las conserbe para pelear contra el mundo, demonio, y carne y le haga mui buen xptiano, que me ha dado palabra de no hazer otra cossa mas de lo que le dijere. Me ha dicho que quiere mucho los Españoles y que se olgara que estubieran aca muchos, pero con circunstancia que an de traher sus mugeres.

Quisiera, Exmo S^r., que con alguna cosa se agasaxara este porque es la cabeza principal de toda esta prouincia. El que hasta ahora se ha procurado agasaxar, con hazer le gouernador, y darle el baston no es mas que *caddi* sujeto con los ócho de estas nuebe naçiones a el gran *xinesi*, y por mucho que se agasaxe a este ha de ser ymposible que el deje de reconocer a el *xinesi* por su señor. Yo se que el bendra bien que se agaseje mas a el *xinesi* que no a el mismo. Haciendolo de esta suerte todos los demas *caddises* que daran mui óbligados por reconozer no hauer reconocido ótro mayor que a el *xinesi*.

Confio con la gracia de el S^r. que en pudiendo los ministros hablar la lengua con perfecion, y con el arrimo, y resguardo de los Españoles se ha de desterrar toda la zizaña que el enemigo mortal de nuestras almas tiene sembrada en esta tierra, y se ha de plantar la feé con mas perfeccion que en otras partes, en particular teniendo el amparo de n^{ro} Catholico Rey, y de Vé que con tanto ardor y fuego diuino procura que esto se fomente, embiando ministros, y todo lo demas que Vé, conoze ser neçeçario por ser cosa mas meritoria y del seruicio de Dios n^{ro} S^r. mas áccepto que no se pierda lo que yá esta empezado no lo permita el S^r. Digo lo todo esto por que el demonio ha de poner muchos estorbos con diferentes lazos y que no se efectue esta causa de el altissimo.

Exmo S^r., bien pudiera con las noticias que tengo correr mas la pluma en todo lo que hasta aqui tengo apuntado en particular de sus ceremonias, ritos, y abusiones que son tantas las que hasta aqui he visto y reconocido que sin éxageracion pudiera llenar media mano de papel. El tienpo no me ha dado mas lugar para concluir con todo, pero lo mas éxenccial es lo que tengo referido hasta aqui. Si Vé. me permite que emplie mas las noticias con mas extencion, estoy mui prompto a éxecutar su horden. Saue él S^r. que nada me muebe de todo esto sino el zela que tengo que ningun alma se condene, y que estos pobres miserables mueran con el santo bauptismo que es cierto que seria grande lastima que esto se perdiera por falta de fomento porque hasta ahora no se ha sauido ni se saue con certidumbre verdadera que hay ótros ynfieles mas politicos, y mas bien poblados que estos y los que estan cercanos a ellos, porque todos siembran. No les falta que comer. Nunca desamparan la tierra, y sus cassas aunque se vaian a la guerra con sus enemigos.

Es gente trabajadora aplicada a qualquier genero de trabajo. Si yó huuiera tenido en este año y tres messes que estoy con ellos algunos cazcabeles, nabajitas, quentas de abolorio y de alguna ropa ázul que ellos aprecian mucho, y alguna trezadillas, y otros trastitos que darles pudiera tener un conbento formado de los materiales mejores que se pudiera podido hauer echo de las cossas y hay aca. Y asi digo que sera mui conbeniente que los miñ^{ros} tengan algo de estas cositas, y que uno solo no lo tenga porque son de un natural los Yndios que no tienen amor sino á aquel que les dá. De tal suerte lo que dizen que solo el que les dá es bueno y los demas son malos, y para administrar el santo sacranento de el bauptismo no an de querer receuirlo sino por aquel que les ha dado mucho. Ni los miñ^{ros} podran valerse de ellos para cossa alguna ni nunca se podra hazer nada én fomentar las misiones, y yó én este año y tres messes que estoy en esta tierra, y diez que empeze esta mision de Vé. del Sant^{mo} Nombre de Maria me he quedado sin trapito ni cossa alguna, solo haciendo pedazos de mis pobres trapos, para dar a algun Yndio que me ayudase. Hazer lo que el S^r. gouerna^r puede ynformar a Vé. de esta su mission.

Mas de todo lo dho no puedo dejar de dar esta breue noticia por estar mesclado en ella muchas abusiones que nonbrarlas cada una de por si hauiase de menester mucho papel. Es que en diferentes tiempos de el año hazen estos ynfieles algunas fiestas festexando los *caddises* a el gran *xinesi* acordandose de sus victorias que an tenido sus antepasados, y por estas fiestas se suelen conbidar unas naçiones á otras rindiendo los capitanes, arcos y flechas, y otras cossas que ellos aprecian, a el capitan, o *xinesi*. Aqui en entonzes se haze la fiesta. Delante de este estan tres dias y tres noches bailandolo y por festejo, y gala. Tiene el que todos los que an benido coman bien, y el quedarse sin comer todos las tres dias, y sin dormir en las tres noches, y no solo deja de comer y dormir mas ni beber, ni tomar resuello, sino siempre meneandolo de una parte a otra como si haciendo el son de el vaile. En estas juntos y fiestas suele hauer mesclado algunas supersticiones. El concurso que se junta es muchisimo porque hombres, mugeres, y niños todos bienen ó van a la fiesta, porque se da mucho se comer.

Confio con el S^r. que en sabiendo la lengua los miñ^{ros} évangelicos han de hazer mucho fructo por ser junta de diferentes naçiones que solo por estas fiestas se juntan en una parte que es a donde si haze esta fiesta ahora sea en esta prouincia de los *Aseney* ó sea la fiesta en otras prouincias comarcanas a esta, éncomiendo que de ningun modo ningun miñ^{ro} evangelico se asiente en el lado de el *caddi*, ó *xinesi* que estan vailando. Lo primero que pediran ha de ser esso, porque se precian mucho detener alguno que ellos conoçen ser de su estimacion para que vean y sepan la estimacion que hazen de ellos. Todos los demas digo que no conuiene no por lo dicho, sino porque Dios no lo quiere, y no es de su agrado que esten alli y miren aquello para sacar motiuo de todo para que despues les pueda desengañar de lo que conociere ser malo y contra el culto y reberencia que se deue, á Dios nro Sr. Esta mui bien mas estar a el lado de el *caddi* es dar a entender que es menos que el y que dan sujecion a el, y puede ser causa que no les tengan la reberencia que se deue. Mas de todo esto es por lo sobredicho, alientense.

Todos los miñros y consuelense, lo primero por ser la lengua de todas estas naçiones façil de aprender y todos los ynfieles de esta parte mui dociles. No se desconsuelen aunque bean algunos tan obstinados que no que eran receuir el santo bauptismo. En dos me ha acontecido a mi que no fue posible poderles reducir a que reciuieran el santo bauptismo y asi se murieron sin el. Algunos cassos an subcedido que es menester mucha prudencia en ello que por alguna cosa indiferente se deje de hazer algun fruto. No digo lo que puede ser porque solo conbiene lo sepan los miñros que pasaran a estas partes que con el exercicio y practica lo bendran á conoçer algunas crueldades han hecho los Yndios que ha sido matar las madres a sus hijos reçien nacidos por no quererlo su padre, y hechando fuego en una casa dejaron quemar dos niños chiquitos diciendo que no hauian de seruir para nada. Exmo. Sr., segun tengo noticias, en la enfermedad que el Sr. embio en este año de 1691 en todo el mes de Marco habran muerto en todas las naciones amigas llamadas *Texias* como tres mill. La enfermedad dio mas de vecio a unas prouincias que a otras á esta. Ya tengo dicho que habran llegado como atreçientos en otras mas, y en otras menos.

Tengo noticias que los *Cadaudachos* estan con esperanzas que los francesses an de boluer porque les dejaron dicho quando se fueron que hauian de boluer quando bolueria el frio, y que hauian de boluer muchos para poblar de una vez la tierra. Esto no es mas que dichos de Yndios aunque se puede rezelar por algunas razones que ellos dizen como es dejarles dicho. Hauian de boluer tan bien por sus conpañeros que hauian quedado por aca. De estos no se otra cosa mas sino que en el mes de Febrero estubieron nuebe o diez en una fiesta que hicieron en una prouincia cercana de esta, como treinta leguas que se llama la prouincia *Nacaos*.

Exmo. Sr., biense que mucho de lo que relato no me ymporta a mi. El hauer puesto algo de cuidado en ello, no ha sido mas que por de este que tengo de dar almas a el Sr. aunque sean muchos los han muerto en todas estas naçiones no faltas mies para quantos vinieren por la sangre de el Sr., y por el Santisimo Nombre de Maria postrado a sus pies le pido todo amparo y aiuda, su Magd. le de mucha salud Pa. que sea amparo de obra tan de el agrado de el Sr.

Para sacar este borron al lo me ha motiuado el pedirmelo el S[r]. Gou[r]. D[n]. Domingo Teran diciendome seria gusto de Vé. le diera algunas noticias.   Vé. perdone por amor de el S[r]. las falsas que como corto en la lengua castellana no he podido poner estos renglones con mas perfecion.   Yó soy Catalan y mui seruidor de Vé.

Reciua Vé., este breue conpendio y con todo rendimiento suplico a Vé. sea su padrino.   Mucho tenga Vé. en que dilatar su vida y n[ro] S[r]. le prospere como desea este su capellan de esta su mision del S[mo] Nombre de Maria, oy a los 15 de Ag[to]. de este dichosisimo año de 1691.

B. los pies de Vé. su mas rendido capellan que mas le ama en el amor de n[ro] dulcisimo Jesu.

Frai Fran[co] de Jesus Maria.

Suplico a Vé. por amor de Dios me ymbie un lienzo de dos varas de alto de el dulcisimo Nombre de Maria para esta mision de Vex[a].

La escriuio

FRAY FRAN[o] DE JESUS MARIA.

AL EX[mo] S[r]. CONDE DE GALUES.

LETTER OF FRAY FRANCISCO HIDALGO TO THE VICEROY OF MEXICO
DATED NOVEMBER 4, 1716

Exmo S^r.

La ocassion de escrebir esta a la grandeza de V. Ex.^{cia} pareciome obligacion precissa, lo primero, porque el ex.^{mo} Sr Virrei, su antecessor me llamo a essa corte para proponerme la entrada de los tejas, el tomar relacion de la tierra, y sus distritos, el que los Yndios de esta nacion me pedian por su ministro; por auerlos conocido antiguamente que me halle en ella, y auer persistido dichos Yndios en esta peticion desde antiguo q' dicha tierra se despoblo, quedando yo desde que me sali pactado con el capⁿ Principal, que ya murio, de volber con ministros; en cuya demanda hallandome ya con tal obligacion; hize con mis Prelados, y superiores, con su Mag^d Catholica, y con el excelentissimo Sr Virrey Duque de Alburquerque todos los empeños possibles, que por incidentes que acaecieron, todo quedo en blanco, sin darse passo a nada. Viendome que todos los medios, que avia tomado fallaron; me ocurrio un buen discurso. Conocia que esta tierra y la demas adentro las iban probando los franceses, siendo conocidas tierras de su Mag^d continentes a el seno Mexicano; y que con gran fuerza se iban apropinquando a lo immediato de essas fronteras de nueba españa: discurri el escribirles dos cartas en diferentes ocassiones que una de ellas llego a manos de ellos, por ver si podia recebir carta de ellos, y remitirla a esse superior Gobierno. La respuesta fue el venir dos francesses a essa corte, con cuyo informe y los que su excia justifico de diferentes personas: determino el que se diesse passo a esta conversion con una mui corta probidencia de 25 hombres, mandando se pongan quatro missiones, inviando los Religiosos por parte de el collegio de la SS^{ma} Cruz de Queretaro, sin darles ningunos probidencias para su manutencion, y mandandome dicho ex.^{mo} S^r. le diese quenta de la tierra y le informase de todo. estos son S^r. ex.^{mo} los motibos, que me assisten para tomar la pluma en la mano, y darle relacion de toda esta tierra de la politica de los Yndios, de su falsa Religion, de los distritos que coge esta nacion, de los frutos que la tierra contiene y de los medios que se pueden dar, para que toda esta tierra se haga un Reyno mui Poblado, y de muchos intereses espirituales y temporales. El dia 21 de enero salimos del collegio de la SS^{ma} Cruz de Queretaro cinco sacerdotes, y aviendonos incorporado en el Saltillo con la compañia de militares, siguiendo nra derrota llegamos el dia 28 de Junio a los umbrales de la prouincia de los tejas de este año presente de 1716 a donde aviendose hecho todas las buenas cortesias, y buena acogida entre dichos Yndios a n^{ros} Españoles como ya de todo y de la possitura de las quatro missiones se dio quenta a esse superior Gobierno: resta ahora el darla de los experiencia y noticias que se han adquirido en la estada de dicha tierra, que por ser ellas tan necesarias: tendra a bien V.Ex^{cia} el atenderlas: para que del conjunto se infiera una buena consequencia. Esta nacion Assinay que llamamos tejas, o texias, contiene muchas parcialidades, llega asta el Rio del *missuri*, segun noticias de los Yndios cogen los Rumbos de norte y leste contienen mayores y menores poblados, por la vanda del Norte se contiene mirando desde essa corte al dicho Rumbo estas quatro missiones de diferentes parcialidades, que haziendo el rostro desde esta primer mission de S. Fran^{co}. de los Texas, unas caen a les nordeste que son las dos primeras, otra a leste en distancias competentes, y otra al nordeste. Siguiendo la cordillera del Norte a cinquenta y tres leguas mas o menos, caen las parcialidades de los Cadodachos, Nazoni, Nacitos, Nadzoos: mas adentro vecinos al Rio del Missuri, caen la Poblacion grande del caynio, tobacana y otras. por la parte del oriente, la poblacion del Nachitoz, que andan empoblarla los franceses, y otras que van a immediar con el poblado de los franceses que estan al desenboque del Rio del Missuri, para entrar a el Rio de la Palizada. Cae esta primer mission de mi P^e. S. Fran.^{co} a 33 grados de Altura de polo en linea recta al norte, y se mira a querertaro linea recta al sur, que se halla en 21 grados. Es esta gente placentera, alegre, de buenas faciones cariaguileñas, y amigables con dos españoles. Siembran Maiz, frixoles, mirasoles diformes de grandes, que es la semilla del porte del mesmo Maiz que la comen en diferentes potajes que hazen con el Maiz y frixol, ay Calabazas, melones, Sandias; cogen cantidad de Nuezes encarceladas, y bellotas para el gasto de su año. Es toda la tierra poblada de diferentes Arboledas, Robles, castaños, pinos, Alamo, Nisperos, ciruelos, y otros muchos que no conozco. Tiene la tierra cepas de vnas silvestres, Granadillas del Piru, Morales, moredas, zarzamoras de dos Generos, lino, cañamo en partes, que ay en esta primer mission: y por parte del camino en grandes cantidades, contiene muchos ojos de agua, Rios grandes y pequeños, es toda la tierra por lo que esta reconocido mui montuosa, y contiene muchas placoletas, vagios, y cienegas a donde estan poblados los Yndios, no se halla en ella parajes competentes para Juntar los Yndios a poblado: sino es que se tome la forma de romper y limpiar los montes. Tiene lagunas en donde se crian diferentes pescados, y tambien en los Rios. Ay Muchas gallinas de la tierra, Benados, y en tiempo de frio Muchos anceres y patos. El Ganado de cibola lo tienen para el Rumbo del poniente y Norueste poco mas de dos dias de Camino: tienen sus enemigos a la vista, y son llanos mui grandes en donde esta nacion Assinay todos los años tienen sus guerras von los dichos por comer la carne, y por la enemistad antigua que ay entre unos y otros. Es toda esta Nacion por lo que esta de presente reconocido, Ydolatra, tienen cassas de Adoracion y el fuego perpetuo, que no lo dexan apagar, son muy abucioneros, y en los Bayles que hazen, el Yndio, o Yndia, que se embriagua con el peyote, o frixolillo, que de propossito lo hazen, creen todo lo que les dizen han visto: tiene Ydolos Mayores y menores, reconocen a el Demonio, y le dan sacrificio entendiendolo, que es su Dios verdadero, y en las pinturas que hazen lo ponen Cornuto con cara de fuego y con otras facciones, que da bien a entender su crecido engaño. No hemos podido conseguir de ellos, aunque al principio consintieron, el poner sus cassas Juntas a la Yglesia. Y assi no ay doctrina christiana, lo primero por la gran renuencia que ay en ellos de todo lo christiana, y por las grandes distancias que ay en las cassas de unas a otras, y por otros motibos y razones que ellos tienen. La repugnancia a el Baptismo desde la vez passada es mui conocida por que han hecho juicio, que el agua los mata: algunos se han baptizado que han muerto de parculos y adultos. Si sacan lumbre de sus cassas no lo quieren consentir por que entienden que se ha de morir alguno de la casa. Las cassas son de zacate bien crecidas y altas y otras de mediano porte, y otras mas menores de el modelo de media Naranja, y en ellas viven muchas familias *respectivo*, tienen el Maiz en tapancos y desvanes, y en cestas grandes de otates, ponen todo su Maiz desgranado, en otras los frixoles, vellotas, y Nuezes. Hazen Ollas mui grandes para hazer los atoles, tener el agua y todos portes, y otras vacijas para su servicio. Hazen petates mui curiosos de otates; que pueden seruir en los estrados de las s[ras] con diferentes colores; petaquillas de lo mismo mui curiosas, y del otate otras cossas menudas que sirven de Zedazo para limpiar y cernir lo que comen. Es esta tierra por las plagas que tiene en tiempo des estio y por las que ay de Perros ladrones, y Nozcones dificultosa de criar ganados menos cabras y obejas; por que la vez passada murio todo lo de este genero, y oy el criar son con muchos afanes. Criar cantidad de caballadas, no se puede por lo montuoso. Lo que se puede criar son chicorros de Ganado Mayor y de cerda y algunos caballos. Siembran estos Yndios de comunidad sus tierras con açadones de palos, y hazen mucho aprecio de los açadones de hierro: hazen las casas de comunidad y tienen hachas de diferentes portes, que adquieren de los franceses. Siembran tabaco todos las Yndias son mas atareadas al tradajo que los hombres. Lo demas del tiempo gastan en passearse, y trazar de sus Guerras: que ordinariamente son por el invierno las guerras de estos Indios. Para las dos funciones dichas reconocen los Yndios superior: en lo demas cada uno es dueño de su Voluntad. Las cabelleras de sus enemigos ponen por trofeo y triunfo pendientes de unos carrizos a la entrada de sus puertas. Entierran sus difuntos y bañados primero los entierran con los triunphos, que han hecho, con las gamuças que tienen, y todos sus parientes le ofrezen, y les ponen de todas sus comidas, y cueras de cibola. Las cabelleras para que sus enemigos les vayan a servir a la otra vida, la comida de matalotaje para el camino, y las gamuzas y demas trastes que tiene para tener que vestir. Mucho estiman la ropa: pero poco les sirue lo que su Mag^d. Les ha dado, porque luego los reparten a otros sus amigos. Esta toda la nacion mui unida continuamente se vissitan unos a otros, es el Gentio quantioso y se dilata por los distritos que tengo ya alegado arriba: No se puede por las cortas fuerzas que han reconocido en nros españoles tratar de ponerlos Juntos en pueblos, y la tierra no ayuda para lo dicho nada por lo montuoso, y demas cossas que le circunvalan: es preciso se considere este punto bien, y a mi corto entender para que todo con el discurso de el tiempo tenga buen exito, esta mi proposicion: necessita de reconocer la tierra de los llanos, que miran al norueste dos dias de camino desde esta mission poco mas, en donde juzgo cae el Rio de la SS ^{ma} Trinidad, segun noticias de estos Yndios. Donde discurro son los temporales, como en esta tierra por lo immediato, en cuyos espacios se podran criar caballadas, Ganados Mayores y menores: y se podra ir poco a poco sacando esta gente con los agasajos y buenas correspondencias, que se tubiere con ella: y sirua de freno la fuerza que se les pussiere. Finalmente el tiempo lo allana todo; y las experiencias que se iran cogiendo iran dando maior methodo, a lo que se debe obrar. Fuera de esta poblacion, se necessita que V.Ex^{cia} de passo a que se puebla la vahia del espiritu Santo, y por lo que yo tengo reconocido por entre los dos Rios de San Marcos y del espiritu Santo antes de Juntarse para entrar en dicha vahia ay espaciosos y grandes llanos, y grandes conveniencias para hazerse grandes poblados de españoles, el temperamento mas benigno que el de el puesto, porque caen grandes elados por el invierno, que en esse tiempo lo reconoci, y del puesto tengo noticias es enfermo por los muchos franceses que murieron, y con muchas plagas que se dize ay en ella; y con la que le circunvalan de Naciones de Yndios enemigos assi dentro de las Ysletas de la dicha Vahia como en los contornos, que todas estan haziendo un cuerpo. Entrando a reconocer el Rio de S. Marcos mas ariba de las ajuntas con el Rio de el espiritu Santo: reconoci una espaciosa laguna, que hizimos juicio, que es desague del Rio de S. Marcos, y echa las olas a poco viento como la mar. Llamanlos Texas, *Sapinay* la preñada. Entrando mas para dichas ajuntas reconocimos el cerrito colorado, que por la vahia antiguamente se reconocio a las margenes del Rio Colorado, o de el espiritu Santo. Ay cintas de montes en partes, y en los Bordos de los dos Rios muchas maderas para edificios. En estos llanos que lindan con la laguna pre-

ñada se puede poner la poblacion, y Juzgo que en un barco se puede
ir por el Rio arriba, y desembocar en la laguna y roconocerla con las
conveniencias que ofrezen aquellos parajes, y por aqui se diese principio al primer poblado de españoles para el comercio de toda la tierra
y a todo rigor para el de la tierra adentro de los Texas. Estara esta
poblacion en lo todo un buen medio para darse las manos a las fronteras del Rio del Norte donde esta el Presidio y Misiones, y para esta
tierra de los Texas, y que por esse puerto de dicha vahia se va ya con
mas fuerza poblando toda la tierra, y se le escuse a su Mag.ᵈ maiores
gastos de los fletes que se tiene por tierra, y maiores dilaciones en los
socorres. Y Juntamente sirue de resguarder el puerto; y de ir suje-
tando los Yndios de esse contorno, y que se allanen los passos y se
pacifique la tierra. Tengo arriba advertido, que solo limpiando los
montes, se puedẽ poner las missiones en la forma que tengo relatada,
y solo se previene este punto porque de despoblar esta tierra para
poblar los llanos, la problaran los franceses (por parte de francia)
que assi se le propuso a su antecesor de V. Ex.ᶜⁱᵃ por parte de francia
los franceses que fueron a essa corte. Sobre estos puntos de jurisdi-
cion y sobre las conveniencias de los pobladores, y militares, y la
sujecion de estos Yndios pide mucho acuerdo, porque a poca diligencia
segun la acceptacion que hazen de los franceses, (a pocas diligencias)
se harian de la parte de francia. Y el methodo que lleban en poblar y
fundar missiones es mui distincto que el que nosotros los españoles
llebamos. Solo quitandoles el puesto de Nachitoz tenia reparo estos
embarazos: y controversias. Como informara de todo el capⁿ Domingo Ramon en la entrada que hizo al Nachitoz como mando hazer
una cruz y lebantar altar a dos franceses que estan alli de retar-
guardia, y se celebro el S.ᵗᵒ Sacrificio de la missa, entrando con la
insignia R.¹ y por estar enfermo, passo su H.ⁿᵒ Diego Ramon por
canoa Rio abajo a rreconocer las poblaciones de la Palizada, y de
alli a rreconocer la mobila. Passo a darle a vexcia una noticia. Noticia que tengo adquirida de los franceses. para mas esplicacion dare
quenta a V. Ex.ᶜⁱᵃ los Rumbos que lleban los Rios. El Rio de la Palizada tiene sus corrientes de Norte a sur, y los dos Rios el de los
Caddodachos que es el mesmo a donde estan mas abajo los indios del
Nachitoz, y los dos franceses: y el Rio grande del Missuri tienen sus
corrientes de poniente a oriente, y desembocan en el sobre dicho Rio de
la Palizada entran de la vanda de aca de lo que nosotros intentamos
poblar, y que francia no se someta mas adentro para nuestras fronteras
de el Nuebo Mexico, parral, y Mar del sur, que cae la prouincia de
Sonora. Advertido esto dire las noticias, que tengo del Rio del Missuri:
en el desemboque de dicho Rio estan dos missiones de PPˢ de la
Compañia franceses, pobladas con los Yndios *Yllinois*, y con poblazon
de franzeses; tienen la mayor parte del Rio arriba sondeado comercian con los Yndios *Caynigua*, *Panni*, que son Yndios blancos:

comercian en Ropas, escopetas francesas, abalorios, y otras cossas: tienen los por suyos, no los han poblado, pero intentan el Poblar todo esse Rio: me han informado que desde los Yllinois a los Indios *Panni* Rio arriba ay ciento y cinquenta leguas: a estos Pueblos de los *Panni* se juntan tres brazos de Rio, que hazen el Rio del Missuri opulento de Aguas y tan grande dizen es como el de la Palizada. Estos Yndios son fronterizos con los *Apaches*, y tienen Grandes Guerras con ellos, y se han reconocido los *Panni* Mayores Guerreros que los *Apaches*: y les han cogido grandes presas, que venden a los franzeses y estos los compran y tiene los por esclavos. Salen los dichos tres brazos de Rio de una grande cerrania que linda con la Mar del Sur de mucha cantidad de ojos de agua. En el brazo del medio adentro, dizen esta una gran ciudad, que años passados reconocio un clerigco frances, y otros seglares de que dieron cuenta al Rey de Francia, y se han hecho despues varias entradas por los franceses por el mesmo Rio aRiba, y he sabido averse perdido ultimamente dos o tres años ha supe entraron ciento y cinquenta franceses, y No he tenido Razon de lo que les ha sucedido. Esta gran ciudad no la habitan Yndios, sino gente blanca, que o han de ser tartaros, o Japones: y de la otra banda de la zerrabia, dize la Relacion nouissima francesa, que desde la cima de la serrania se ve la costa y mar del sur y muchas embarcaciones. De esta gente blanca refiere el P^e. Fr. Ju^o. Torquemada en su Monarchia indiana, y las diligencias que por mar y tierra se mandaron por el excellentissimo Sr Virrey de Mexico hazer en aquel tiempo con todo este conjunte de noticias vea Vex.^cia en que estado nos van dexando los franceses: por las espaldas se nos van entrando con silencio: pero Dios ve las intenciones. Exce^mo S^r. todo esto pide un Gran reparo, y si fuera possible aunque se quitaran algunos Presidios de la Vizcaya y reparar este tan gran daño que se nos entra por nras puertas. Mobera mas a emprender esta impresa el dote que dios ha puesto en esta tierra, para que con el tiempo ella se pueda costear por si: Por algunos de los que hizieron esta ultima entrada han reconocido en estos Payses, que tienen la inteligencia en metales: que es toda esta tierra de Minerales, y no se reconoce otras piedras, sino los de metales, y las aguas nacen todas de minerales: no se ha podido hazer la experiencia por hallarnos mui atrasados con enfermos y otros accidentes que han acecido, por cuya causa esta suspensa la materia. Para el establecimiento de poner los Pueblos, y Juntar los Yndios a mejor forma de poblado: seruiran Yndios christianos, que sepan la lengua castellana y los de esta nueba españa. Y para beneficiar las minas españoles que tengan curia en metales. y para los cañamos, y linos beneficiarlos se de passo despues y pedirle y informarle a Su Mag^d la gente de españa que fuere mas al propossito, y lo mismo las viñas: supuesto el bene-

placito de Vex ^{cia} y de ese superior Gobierno.   Y lo mismo digo acerca
de beneficiar las sedas, pues ay tanto moral y moredas en esta tierra.
Estos Yndios *Thejas* no nos dan ningun seruicio, solo se contentan con
vissitarnos.   Las necessidades que padecemos en lo necessario que hemos
menester de seruicio, y mantenimientos.   Las referimos a dios que assi
lo ha ordenado, y Juntamente ceda todo en la mayor honrra y gloria
de Dios, por cuya soberana Mag ^d los hemos padecido.   Escusome de
reproducir mas noticias acerca de la entrada del Nachitoz, lo poblado
y distritos de tierra del camino: y lo demas de noticias que repⁿ,
adquirira de la entrada de su H.^{no} el Alpherez a la palizada y
mobila: que esso le toca oficio el darlas.   Lo que discurro no reco-
nocera ahora el dicho Alpheres Diego Ramon es el desemboque del Rio
del Missuri a donde ay poblacion de franzeses, y de los Yndios
Yllinois como ya arriba he relatado a la Grandeza de Vex.^{cia} importa
hazer tambien este reconocimiento, y ponerles frontera para que no
passen Rio aRiba a descubrir a la grandeza de poblados, que pretenden
poblar.   Toda su comunicacion es por los Rios: y poniendoles frontera
aqui Junto a los *Yllinois*, en el *Nachitoz*, y en la vahia de el espiritu
Santo: quedan circunvalados los franceses, que estos tienen tambien
a los Yngleses de la nueba Carolina rodeados.   Y aunque el poblado
de Panzacola tienen los franceses a espaldas, es muy preciso el con-
servar aquel puerto y fortificarlo mas con un buen castillo y muralla
aunque se gaste en esto mucha hazienda Real; que como esta ahora de
ofrecerse Guerras con franzia a poca diligencia lo ganaban los franceses: y assi lo he oido decir a ellos, y en estas guerras passadas hu-
biera perdido españa este puerto, y los Yngleses lo ubieran ganado, si
los franceses de la mobila no ubieran dado diferentes ayudas de costa:
el Puerto de Panzacola es el mejor puerto que de Varra a varra tiene
nro Rey Catholico en las Yndias, para resguardo de muchas armadas:
como se lo oy decir al cosmografo de su Mag ^d en tiempos passados que
se fue a rreconocer por la mar.   Con todas estas prebenciones assegura
Su Mag ^d un Gran Reyno en estas dilatadas prouincias con grandes
riquezas.   Dios nro S^r. conserue la vida de Vex^{cia} por muchos años
para la propagacion de las Sta fe, y aumento de la R^l. corona. Es fha
en esta Mission de S. Fran^{co} de los tejas oy 4 de Nobiembre de 1716
años.

Siervo de Vex ^{cia} que B. S. M.

FR. FRAN^{co}. HIDALGO.

Exmo S^r. MI S^r.

EXTRACTS FROM THE CRÓNICA DE LA PROVINCIA FRANCISCANA
DE LOS APÓSTOLES SAN PEDRO DE MICHOACÁN BY FRAY ISIDRO
FELIX DE ESPINOSA, PUBLISHED UNDER THE EDITORSHIP OF DR.
NICOLAS LEON (PP. 419–442)

CAP. IX.

DESCRIPCION DE LA PROVINCIA DE LOS TEXAS, COSTUMBRES DE LOS INDIOS,
Y LA VARIEDAD DE SUS RITOS, IDOLATRIAS, Y SUPERSTICIOSAS CEREMONIAS.

La Provincia de los Assinais, vulgo Texas, se halla en distancia de
mas de quinientas leguas de la Ciudad Imperial de Mexico, por el
camino que han frequentado hasta aora nuestros Españoles, y por linea
recta, respecto de dicha Ciudad, caè al rumbo de Nornordeste, y se halla
en altura de Polo el sitio de las primeras Missiones, de treinta y tres
grados y medio, y algunos minutos. Contiene muchas parcialidades
esta Nacion Assinai, que por evitar confussiones, no las nombro en su
proprio Idioma, y se estiende por los quatro rumbos principales, en
distancia de mas de cien leguas por cada viento, hasta las orillas del
Rio Missuri, que desemboca en el de la Palizada, tirando las lineas del
Norte, en que ay muchas Naciones politicas, que siembran; y de una
ǫ está poblada por el Rio Missurî corriente arriba, hai noticia de la
Nacion Arricarà, ǫ son quarenta y ocho Pueblos, en termino de diez
leguas; y de tanta multitud de Naciones, solo se han sujetado al
Dominio del Rey Catolico las que tuvieron la dicha de seis Missiones,
ǫ se plantaron en los años de 16. y 17. Es toda esta Gente placentera,
alegre, de buenas facciones por lo comun, y muy amigable cõ los
Españoles. Tienen politica para hacer sus siembras de maiz, frisoles,
calabazas, melones, y sandias; y siembran tambien cantidad de Gyrasoles, que se dàn muy corpulentos, y la flor muy grande, ǫ en el centro
tienen la semilla como de piñones, y de ella mixturado cõ el maiz, hacen
un bollo, ǫ es de mucho sabor, y substancia. Cogen cantidad de Nuezes
encarceladas, y de Bellotas, para el gasto de su año. Toda la tierra
està poblada de diferentes Arboledas, como son Robles, Pinos, Alamos,
Encinas, Nogales muy gruessos, que dàn la Nuez encarcelada; y otra
especie de Nogales de Nuez pequeña, y mollar, de ǫ se abastecen los
Indios. De los Arboles frutales, fuera de las Nueces, hai Nisperos,
Ciruelos, Parras sylvestres, y muy gruessas, y entre ellas Uba blanca,
que parece moscatel, y solo les falta el cultivo para ser tã buenas como
las domesticas.

Hai multitud de Morales, y Moredas, Zarzamoras muy gruessas,
y muy suaves, Granadillas como las de China, en abundancia, y

muchos Castaños, aunque es pequeño el fruto q̃ dàn, como el de una bellota de las blãcas. Los pastos, y tierras son en todo parecidas a las de la Florida, que es tierra continente cõ la de Texas; y todo lo q̃ se leè de aquella Provincia en su amenidad, y fertileza, se puede adaptar á esta otra, con poca diferencia. Por la mayor parte es tierra llana, aunque en partes muy montuosa, y no se hallan serranias por todo Texas, pues solo se encuentran algunas listas de lomeria, tirando al Norte. La piedra anda siempre muy escasa, y se halla solamente en algunos respaldos de Arroyos secos, conque no es facil el fabricar de calicanto, aunque se quiera. El temperamento es muy parecido al de España, pues comienza â llover desde Septiembre, y duran las aguas hasta Abril; y los quatro meses restantes, son muy excessivos los calores, y muy raros los aguazeros de este tiempo; y como para lograrse las simenteras, ha de ser con el beneficio de las aguas del Cielo, en siendo escasas, lo son tambien las cosechas. Tiene toda la tierra Rios, y Arroyos perennes, y abundantes, y muchos ojos de agua; pero en el Verano corren tan profundos, que no dàn lugar para sacar sus aguas en assequias; y como la tierra es tan montuosa no descubre lugares cõpetentes para poder cõ la industria regarse; y esta ha sido en todos tiempos la mayor dificultad para q̃ se congreguen los Indios. Hai muchas Lagunas en q̃ se cria abundantemente el Pescado, y estas no son continuas en algunas partes, sino que se forman de las crecientes de los Rios, y Arroyos, por el Invierno; y quando calienta el tiempo, se vàn los Indios à ellas con sus familias, y se mantienen algunos dias, de pescado, y llevan para sus casas muchos Pezes assados en la lumbre, de que participé alugnos, y entre ellos el Pez que llaman Dorado. Lo q̃ mas abunda en aquellos Montes, son los Ciervos, ó Venados, de que tienen su continuo bastimento los Indios, y juntamente con los Pabos de la tierra, á que se juntan por el Invierno muchas Abutardas, Grullas, y en todo el año Perdices, y Codornices, en abundancia.

No viven estos Naturales en congregaciones reducidas à Pueblo, sino q̃ cada parcialidad de las quatro principales, en q̃ se plantaron las Missiones, estàn como en ranchos, dispersos unos de otros, siendo de esto el principal motivo, el que cada familia busca paraje competente para su siembra, y que tenga agua de pie para su gasto, y para bañarse, que es en todos ellos muy continuo. Las casas forman de maderas, con latas muy flexibles, y muy altas; y el modo que tienen para fabricarlas, es de esta suerte: Los dueños de la Casa, quando ya quieren renovarla, avisan à los Capitanes, que llaman en su idioma CADDÍ; y estos, señalado el dia, ordonenan à los Procuradores, que llaman TAMMAS, que corran todas las Casas, dando aviso para que acudan à la fabrica. Suben los dos mandaderos en sus Caballos, que tienẽ ya todos los Texas muchos, desde la primera entrada de los Españoles; y llevando en una mano tanto numero de palillos, como han de ser las latas para la Casa; vàn corriendo la posta, y en cada rancho dàn uno de aquellos palillos, para q̃ el que lo recibe tenga cuidado de cortar su lata, y llevarla limpia, hasta clavarla en el hoyo que le toca. A otro de la Casa, le encarga los varejones correspondientes para irla texiendo; y la correa, que es de cascara de Arbol, y tan fuerte, q̃ por delgada que sea, no se rompe á dos manos. A las Indias, una, u dos de cada casa, les encomiendan el llevar cada una su carga de zacàte, que es mas crecido que los mayores trigos, para cubrir todo el enmaderado. Hecha esta prevencion, se vàn los Tammas à dormir al sitio donde se ha de fabricar, donde los regalan los Caseros; y quando salta la Aurora, comiẽzan â dar voces para concovar la gente prevenida. Al ir rayando el dia, vàn viniendo los Capitanes, y toman sus assientos, sin poner mano en toda la obra, mas que con authorizarla. Salido el Sol, a la primera voz que dà el Mandón, và cada uno corriendo con su lata ombro, y la pone en el hoyo que antes tenia hecho. En medio de las latas, que estàn puestas en figura circular, clavan un madero muy alto, con horquillas, para figura circular, clavan un madero muy alto, con horquillas, para subir por èl; y puestos en lo alto dos Indios, sobre una pequeña cruz de dos maderos, tirando cada uno un lazo, prenden la lata por la punta, en correspondencia una de otra; y assi las vàn atando, como quien forma una media naranja.

Despues ván armando las latas con varejones, todos á un tiempo, y con tanta destreza, que subiendo cada uno por su lata, no tardã una hora en formar la escala de abajo arriba. Entran otros de refrezco cubriendo la casa de zacàte, del gruesso de tres quartas, comenzando à ponerlo de abajo arriba, al contrario de las casas pagizas, que usan los Españoles; y con tanta velocidad, q̃ poco despues de medio dia, estan coronando el Xacal, formando del zacáte bien atado, la figura que les sugiere su imaginativa. Concluida la fabrica, cortan por el pie el horcon dèl medio, y queda figurada la vivienda en el ayre. En todo este tiempo andan los Mandònes cõ sus varas de dos, ó tres ramales, frezcas, y correosas, avivando la gẽte; y el hombre. ó muger que llega tarde, despues de aver comenzado la obra aunque traiga el material que se le avia encomendado, lo sale á recibir; y si es hombre, le dà por los pechos quatro, ô cinco, varazos; y si es muger le descubre la espalda, y hace lo mismo; y esto es, sin excepcion de personas, pues si su misma muger, ó hermana caè en la falta, lleva su penitencia; y ninguno hace duelo de ello, antes se quedan riendo. En todo el tiempo que trabaja el Pueblo, todos los dueños de la Casa estàn ocupados en disponer la comida para todos, teniendo antes prevenida mucha carne de Venados, ó Ciervos, y muchas ollas de maiz molido, que en estas Indias se llama Atóle, y vàn repartiendo desde los Capitanes hasta el ultimo, cõ abundancia, orden, y concierto, porque tienen cajetes de barro mayores, y menores, para dar à grandes, y pequeños; y con esto se disuelve la junta, y se và cada uno á su casa muy contento. La diferencia que hai en fabricar estas Casas es, que para los Capitanes, y principales, se ponen mas latas que las ordinarias, y assi son mucho mayores; pero no se exime, aunque sea el Capitan principal, de darles de comer à todos los q̃ cõcurren; antes sì es cõ mas abũndancia el banquete, y se previene cõ mas tiempo, para quedar sobre todos mas ayroso.

Las sementeras, que hacen los Assinais, son tambien de Comunidad, y comienzan la primera en la Casa de su CHENESI, q̃ es su Sacerdote principal, y el q̃ cuida de la Casa del Fuego, que despues hablarè de ella en su lugar. Despues và à sembrarle al Capitan principal, y se vàn siguiendo todos los demàs por su orden, segun lo determinan los Capitanes en sus juntas. Lo que hacen los Indios juntos, es solo limpiar la tierra, y dejarla cabada cosa de una quarta, que al principio hacian todo esto con Azadones de madera de nogal tostado, y despues con Azadones de fierro, q̃ han adquirido de los Españoles, y de los Franceses, que estàn en Nachitòs. Acabada esta funcion en dos, ó tres horas, los dueños de la casa les dàn su comida con toda abundancia, y se mudan à otra parte para hacer lo mesmo. El sembrar el maiz, y frisoles, con las otras semillas, toca à los Caseros; y de ordinario, quien lo hace, son las Indias viejas, que por ninguna manera permiten el q̃ les ayude alguna India preñada, porque dicen se ha de malograr la cosecha. Dos siembras tienen cada āño: la primera, à fines de Abril, que es quando allà cessan las aguas, y entonces siembran el maiz pequeño, que no sube la caña una vara de altura; pero desde el pie hasta la punta està cargada de mazorquitas muy granadas, y muy pequeñas. A fines de Mayo lavantan esta cosecha, q̃ les sirve de mucho alivio, quando el año ha sido esteril; y en la misma tierra, limpiandola de nuevo, hacen la siembra grande, que no dura para llegar á madurèz mas que hasta fines de Julio, como yo lo experimentè los años que assisti en aquellas Missiones. El frisol siembran con mucha curiosidad; y para que se enrede, y estè libre de animalejos, y de la humedad, le ponen à cada mata su carrizo clavado en tierra, y assi se carga mucho mas, y no les cuesta trabajo al recogerlo, porque lo arrancan con el carrizo, y todo junto lo conducen à sus casas. Tienen en sus viviendas hechos canastos de otatilllos muy grandes, en que recogen el maiz desgranado, y el frisol; y para q̃ no entre la polilla, le van echando sus capas de ceniza bien cernida, y cubren los canastos para libertarlo de los ratones.

Son estos Indios tan providos, que de las mejores mazorcas del maiz, dejandole la hoja, hacē unos atados como trenza, y la cuelgan en un palo cõ horquetas dentro de la casa, en parte que le estè dando el humo; y para esto separan la cantidad que necessitan para sembrar dos años, porque si fuere esteril el primero, no falte semilla para el segundo; y de esto, no tocarán à un grano, aunque les falte del todo el maiz que tenian para el gasto, y mas aína van à buscarlo, haciendo sus cambios en otras rancherias, que lograron cosecha mas abundante. En los años de esterilidad, suplen la falta de mantenimiento cõ la caza de Animàles, y Aves diversas, y con buscar Pescado en los Rios, y Lagunas; y para hacer sus poleadas, muelen una semilla que dà el carrizo, q̃ mas es otatillo hueco; y bien tostada la semilla, que es como granos de trigo, suple por el maiz en sus comidas. El Ganado de Sibola está distante de los Texas mas de quarenta leguas; y para hacer provision de zezinas, van todos los Indios bien armados; porque en esse tiempo, si se encuentran con los Apaches, se matan inhumanamente unos à otros. En estas ocasiones, que de ordinario es por el Invierno, suelen matar muchos Ossos, que hai por la parte del Norte, y traen muchas pellas, embueltas en heno, cargadas en sus Caballos; y despues de derretidas conservan la manteca en ollas, para sus guisados de todo el año. Estos Ossos se mantienen de nuezes, y bellotas, de que abundan todos aquellos Payses, y solo se véèn en Texas, y sus cercanias, quando ha sido poca la nuez, y bellota por la parte del Norte, por los muchos, yelos, y nevadas, como sucedió el año de 22. que fue la primera vez que los alcancé à vèr vivos, tan cerca de la Mission donde estaba, que sin q̃ sirva de jactancia, acompañado de muchos Indios, que con sus Perros tenian subidos dos Ossos en los Arboles: â tiro de escopeta cayeron dos de mi mano, con vala rasa, y otro que venía solo por una vereda, teniendo un roble por resguardo, acerté à darle en la cabeza; y de todos ellos, hicieron su particiõ los Indios, y me dejaron providẽcia de manteca para muchos dias; y es cierto, q̃ para guisar qualquiera cosa, no hace falta con ella otra grossura.

CAP. X.

PROSIGUE LA MATERIA DEL PASSADO, SOBRE LAS SUPERSTICIONES, È IDOLATRIAS DE LOS ASSINAIS

Aquellos Infieles, con quienes anduvo prodiga la naturaleza, haciendolos de buena disposicion, y de hermosas facciones, si con sus costumbres degeneran, siendo en lo interior disformes, son, de Sentencia de Clemente Alexandrino, semejantes à los Templos de los Egypcios. Estos resplandecen en las paredes de piedras muy pintadas por defuera, y en toda la fabrica se encuentra mucha cultura, y adorno; pero si se registra lo interior de los Templos, no se encuentra Dios, aunque se busque, sino un Cocodrilo, una Serpiente, ú otra bestia, ó fiera indigna del Templo, y mas à proposito para tener su habitacion en una inmunda gruta. Tales son todos aquellos, que haciendolos Dios de

buenas facciones, no resplandece en sus almas la hermosa Imagen de
Dios, que como sus criaturas tienen; porque no le adoran, ni conocen,
sino que en su lugar tienen Leones, Ossos, Simias, y otros inmundos
Simulacros de los demonios, á quienes adoran, y dàn culto en su corazon.   De esta calidad contempla mi compassion á los Indios Assinais,
y otras muchas Naciones, q́ hai por aquella parte del Norte; pues
todas, por lo general, son de muy buena disposiciõ corporal, y mucho
mas blancos que los Mexicanos, y Tlascaltecas, naturalmente politicos,
y de buenos entendimientos; pero todas estas prendas las desfiguran
por las muchas idolatrias, y supersticiones, cõ que los tiene ilusos el
demonio, originãdose de Padres à Hijos la falsa creécia de sus herrores;
pues hasta los Niños pequeños, luego que les despunta la razon, estàn
instruidos en las falsedades de sus mayores, que me causaba admiracion
el oìrles razonar todos los Ritos, y supersticiones en q̃ los avian criado
sus Padres.   En toda esta numerosa Nacion de los Assinais, q́ tienen
con el mismo Idioma mas de catorce, ó quince Parcialidades, se tiene
creido, que ay un Capitan Grande allà en el Cielo, à quien llaman
CADDÌ, ò AYO, que es lo mismo, q́ el Capitan de allà arriba; y dicen, q́
este lo crió todo; y para q́ se vea lo inconsequente q̃ proceden, lo
cuentan en esta forma.   Dicen, que en los principios del mundo huvo
una sola muger, y q́ esta tenia dos Hijas, la una doncella, y la otra que
estaba en cinta, sin señalar ni para la Madre, ni para la Hija, hombre
alguno de quien pudiessen procrear.   Un dia, que las dos Hermanas
estaban solas sin la Madre, y la preñada estaba recostada en el regazo
de la doncella, que la espulgaba, se la arrebataron de delante; y fue
assi el sucesso:
    Apareció de repente un Hombre agigãtado, y descomunal, de feroz
aspecto, y con unos cuernos, que no se véian de altos, y á este le
llaman CADDAJA, diablo, ò demonio; y acometiendo â la preñada, la
desgarro cõ sus uñas, y masticandola, se la engullò: entretanto, la
doncella se subió à la copa de un Arbol muy alto; y quando acabó
el diablo de comerse à la Hermana, levantó los ojos á buscar à la
dõcella para hacer lo mismo, y forcejaba por subir; mas no pudiendo,
comenzó con dientes, y uñas a querer cortar el Arbol.   Yo les replicaba
quãdo me contaban esto, quo como siendo tan grandes los cuernos,
q́ se perdian de vista, no alcanzaba con ellos?   Y nunca sabian dar
respuesta.   La doncella, viendo el aprieto en que estaba, se dejò
caer en un charco profundo de agua, que estaba al pie del Arbol,
y zambullendose en èl, fue à salir muy lejos, y se escapó hasta
dõde estaba su Madre.   El descomunal gigante comẽzò á sorver la
agua para agotarla, y hacer pressa de la doncella; pero se halló
burlado, y se fue de aquel puesto.   Diò noticia la doncella à su
Madre de todo lo sucedido, y fueron juntas al sitio donde
avia muerto la otra, y registrando el rastro de la sangre, q́

desperdiciaba el diablo al masticarla, encontrò en una casca-
rilla de bellota una gotilla de sangre, y cubriendola cõ
otra media cascara de lo mismo la abrigò en el seno, y se la llevò
á su casa. Metióla en una tinagita, y bien tapada la boca, la puso
en un rincon; à lo noche sintiò ruido, como q̃ roían la tinaja; y yendo
à registrarla, hallò, que de la sangre se avia congelado un Niño, tan
pequeño como un dedo, Bolvió à taparla, y oyendo el mismo ruido
la noche siguiente, halló q̃ avia crecido hasta la estatura de Hombre
grande: quedó muy gustosa, y le hizo luego su Arco, y sus flechas,
y preguntò por su Madre: dixeronle como se la avia comido el diablo,
y saliò á buscarlo; y quando lo encontró, con la punta del Arco lo
tiró tan lejos, q̃ no pareciò mas. Vinose can su Abuela, y Tia, y les
dixo, que no era bueno estár en la tierra, y se subiò con ellas al
Cᴀᴄʜᴀᴏᴀʏᴏ, que assi llaman al Cielo; y desde allá està desde entonces,
governando todo el mundo; y esta es la primera deidad que reconocen, y à quien ofrecẽ cultos, y temen q̃ les puede premiar, y castigar en
lo bueno, y malo que hicieren.

Tienen con el Fuego particularissimas abusiones, y le tributan
culto. Para esto ay una Casa destinada, en q̃ siempre hai fuego
perpetuo, y tienen destinado un viejo, que tiene cuidado de cebarlo,
y este es el Cʜᴇɴᴇsɪ, ó Sacerdote grande de ellos. Dicen, q̃ en apa-
gandose, se han de morir todos. Esta Casa, q̃ el año de 1716. por
Diciembre renovaron, està entre los medios de los Nᴀɪᴄʜᴀs, y Aɪɴᴀɪs,
y es comun à ambos Pueblos, y dicen ser la Casa del Capitan grande.
Es rotunda, capaz, pajiza, y tiene dentro un docel con estèras formado, y en el assiento de la cama tres petates, dós de ellos muy
pequeños; y á un lado de la puerta sobre tapextles otras estèras embueltas á rollo. Delante de la cama un banquito cõ quatro pies, y
quadrado, de una pieza, algun tanto levantado sobre tierra; y sobre
el banquillo suele aver tabaco, y pipa con algunas plumas, y tiestos
de barro, q̃ demuestran ser incensarios q̃ nutren de cebo, y tabaco.
El fuego, o foguera, la forman siempre, de quatro troncos muy largos,
y pesados, que miran à los quatro vientos principales: la leña le
trae menuda, y està en pyras de la parte de afuera. Aqui se juntan
los Ancianos à sus consultas, y bayles para las guerras, y faltas de
agua para los sementeras, q̃ ordinariamente salen fallidas sus suplicas, y todo fabulas. La ceniza de este fuego, se va amontonando
afuera; y quando hacen traslado de huessos de los enemigos, que han
muerto, los sepultan en estas cenizas. Cerca de esta Casa hai otras
dos pequeñas, a distancia de poco mas de un tiro de escopeta; y
llaman las Casas de los dos Cᴏɴɪɴɪᴄɪs. Estos, dicen, son dos muchachos, ò niños pequeños, q̃ embiò desde el Cᴀᴄʜᴀᴏ ᴀʏᴏ, ò el Cielo, su
gran Capitan, para q̃ consultassen sus dudas con ellos; y fingen, que
estuvieron en estas Casas, hasta que avrà poco mas de dos años,

segun unos (y fue al tiempo que se hallaban en Mexico dos Religiosos
de la Cruz, negociando la entrada á los Texas) ò segun la India
Interprete quãdo los enemigos Yojuanes quemaron estas Casas,
dicen, los vieron subir por el humo arriba, y no han bajado mas.
En estas casillas estàn dos petaquillas como de tres quartas cõ sus
tapaderas de carrizo pintado, y curiosas, levãtadas sobre uno como
Altar de madera, cõ quatro horconcillos.

Dentro, registré con otro Religioso, aver en las petacas quatro, ò
cinco platillos, ó vasijas de madera negra, como escudilla rotunda, y
todo muy curiosamente labrado, con sus quatro pies, unos de hechura
de Patos pequeños, cõ cabeza, y cauda de Pato: otros con cabeza, cauda,
y pies de Caymàn, ó Lagarto. Ademàs de esto, muchas plumas de
todos tamaños, y colores; y unas martas de plumas de Pavos terrestres,
pluma blanca de pechuga suelta, y algunos emboltorios de penachos
de plumas, coronas de pieles, y pluma, y virrete de lo mismo, con
muchos huessecillos de Grullas, que sirven de flautas, ò pifanos, y
otras de carrizo, laborcadas, y cõ sus agujerillos al proposito, y otros
muchos instrumẽtillos, que usan en sus mitotes, ó bayles. Está una
de estas casillas muy bien barrida, y cuidada, donde estan estas dos
petaquillas. La Casa del Fuego es la de los Ainais como la Parro-
quia, ò Cathedral; y otra en los Naichas, y otra en los Nacocdochis,
y Nazonis; y de este fuego se llevo á aquellas Casas: lo ordinario es,
juntarse en Mezquita los Naichas, y Ainais: y los Nacocdochis, y
Nazonis en la otra Mezquita que hai en Nacocdochi, à sus particulares
Fiestas de el Año. Todas las Casas, ò las mas de ellas, se sirven de
el fuego de aquella principal Casa, no por q́ lo lleven todos los dias de
ella, sino porque quando se fabricaron, se llevó de alli, y lo cõservan; y
si alguna vez se apaga, tienen por presagio de averse de morir toda
aquella familia; y lo traẽ de nuevo de la Casa de la Mezquita con
muchas ceremonias, que dirè en su lugar. Al fuego lo temen mucho
q́ se enoje, y le tributan el primer Tabaco, primicias del maiz, de la
carne que matan, y de todas sus cosechas: dàn á entender q́ el fuego
los criò à ellos. Aũque alucinados, tambien dicen, q́ salieron los Hom
bres del Mar, y se repartieron por toda la tierra: à estos Criadores
llamã Niacaddi, al Agua, y Fuego; mas siempre acuden al fuego en
todas sus funciones. Dicen, que en los principios avia en la tierra
muchos demonios q́ los mataban, y haciã muchos daños, q́ eran agigan-
tados, y horribles: y tambien dicen ser ellos descendientes de Ossos,
otros de Perros, otros de Nutrias, y otros de Coyotes, ô Raposas; y
preguntandoles la razon, respondian:

Que sus antepassados, viendo los males que les hacian estas Fantas-
mas, ò demonios, se transformaron en dichos Animàles; y con todo
esso, eran hombres, mugeres, y niños racionales. Tienen estos Indios
mucha luz de la inmortalidad de la Alma, y la confiessan: y se conoce

esto, en los entierros, y honras funerales que hacen, en esta forma:
Amortajan el cuerpo difunto, bañandole primero, cõ las mejores ropas
que tienen, ó con gamuzas nuevas; y teniẽdolo algunas horas en su
propria casa, donde hai, entretanto, muchos lamentos, le previenen
mucho pinóle, maiz, y de todo lo que hai comestible; y juntamente, si
es hombre, le aparejan su Arco, y flecha, y cuchillo, con lo demàs que
acà necessitaba; y si es muger, todos sus ministriles mugeriles de canas-
tillas, instrumentos de moler, y vasijas de barro; porque dicen los
han menester allà dõde vàn.   Y preguntandoles adonde vàn las Almas
de los que mueren?   Dicen, ǵ caminan luego que salen de los cuerpos
ázia un lado del Poniente, y de allá suben otra vez por el ayre, y passan
por cerca de donde esta el Capitan grande, que nombran CADDI AYO; y
de alli van à parar â una Casa, sita à la parte del Sur, que dicen
es la Casa de la Muerte.   Y què muerte sera sino la eterna?   Alli
imaginan, ó los persuaden sus viejos, ǵ estàn todos muy contentos, y
que no hai hambre, enfermedades, ni otras penas; y que se quedan todos
en el estado que los cogió la muerte: desuerte, ǵ si una muger murió
estando en cinta, siempre está allá ocupada; y si murió con una criatura à los pechos, allà la anda cargando; y á este modo otras erroneas
inconsequencias.   Mas no dicen buelven marido, y muger à hacer vida
maridable.   Preguntè con advertencia, si todos iban á este lugar sin
pena?   Y me dixeron que sì: menos los malos; y solo tienen por tales
á sus enemigos, que estos vàn â la Casa del TEXINO, ǵ es el diablo; y
allà los castiga mucho: no tienen por dignos de el Infierno á los adul-
teros, sodomiticos, y concubitores, ni ladrones, sino solo concibẽ maldad
sensible, en quanto al corporal agravio: y assi todos los ǵ quãdo mueren
se les hace su entierro cõ las fingidas deprecaciones de sus Santones,
dicen vàn al descanso, y se les acaba lo malo que hicieron: mas si no les
rezan, los lleva el diablo à su casa: mas de una, ù otra manera, allà
van â dar.

Las honras, ó funerales de los que murieron en la guerra, ò ausentes
de sus casas, las hacẽ en esta forma: Combidan toda la gente para el
dia señalado, y previenen bastante comida de lo que dà el tiempo;
y distante como un tiro de piedra de la casa, disponen una pyra de
leña menuda; y juntos todos, estàn hombres, y mugeres dolientes tira-
dos en sus camas, muy desgreñados; y entrãdo un Capitan de los Santones, habla pocas razones con ellos; y luego comienza un llanto, mas
proprio le dirèmos ahullido, á que corresponden las mugeres todas
plañidoras.   Salen hasta siete hombres fuera de la casa, y bueltos de
cara al Oriente, rezan sus oraciones, teniendo delante una basija
pequeña cõ maiz molido, y mojado; y acabada la deprecacion del viejo
principal, toman de la ollita parte del maiz mojado, y lo esparcen à
los quatro vientos, y lo restante se lo comen tres de ellos, que sirven
de Padrinos del funeral, y bueltos adentro, renuevan el clamor los

dolientes. Sientanse todos los Capitanes por su orden, y los Padrinos se assientan jŭto á los del duelo, y vàn ofreciendo à un viejo Santon, tabaco, y arina de maiz; y tomandolo, dà una buelta al fuego, que està en medio de la casa, reza su embolismo, y echa en el fuego algo del tabaco, y harina, y buelve à entregarlo à los Padrinos. Passado esto, salen dos, ó tres Indios, y entriegã un Arco, y flechas á la muger, ò Madre del difunto; y luego, desde los Capitanes, uno por uno, vàn ofreciendo â los del duelo, ya seis, ya ocho flechas, segun el afecto de cada uno. Siguense las mugeres, q́ van dando el pesame, y cõtribuyendo sus sartas de abalorio, cuchillo, ó ropa; y de todo junto, añadiendo gamuzas muy buenas, y todas las alhajas que fueron del difunto, hacen su emboltorio, y lo cubren con una estèra, q́ hace rollo; y entretãto, està cantando un viejo, y otro mancebo, en tono muy funesto, y á compàz; y uno de los Padrinos saca en ombros el emboltorio: otro lleva fuego, y otro un manojo de zacáte seco, y llegãdo à la pyra prenden por todas partes fuego, y echan encima la estèra cõ todas las flechas, y ropa, y las reducen â cenizas, sirviẽdo de doble de campanas la confussa griteria de los dolientes, y amigos, miẽtras otros del corrillo están riendo, y chacoteando. Corona toda la funcion la comida q́ repartẽ â todos, y acabada queda la compañia deshecha. Todo esto dicen, es para que vaya la alma à la casa del descanso, ó para q́ quando venga â vèr su cuerpo, halle lo que se hizo con él.

CAP. XI.

OTROS VARIOS RITOS, QUE OBSERVAN CON MUCHA PUNTUALIDAD ESTOS INDIOS ASSINAIS

Desde que nace una Criatura, comienzan á exercitar con ella los Santones diversas ceremonias, que parece querer remedar con ellas el bautismo. A los seis, ú ocho dias del nacimiento, avisan á uno de sus Sacerdotes; y viniendo à la Casa, toma su particular assiento, y le ponẽ en las manos el recien nacido, à quien hace muchas caricias, y le està hablando á la oreja mucho rato: despues lo baña todo entero en una grande basija, y le pregunta à sus Padres, q́ nombre se le ha de poner; y de ordinario, el que le señalan es diminutivo del q́ tienen sus Padres: si es muger, hace este mismo oficio con ellas una vieja decrepita, que es tambien saludadora; y de toda esta chusma hai bastante copia, que tienen como repartidas sus feligresias; y para concluir la funcion, les tributan sus regalos por modo de obenciones; y aquel dia se come de lo que tienen, esplendidamente. Entre estas Gentes dura el matrimonio miẽtras no desconforman las voluntades; q́ entonces, se buscan ambos otro cõsorte. No se celebra con particulares ceremonias la mutua entrega, aunque anteriormente se grangean las voluntades de los Padres, o Hermanos de la Novia, con traerles algunos Ciervos, ó Venados, que les dejan â la puerta de su casa, sin hablar otra palabra; y si lo meten adentro, y lo comen, es la señal mas cierta de que prestan su consentimiento; y no hai que esperar la espontanea voluntad de la Novia, pues esta se refunde en el querer de sus Padres: conque se juntan, como dice el Padre Acosta de los del Perú, al modo de los Animàles. En quanto á la fidelidad, algunos hacen duelo si se les falta en ella, y castigan à sus mugeres con azotes; otros, ó no hacen caso, o se hacen de la vista gorda; pues ordinariamente, entre los mismos Indios hai poco reparo en q́ sus mugeres tengan llanezas, y juegos cõ los de su misma Nacion; y no se hace caso de que hablen con toda libertad unos con otros, cõ chanzas, y donayres provocativos, antes lo celebran como si fuessen chistes muy agudos, en q́ se conoce la mucha obscenidad en que viven sumergidos.

De la peste de Curanderos, y Medicos sylvestres, està contaminada toda esta tierra, y estos son un mixto de abusion, y mentiras, con mucha parte de brujeria, que hasta aora no se sabe si es formal. Tienen estos mata-sanos particulares insignias, de plumeros en la cabeza, y gargantillas curiosas de pieles de viboras, muy pintadas, y en las casas su banco señalado, q́ es mas alto que el de los Capitanes. Para curar un enfermo, hacen una quantiosa hoguera, previenen sus pifanos, y un abanico de plumas: los instrumentos son unos palillos labrados, y con fizuras, al modo de un cascabel de vibora; y este palillo puesto en hueco sobre un cuero, hace consonancia de nada menos, que infierno. Antes de tocarle, beben sus yervas recocidas, cõ mucha espuma, y comienza à hacer su bayle sin mudarse de un puesto, y acompaña la musica de infierno, canto de cõdenado, que solo allà tendrà simil la desentonada algarabia, q́ hace el Curandero; y dura la funcion desde media tarde hasta cerca de la Aurora. Interpola el canto para hacer sus crueles medicamentos; pues al triste paciente, que ya lo tienen en parrillas con muchas brasas, que estan cebando debajo de las camas, le comienza à chupar las entrañas, aziendole del estomago, con los labios, q́ le pegan al espinazo, con la cabeza; y entre tristes quexidos, dà á entender el blando medicamento q́ le aplican. Vàn los Medicos chupando, y escupiendo; y llevando prevenida sangre, ó gusanos, los toman en la boca, y dicen los sacan del cuerpo del enfermo. Lo cierto es, que le chupan la substancia corporea, de quantas cosas apetecibles tiene, conque les pagan (viva, ò muera el enfermo) sus crueles curaciones, que duran mientras hai mucho que comer, y que agarrar. A otros enfermos los sajan con pedernales, por el higado, y les chupã en realidad la sangre: y lo mismo hacen cõ los picados de viboras, escupiendo lo que entre los labios aprietan; y esto, aún es tolerable, pues surte naturalmente su efecto. Ellos adivinan (segũ dicen) si es de muerte el enfermo; y si es algun principal, hai junta de Medicos, y cada uno hace empeño de hacer su desatino.

Bien es verdad, q̃ entre tanto desvario, algunas curaciones puedẽ suceder naturalmente; por quãto aplican yervas medicinales, de que abunda la tierra, q̃ es continente con la de la Florida; y en esto tienen mucho conocimiento de ellas: pero los cantos, y bayles, no pueden ser curacion de los enfermos.

La abundancia de bebidas amargas, que toman los Curanderos, fingiendo ser de provecho a los dolientes, es ilusion fantastica; pues solo se reservò este modo de curacion, para aquel Divino Medico, que para sanar nuestras dolencias, tomó à pechos la amarga pocion de la hiel, y vinagre; y siendo su Magestad el desangrado, fuimos nosotros los q̃ logramos una salud eterna. Acontece tambien, ser el dolor, ó enfermedad por algũ tumor, ò hinchazon; y á estate dolencia aplican el madurativo del pedernal, y la ventosa de sus labios. Hacen creer estos à toda la Nacion, que las enfermedades tienen origen de maleficio, q̃ les hacen los Indios comarcanos de las Naciones BIDAIS; AYS, y YACDOAS, que abundan de mata-sanos, Estos (dicen los ASINAIS) por ser malevolos, ó Brujos, vienen ocultamente, ó envian desde sus tierras la enfermedad q̃ llaman AGUAIN: y para saber su ethimologia, es una cosa aguda, ò q̃ tiene punta azicalada como saeta, y esta viene disparada del Arco del que llaman TEXINO, y nosotros llamamos diablo, que la assesta al doliente; y para sacar esta punta, ó saeta, que dicen es como una aguja gruessa de color blanco, y pequeña, son los bayles, cantos, y madurativos, que vàn insinuados: y antes de hacerlos, invocan à los Curanderos BIDAIS, en su ayuda; y dicen, vienen â socorrerlos en forma de Buhos, ò Tecolotes, que el demonio les trahe en semejantes ocasiones; y son en tres especies en esta tierra; y al oìr el èco del Buho, levantan la algazara, como si ya huviessen conseguido una victoria. Añaden à este, otro desatino, de que el falso Dios, que llaman YNICI, viene movido de sus cantos, y deprecaciones, à auxiliarlos. Son estos Curanderos el mobil de todas sus estratagemas, y embustes. Ellos recitan, ó regañan entre dientes unos desatinados disparates, puestos de cara à un palo de los de la casa; y despues tomando Tabaco, lo echan al fuego; y de la carne q̃ trahen de Cybola, parten una pitanza, y esta và à el fuego, y otros menudos pedazos tiran àzia los quatro vientos, á quienes hacen la salva en todas sus funciones al chupar, arrojando una bocanada de humo à cada viẽto; y el primero es â lo alto al Capitan de arriba, que no es otro, que el q̃ cayò de lo alto en el abysmo.

Toca à estos Curanderos tomar la mensura para fabricar las Casas; hallarse en la bẽdicion de las nuevas fabricas, y ser de los primeros en todas las funciones de atragantarse. Siendo tãta la copia de estos embaydores, aun sin cortar la muerte alguna cabeza à esta Hydra, le brotan á cada passo cabezas, en nuevos Ministros de la mentira, que lo son unos Mocetones, que apenas llegan à los veinte años; y por aver quiẽ quiera graduarlos, les sobrã meritos para salir

muy perítos. Juntãse muchos viejos de los Recitantes, ò Santones,
con chusma de Cirujanos, y vestidos de fiesta con lo que tienen, dán
sus bebidas al nuevo Matasanos, y le brindan mucho tabaco, ỹ junto
con las bebidas, le hace perder el juicio, hacer visajes, y caer en tierra
como un ebrio; quedalo, ó en realidad, ó en ficcion, y assi està veinte
y quatro horas tenido por muerto, hasta que le dâ gana de bolver
en sî, suspirando; y cuenta lo que soñò, ó lo que le sugerió la imagi-
nacion; y dicẽ se fue muy lejos la alma. Despues comienza su canto,
y musica desconcertada, que vâ continuando por ocho dias, ayudado
de otro tal Cirujano, interpolando las mugeres concurrentes alarido
confuso; y entre estas canciones, dàn assalto à las ollas, ỹ nunca cessan
de atizar à la lumbre, festejãdo sus vientres, miẽtras el nuevo Medico
alegra con sus bayles, y cantos al cõcurso. Estos Medicos son muy
atendidos, y respectados de todos, y en su estimacion son los oraculos
de sus embaymientos: y en la verdad, no pudo el demonio, ỹ es el
Cathedratico de esta fulleria, dexarles mejor patrimonio para desfru-
tar de los ASSINAIS la mejor carne, las primicias de los frutos, y el
que les fabriquen sus casas, y acudan cõ presteza à sus siembras, ỹ
es entre las miserias de estos Naturales, la mayor felicidad à que
aspiran. Entre los NACOCDOCHES, que son tambien ASSINAIS, suele la
Medicina tener por remuneracion la muerte, quando, ò no se acierta la
cura, ò vuela la fama de ser maligno el Curandero; que entonces
los parientes del que murió à manos de sus ruines medicamentos,
estrenan en el Medico sus garras, dandole con un madero en las sienes,
sin darle lugar á que se cure. Son, en fin, estos Cirujanos, el mayor
obice à la conversion de muchos, que si no temieran sus amenazas,
recibieran con amor el Santo Bautismo.
    Persuaden â los dolientes, que con la agua Santa del Bautísmo se
les quita la vida; y quando à escusas de ellos se ha bautizado alguno,
suelen desampararlo, pretextando, que por averles echado la agua
Santa, avia tomado tãto cuerpo la enfermedad, que no podia desvara-
tarlo todo su estudio. Muchos de estos desamparados, acudian à
buscar algun remedio entre los Españoles; y por misericordia de
Dios, despues de deshauciados de los suyos, los vimos convalecer, y
cobrar salud perfecta. De todo finge el demonio; y de Medicos, ó
Cirujanos, hace que se gradùen sus discipulos de Astrologos. Por
el Mes, ò Luna de Febrero, à quiẽ llaman SACABBÍ, se hace una junta general de todo el Pueblo; y aviẽdo prevenido caza de Conejos,
Gatos montezes, Venados, Pavos sylvestres, Tejones, y carne seca,
ỹ guardan entre año: y las Indias, su porcion de maiz remolido,
hecho arina, y otros, ministriles de bocolica, ỹ dà la tierra, comiẽzan
su funcion á la mañana, estando dentro de la Casa, donde concurren
todos los Capitanes, y Cirujanos viejos, y perítos: dos, ó tres de estos,
passan la mañana en apurar la CASINA, ỹ son hojas de Laurel reco-

sidas, y tocan sus tragadas los Viejos de la Mesta: y despues, bueltos
de cara à un madero de la Casa, hacen sus deprecaciones, dirigidas al
Capitan de lo alto; y tomando una ala de Aguila, que llaman Ygui,
hacen con ella sus cantos, y bayles, y la tienē muy compuesta: saludan
entretanto al fuego, cõ echarle tabaco molido, y anda continuamente
de mano en mano la pipa de tabaco; y despues hacen demonstracion
de q̃ aquella Aguila de quien son las plumas, sube á lo alto à consultar
con el Capitan que allá està, el pronostico del año; y aviendo los
viejos hecho su Almanaque à solas, y entre dientes, salen á manifes-
tarlo, ó divulgarlo á lo publico: diciendo, v. g. que este Año (como
me lo dixeron) de 718. ferá muy abundante de nuezes, y bellotas; pero
no de maizes, por q̃ faltarian al mejor tiempo las aguas.   El año que
hai muchas garrapatas (y las hai todos los años) dicen, que avrà
abundancia de frisoles.   En lloviendo mucho por Marzo, y Abril,
dicen, seràn por Junio, Julio, y Agosto, muy cortas las aguas: y salen
tan verdaderos sus pronosticos, que suelen perderse, por abundancia
de lluvias, las simenteras.

Por muchas cosas, que naturalmente suceden, pronostican futuros
contingentes.   Si al tiempo q̃ la gente anda en busca del ganado de
Cibola, ó en demanda de sus Enemigos en la guerra acontece venir
muchos paxarillos pequeños, dàn por assentado vienen ya cerca
los ausentes: llaman à estos paxarillos Banit.   Quando salen à
la guerra, hacen juntas generales en casa de un Capitan, y dán bebe-
dizos à uno de los tenidos por mas valiente, hasta que pierda, ó
finja perder el juicio; y este, despues de un dia, y noche, dice,
viò donde estaban los enemigos, y si prevenidos, ó no: y de aqui
presagian sus fingidas victorias.   Hacen lo mismo en el camino,
quando salen à sus jornadas, y cõ una cola de Zorra formã Astro-
labio, para vèr los sucessos futuros: y todos sus bayles, deprecaciones, y loquelas à la lumbre, surten tan buen efecto, que el Año
passado siendo el pronostico, de que vencerian á los Yojuanes sus
contrarios, salieron los de Naicha apocados, desbaratados, y con per-
dida de muchos que quedaron cautivos.   Tienen por cosa assentada,
q̃ si por el Invierno soplan la lumbre cõ algun aventador, ó abanico
de plumas, que luego vendrà tal nieve, ó frio, q̃ los acabarà á todos; y
muchas veces viendonos à nosotros avivar la lumbre cõ alguno de
estos instrumentos, nos lo querian quitar de las manos, y decian que
eramos necios, ó locos en hacer tal cosa; y que no temiamos, porque
estabamos cubiertos de ropa: aprentandoles con razones de su abusion, decian, que era otra lumbre, ó fuego el nuestro, por ser sacado
con pedernal, y fierro, y el de los Assinais con palos, estregado uno
cõ otro.   Poco tiempo hà, que preguntanadoles la causa de no ausen-
tarse todos de sus casas en estas Missiones de Ainai, y Naicha,
aunque sea el tiempo de la Cibola (como se ausentan los Nazonis, y

Nacocodochis) me respondió un Santon, que por no dejar perecer el fuego, si le faltasse el nutriměto; y ques los Nazonis, y Nacocdochis tenian otro fuego diverso, q̃ sacan de dos palillos, estregando uno con otro; y este fuego en virtud, dejaban en sus casas colgado; y por esso no se moriã: mas los Ainais, y Naichas, tenian fuego de sus ante-passados; y esta tradicion conservan hasta aora.

CAP. XII.

En que se incluyen otros Ritos, y se describen las funciones publicas.

Para comenzar à comer del maiz nuevo, llaman de cada casa uno de los Santones; y mientras, arrimado â un poste de la casa, martaja entre diětes sus deprecaciones, se corta alguna porcion de los nuevos frutos: parte se assa, y parte se muele en los morteros para atóles; y acabada la deprecacion, presentan de aquellas viandas al Anciano, que echando particulas de la pitanza al fuego, se echa à pechos lo restante, que suele hacer pausa para concluir, por ser la porcion considerable; no faltan à esta funcion conocidos, y familiares, assi de la parentela, como de casa del Santon; y todas juntas quedan ya dadas estas primicias, con salvo conducto para dar, y comer quãto gustaren. Tienen dichos Santones, muy assentada entre estos Indios, la creencia, que si antes de hacer ellos su depreccacion, alguno grande, ó pequeño, corta de las simenteras elote, ú hoja de la caña del maiz, sin duda serà mordido de culebra: y hasta à los Perros alcanza esta cõminacion, ó entredicho; y assi, para que no coman del maiz, les atan la una mano, ó brazuelo al cuello, y andãdo en tres pies, andan de hambre à la quarta, por que no alcanzan à los elòtes, de que son aficionados en extremo. Y como tal vez, por accidente, acontece picar à alguno una vibora, aviendo comido, antes de la referida diligencia, confirman con este acaso, ser cierto el fingido embaymiento. Antes de salir á cazar Venados ponen en un poste de sus casas pajizas, una cabeza de Venado seca, con cuello, y hastas, y estan deprecando á su Caddi Ayo, les ponga á las manos la pressa; y à pausas, de tabaco molido, q̃ alli previenen, echan parte al fuego; y hecha esta diligencia, (que dura mas de hora) ponen à la puerta del Xacal dicha cabeza; y con otra en la misma forma, vàn al campo à cazar, envijandose de tierra blanca el cuerpo desnudo; y en aviendo hecho caza, parten al Venado muerto, y le estan algun tiempo hablando al oìdo (no sé què enigma encierra esto) y cargan con èl para casa, arrojandole de golpe cerca de la puerta, mientras los caseros hacen anotomia de èl; y observan, q̃ el q̃ lo mata no lo come, sino es q̃ otro le combide, o no tenga otra cosa conque saciar su vientre.

Antes de comenzar la simentera, se dá aviso à todas las mugeres para prevenir sus comidas en dia señalado; y se juntan todas,

ancianas, mozas, y niñas; y de corteza menuda del carrizo, ꝗ està para
este dia prevenida por una vieja, que es la que capitanèa esta fiesta,
forman dos, ò tres estèras, y las entriegan á un Indio Capitan, quien
las ofrece á la Casa del Fuego, para ꝗ aquel año aya buenas cosechas:
y concluye la funcion con comer juntos lo que en particular traìan
de sus casas â este intento; y assi se disuelve la junta. Tambien hai
junta general de hõbres, y mugeres, en casa de un Capitan, donde hai
casa pequeña del fuego, y alli cortan madera para hacer azadones,
que es de nogal negro, limpian un espacio de tierra, como tiro
de piedra en circuito, recojen mucha leña, que dejan hecha pyra; y de
Venados assados, harina de maiz, y otras cosas comestibles ꝗ traen
prevenidas, reparten gustosos, y se van para sus casas muy festivos.
Del primer corte del tabaco (ꝗ nunca dejan llegar â sazon) anda
muy diligente un TAMMA, ꝗ es mandón, ú oficial entre ellos, reco-
giendo las primicias, que entrega â un Capitan, á quien toca repeler
las tempestades con sus conjuros, hacer suplicas para las lluvias, y
ser el primero en bẽdecir à su usanza los nuevos frutos; y à este,
respectan mucho, y cuidan de assistirle â su simentera. Funcion
despues de las cosechas, es una junta entre los Indios, la mas celebre,
y de mayor cõcurso, porque solo quedan uno, ú dos en las casas à
cuidarlas, de las viejas, ó enfermos. Dase aviso por los Mandones,
algunos dias antes, para ꝗ vengan de todas las familias los que han
de ofrendar en la fiesta. Concurren primero, seis dias antes, los
hombres, à casa de un Capitan (que es donde hai Mezquita pequeña,
y donde antes tenian despejado el sitio) y estando dentro solos los
viejos recitantes, y los que les ministran sus bebidas de Cazina tibia,
y espumosa, ordena el viejo, ꝗ hace oficio de CHENESI, ó Sacerdote,
salgan por todos vientos â cazar Venados los mozetones, y gente
fuerte, assegurandoles los cogeràn breve, por quedar èl haciendo
suplicas, con los viejos, â su Capitan de arriba, ó CADDI AYO: y si
cazan dos, ò tres, todos vienen á dicha casa; y lo mismo hacen los dias
siguiẽtes; y excepto las entrañas, y cabeza: lo restante de carne, se
prepara astada para la futura funcion. Venido el dia de ella, sacan
todo lo mejor ꝗ tienen de ropas de bayetas, que guardan intactas, à
este intento, gamuzas muy tiernas, y con fluecos orlados de cuentecillas
blancas, y otras gamuzas muy negras, curiosamente salpicadas de
dichas cuentas, pulseras, y gargantillas, que solo este dia, y en dias
de funcion les sirven; y van concurriendo á la Casa dicha, donde
la tarde antes estàn prevenidas las cosas necessarias â la fiesta.
    Es de noche, por la Luna creciente de Septiembre, y â prima noche
yá està dentro de la casa el concurso de viejos Santones, Medicos, y
Capitanes del Pueblo, los domesticos, y oficiales que se necessitan; y
los demàs que van llegando, se alojan à la parte de afuera por sus
familias: donde forman luminarias, assi para alumbrarse, como para

el frio, q̃ comienza ya á sentirse.   Despues de recitar entre dientes dos
de los viejos sus oraciones, puestos en pie por mas de hora, toman
tabaco, y echan al fuego, q̃ està en medio de la Casa, y de la carne
assada alguna partecilla; y sentados en sus bancos, dán al resto de
carne prevenida, un assalto entre todos los Capitanes, Medicos, y
Ancianos, y vàn interpolando sus bebidas de Azebuche recocido, q̃
les dán en un Vaso de barro hasta tres y quatro porciones, y descansan
en sus bancos, sentados por su orden, tomando pipas de tabaco, que
corre por todos, cebandola á pausas; y arrojan de la primera bocanada,
humo, primero ázia arriba, luego àzia la tierra, y despues â los
quatro vientos: entretanto, junta toda la gente, se và aproximando la
media noche, y cerca del Galicanto, comienza un pregonero â llamar
por su orden de todas las familias, van entrando de tres en tres una
muger de cada casa, y entriegan una olla pequeña, ó canastilla de
maiz hecho harina, muy remolida, y algunas bolas, que llaman BAJAN,
hechos à modo de alfajor duro (y se componen de maiz tostado,
y semilla de Gyrasoles) y vàn los mayordomos depositandolo todo
en dos canastos grandes de por sì; y por este orden vàn llamando,
y ofreciendo todas las casas, y familias.   Esto concluido, se reparte
aquella ofrenda entre viejos, Capitanes, y Oficiales del Pueblo: y
pausa algun tiempo la funcion, mientras unos mozetones duermen,
y otros en chusma cantan con sus instrumentos para espantar el sueño,
porque hai en no dormir aquella noche, mucho esfuerzo.

De media noche en adelante, està de vigilia, ó centinela, un Indio de
los mandones, observando quando las Cabrillas se ponen perpendicu-
lares en el Cielo, respecto del sitio de la Casa, (llaman á estas Estrellas
las SANATES: esto es, las mugeres, porque les finge el demonio, que las
siete Estrellas son gente) y entonces avisa al viejo Santon principal,
que và con otro tal, à un circulo, q̃ tienen formado de carrizos verdes,
clavados en la tierra, y una gran foguera, que atizan continuamente,
tres, ó quatro mozetones; y sentados en cabezera los dos Ancianos, que
sirven de Maestros de Capilla: siguense por su orden, à la mano
siniestra, las mugeres ancianas, en primera ala, ò fila, detràs las casadas
mozas, y solteras; y arrimadas al circulo las de menor edad, y las
niñas enfrente de este circulo: à la parte del Levànte està una enramada,
con hoguera dentro, donde salen uno en pòs de otro, tres viejos, con
lo mejor q̃ pueden, de vestidos, ó cibolas curiosas, y comienza el canto de
los del circulo, viejos, y mugeres, mientras con gran pausa, passo à passo
baylando, se acercan los tres viejos al circulo; y luego que entran, pausa
el canto de dentro, y el viejo delantero hace un razonamiento de pura
algarabia, en vóz apresurada, y alta, sin decir razon concertada; y al
punto presentan delante, sin lenvantarse las Indias, ollitas de harina
de maiz, y bollos de varios granos, cada una la suya; y prosigue el
canto de los de adétro, y los viejos se buelven en silencio: mientras, los

mozetones à carrera cargan al sitio frontero con las ofrendas. Esto mismo repiten passada una hora, poco menos, y solo el canto, y musica de los dos viejos, y mugeres, es mas continuado, aunque passan algunos ratos, hasta que llega la Aurora, que entonces avivan mas los unos, y los otros, con musica de guaje, ô calabaza con piedrecillas dentro, conque forman el són, y acompañan con voces. Luego que va amaneciendo, cessa este canto, y reparten entre estos cinco viejos lo que se há congregado de las ofrendas. Passada esta cantilena, mudan de jornada, esperando todos la venida del Sol de aquel dia, embian algunos mozos, y muchachos que andan en el monte proximo, como llamando, ò dando voces al Sol, para que apressure su venida; y luego al punto que comienza à rayar, salen todos corriendo cõ algazara, muy festivos; y parece, que, o le dàn gracias por la passada cosecha, ó le convidan para que assistan à sus carreras, q̃ comienzan luego, estando en ala todos los de una estatura, ó edad; y dando señal de partirse, todos corren á quien mas puede, y dán buelta á un Arbol, q̃ estarà mas que tiro de Escopeta, y buelven adonde salieron, y continúan dos, y tres bueltas, hasta q̃ serinden; y à su proporcion los muchachos, y niñas hacen despues lo mismo.

Estàn todos los parientes muy atentos à quien aventaja, y este lleva los lauros de fuerte; y por los q̃ quedan traseros, ó cansados, sin perficionar la carrera, levantan sus mugeres, y parientes, un doloroso llanto; porque dicen, q̃ aquellos quando salgan á la guerra, por poco agiles, quedaràn, ó presos, ò cautivos, ò muertos de sus enemigos. Dura esto como mas de hora: despues, teniendo un madero enterrado, y en hueco, y cubierto de verdes ramas por cima, eligen ocho Indias robustas, que sentadas à proporcion con unos maderos, à dos manos, forman atambor del madero hueco, al compàz de la calabaza, que tocan los viejos, y los cantores, y cantatrices, q̃ seràn mas de veinte; y toda esta musica es, para el bayle, que hace todo el concurso, ancianas, mozas, hombres, niños, y niñas: puestos à circulo, los hombres en parejo de las mugeres, de cara, sin dar saltos mas que con los pies, à un tiempo; y en esta honrada friolera cõsumen el tiempo, hasta medio dia, que bien fatigados, y somnolentos, parte cada uno para su casa á tomar descanso de el penoso entretenimiento.

En las ocasiones, que estos Indios alcanzan victoria de sus contrarios, traẽ las cabezas por despojo, y las tienen juntas en un Arbol, pendientes, hasta que con decurso de tiempo, determinan darles sepultura. Para esto, se cõgregan una noche señalada, hombres, y mugeres, en el sitio donde estàn las calaberas, forman varias fogueras; y preparados los instrumentos lugubres y funestos, se disponen los Cantores, y Capilla, tiznados de carbon; y assentados en tierra, con voz muy triste, è inclinada la cabeza, cantan à compàz, y cubiertos de pieles de pies à cabeza, baylan, sin moverse de un lugar, las mugeres en ala, y à parte los hombres; y dura esto, la mayor parte le la noche: siguese despues, q̃ un decrepito anciano, con otros mozetones, al rededor del Arbol donde estàn las calaberas, can una flecha en la mano, puestos á uno de los vientos dàn una voz ó alarido: passã assi à los otros vientos, y hacen lo mismo: y de quando en quando disparan una escopeta ázia las calaberas, y levantan al traquido confussa vozeria todos juntos. Llegada la mañana, se envijan de tierra blanca los rostros, y brazos, y llevan à sepultar las calaberas al Cenizero, q̃ està immediato à la Mezquita del Fuego, en que gastan en varias ceremonias lo restante del dia: toda la funcion parece cosa de Infierno, assi en los cantos, como en el aparato q̃ se representa: y ofrecen á las calaberas pinole molido, y de otras cosas comestibles, q̃ en lugar de los muertos consumen los vivos, despues de hechas sus deprecaciones, y supersticiosas ceremonias.

Tienen estos Indios una fiesta por los principios de Mayo, muy parecida á la que usan algunas Aldeas de la Europa; pues segun refiere el Thesoro de la Lengua Castellana, suelen los mozos Zagàles, el primer dia de Mayo, poner en la Plaza, ú en otra parte, un Olmo desmochado, con solo el remate vestido de hojas, y se festejan en èl con varios juegos, y carreras, diciendo aver celebrado el Mayo. A este modo los Indios Texas, para celebrar esta funcion del Mayo, previenen un Pino muy alto, delgado, y muy derecho; y despues de averlo descortezado, dejando solo el remate, lo clavan en la tierra en medio de un campo muy llano, y forman dos veredas muy dilatadas, limpiando el suelo para correr con mas ligereza, y estas vàn à rematar por detràs del Arbol, formando circulo; y juntos innumerables Indios, al salir del Sol, comienzan unos tras otros à correr por las sendas, escogiendo para esto los mas robustos, y ligeros; y el q̃ sin pausar dà mas bueltas al Mayo, esse es el que victorean, y el q̃ se lleva entre todos los aplausos. Despues de bien cansados, toman todos generalmente su resfuerzo, que llevan prevenido las Indias; y este dia es muy celebrado de todos, porque sirve de ensaye, para saber correr quãdo pelean con sus enemigos.

CAP. XIII.

POLITICA, Y PROPRIEDADES NATURALES DE ESTOS INDIOS

Ya q̃ hemos expressado la multitud de errores con q̃ viven aluzinadas estas Gentes, será razon mezclar algunas propriedades buenas, que les assisten, y de la Politica conque se goviernan. Son por lo general los Indios Assinais, naturalmente vivos, perspicazes, amigables, altivos, y de no bajos pensamientos. En las facciones bien dispuestos, corpulentos, ligeros, y robustos; y prontos para las expediciones belicas, y de gran corazon. Con sus amigos conservan una paz inalterable, y con sus enemigos nunca dàn treguas, ni admiten cõcordia. Tienen todos los Pueblos su principal Capitan, y este es perpetuo; y hereda el oficio uno de sus Hijos, ò el Pariente mas cercano; y en esto no se ofrece litigio, ni controversia. Si sucede morir el Capitan principal, dejando solo un Hijo pequeño, á este lo reconocen por cabeza; y mientras duran los años de su minoridad, le ponen un Ayo de los Cazíques, que suple sus veces, y trae à todas las juntas al Zagalejo, y le dán el primer assiento, que de ordinario mientras los grandes hacen sus consultas, se està durmiendo, ò traveseando. Fuera de estos Capitanes, eligen todas las parcialidades uno, que sirve de General en la guerra, y á este obedecen quando salen á la Campaña, sin faltar un punto de sus ordenes; y aunque ayan caminado todo el dia sin tomar alimento, ni aun refrezcan la lengua al passar por los aguajes, hasta ḙ el Capitan hace alto, despues de explorar si hai algunos enemigos cercanos. Despues de aver conseguido alguna victoria de sus cõtrarios, và remitiendo la gente ḙ llevó consigo, y èl se queda con otros Indios esforzados, defendiendo la retaguardia. En estas guerras de unos Indios cõ otrós, usaban antiguamente de los Arcos, y flechas, con sus adargas; pero yá en estos tiempos, han adquirido tantos fusiles, con la vecindad de los Franceses, que saben manejarlos con destreza, y les sirven en la guerra, y quando està en sus Pueblos para la caza; y siempre andan cargados cõ su Escopeta.

En tiempo de calores andan los hombres con solo un cendal, que los cubre por delante, sin otro vestimento; y en tiempo de frio, andan abrigados con pellejos de Cibolas, muy bien pintados, y curtidos. No usan el cabello largo, porque todos se lo cortan à cercen, y les queda como de dos dedos, muy parejo, y bien assentado. Gustan mucho los hombres de traer colgadas algunas curiosidades en las orejas; y quando adquieren zarzillos, abalorios, y gargantillas, se los ponen en sus fiestas en los cuellos, muñecas, y rodillas; y el rostro se tiñen cõ bermellon, y unto de Osso, para que quede mas terso, y rosagante. En medio de la cabeza se dejan criar una trenza delgada, como los Chinos, y en ella se atan con curiosidad algunas plumas de las mas exquisitas, y cõ esto les parece, que cada uno està como un pimpollo. Quando veían algunas plumas de los Gallos de Castilla, que nosotros criabamos, no paraban hasta coger la mejor pluma de color, y la guardaban en un cañuto, para salir cõ ella en sus lucimientos. Por el contrario todas las mugeres, en todo tiempo del año se visten con mucha honestidad, pues hacen de dos cueros de Venados curtidos su vestidura, hasta la garganta del pie, enteramente cubiertas; y estas gamuzas son muy negras, y de lustre, ḙ solo alli las saben teñir, y parecen un paño fino; y para darle mas gracejo, bordan todas las orillas con cuentecillas blancas muy pequeñas, que se dàn naturalmēte en algunas yervas, y abujerandolas sutilmente, las cosen con facilidad en sus gamuzas. De otra gamuza grande, bien teñida,

abierta por medio, quanto quepa por la cabeza, cubrē el pecho, y
espalda hasta la cintura, y en todas las orillas la cortan como flueco,
conque queda el trage muy vistoso. El cabello traen siempre atado,
muy peynado, y compuesto, y de èl forman una trenza, que despues
recogen, atandola curiosamente al celebro, con un cordelillo muy en-
carnado de pelos de Conejo, que tiñen al proposito, con una yerva que
se dá en toda aquella tierra. No tienen todas estas Indias mas que
una raya en medio del rostro; pero se labran con mucha curiosidad
los pechos, y los brazos; y esta labor de la espina, se hace quando son
niñas tiernas.

Todo el trabajo de la Casa carga sobre las pobres mugeres, pues
ellas son las ꝗ muelen el maiz en sus morteros, que tienen de madera,
muy curiosos, ellas ponen á cozer en ollas muy grandes, la carne,
que cazan sus maridos, y de su mano labrā de barro todo quanto han
menester para su servicio manual: ellas recogen las cosechas, las limpian, y guardan con mucho asseo; y en tiempo de frio salen à los
Montes á recoger Nuezes, y Bellotas para todo el año; y son tan
providas, que á qualquier hora del dia, ꝗ llega un huesped à su
casa, al punto le ponen en las manos una escudilla grāde de comida,
de lo ꝗ se previno con abundancia por la mañana. Son, en suma,
estas pobres Indias de Texas, de buenas facciones, y de color mas
blāco, que pardo, naturalmente honestas, y siempre inclinadas á lo
bueno; pues quitadas algunas ancianas, que estaban recosidas en
supersticiones, toda la gēte moza, oía con mucha atencion todo lo
que se le proponia por los Ministros Evangelicos, assì para ser
honestas, como para no dar assenso à las fabulas en que las avian
nutrido sus Santones. Es cierto, ꝗ todas estas gentes, por no aver
rayado en ellas la clarissima luz del Evangelio, viven entre sombras
de muerte, ofuscada la vista de sus almas cō supersticiosos errores;
pero quien se hiciere cargo de ꝗ Gentes tan racionales como nuestros
antiguos Españoles, antes de la venida del Apostol Santiago cometian
mayores abominaciones; y que en estas, y mayores, incurrian los
que se preciaban de Sabios entre los Areopagitas, en lugar de tener
enojo contra estos pobres Gentiles, verá con toda claridad, que
respecto de la barbaridad de los Gentiles que huvo en aquellos tiempos en Europa, y la ꝗ despues se descubriò en esta America, puedē
tenerse por menos engañados con las falacias del demonio los Indios
Texas; y por consiguiente, queꞌ estan mas capaces de enterarse en
todas las verdades Catolicas; puesto, que son de aquellas Gentes
que menos atropellan la ley natural, y que positivamente no re-
pugnan lo que se les propone para su eterna salvacion. Dotò el
Señor à estas Gentes, de entendimiento despejado; y teniendolo muy
perspicaz para discurrir en cosas materiales, es facil, ꝗ ilustrados,
levanten sus pensamientos á lo eterno.

Con las Naciones circunvecinas mantienen estos Texas una paz inviolable, y se guardan unos á otros sus fueros, sin que se dè caso, que motive à rompimiento; pues quando sucede, que algun particular hace algun daño, ò les roba algun Caballo de los muchos q̃ tienen, remiten á aquella parcialidad uno de los principales can la noticia, y al punto hacen junta los Cazíques, y mandan al delinquente, que traido à su presencia buelva lo q̃ avia tomado, y la dàn una reprehension muy acre, amenazandole, que para otra vez que se desmáde, ó lo desterrarán de su Pueblo, ó haràn con èl un exemplar castigo. Entre sí mismos observan mucha rectitud en la justicia; y quando unos à otros se han usurpado alguna cosa, no toman la demanda los particulares, sino que dàn su querella al Capitan principal; y este, con parecer de los otros Capitanes, y Ancianos, hace que se dè satisfacion muy cumplida, y deja las partes bien compuestas, sin que les quede motivo de disencion en adelante. En lo que mas descubren su politica es, en las embajadas, q̃ embian de unos á otros Pueblos, especialmente quando se quieren convocar para la guerra; y el que và de Embajador, le reciben los Capitanes con mucha honra, y le dàn assiento principal, tratandolo cõ mucho regalo del que ellos usan, mientras confieren la respuesta, que han de dar; y son tan puntuales en lo que dejan pactado, que no faltan un dia del plazo señalado, en que se juntan todos para marchar en busca de sus enemigos, q̃ los mas declarados son los Apaches. En ocasiones, que de quarenta leguas vienen á los Texas los Cadodachos, q̃ caen à la parte del Norte, remiten un mensajeto por delante, dando aviso de su venidas; y luego les previenen hospedage, y dàn aviso à todas las Casas del Pueblo, para q̃ prevengan el bastimento necessario, que cada uno dà con mucha liberalidad, y salen con su Capitan todos los Cazíques à recibirlos algunas leguas antes del Pueblo, todos vestidos de gala, á su modo; y despues de llegar â sus Casas, les hacen bayles, y festejos, y unos â otros se presentan sus dones de lo q̃ abunda en sus tierras; y cõ esto se renuevã las amitades, y hacen pacto de defenderse unos à otros de sus enemigos.

Esta misma politica usan con las Naciones que caen á la parte del Sur, y viven muy cercanos à las Playas del Seno Mexicano, que acostumbran venir por auxiliares de los Texas en tiẽpo de guerra; y para tenerlos gratos, los hospedan todos los años despues de las cosechas, que es el tiempo en que vienen muchas familias de hombres, y mugeres, à visitar á los ASSINAIS; y es el tiempo en q̃ comercian unos con otros todas aquellas cosas de que carecen en sus Pueblos. Con los Indios que estàn sugetos à los Franceses se conservan con mucha amistad, y quãdo de una parte à otra se visitan, son mucho mayores los obsequios, y el aparato conque los reciben; porque estando tan industriados de los Franceses sus Indios en

ceremonias politicas, procuran nuestros Indios no dejarse vencer
de ellos en carabanas, y cortesias; y no les rindẽ parias en mostrarse
valientes, y guerreros; y para esto hacen alarde de manejar las escopetas con destreza, y de correr en sus Caballos con suma ligereza;
pues aunque los NACHITOCHES tienen mas abundancia de fusiles, q̃ los
Texas, son muy contados los Caballos q̃ tienen; y assi marchan à
pie, y los Texas todos montan à Caballo, con tanta destreza, q̃ llevando
sueltos los pies, corren con suma velocidad, y goviernan la bestia
con solo un cordelillo delgado, que les ajustan en lugar de freno en
la boca, que los campistas llaman barbiquejo.   Con nuestros Españoles
se han mostrado siempre afables, y cariñosos; y aunque por sus in-
teresses se careã mucho â la amistad de los Franceses, no tienen con
ellos aquella intimidad que muestran cõ los Españoles, en quienes
es mas lizo el trato, y menos interessado el commercio, como conocerà
sin passion, quien libre de ella, huviere estado donde comercian los
Indios con ambas Naciones.   El amor que estos Indios Texas han
mostrado siempre à la Gente Española, no es necessario dar para
ello mas pruebas que las mismas experiencias de los q̃ algun tiempo
han vivido entre ellos; pues no hè visto hasta aora alguno, q̃ despues
de salir de aquella tierra, no se haga lenguas del mucho agasajo de
aquellos pobres Indios.

Muchas otras cosas pudiera conglomerar sobre este assunto; pero
escusando proligidad, porque no parezca passion lo que es realidad,
quiero concluir con una accion del todo politica, y digna de
estamparse en los moldes, de que fui testigo ocular; y passó en esta
forma: Estando yo de Presidente en la Mission de la Concepcion
Purissima de los Texas el año de 1718, con ocasion de entrar por
Governador de aquella Provincia el General D. Martin de Alarcon,
se le diò aviso à los Indios, y se juntaron todos para hacerle el
recibimiento, muy festivos, y gozosos.   Llegaron à encontrarse con
el Governador, que estaba ya prevenido de dejarse recibir à la usanza
de los Indios; y un tiro de escopeta antes de la Mission, lo apearon
del Caballo los Capitanes, y uno le quitaba las espuelas, otro el
espadin, otro el baston, y luego lo cargó en ombros uno de los Cazíques
principales, y otro lo iba sosteniendo de los pies, llevando el Caballo
de diestro uno de los mismos Indios; y assi llegó cargado à la Mission.
Tenian yá dispuesto el assiento con muchas Cibolas curiosas, que
servian de Alfombras; y antes de sentarlo le labaron la cara cõ
mucha suavidad, y limpieza, y le dieron la pipa de paz con tabaco,
que es la ceremonia, conque declaran à uno por Capitan General de
todos ellos.   Despues le hicieron un parlamento en nombre de toda
la Nacion, y le dixeron, que de alli á dos dias vendrian á darle la
obediencia todos los Pueblos.   Convocados, al tercer dia se juntó
una multitud copiosissima de hombres, y mugeres, de las quatro

Missiones, con sus Capitanes; y entrada la noche, se encendieron muchas luminarias, y pusieron en un Portal assiento muy bien esterado, para darle al Governador la envestidura: pusieronle en la cabeza una pluma muy curiosa; y sentado, conmenzaron á cantarle en dos Coros, hombres, y mugeres, con sus pifanos, y atabales; y despues successivamente, en nombre de cada Pueblo, le hacian un razonamiento en su lengua, y le iban ofreciendo pieles muy bien curtidas, y muchos canastos de cosas comestibles; y duró esta funcion hasta mas de media noche, con tanta alegria, que querian los Indios amanecer en ella: pero á instancias mias, les persuadi, que prosiguiessen ellos en su fiesta, y nos dejassen ir à descansar, como lo hicieron; y en nombre del Governador les hice en su lengua un parlaméto, agradeciendo su obsequio, y prometiendoles los favorecerian siépre los Españoles: conque quedaron todos muy gustosos, y prosiguieron cantando hasta el dia siguiente.

CAP. XIV.

EMPLEO QUE TUVIERON LOS MISSIONEROS EN ESTOS PRIMEROS TIÉPOS; Y LAS MUCHAS PENALIDADES, QUE SE LES FUERON OFRECIENDO

Muy desde los principios comenzaron los Missioneros à sustentarse con el pan de lagrimas, y de tribulaciones; pues lo mismo fue llegar à aquella Provincia, q experîmentar innumerables trabajos en ella. El primero fue, que de veinte y cinco Soldados, que entraron para escolta, siete de ellos hicieron fuga, y nos desampararon, llevandose de camino algunas bestias de las q servian à los Religiosos. Señalado el sitio para cada Mission, y compartidos los Religiosos, quedaron solos, componiendo su vivienda pajiza; y como las providencias para el mantenimiento no se llevaron por delante, al primero dia comenzò la abstinencia; y sin ser Quaresma hacia el plato una poca de legumbre de verdolagas, cogidas de las simenteras de los Indios, con solo el condimento de un poco de sal, y pimientos. Solian traer tal vez los Indios un poco de harina de maiz, y frisoles, con otras frutas, que servian para divertir, mas que para sustentar la hambre. Raras veces se alcanzaba un bocado de carne, y llegó ocasion en que una Cabra, que se avia enfermado de una pierna, se la hicimos cortar, y con lo restante nos mantuvimos mas de una semana. El chocolate, que suele ser el suple faltas de la comida, fue con tanta escazés, que entre cinco Religiosos, que eramos de este Colegio de la Santa Cruz, solo tuvimos q partir dos arrobas; y dejando de lamentar necessidades, para adelante, q fueron mayores, voy à lo principal, q es dàr noticia del empleo Apostolico de los Missioneros. Aunque todos, unos mas, y otros menos, tenian sus penalidades, vivian muy gustosos, y no se les passaba dia sin celebrar el Santo Sacrificio de la Missa, pidiendo à el Señor la conversion de aquellas Gentes.

Como los Indios viven tan dispersos, todo el empeño de los Missioneros era, persuadirlos á que se juntassen; y aunque daban esperanzas de hacerlo en levantando sus cosechas, eran tantas las dificultades que se ofrecian para efectuarlo, que en veinte años no pudo lograr ninguno de los Ministros el consuelo de tener todos los de su Pueblo juntos. Mudaronse las Missiones â parajes mas espaciosos, con el designio de congregar los Indios; pero no ofrecia el terreno toda aquella capacidad, que era necessaria para cerca de mil personas, que avia en cada Pueblo. Todos los mas dias venian los Indios à visitar à los Padres; y como ya sabian mucho de la lengua del País, los procuraban ir desengañando de sus errores, y les persuadian la suma importancia de recibir el Santo Bautismo, confessando la verdad de un Dios Trino, y Uno; y haciendoles conocer la mucha ceguedad en que avian vivido; pero todo esto lo tomaban como cosa superficial; porque estàn tan creidos en lo que heredaron de sus mayores, que es menester todo el auxilio Divino, para arrancarles del corazon aquellas vanas credulidades cõque se criaron desde niños. En una ocasion q̃ estuvo un Ministro hablando muy de espacio cõ uno de los principales Maestros de sus errores, quando ya estaba en la lengua muy períto, lo llegó á convencer de tal suerte, q̃ no teniendo ya razones para evadirse de las verdades Catolicas, que se le proponian, confessó de plano, que sus observaciones, no tenian mas fundamento, que el averlas heredado de sus mayores; y que èl, y los demàs tenian buen corazon, y desseaban entender bien lo que los Padres les proponian, que entonces abririan los ojos, y seguírian el mismo camino que los Ministros enseñaban. En las mugeres se encontró mucha mas docilidad para ser enseñadas en la verdad de nuestra Santa Ley; y assi fueron muchas las que estando ya algo ilustradas, lograron el Santo Bautismo en el articulo de la muerte; dandoles à entender lo que les faltaba para su digna recepciõ; y murierõ muchas, dejando bien fundadas esperanzas de aceptar este singular beneficio de Dios, sin ficcion alguna. En los parvulos se cogió à manos llenas el desseado fruto, pues todos los que morian, raro se fue sin el Santo Bautismo.

Para que estos no malograssen tan soberana dicha, tenian los Missioneros hecha lista de las casas, ó ranchos de los Indios, con el numero de adultos, y pequeños, y el nombre de los sitios; y quando llegaba algun Indio á visitar à los Padres, le preguntaban cõ curiosidad, si estaba buena toda su familia; y en sabiendo q̃ avia algun enfermo, mostraban que lo sentian, y que irian luego à visitarlo; y esto lo hacian, no solo por el consuelo de los mismos dolientes, sino principalmente por catequizar al enfermo, y persuadirle â que recibiesse la saludable agua del bautismo; y aunque costaba dificultades, por q̃ muchos les persuadian que aquella Agua Santa les quitaba la vida, los desengañaban cõ eficaces razones los zelosos Ministros, y los enfermos movidos de lo Alto, recibian voluntariamente el Bautismo; y los mas, morian despues de averlo recibido. Suele, à tiempos, aver enfermedades generalmēte entre estos Indios; y la mas comun que se lleva à muchos, es la dissenteria de sangre, que les proviene de q̃ en todo el Invierno acostumbran echar·debajo de las camas muchas brasas ardiendo, para templar en parte el mucho rigor del frio, teniendo las camas en alto; y no bastando los pellejos de Cybolas para calentarlos, suplen con el fuego lo que les falta de abrigo; y esto es ocasion de q̃ los mas adolezcan de dicha enfermedad; y si no frequentaran bañarse en todo el año, aùn quando està nevando, fueran muchos mas los q̃ murierã por tener la sangre requemada. En ocasion que corre esta epidemia, no esperan los Misioneros á ser llamados, sino que en diciendo Missa, montan en un Caballo, y vàn visitando todas las rãcherias; y aunque les cueste mucho trabajo, no se buelven á su Mission sin aver bautizado los moribundos; y si han encontrado resistencia, repiten otro dia la visita, clamando al Cielo para que les abra los ojos de la alma; y el Señor, movido de su piedad, y de que aquellos pobres fon precio de su Sangre, facilita reciban el Bautismo.

Las muchas penalidades, que esta importante diligencia ocasionaban en los Ministros, se viene à los ojos, con solo hacer reflexion, de que los ranchos de los Indios estàn tan separados, que algunos distan de la Mission seis, y siete leguas por cada viento, aunque otras estàn en mucha menos distancia; pero no es dable, aunque uno fuesse corriendo, visitar la mayor parte en un dia; y mucho mas, por ser necessario detenerse largo tiempo en catequizar los moribundos, y convencer à los sanos, para que no le impidan al enfermo su salvacion eterna. Para aliento de sus Ministros, y premiar su zelo, obrò el Señor cosas bien raras, que de muchas, solo apuntarè algunas pocas. El primer año que se plantaron las Missiones, enfermò el Capitan General de los Indios Texas, y en su misma Casa, al mismo tiempo, otro Capitan, paríente suyo. Eran ambos ya muy ancianos, y tan estimados de todo el Pueblo, que reconociendo estár cercanos à la muerte, se congregaron para assistirles multitud de hombres, y mugeres, yendo unos, y viniĕdo otros, sin que faltasse el concurso de dia, ni de noche: da tal suerte, que estaba el sitio de la Casa cercado de barracas con mas de quinientas personas. Tuve yo noticia del grave peligro en q̃ estaba el Capitan; y subiendo à Caballo, por estàr distante mas de cinco leguas, fui á verlo, con el pretexto de saber de su enfermedad, y por consolar al Pueblo, que estaba muy contristado, aunque mi principal designio era, que no muriesse sin bautizarse. Luego q̃ le vi, le di à entender en su idioma, lo mucho que sentia el que me faltasse, porque nos queria mucho á los Religiosos; y de camino le fui suavemente proponiendo la necessidad del Santo Bautismo para salvarse, y lo que debia creer, para q̃ surtiesse su efecto, detestando los errores de sus antepassados. A todo me dió grato oído, y me pidiò tiempo para responderme. Cinco dias repeti la visita, y al cabo de ellos, mandó traer Agua en una basija, y delante de los que assistian, bajó la cabeza, y me pidiò que lo bautizasse, lo qual hice, aumentando con la agua de mis ojos, la de la basija.

A este Capitan, que por las circunstancias de su bautismo llamarè dichoso, le puse por nombre Francisco; porque desde que comenzè à catequizarlo, invoquè en mi auxilio el de mi Serafico Patriarca; y espero, que con tal patrocinio, se lograria aquella alma. En lo humano me sirvió de consuelo, el que antes de morir dió muchos consejos á su hijo, y le encargò cuydasse mucho de los Padres, y que ellos sabian la verdad, y venian á buscarlos de tan lejas tierras: con otras razones, que daban á entender avia hecho efecto en su alma el Santo Bautismo. Yà bautizado el Capitan principal, todas mis ancias eran, porque lograsse la misma dicha el otro enfermo, pues advertia, que aquel viviente esqueleto, estaba ya para derribar en tierra los huessos. Teniale ya catequizado, y me pedia treguas, dilatandolo para quando se viesse mas á lo ultimo. Un dia, que por estàr el Sol muy claro, y la mañana muy serena, saliò à que lo bañasse su muger, sentado al Sol en un banquillo, me parecio ocasion oportuna para q̃ se labasse su alma, quando le bañaban el cuerpo. Lleguéme à èl, y con mucha suavidad le dixe en su lengua, que si queria labarse su alma, como se lababa el cuerpo, no era menester otra cosa mas q̃ dar credito à lo que le tenia dicho; y en breve le repeti de nuevo, admitiendo de voluntad el labatorio Santo; y me respondiò, que lo hiciesse. Su muger, ignorante de lo que yo intentaba, no queria darme la basija c̃que lo estaba bañando; pero èl, seriamente mandó, me la entregasse llena de agua; y bajando la cabeza, me hizo señal se la bañasse, diciendole lo que le avia enseñado; y con el nombre de Francisco, lo bautizè muy à mi satisfacion, y le expliquè despues como avria quedado su alma si avia creido lo q̃ yo le avia propuesto. A dos, ó tres dias, con diferencia de pocas horas, murieron mis dos Franciscos, y fueron muy llorados del Pueblo, q̃ gastó ocho dias en hacerles sus funerales exequias.

Entre los Indios, que conservan mas autoridad entre los Texas; y aún son primero q̃ los Capitanes, son sus Sacerdotes, á quienes llaman CHENESI. El primero de estos, que es el que cuida la Casa del Fuego, y tiene cerca su casa, para q̃ nunca falte á la llama nutrimento, era el mas opuesto à los Sacerdotes de Christo, y el q̃ impugnaba con acrimonia el Santo Bautismo, persuadiendo â los enfermos, que aquella Agua que los Padres llamaban Santa, les abreviaba la vida. Su mismo nombre daba á entender ser en todo c̃trario à los Españoles, pues se llamaba SATA YAEXA: Sata, ó Satán, yá sabe el Erudíto, que es contrario; y la voz YAEXA, quiere decir Español; y todo junto sin violencia, el contrario de los Españoles; como lo era en realidad, oponiendose siempre á los Ministros Evangelicos. Este fingido Sacerdote enfermó de muerte, y llegando á mi noticia el peligro de perderse aquella pobre alma, formè concepto, de que el reducirlo â que se bautizasse, era empressa del brazo poderoso de Dios; y que necessitaba de especialissimos auxilios, y socorros del Cielo. Era dia de la Conversion de S. Pablo, y acordandome de lo que hizo el Señor con este perseguidor de los Christianos, desconfiado de mis fuerzas, me vali de mi humilde Compañero, que lo era â la sazon el P. Fr. Gabriel de Vergara, Hombre por sus virtudes venerable; y para alentarlo á la empressa, le mandè por santa obediencia fuesse à la casa del enfermo, que distaba mas de tres leguas; y procurasse desengañarle de sus muchos errores, y persuadirle, que la unica puerta para entrar en el Cielo, es la de el Santo Bautismo. Obedeciò el humilde Religioso, y comenzò cõ grande prudencia, y madurèz á desbaratar la dureza de aquel corazon empedernido. Concibió esperanzas de lograr su intento; y repitiendo la visita, á fuerza de baterias amorosas, y persuaciones, hijas de su espiritu, libre, y espontaneamente pidió el Bautismo; y á instancia de el zeloso Ministro, el nuevo Pablo (que assi se llamó) hizo juntar los Indios, y les dixo claramente, que todas sus cosas eran mentiras; y que solo era verdad lo que el Padre decia. Sea Dios alabado eternamente.

BIBLIOGRAPHY

ABEL, ANNIE H. *See* SIBLEY, JOHN, 1922.
ALMONTE, FRAY JUAN N.
    1925. Statistical report on Texas. Translated by C. E. Castañeda. Southwestern Hist. Quart., vol. 28, No. 3, pp. 177–222. ("Document translated here was published in February 1835.")
AMERICAN STATE PAPERS
    1832, 1834. Documents, legislative and executive, of the Congress of the United States. Class II, Indian Affairs, vols. 1–2.
    1834, 1859, 1861. Documents of the Congress of the United States, in relation to the Public Lands. Class VIII, Public Lands, vols. 3, 4, and 8.
BANDELIER, AD. F., EDITOR
    1905. The journey of Alvar Nuñez Cabeza de Vaca . . . translated from his own narrative by Fanny Bandelier. Trail Makers (series). New York.
BEAURAIN, LE SIEUR. See LA HARPE, BERNARD DE, 1831.
BIEDMA, LUIS HERNANDEZ DE. *See* BOURNE, EDWARD GAYLORD, EDITOR.
BIENVILLE, JEAN BAPTISTE LE MOYNE, SIEUR DE
    MS. Memoir. Copy obtained from the Newberry Library, Chicago. *See also* Margry, Pierre, vol. 4, pp. 432–444. Paris, 1880.
BOLTON, HERBERT EUGENE
    1908. The native tribes about the East Texas missions. Quart. Texas State Hist. Assoc., vol. 11, No. 4, pp. 249–276.
    1912. The Spanish occupation of Texas, 1519–1690. Southwestern Hist. Quart., vol. 16, No. 1, pp. 1–26.

1914. Athanase de Mézières and the Louisiana-Texas frontier, 1768–1780. Documents published for the first time from the original Spanish and French manuscripts, chiefly in the archives of Mexico and Spain; translated into English; edited and annotated, by Herbert Eugene Bolton . . . 2 vols.   Cleveland.

1915. Texas in the middle eighteenth century. Studies in Spanish colonial history and administration. Univ. Calif., Publ. Hist., vol. 3.

1916. Spanish exploration in the Southwest, 1542–1706. *In* Original narratives of early American history. Charles Scribner's Sons. New York.

BOURNE, EDWARD GAYLORD, EDITOR

1904. Narratives of the career of Hernando De Soto. 2 vols. Trail Makers (series). New York.

BUCKLEY, ELEANOR CLAIRE

1911. The Aguayo Expedition into Texas and Louisiana, 1719–1722. Quart. Texas State Hist. Assoc., vol. 15, No. 1, pp. 1–65.

BUGBEE, LESTER G.

1898. The real Saint-Denis. Quart. Texas State Hist. Assoc., vol. 1, No. 4, pp. 266–281.

BUSHNELL, DAVID I., JR.

1927. Drawings by A. DeBatz in Louisiana, 1732-1735. Smithsonian Misc. Coll., vol. 80, No. 5.

CABEZA DE VACA, ALVAR NUÑEZ. *See* BANDELIER, AD. F., EDITOR.

CASAÑAS DE JESUS MARIA, FRAY FRANCISCO

1926-27. Descriptions of the Tejas or Asinai Indians. 1691-1722. Translated from the Spanish by Mattie Austin Hatcher. I. Fray Francisco Casañas de Jesus Maria to the Viceroy of Mexico, Aug. 15, 1691. Southwestern Hist. Quart., vol. 30, pp. 206-218. Ibid.; II. vol. 30, pp. 283-304. (Spanish text given above on pp. 241-263.)

CASIS, LILIA M., TRANSLATOR

1899. Carta de Don Damian Manzanet á Don Carlos de Siguenza sobre el Descubrimiento de la Bahía del Espíritu Santo. Quart. Texas State Hist. Assoc., vol. 2, No. 4, pp. 253-312.

CASTAÑEDA, CARLOS E.

1931. Myths and customs of the Tejas Indians. *In* Publ. Texas Folk-Lore Soc., vol. 9, pp. 167-174.

1936, 1938. The Mission Era: Vol. 1, The finding of Texas, 1519-1693; vol. 2, The winning of Texas, 1693-1731; vol. 3, The missions at at work, 1731-1761. *In* Our Catholic Heritage in Texas, 1519–1936 (7 vols.), prepared under the auspices of the Knights of Columbus of Texas, Paul J. Foik, editor. Austin, Tex. *See also* Almonte, Juan N.; Morfi, Fray Juan Agustin, 1935; Sanchez, Jose Maria.

CHABOT, FREDERICK M. *See* MORFI, FRAY JUAN AGUSTIN DE, 1932.

CHARLEVOIX, PIERRE F. X. DE

1866–1872. History and general description of New France. Translated with notes, by John Gilmary Shea. Vols. 1–6.

CLARK, ROBERT CARLTON

1902. Louis Juchereau de Saint-Denis and the re-establishment of the Tejas missions. Quart. Texas State Hist. Assoc., vol. 6, No. 1, pp. 1–26.

COX, ISAAC JOSLIN, EDITOR

1905. The journeys of Réné Robert Cavelier, Sieur de La Salle. 2 vols. Trail Makers (series). New York.

COXE, DANIEL
  1850. A description of the English province of Carolana, by the Spaniards
        called Florida, and by the French La Louisiane . . . *In* Historical
        collections of Louisiana, . . . compiled with historical and biograph-
        ical notes, and an introduction, by B. F. French . . . Pt. 2, 2nd
        ed., pp. 221–276. Phila.
CULIN, STEWART
  1907. Games of the North American Indians. 24th Ann. Rep. Bur. Amer.
        Ethnol., 1902–1903.
CUSTIS, PETER. *See* FREEMAN, THOMAS, and CUSTIS, PETER.
DE MÉZIÈRES, ATHANASE. *See* BOLTON, HERBERT EUGENE, EDITOR, 1914.
[DERBANNE, RELATION OF THE SIEUR]
        Description du Chemin suivi par les Francais et les Espagnols dans leurs
        desseins d'occuper certaines parties du Texas. *See* Margry, Pierre, vol. 6,
        pp. 214–220. Paris, 1886.
DE SOTO, HERNANDO. *See* BOURNE, EDWARD GAYLORD, EDITOR; ROBERTSON, JAMES
        A; and U. S. DE SOTO EXPEDITION COMMISSION.
DORSEY, GEORGE A.
  1905. Traditions of the Caddo. Carnegie Inst. Washington, Publ. No. 41.
  1905 a. Caddo customs of childhood. *In* Journ. Amer. Folk-Lore Soc., vol. 18,
        pp. 226–228.
DORSEY, JAMES OWEN
  1897. Siouan sociology: a posthumous paper. 15th Ann. Rep. Bur. Ethnol.,
        1893–1894, pp. 205–244.
DOUAY, FATHER ANASTASIUS
  1905. Narrative of La Salle's attempt to ascend the Mississippi in 1687 . . .
        In Journeys of La Salle, edited by Isaac Joslin Cox, vol. 1, pp.
        222–247.
ELVAS, NARRATIVE OF THE GENTLEMAN OF. *See* BOURNE, EDWARD GAYLORD, EDITOR;
        and ROBERTSON, JAMES A., TRANSLATOR AND EDITOR.
ESPINOSA, FRAY ISIDRO FELIS DE
  1927. Descriptions of the Tejas or Asinai Indians, 1691–1722. Translated
        from the Spanish by Mattie Austin Hatcher. IV, Fray Isidro
        Felis de Espinosa on the Asinai and their allies. Southwestern Hist.
        Quart., vol. 31, pp. 150–180. (Spanish text of Chapters 9–14 given
        above on pp. 273–300.)
FLETCHER, ALICE C., and L(FLESCHE, FRANCIS
  1911. The Omaha tribe. 27th Ann. Rep. Bur. Amer. Ethnol., 1905–1906,
        pp. 17–672.
FOREMAN, GRANT
  1930. Indians and pioneers, the story of the American Southwest before
        1830. Yale University Press.
  1930 a. A traveler in Indian territory. The journal of Ethan Allen Hitch-
        cock, late Major-General in the United States Army. Edited and
        annotated by Grant Foreman. Cedar Rapids.
  1933. Advancing the frontier, 1830–1860. Univ. Okla. Press, Norman.
  1934. The five civilized tribes. Univ. Okla. Press, Norman.
FREEMAN, THOMAS, and CUSTIS, PETER
  1806. An account of the Red River in Louisiana, drawn up from the returns
        of Messrs. Freeman and Custis to the War Office of the United
        States, who explored the same in the year 1806. Washington.
FREIRE-MARRECO, BARBARA. *See* ROBBINS, WILFRED WILLIAM.

GALLATIN, ALBERT
1836. A synopsis of the Indian tribes within the United States east of the
Rocky Mountains, and in the British and Russian possessions in
North America. Trans. and Coll. Amer. Antiq. Soc., vol. 2.
GARCILASO DE LA VEGA (EL INCA)
1723. La Florida del Inca. Historia del Adelantado, Hernando De Soto,
governador, y capitan general del reino de la Florida y de otros
heroicos caballeros, Españoles, e Indios. Madrid. (Also Lisbon,
1601.)
GATSCHET, ALBERT S., EDITOR
1891. Two Indian documents. I, Migration of the Wichita Indians. Amer.
Antiquarian, vol. 13, No. 5, pp. 249–252.
HABIG, MARION A.
1934. The Franciscan Père Marquette; a critical biography of Father Zénobe
Membré, O. F. M., La Salle's chaplain and missionary companion
1645(ca.)–1689, with maps and original narratives. Franciscan
studies, No. 13. Joseph F. Wagner, Inc., New York.
HAMMOND, GEORGE P., and REY, AGAPITO
1940. Narratives of the Coronado expedition, 1540–1542. Coronado cuarto
centennial publ., 1540–1940, edited by George P. Hammond. Vol.
2, Univ. New Mex. Press, Albuquerque.
HARBY, MRS. LEE C.
1895. The Tejas: Their habits, government, and superstitions. Ann. Rep.
Amer. Hist. Assoc., 1894, pp. 63–82.
HARRINGTON, JOHN PEABODY. See ROBBINS, WILFRED WILLIAM.
HARRINGTON, M. R.
1920. Certain Caddo sites in Arkansas. Ind. Notes and Monogr. (Misc. 10),
Mus. Amer. Ind., Heye Foundation. New York.
HATCHER, MATTIE AUSTIN.
1927. Myths of the Tejas Indians. Publ. Texas Folk-lore Soc., vol. 6, pp.
107–118.
See Casañas; Espinosa; Hidalgo; and Padilla.
HEUSINGER, EDWARD W.
1936. Early Explorations and mission establishments in Texas. The Naylor
Co., San Antonio.
HIDALGO, FRAY FRANCISCO
1927. Description of the Tejas or Asinai Indians, 1691–1722. Translated
from the Spanish by Mattie Austin Hatcher. III, Fray Francisco
Hidalgo to Fray Isidro Cassos, November 20, 1710. (Extract.)
Fray Francisco Hidalgo to the Viceroy, November 4, 1716. South-
western Hist. Quart., vol. 31, pp. 50–62. (A photocopy of the orig-
inal is in the possession of the Univ. Texas, and a typewritten copy
in the Library of Congress, from which the Spanish is reproduced on
pp. 265–271 above.)
HITCHCOCK, ETHAN ALLEN. JOURNAL. See FOREMAN, GRANT, 1930 a.
HODGE, FREDERICK WEBB, EDITOR
1907, 1910. Handbook of American Indians north of Mexico. Bur. Amer.
Ethnol. Bull. 30, pts. 1 and 2.
IBERVILLE, PIERRE LE MOYNE D', JOURNAL DE. See MARGRY, PIERRE, vol. 4, pp. 178–179.
Paris, 1880.
INDIAN AFFAIRS (U. S.)
1825–1939. Indian Affairs (U. S.). Office of Indian Affairs (War Depart-
ment). Reports, 1825–1848. Reports of the Commissioner of
Indian Affairs (Department of the Interior), 1849–1939.
INDIAN TREATIES. See TREATIES

304   BUREAU OF AMERICAN ETHNOLOGY   [BULL. 132]

JOUTEL, HENRI, RELATION DE. *See* MARGRY, PIERRE, vol. 3, pp. 89–534. Paris, 1878.

KOCH, CLARA LENA
    1925. The Federal Indian policy in Texas, 1845–1860. Southwestern Hist.
        Quart., vol. 29, No. 2, pp. 98–127.

KRESS, MARGARET KENNEY, TRANSLATOR. *See* SOLÍS, FRAY GASPAR JOSÉ DF.

LA BARRE, WESTON
    1938. The Peyote cult. Yale Univ. Publ. Anthrop., No. 19.

LA FLESCHE, FRANCIS. *See* FLETCHER, ALICE

LA HARPE, BERNARD DE
    1831. Journal historique de l'établissement des Français a La Louisiane.
        Nouvelle-Orléans and Paris. (Probably in reality the work of the
        Sieur de Beaurain.)
    1886. Relation du voyage . . . *See* MARGRY, PIERRE, vol. 6, pp. 243–306.
        Paris.

LA SALLE, RÉNÉ ROBERT CAVELIER, SIEUR DE. *See* COX, ISAAC JOSLIN, EDITOR.

LE PAGE DU PRATZ, ANTOINE S.
    1758. Histoire de la Louisiane. 3 vols., Paris.

LESSER, ALEXANDER, and WELTFISH, GENE
    1932. Composition of the Caddoan linguistic stock. Smithsonian Misc.
        Coll., vol. 87, No. 6.

MARGRY, PIERRE
    1875–1886. Découvertes et établissements des Français dans l'Ouest et dans
        le sud de l'Amérique septentrionale (1614–1754). Mémoires
        et documents originaux recueillis et publiés par Pierre Margry.
        6 vols., Paris.

MASSANET (OR MANZANET), DON DAMIAN. *See* BOLTON, HERBERT EUGENE, 1916;
    and CASIS, LILIA M.

MOONEY, JAMES
    1896. The ghost-dance religion, and the Sioux outbreak of 1890. 14th Ann.
        Rep. Bur. Ethnol., 1892–1893, pt. 2.

MORFI, FRAY JUAN AGUSTIN DE
    1932. Excerpts from the Memorias for the history of the Province of Texas,
        being a translation of those parts of the Memorias which partic-
        ularly concern the various Indians of the Province of Texas; their
        tribal divisions, characteristics, customs, traditions, superstitions,
        and all else of interest concerning them. With a prolog, appendix,
        and notes, by Frederick M. Chabot. Privately printed. (The
        Spanish original has also been consulted.)
    1935. History of Texas, 1673–1779. Translated, with biographical intro-
        duction and annotations, by Carlos Eduardo Castañeda. 2 pts.
        Quivira Soc., Albuquerque.

MUCKLEROY, ANNA
    1922, 1923. The Indian policy of the Republic of Texas. Southwestern
        Hist. Quart., vol. 25, No. 4, pp. 229–260; vol. 26, No. 1, pp. 1–29;
        vol. 26, No. 3, pp. 184–206.

NUÑEZ CABEZA DE VACA, ALVAR. *See* BANDELIER, AD. F., EDITOR.

NYE, CAPTAIN W. S.
    1937. Carbine and lance, the story of Old Fort Sill. Univ. Okla. Press,
        Norman.

OVIEDO Y VALDÉZ, GONZALO FERNÁNDEZ DE (EL CAPITAN)
    1851–1855. Historia general y natural de las Indias. 4 vols. Madrid.

PADILLA, JUAN ANTONIO
    1919. Texas in 1820. Translated by Mattie Austin Hatcher. I. Report on
        the barbarous Indians of the Province of Texas. Southwestern
        Hist. Quart., vol. 23, No. 1, pp. 47–68.

PARSONS, ELSIE CLEWS
1941. Notes on the Caddo. *In* Mem. Amer. Anthrop. Assoc., No. 57, pp. 1–76.
PÉNICAUT, RELATION DE. Les premiers postes de la Louisiane. *See* MARGRY, PIERRE, vol. 5, pp. 375–586, Paris, 1883.
PETRULLO, VINCENZO
1934. The diabolic root, a study of Peyotism, the new Indian religion, among the Delawares. Univ. Pa. Press, Phila.
POWELL, J. W.
1891. Indian linguistic families of America north of Mexico. 7th Ann. Rep. Bur. Ethnol., 1885–1886, pp. 1–142.
RANJEL, RODRIGO
A narrative of De Soto's expedition based on the diary of Rodrigo Ranjel. *See* Bourne, Edward Gaylor, Editor. Narratives of the career of Hernando De Soto, vol. 2, 1904.
REY, AGAPITO. *See* HAMMOND, GEORGE P.
ROBBINS, WILFRED WILLIAM; HARRINGTON, JOHN PEABODY; and FREIRE-MARRECO, BARBARA
1916. Ethnobotany of the Tewa Indians. Bur. Amer. Ethnol. Bull. 55.
ROBERTSON, JAMES A., TRANSLATOR AND EDITOR
1933. True relation of the hardships suffered by Governor Fernando de Soto and certain Portuguese gentlemen during the discovery of the Province of Florida, now newly set forth by a gentleman of Elvas. Publ. Florida State Hist. Soc., No. 11, vol. 2. De Land.
ROBLES, VITO ALESSIO
1938. Coahuila y Texas en la epoca colonial. Editorial Cultura, Mexico, D. F.
ROYCE, CHARLES C.
1899. Indian land cessions in the United States, compiled by Charles C. Royce, with an introduction by Cyrus Thomas. 18th Ann. Rep. Bur. Amer. Ethnol., 1896–1897, pt. 2.
SANCHEZ, JOSÉ MARÍA
1926. A trip to Texas in 1828. Translated by Carlos E. Castañeda. Southwestern Hist. Quart., vol 29, No. 4, pp. 249–288.
SAUER, CARL
1934. The distribution of aboriginal tribes and languages in northwestern Mexico. Ibero-Americana: 5. Univ. Calif.
SCHMITT, REV. EDMOND J. P.
1898. Sieur Louis de Saint Denis. Quart. Texas State Hist. Assoc., vol. 1, No. 3, pp. 204–215.
SCHOOLCRAFT, HENRY R.
1851–1857. Historical and statistical information respecting the history, condition and prospects of the Indian tribes of the United States. Collected and prepared under the direction of the Bureau of Indian Affairs. Vols. 1–6. Philadelphia.
SHEA, JOHN GILMARY
1852. Discovery and exploration of the Mississippi valley. New York. *See also* Charlevoix, PIERRE F. X de.
SHELBY, CHARMION CLAIR
1923. St. Denis's declaration concerning Texas in 1717. Southwestern Hist. Quart., vol. 26, No. 3, pp. 165–183.
1924. St. Denis's second expedition to the Rio Grande, 1716–1719. Southwestern Hist. Quart., vol. 27, No. 3, pp. 190–216.

SIBLEY, JOHN
  1832. Historical sketches of the several Indian tribes in Louisiana, south
        of the Arkansas river, and between the Mississippi and river
        Grande. *In* American State Papers, Class II, Indian Affairs, vol. 1,
        pp. 721–731.
  1922. A report from Natchitoches in 1807. Edited, with an introduction,
        by Annie Heloise Abel. Ind. Notes and Monogr., Mus. Amer. Ind.,
        Heye Foundation. New York.
SOLÍS, FRAY GASPAR JOSÉ DE
  1931. Diary of a visit of inspection of the Texas missions made by Fray
        Gaspar José de Solís in the year 1767–1768. Translated by Mar-
        garet Kenney Kress, with introductory note by Mattie Austin
        Hatcher. Southwestern Hist. Quart., vol. 35, pp. 28–76. (Original
        recorded in Memorias de Nueva España: Documentos para la his-
        toria eclesiastica y civil de la Provincia de Texas. vol. 27, pt. 2, pp.
        248–297. Transcript Library, Univ. Texas.)
SPIER, LESLIE
  1924. Wichita and Caddo relationship terms. Amer. Anthrop., n. s., vol. 26,
        No. 2, pp. 258–263.
STANLEY, J. M.
  1852. Portraits of North American Indians, with sketches of scenery, etc.,
        painted by J. M. Stanley. Deposited with the Smithsonian In-
        stitution. Smithsonian Misc. Coll., vol. 2, art. 3.
SWANTON ANNIVERSARY VOLUME
  1940. Essays in historical anthropology of North America, published in
        honor of John R. Swanton, in celebration of his fortieth year with
        the Smithsonian Institution. Smithsonian Misc. Coll., vol. 100.
SWANTON, JOHN R.
  1928. Social organization and social usages of the Indians of the Creek
        Confederacy. 42nd Ann. Rep. Bur. Amer. Ethnol., 1924–25, pp. 23–472.
  1928 a. Social and religious beliefs and usages of the Chickasaw Indians,
        44th Ann. Rep. Bur. Amer. Ethnol., 1926–1927, pp. 169–273.
  1931. The Caddo social organization and its possible historical significance.
        Journ. Wash. Acad. Sci., vol. 21, No. 9, pp. 203–206.
TONTI, HENRI DE. Memoir. *In* Journeys of La Salle, vol. 1, pp. 1–65, 1905.
        See Cox, Isaac Joslin, Editor.
TREATIES
  1837. Treaties between the United States of America and the several
        Indian tribes, from 1778 to 1837, compiled and printed by the
        direction, and under the supervision, of the Commissioner of
        Indian Affairs. Washington.
U. S. DE SOTO EXPEDITION COMMISSION
  1939. Final report of the U. S. De Soto Expedition Commission. House
        Doc. No. 71, 76th Congress, 1st session.
WALKER, WINSLOW M.
  1935. A Caddo burial site at Natchitoches, Louisiana. Smithsonian Misc.
        Coll., vol. 94, No. 14.
WELTFISH, GENE. *See* LESSER, ALEXANDER.
WINSHIP, GEORGE PARKER
  1896. The Coronado Expedition, 1540–1542. 14th Ann. Rep. Bur. Ethnol.,
        1892–1893. Pt. 1, pp. 329–613.
ZAVALA, A. DE
  1916. Religious beliefs of the Tejas or Hasanias Indians. Publ. Texas Folk-
        Lore Soc., vol. 1, pp. 39–43.

The following material bearing on "Caddo customs of childhood" was obtained by the late G. A. Dorsey in 1905 from the informant White-Bread mentioned elsewhere, but was overlooked in the preparation of the above material:

The lodge is always placed so that it faces the east. This is done that the sun, as it arises out of the east to shine upon another day and bless all things, may bless the inmates of the lodge. When a child is born it is carried to the door of the lodge and held there as the sun rises that it may see the child and bless it. Then, if the child be a boy, the father places a tiny bow and arrow in his hands that it may grow to a good hunter and ward off dangers. Before the child is born a bright fire is kindled and kept burning for ten days and nights after the birth to keep away evil. There is a great animal with wings who eats human beings, especially babies, but the animal cannot come near the light. A greater monster than this is the cannibal person. In every tribe there are some of these wicked people. They look like anyone else, but at night, when it is dark, they set forth and steal human children to eat. Like the animal who eats human beings, they cannot go near the light, and so people keep the fire kindled to frighten them away. Then, too, the fire is related to the sun, because it gives heat and light, and so it gives a blessing to the child.

At the end of the tenth day the mother and father carry the child to the river, and all bathe. After that the fire is allowed to smoulder, but it is not put out entirely until after the child is two years old. From that time until the child is eight or ten it is allowed to play and grow in its own way. Then the grandmother, or some old person, calls the child into the lodge and, telling it to sit still and behave, she teaches it. If the child is a boy, she tells him how to take care of himself so that he will grow up to be a strong man. She tells him how to act that he will gain the good will of the tribe, and she tells him stories about boys who would not listen to the teachings of their grandmothers, and the trouble that they caused when they grew to be men. And she tells them about boys who have listened to their grandmothers, and how they grew up to be great and wonderful men. Then she tells the boy to go to the river every morning to swim and bathe, no matter how cold the water is. He is taught to say his prayer to the water: "Grandfather, make me strong to endure all things, that heat and cold, rain and snow may be as nothing to my body." As he returns to the lodge he is taught to pick up a stick and carry it to the fire, saying: "Grandfather, help me to live and become a good man, and to help others to live." To the rising sun he is taught to pray: "Grandfather, protect me, keep me from dangers and give me a long life and success."

At another time the boy is taught that there are many bad and dangerous places on the road leading to the spirit-land, and that he will be caught in some of these places if he does not heed what is taught him. She says, "There are six bad places on the way to the spirit-land. The first place is where the dogs stay. If you whip or mistreat or kill a dog, the dog, when it dies, goes to its people and tells what you have done. When you die, you have to pass the place of the dogs, and the chief of the dogs goes and sits by the road and waits for you. When you come he tells you to look for fleas on his head, and when you find one he tells you to bite it. When you bite it, you become a dog. Then he takes you to where the dogs stay, and there they mistreat you as you mistreated them on earth. They keep you there and never let you get away, so that you cannot continue your journey. For this reason we place a bead on the little finger of a dead person, so that he may bite it instead of the flea and so fool the dog and escape him. Along the road there is another place where you hear some one calling you. If you form the habit during life of standing about talking about people, you will turn your head and wait for the person who is calling. Then you will stand and say mean things about some one until you forget that you are going on a journey and become a tree by the road side. If you learn to go through life attending to your own affairs, you will not pay any attention to the voice, but go straight ahead. Soon you will come to a place where there are two large rocks pounding each other. You will have to pass between these rocks. If you listen well to all that you are told, and remember that you were told about the rocks, you can pass through. If you forget what you have been told, you will be crushed by the pounding rocks. Next you will come to a stream of water that looks very small; but it is not small, for the banks stretch away, and it becomes a great river. If you are quick to do all that you are told in this world, you will reach the stream when the banks are close together and you can jump across; but if you are slow to do what you have to do on this earth, you will reach the river after the banks have spread and you will be too late to jump across, but will fall into the water and become a fish. As you journey on the other side of the river, should you get across, you will come to persimmon-trees. If in this world you want everything you see and always try to get things that you do not need, just because some one else has them, you will stop under a tree to gather persimmons. Then you will wander to the next tree and the next, until you lose your way and forget that you are on a journey. Then you will become a raccoon and live forever among the trees. Should you escape the persimmon-trees, you will soon meet a person along the road. He will ask you to help him do some work. If you are forgetful in life and begin one thing and do not finish it, but go off about something else, you will forget that you are on a journey and you will stop and help this man. You will work until you are nothing but skin and bone. Then you will die, but you will soon come to life only to work yourself to death again. Then you will come to life again, and so on. There is no end. This is the last danger that you meet on the way."

After the boy has been taught about all the dangers that beset him on the way, and entreated to follow closely the teaching of his elders that he may escape those evils, he is taught what is in store for him when at last he reaches the end of his journey. All this is done to encourage him to lead a good life and grow up to be a good man. [Dorsey, 1905 a.]

Kiowa—Continued
 fight with Caddo, 114
 names applied to Caddo by, 6
 Satank, chief of, 116
 Satanta, chief of, 116
Kiowa Agency, consolidated with Wichita Agency, 117
Kiowa Apache, Caddo name for, 7
KI'sî, unidentified river, 26
Koasati, Cutchates identified as, 88
 Freeman-Custis expedition visits, 77
Koch, Clara Lena, on Federal Indian policy in Texas (1845–60), 102–104, 105–107
 on Indian aid to U. S. troops, 107
Kullituklo, 85
Koroa, salt industry, 193
La Bahia, 64, 65
La Barre, Weston, on John Wilson, 121
 on Peyote cult, 121
Labor, division between sexes, 162–163
Lacane, division possibly of Nacono, 11
 identified with Hacanac and Nacanish, 32
 mentioned in De Soto narratives, 8
 province visited by De Soto expedition, 32
 synonym for Nacanish, 8
Lac de Muire, 76
Lac Macdon, 75
Laffitt, Pierre, 85
La Gran Montaña, 67
La Harpe, Bernard de, expedition into Caddo country, 56–59
 on Naouydiche, 11
 on population, 20, 21, 25
 post erected at Nasoni village, 57
 salt obtained, 139–140
La Junta, 37
Lake Bastiano. See Lake Bistineau.
Lake Bistineau, 77, 84
Lake Caddo, 94
Lake Macdon, 85
Lake Pontchartrain, 135, 141
 location of Acolapissa on, 51
 location of Natchitoches on, 51
Lake St. Joseph, Taensa towns on, 50
La Mothe, M. de, 53
Language, conclusions regarding, 234
La Salle, Réné Robert Cavelier, Sieur de, explorations in Hasinai country, 38–40
 murder of, 40
Lavaca Bay, 38
Lawrie Tatum, delegate to messiah, 118
Leavenworth, an officer, 89
Leeper, Agent, 112
 wounded by Indians, 113
Legends. See Myths.
Leon, Dr. Nicolas. See Espinosa, Fray Isidro Felix de.
Le Page du Pratz, Antoine S., on trade of Avoyel Indians, 37
LeRoy, Coffee Co., Kans., 114
Lesser, Alexander, and Weltfish, Gene, authorities on living Caddo, 13–14

Lesser and Weltfish—Continued
 enumeration of Caddo tribes, 13–14
 investigation of Caddoan languages, 2
 on Hainai dialect, 14
 on relationship, terms of, 168
Lipan, 86, 95, 124
 Caddo name for, 7
 mentioned by Casañas, 10
Little Boy. See Show-e-tat.
Little Caddo, 70
 population, 20
Little Kadohadacho, Gaignard' visit to, 71
Little River, 80
Little Washita, 110
Lopez, Father Nicolas, on ambassadors from the Texas, 38
Los Adaes, Presidio del Pilar de, 66, 67
 abandonment of, 68
 capital of Texas, 65
 capital of Texas moved from, 69–70
 provisions from Mexico, 64–65
 relations with Natchitoches post, 66, 68
 St. Denis agreement to withdraw from, 61
 Spanish occupation, 63–65
Louchetehona, identified as Doustioni, 55
Louchetehonis, mentioned by Bienville, 56
 See also Doustioni.
Louisiana, annexed to Spain, 199
 belonging to France, 73
 cession to Spain, 67, 68
 claims to land, 92–94
 French colony, 50
 Purchased by United States, 73
Macarti, Cavallero, Commandant of Natchitoches post, 27, 164
 on Kadohadacho clans, 164
McCurtain County, Okla., 85
Mackenzie Basin Type, relationship system classified with, 167, 237
Madargoes, mentioned by Robert M. Jones, 96
 See also Anadarko.
Maligne, 40
Manufactures, 154–159, 236, 239
 See also individual items, such as, Pipes; Musical instruments, etc.
Manuel, Father, 56
Manuscript Memoir (Bienville). See Bienville.
Many, Col. James B., 88–89
Marcy, Capt. R. B., 100
 on condition of Caddo at Brazos Reserve, 104
 on José Maria, character of, 124
 surveyor of land for Brazos Agency, 102–103
Maréchal-d'Estrées, le, 59
Margil, Padre, 53, 58, 62, 69
 death of, 65
 in charge Mission of Nuestra Señora de Guadalupe, 54
 in charge San Miguel de los Adaes, 64
 with Aguayo expedition, 59

Nacogdoche, 88
  character of, 123, 124
  distinctive features, 147
  fire temple, 214, 215
  gifts from Spaniards to, 62
  mentioned by De Mézières, 71, 72
  mentioned by Lesser and Weltfish, 13
  mentioned by St. Denis, 10
  mentioned by Sibley, 74
  mission for, 54, 62
  Nacodissy identified as, 8
  Nazadachotzi identified with, 9
  Neticatzi identified with, 9
  outsiders among in 1716, 55
  population, 18, 19, 20
Nacogdochitos Indians, Sanchez' visit to, 88
  See also Nacogdoche.
Nacondiché, mentioned by Tonti, 43
  See also Nacogdoche.
Naconicho, creek, 11
  division possibly of Nacono, 11
Nacono, chief, account of, 60
  divisions of, 11
  food of, 61
  gifts from Spaniards to, 61
  identified with Nacanish, 9
  Lacane, division of, 11
  mentioned by Casañas, 9, 171
  mission for, 54
  Nacao, division of, 11
  Naconicho, division of, 11
  Nakanawan, division of, 11
  welcome to Aguayo, 60–61, 198
Nacoz, identified with Nacachau, 9
  mentioned by Casañas, 9
Nactythos, mentioned by Iberville, 50
  See also Natchitoches.
Nadaco, associated with Hasinai, 11
  character of, 124
  identified as possibly Anadarko, 8
  location of, 12, 57, 75
  mentioned by Joutel, 8
  mentioned by Sanchez, 88
  population, 18
  See also Anadarko.
Nadacocos, identified with Anadarko, 10
  mentioned by St. Denis, 10
Nadacogs, mentioned by De Mézières, 71
  See also Anadarko.
Nadaho, identified with Adai, 9
  mentioned by Joutel, 9
Nadamin, identified with Sadamon, 9
  mentioned by Joutel, 9
Nadan, identified with Anadarko, 9
  mentioned by Casañas, 9
  synonym for Anadarko, 11
Nadas, relation to Adai, 13
  Tonti visit to, 42
  village mentioned by Tonti, 13
Nadote chief, 68
Nadote village, hostility to Spaniards, 68
Naguatex, branch tribe of Namidish, 8
  interpretation of name, 32
  meaning of word, 8, 139

Naguatex—Continued
  mentioned in De Soto narratives, 8, 11
  Moscoso visits, 32
  pronunciation of, 8
  See also Namidish; Nawatesh.
Nahacassi, identified with Yatasi, 9
  mentioned by Joutel, 9
Nahouidiches, on La Harpe expedition, 58
  See also Nawatesh.
Naichas. See Neches.
Nakanawan, division possibly of Nacono, 11
  mentioned by Mooney, 14
  synonym for Hainai, 11
Nakasa, Bienville's visit to, 50
  discussion of, 13
  mentioned by Beaurain, 13
  mentioned by Bienville, 13
  tattooing, 143
  See also Nataché; Natchés.
Namidis, interpretation of name, 12
  mentioned by St. Denis, 10
Namidish, foods of, 127
  location, 57
  Nabiti identified with, 9
  Naguatex branch tribe of, 8
  Naviti identified with, 9
  salt, 139
  See also Amediche; Naodiche; Naondiché; "Ouidiches."
Naming ceremony, 160
Nanatscho, white settlement at, 85
  See also Nanatsoho.
Nanatsoho, chief of meets La Harpe, 57
  Kadohadacho tribe, 6
  Natsohos identified as, 8
  Natsoos identified with, 9
  Natsvtos identified as, 50
  See also Natsohos; Natsvtos.
Nandacos, mentioned by Sibley, 82
  See also Anadarko.
Nandakoes, mentioned by Sibley, 74, 75
  See also Anadarko.
"Naondiché," 42
  See also Namidish; Nawatesh.
Naodiche, visited by Joutel, 40
  See also Namidish; Nawatesh.
Naordiche. See Namidish.
Naouadiché, mentioned by Tonti, 43
  See also Namidish; Nawatesh.
"Naoudiches," food of, 58
  See also Namidish; Nawatesh.
Naouidiche, meaning of name, 139
  See also Namidish; Nawatesh.
Naovediche, mentioned by Tonti, 43
  See also Namidish; Nawatesh.
Naouydiche, identified as Noadiche, 11
  location, 11
  peace with Kadohadacho, 57
  See also Namidish; Nawatesh.
Naquiscoça, mentioned in De Soto narratives, 8, 10
  Nacachau possibly identified with, 10
  province visited by Moscoso, 32

Natsvtos, mentioned by Iberville, 50
  See also Nanatsoho.
Navasota River, 40
Navedachos, described by De Mézières, 72
  mentioned by St. Denis, 10
  See also Nabedache.
Naviti, identified with Namidish, 9
  mentioned by Casañas, 9
  See also Nabiti.
Nawadishe, synonym for Nabedache, 12
Nawatesh. *See* Naguatex.
Naytanes, identified with Comanche, 70
  mentioned by De Mézières, 70
Nazadachotzi, identified with Nacogdoche, 9
  mentioned by Casañas, 9, 171
Nazones, identified with Nasoni, 9
  mentioned by Casañas, 9
  See also Nazonis.
Nazonis, mission for refounded, 62
  See also Nasoni; Nazones.
Necan, identified with Nacanish, 9
Necha, identified with Neches, 9
  mentioned by Casañas, 9, 171
Nechavi, mentioned by Casañas, 9, 171
Neches, Aguayo visit to, 60–61
  fire temple, 214, 215
  gifts from Spaniards to, 61
  mission for, 54, 61
  Necha identified with, 9
  Nesta identified with, 9
  Nouista identified with, 9
Neches River, 54, 61
  Caddo name of, 16
Neighbors, Maj. Robert S.
  account of removal of Indians from Brazos Agency, 112
  murdered, 113
  on cause of uprisings, 108
  on condition of Caddo tribes (1846), 98
  on population, 19, 20
  on progress of settling Indians on Brazos Reserve, 104–105
  peace between enemy tribes negotiated by, 98
  removes Texas Indians to territory north of Red River, 111–113
  report of land cultivated at Brazos Agency, 106–107
  Special Commissioner to Texas Indians, 98
  surveyor of land for Brazos Agency, 102–104
Nesta, identified with Neches, 9
  mentioned by Casañas, 9
Netches. *See* Neches.
Neticatzi, identified with Nacogdoche, 9
  mentioned by Casañas, 9
Nĭshkû'ntŭ. *See* Wilson, John.
Nisohone, synonym for Nissohone, 8
Nissohone, identified as Nasoni, 8
  mentioned in De Soto narratives, 8
  province visited by De Soto expedition, 32.
  See also Nasoni.

Nadacao. *See* Anadarko.
Noadiche, found by Joutel, 11
  Naouydiche, identified as, 11
Nevadizoes, mentioned by De Mézières, 71
  See also Nabedache.
Nondacao, identified as Anadarko, 8, 32
  mentioned in De Soto narratives, 8
  province visited by Moscoso, 32
  synonym for Nadan, 11
  See also Anadarko.
Nondacau, mentioned by Casañas, 10
Nondaco, identified as Anadarko, 8
  mentioned by Joutel, 8
Nondako, Nadacao identified as, 32
  See also Anadarko.
Nose ornaments. *See* Adornment, personal: ornaments.
Nouista, identified with Neches, 9
  mentioned by Joutel, 9
Nouydiches, identified as Nahouidiches, 58
  mentioned by Du Rivage, 58
  See also Namidish; Nawatesh.
Nuestra Señora de Guadalupe de Albuquerque de los Nacogdoches, 65
  abandonment, 70
  description, 69
  difficulties of, 72
  establishment, 54
  refounding, 62
Nuestra Señora de la Assumpción, arroyo of, 62
Nuestra Señora de la Purisima Concepción de Acuña, founded, 65
Nuestra Señora de la Purisima Concepción de los Hainai, establishment, 54
  refounding, 61–62
  transferred and renamed, 65
Nuestra Señora de los Dolores de Benavente de los Ays, 65, 125–126
  abandonment, 70
  description, 69
  difficulties of, 72
  establishment, 54
Nuestra Señora de los Dolores de los Texas, Presidio of, 54
  fortifications outlined, 65
Nuestra Señora del Pilar de los Adaes, 65
Nuevo Leon, 55, 65
Nuts. *See* Foods, vegetable.
Nye, Capt. W. S., on Show-e-tat, 116
"Old Caddo village," 12
Olivares, Antonio de San Buenaventura, 51
  on paint, green, 144
Omaha, 122, 198
  clans, 166
  name applied to Caddo by, 6
Onadakoes, mentioned by Neighbors, 98
  See also Anadarko.
O'Reilly, Governor, 203
Origin legends, 25–29
Orleans Territory, 73

326 INDEX

Ornamentation, conclusions regarding, 236
Ornaments. *See* Adornment, personal.
Orobio y Basterra, Don Prudencio de, 67
Orreilli, Señor Conde de, 199
Osage, 43, 81, 82, 198
  Annaho identified with, 9
  Big Moon cult among, 121
  enemy of Kadohadacho, 71, 74, 78, 79, 85
  leave-taking, method of, 97
  name applied to Caddo by, 6
Osage orange. *See* Bois d'arc.
Ouachita, Bienville's visit to, 50
  description of in 1699, 50
  population, 21
  temple, 216
  Tonti's visit to, 42
  Yesito identified as, 50
Ouachitas River, identified as Boggy River, 57
Ouasita. *See* Quachita.
Ouchita, in Natchitoches group, 12
"Ouidiches," Father Anastasius mentions, 41
  See also Namidish; Nawatesh.
Padilla, Juan Antonio, on Caddo tribes, distinctions between, 146–147
  on condition of Caddo, 86
  on Eyeish, character of, 126
  on foods, animal, 134
  on houses, 152
  on Kadohadacho, morals of, 124
  on Kadohadacho trade, 197
  on nose ornaments, 146
  on painting of body, 145
  on physical characteristics of Caddo, 122
  on population, 18, 20, 22
Painting, 159
Painting, body. *See* Adornment, personal.
Paints, 144, 145
Palmer, Dr. Edward, specimens for U. S. National Museum, 154, 158
Palo Guacho, 63
Panis, 77, 78, 81
Parker, William B., letter to Schoolcraft, 28
  on houses, 152
Parsons, Dr. Elsie Clews, authority on modern Caddo, 3, 14
  on burial customs, 209–210
  on clans, 166
  on games, 175
  on hunting, bear, 137
  on marriage, 162
  on present government, 173
  on relationship, terms of, 168
  on religious ceremonies, 234
  on war dance, 192
Patroon, 63
Pauit, 36
Pawnee, 38
  Caddo name for, 7
  inclusion in Caddoan stock, 6

Pawnee—Continued
  influence on Caddo religious beliefs, 238
  legend of, 28
  names applied to Caddo by, 6
"Pawpaw People," 26
Pearl River, 51
Pease, E. M., Governor of Texas, 102–104
Pecan Point, 85, 88
Pecos, Cicuye identified as, 34
Pecos River, 102
  Caddo name of, 16
Pénicaut, leads Natchitoches to St. Denis, 52
  on burial customs, 208, 238
  on clothing, 141
  on eating, 174
  on fire making, 155–156
  on fishing, method of, 138
  on foods, vegetable, 133
  on hunting, 135
  on St. Denis, 51
  on tattooing, 142, 235–236
  on temple, Acolapissa and Natchitoches, 216
  on war customs, 188–189
  on war paraphernalia, 147
People of Bayou Dauchite, Dotchetonne identified with, 9
Pequeños Cados, annual present to, 200
  See also Petit Caddo.
Perrier, 66
Petit Caddo, De Mézières expedition to, 70
  trading depot, 67
Petrullo, Vincenzo, on John Wilson, 120–121
Peyote cult, 120–121
Peyote meeting, 210
Phillips, Rev. John W., mission school, effort to establish, 105
Physical characteristics. *See* Characteristics.
Pichardo, José Antonio, on interpretation of Natchitoches, 26
Pipes, 158
Piseros, Juan, contract with De Mézières, 200–202
Pita, Friar José, with Aguayo expedition, 59
Plains culture, 197–198
Plains people, description of, 33–34
Planting. *See* Agriculture: communal planting.
Platters, 214, 215
Plummer, Captain, 112, 113
Ponca, 198
Pope, John, Governor of Arkansas, 88
Population, 16–25
Porter, Peter B., on population, 20
Pottery, 157–158, 159, 239
Pouch, tobacco, 158
Powell, J. W., on designations, 6
Pow-iash, second chief of Caddo, 98
"Prairie des Ennemis," 20
  Gaignard's visit to, 71

Waco—Continued
  removed to Brazos Agency, 104
  Stem's enumeration of, 101
War, 184–192
  customs, conclusions regarding, 237
  paraphernalia, 147
  preparation, painting of body, 144
War dance. *See* Dances.
Warfare, of Teyas, 34
  of Tula, 29, 30, 31
Washita River, Caddo name of, 16
Washita Valley, 126
Weltfish, Gene. *See* Lesser, Alexander, and Weltfish, Gene.
White Bread, informant, on clans, 164–165
  on customs of childhood, —
  on relationship of Caddo tribes, 15
White Chief, guide of St. Denis, 50
White Deer, prominent Caddo, 117
White Moon, informant, 210
  quoted on relationship, terms of, 168
White Woman, 173
Wichita, 38, 56
  assistance to Texas Rangers, 114
  Caddo living with, 107
  De Mézières expedition to, 70
  depredations on Caddo, 98, 99
  Ghost dance, 118
  houses, 153
  inclusion in Caddoan stock, 6
  influence on Caddo religious beliefs, 238
  inhabitants of Quivira, 35
  mentioned by Casañas, 10
  names applied to Caddo by, 6
  Taouyaches identified as, 70
  traditions on tribal movements, 29
Wichita Agency, 114
  Kiowa and Comanche Agency consolidated with, 117
Wichita Confederation, Tawakoni member of, 59
Wichita Mountains, 109, 112
Wild Horse Creek, 100
Williams, Indian agent, 98
Williams, Col. L. H., interpreter, 99
Williams, George, assistant interpreter at Brazos Agency, 106
Wilson, Billy, delegate to messiah, 118
Wilson, John, leader Caddo Ghost dance, description of, 118–121
Women, artistic ability, 159
  aquidau, wives of officials, 170
  childbirth, 159–160
  clothing, 140–141, 147
  drummers, 156
  duties at erection of house, 150
  hair dressing, 142
  industry of, 123
  Kadohadacho ruler, 173
  marriage, 160–162
  Nabedache "queen," 173
  painting of body, 144
  physical characteristics, 122

Women—Continued
  pottery industry, 158, 159
  relationship, terms of, 168
  tattooing, 143–144
  wives exchanged or bartered, 161
  work of, 163
Wood, products made from, 155–156
Wortham, James, 115
Xacatin, synonym for Soacatino, 8
Ximena, identified as Galisteo, 34
  village visited by Coronado, 34
Xinesi. See Government: officials.
Xuacatino, synonym for Soacatino, 8
Yatacé, mentioned by Bienville, 55, 56
  See also Yatasi.
Yataché, mentioned by Iberville, 50
  Tonti's visit to, 42
  village mentioned by Tonti, 13
  See also Yatasi.
Yatasi, 70
  agreement with Spaniards, 70
  Chickasaw, severe treatment by, 57
  chief of, 70
  Choye identified with by Tonti, 9
  conflict with Spaniards, 75
  crops, 75
  decimation, amount of, 57
  dialect, examples of, 15
  discussion of, 13
  divisions of, 10–11
  in Kadohadacho region, 56
  living with Kadohadacho, 57
  location, 7, 50, 75
  mentioned by Lesser and Weltfish, 13
  Nacassa identified with, 9
  Nahacassi identified with, 9
  Natassee identified as, 71
  Natchitoches, living with, 57
  part settling with Kadohadacho, 10
  part settling with Natchitoches, 10
  population, 21
  Sibley on condition of, 75
  speech of, 75
  temple, 216
  trading depot at, 67
  See also Yatacé; Yataché; Yattassees.
Yatasse, annual present to, 200
Yatay. *See* Adai.
Yattassees, mentioned by Sibley, 74, 75
  See also Yatasi.
Yesito, mentioned by Iberville, 50
  See also Ouachita.
Yguanes, mentioned by Sanchez, 88
Yojuane Indians, 52, 214, 215
Yowani Choctaw, mentioned, 14, 89, 124
  possible identity of Yguanes with, 88
Yuganís, character of, 124
  distinctive features, 146–147
  mentioned by Padilla, 18
  population, 18
Zacatecan, missionaries, 53, 54
  missions, 66
  See also individual names of missions; College of Zacatecas.